Religion and Public Health during the Time of COVID-19

Religion and Public Health during the Time of COVID-19

Editors

Andrew Flescher
Joel Zimbelman

MDPI

Basel • Beijing • Wuhan • Barcelona • Belgrade • Novi Sad • Cluj • Manchester

Editors
Andrew Flescher
State University of New York
Stony Brook, NY, USA

Joel Zimbelman
California State University
Chico, CA, USA

Editorial Office
MDPI
St. Alban-Anlage 66
4052 Basel, Switzerland

This is a reprint of articles from the Special Issue published online in the open access journal *Religions* (ISSN 2077-1444) (available at: https://www.mdpi.com/journal/religions/special_issues/covid19_and_religious_issues).

For citation purposes, cite each article independently as indicated on the article page online and as indicated below:

Lastname, Firstname, Firstname Lastname, and Firstname Lastname. Article Title. *Journal Name* **Year**, *Volume Number*, Page Range.

ISBN 978-3-0365-8572-7 (Hbk)
ISBN 978-3-0365-8573-4 (PDF)
doi.org/10.3390/books978-3-0365-8573-4

Cover image courtesy of Rachel Foxman

Contents

About the Editors

Andrew Flescher

Andrew Flescher is Professor of Public Health and a Professor of English at Stony Brook University. He specializes in medical ethics, medical humanities, public health, transplantation ethics, health care policy, and comparative religious ethics. He chairs the ethics committee for the Organ Procurement Transplant Network/United Network for Organ Sharing (OPTN/UNOS) and serves as the medical ethicist on the New York State's Transplant Council. In addition to writing several articles and book chapters, he is the author of four books: Heroes, Saints, and Ordinary Morality (2003, Georgetown University Press), The Altruistic Species (2007, Templeton Press, winner of the Choice Award), Moral Evil (2013, Georgetown University Press, winner of the Prose Award), and The Organ Shortage Crisis in America (2018, Georgetown University Press).

Joel Zimbelman

Joel Zimbelman is Professor Emeritus of Religious Ethics in the Department of Comparative Religion and Humanities at California State University Chico. His research interests include comparative religious and applied social ethics, the history and development of Christian ethics, religious and philosophical perspectives on biomedical ethics, ethics and biotechnology, and public health policy. He is the author, along with Becky White, of *Moral Dilemmas in Community Health Care: Cases and Commentaries* (Pearson Longman 2005).

Preface

It has been well over a year and a half since we began discussions on the potential publication of a series of journal articles around the topic of the encounter between religious practice and COVID-19. After significant effort and wonderful collaborations across many miles, months, and continents, we have finally completed the project. Many dimensions of the recent COVID-19 pandemic and its amelioration have been discussed in the literature—basic and applied scientific research, public health and public policy challenges, legal issues, the psycho-social dimensions of ongoing health risk and the treatment of the ill and dying, financial issues, fiscal policy, and national security issues. To date, however, there has been scant attention given to the thorny moral issues presented by COVID-19 in connection with the religious beliefs, mores, history, practices, and communal identity in assessing and evaluating responses to the pandemic. Our goal in this Special Issue of *Religions* was to address this gap and to reveal how important—indeed, definitive—such beliefs and practices are (and should be) to stakeholders and policy makers, and to those afflicted by this pandemic.

The collection of essays in the Special Issue includes treatments of religious freedom and the argument from autonomy; religious exemptions to vaccination requirements; social justice and the claims of the other (with regard to mitigation measures, vaccines, and public health policy); nationalism versus globalism in the context of pandemics generally; the impact of colonialism on developing regions of the world; and the adjudication of the debate over the extent to which religious insiders should be permitted to speak in their own voices and act independently within the context of the larger state. All of these essays examine the appropriate balance that we should strive to maintain between individual liberty and population health and flourishing. They probe the extent to which religious practices in a variety of cultures stood as impediments to implementing public health measures, while, at the same time, serving as resources for morally imagining solutions to crises precipitated by the COVID-19 pandemic. These essays may be said to reflect "pandemic narratives," that is, idiosyncratic accounts of how various sub-populations across the globe have striven to process the challenges and a new world order that the pandemic brought about.

In an undertaking this ambitious and far-reaching there are many to thank without whom we would not have had the tenacity to see this project through to its timely completion. We are grateful to a cohort at Stony Brook University who in the summer of 2020 began the "Pandemic Narratives Project" to study the impact of illness on human communities and explore global pandemics as objects of historical and contemporary concern. Our goal in that initiative was to inquire how we might access perspectives traditionally muted during health crises while paying particular attention to the lived experience of vulnerable groups. Our method was to integrate new insights from the STEM fields, humanities, and social sciences into an interdisciplinary whole. Special thanks go to Lisa Diedrich, Nancy Tomes, Karen Lloyd, and Susan Scheckel for their ongoing innovation and constant inspiration. Diana Cates, a mentor and wonderful colleague, helped us to navigate the labor-intensive task of editing, providing enormously valuable advice for how to bring forth with clarity and power disparate authorial voices. We would like to acknowledge and express gratitude towards Rachel Foxman for providing a poignant and an original image which adequately captured the two intersecting spheres that constitute the subject of our Special Issue: religion and public health. We would finally like to thank Moira Li and the expert and professional team at MDPI who helped us to develop the original idea for the Special Issue and encouraged us through the early conceptual stages right to the end of the project.

We have never been part of such a large, collaborative endeavor that drew from such a diverse group of scholars, but also that drew from experts on at least four continents. We could not have pulled off this project but for the ability of our authors to recognize the potential that such a publication could have and their willingness to contribute their time, energy, enthusiasm, creativity, and intellectual imagination to tackling these issues. Both of us are forever in their debt.

Andrew Flescher and Joel Zimbelman

Editors

religions MDPI

Editorial

Looking at the Impact of COVID-19 on Religious Practice and the Impact of Religious Practice on COVID-19

Joel Zimbelman [1,*] and Andrew Flescher [2,3,4]

1 Department of Comparative Religion and Humanities, California State University, Chico, CA 95929-0740, USA
2 Department of Family, Population, and Preventive Medicine, State University of New York, Stony Brook, NY 11794-8338, USA; andrew.flescher@stonybrook.edu
3 Core Faculty in Public Health Program, State University of New York, Stony Brook, NY 11794-8338, USA
4 Department of English, State University of New York, Stony Brook, NY 11794-8338, USA
* Correspondence: jzimbelman@csuchico.edu

1. Religion and Health Care Policies in the Era of the Pandemic

As this collection of essays on the manner in which religion and public health policy have impacted one another in the COVID-19 era goes to press, both the United States' Centers for Disease Control (CDC) and the United Nations' World Health Organization (WHO) have recently declared the end to the pandemic (CDC 2023b; UN 2023b; Williams 2023; Siddiqui et al. 2022). The easing of various legal and policy restrictions, disappearance of financial support initiatives, and dismantling of some infrastructures for the delivery and dissemination of tests, vaccines, and medications, as well as altered case reporting protocols, are significantly changing or ending in many countries. Still, COVID-19 cases, deaths, and costs continue to be a crushing burden in many global communities (Johns Hopkins Coronavirus Resource Center 2023; *Our World in Data* 2023; Harvard Global Health Institute 2023; Dartmouth College 2023; American Public Media 2023; UN 2023a; *New York Times* 2023; *Washington Post* 2023; *Towards Science Data* 2023; European Union 2023).

One of the great underreported stories of the global coronavirus tragedy was the way in which this public health crisis was, on the one hand, uniquely experienced by specific religious and culturally distinct communities, and, on the other, how the responses of these communities either contributed to or exacerbated the public health challenges and muted successes in battling the pandemic. Even a cursory review of most documented timelines of the pandemic reveals the extent to which religion was not initially considered an important variable in appreciating how various publics perceived and reacted to COVID-19 (CDC 2023a; WHO 2023; Kantis et al. 2023). In 2020, the scholarly voices and media addressing these issues were few and far between, but wider interest and sustained coverage and analysis appeared shortly thereafter and has been increasing since early 2021 (Levin 2020; Hartford Institute for Religion Research 2021; Levin et al. 2022; Levin and Bradshaw 2022; Majumdar 2022; Witt-Swanson et al. 2023). A number of university-supported and state-sponsored centers and institutes (some with religious affiliations) have established research agendas for conversations that address the intersectionality of religion and COVID-19 (Georgetown University 2023a, 2023b; Hartford Institute for Religion Research 2023; Pew Research Center 2023).

Each of the ten essays which appear here explores these concerns in a sustained and representative way. Together, they provide the first significant attempt to examine comparatively a sizeable complement of scholars willing to address both the experiences of particular religious communities and to interrogate those experiences from the perspective of the comparative and multi-disciplinary academic study of religion. The essays originate from disparate global regions and distinct religious communities, and include additional insights from the related fields of comparative religious ethics, public health, literature, sociology, history, and anthropology. We believe it is an important resource that will invite

Citation: Zimbelman, Joel, and Andrew Flescher. 2023. Looking at the Impact of COVID-19 on Religious Practice and the Impact of Religious Practice on COVID-19. *Religions* 14: 933. https://doi.org/10.3390/rel14070933

Received: 2 June 2023
Accepted: 7 July 2023
Published: 19 July 2023

a larger and developing discussion of the experience most communities have been through since the end of 2019 coping with a pandemic which shook the stability and collective mental health of whole societies worldwide. Some of these essays emphasize the partisan and self-referential motivations of individuals in their faiths and communities, but they also bear witness to the common humanity, vulnerability, and aspirations for life and sense of purpose that bind us together. It is such shared experiences that makes challenges like the COVID-19 pandemic an opportunity for putting into collective practice the basic norms of justice, compassion, and human flourishing felt across particular communities.

There are two foundational claims that the selected essays within this collection reflect. The first is that attention should be given to the relationship that exists de facto between religious beliefs and practices and the lived experiences of those suffering the mental and physical health consequences of the COVID-19 pandemic. These connections fly under the radar and are often easy to miss, but our contention is that the modern human experience of COVID-19 cannot be fully appreciated without attention to these connections.

A second claim is that insights from the humanities and social sciences are indispensable to the project of analyzing and interpreting the full range of lived human experiences—spiritual and psychological, social and communal, and political—that communities confront with challenges like COVID-19. There were missed opportunities in the first three years of the pandemic to fully appreciate the insights, challenges, and resources that religious communities would present as this catastrophe unfolded (Pankowski and Wytrychiewicz-Pankowska 2023). That failure diminished our appreciation of the complex ways that public health functions and of its dependence for success on broad community and culturally inflected collaboration (Volet et al. 2022).

The first issue that crowded out religious voices and the analytic and cautionary message of these disciplines was the declaration of an "emergency" and the positioning of the main players on the chess board for what was to come. As the pandemic broke in the first days of 2020, it was the concerns of politicians which seemed to surface first and which monopolized media coverage, though a broad consensus on policy responses appears to have held for several months across disparate politically defined communities in the US and elsewhere (Covid Crisis Group 2023; Wallace-Wells 2023). At the same time, the WHO, CDC, the US Food and Drug Administration (FDA), the US Department of Health & Human Services (HHS), and the National Institute of Allergy and Infectious Diseases (NIAID), along with other national health agencies and state public health departments sought to orchestrate a narrow and crisis-informed public health response, slowing or stopping the spread of this unknown virus through continuing research and initiatives at various levels. While lip service was paid to the importance of pacing policy development in ways that would be acceptable to various parties and communities which might have a likelihood of achieving broad compliance, a technical public health focus tended to dominate initial policy efforts. Vaccine research and design, production, and phased drug trials moved to center stage in the first five months as a long-term response and as "our best hope" to addressing the acute crisis. Press conferences, evening news reports, and data management and dissemination coalesced around these same priorities, with less attention initially given to psycho-social concerns, distinct issues experienced locally by various communities, socio-economic challenges, and the demands of distributive justice.

The second development that crowded out religious and community-based concerns was the speed and tenacity with which the conflict between public health imperatives and civil rights claims solidified as a polarized either/or proposition. A plethora of constituencies, largely driven by political or religious identities, took sides in that debate in short order. Forty years ago, it was HIV/AIDS, not COVID-19, that was the first major public health crisis to emerge in the era of modern civil rights. However, the velocity of spread of the COVID-19 pandemic particularly its initially elevated R0 (pronounced "R-naught"), as well as the fact that everyone, and not just a handful of narrow populations, was assaulted by indeterminate rates of morbidity and mortality arguably made the experience of COVID-19 more tangible, frightening, and pervasively disorienting to a broader population of individuals (Eisenberg 2020). No one had the luxury of being spared in the second great pandemic of the contemporary era, as they had been in the first. Complicating matters was the final design and production of families of likely successful vaccines commencing very early in the process. Within a year of our discovery of the SARS-CoV-2 virus, debates about how to pay for and mobilize production of the vaccines which would counter it; who to prioritize for vaccination; how to assure just and efficacious distribution of vaccines; and how to address vaccine-refusal prevalent in several quarters of the globe all quickly surfaced among the major concerns of many of the players just identified. Meanwhile, rarely at this stage of policy formation, which included bickering among agencies and government entities, did one hear of substantive consultation with local faith or ethnic communities. Largely absent as well were community-led discussions and debates (as opposed to insular sectarian pronouncements) that might have informed vaccination priorities in those settings.

These developments meant that little public attention was paid to the fact that all human beings live in and have their identities and moral visions largely shaped by the religious and social communities of which they are a part. The trenchant research and observations of scholars such as Robert Wuthnow and Nancy Ammerman have helped us to appreciate the unassailable power that religious identity has on worldview as well as on the mundane, everyday practices of human life (Wuthnow 2022; Ammerman 2021; Wuthnow 2010). In other words, the discussions, debates, sermons, teachings, rituals, and evolving practices of thousands of these different religious communities inevitably informed billions of people's attitudes, dispositions, and responses to the pandemic in ways that were subtle yet profoundly significant. This lack of engagement meant that many developing and essential viewpoints informing policy were lost on the policymakers. Sometimes these religious attitudes diverged from the secular public health narratives and prescriptions (Martens and Rutjens 2022; Bartkowski et al. 2023). However, additional analysis reveals that the preponderance of religious communities and their leadership embraced positions that in significant ways dovetailed with, and even reinforced, evolving and "best-practice" public health policies (Idler et al. 2022; Nortey 2022). Indeed, studies seeking to determine the factors informing variations in morbidity and mortality across communities in the first year of the pandemic noted that religious belief was not a statistically significant factor in accounting for such differences (Chang et al. 2022). The failure to focus adequate attention on the religious beliefs and practices of various communities meant that public health professionals, the general public, and the mainstream media were blind to important insights into specific motivations and behaviors of their constituencies. They missed nurturing partnerships with particular communities for successful public education (Majumdar 2022). They failed to ameliorate suspicion and anxiety about both the pandemic itself and the efficacy of vaccination (and testing, masking, distancing, quarantine, and treatment) (Sisti et al. 2023). And so, over a period of two to three years, they tended to solidify policies that at times reinforced, but could also be antagonistic toward, the realities on the ground.

Web-based data resources and various well-regarded publications have estimated the numbers of excess deaths that occurred during the pandemic as one statistically significant proxy for its virulence and toll (Woolf et al. 2020; *Economist* 2021, 2023; COVID-19 Excess Mortality Collaborators 2022; Stoto and Wynia 2020). Certainly, better public policy and more focused and targeted vaccine access could have significantly reduced those numbers. However, our most basic contention is that the pain of the pandemic in its first three years, its morbidity and mortality rates but other dimensions as well, was exacerbated by the disconnect between the public health, national political, and broad media discourse on the one hand, and the rich reflections and insights of various religious communities that span the globe, on the other.

It is not too late to engage both the pandemic perspectives and biases of religious communities as a way to ameliorate our current situation. Unlike the pestilence gripping Camus' Oran, it is unlikely that our virus will just exit the city and dissolve into the sea, or that the populations most impacted by COVID-19 will hit a magical "herd immunity" status that confers significant protection against infection. Best current estimates reflect that someone still dies from COVID-19 every four minutes, even after the infection has claimed over 20 million lives globally (Cortez 2023). Health precautions and testing, vaccines and boosters, medications, and altered social arrangements will be with us for years to come. In such a situation, we will have to better account for how religious people and communities engage and think about health care crises; how radically divergent their ideas can be; how they still retain or have abandoned respect for public health and political institutions; how best to engage the most eloquent and compelling voices from within these communities to further discussion and debate; and how the discipline of the academic study of religion, and cognate fields, can help to frame our analysis. These will each be important tasks to take on in the coming years. In the same way that emerging moral dilemmas in a health care context reinvigorated the disciplines of religious studies and philosophy fifty years ago, COVID-19 may provide scholars in various fields, including potentially all of the humanities and social sciences, an opportunity to be part of larger and more vigorous policy conversations.

The challenge we face can be framed in more practical terms. A crucial component of claiming to deal successfully with a challenge like COVID-19 must be the establishment of effective health care policy. Even now, policy making in this context continues to be somewhat inchoate, inconsistent, weak on benchmarking, and short of sufficiently effective outcomes. We anticipate that a series of detailed monographs and comprehensive reports in the coming years will be used to conduct an analytic and exhaustive post-mortem on our global response to the pandemic. It will acknowledge some of our imaginative decisions and at the same time excoriate us for our blind spots, mixed allegiances, and selfishness. Most importantly, it will situate this acute health care crisis in the context of larger and growing concerns of global sustainability and interdependence (Ebi et al. 2020). Along with a few other works starting to appear (Covid Crisis Group 2023; Blumczynski and Wilson 2023), our collection of essays will hopefully arm us with resources and deeper understandings of our human capacity to fight the next battle better on behalf of its victims—a population that ironically is so often left out of these debates.

2. Our Contributing Authors

One of the things which becomes immediately clear in looking at this collection of essays in their entirety is the extent to which they balance one another. The reader will encounter just as many examples of religion and the appeal to the resources within religious communities serving to alleviate the major health stresses and burdens precipitated by the pandemic as ones in which the influence of religion has stood as an impediment to achieving desired health outcomes. In the majority of cases, this balance is reflected within the essay itself. Indeed, it was not lost on our authors that religion turns out more often than not to be a double-edged sword, both an extra demand in encountering, and a surprising remedy in service of managing, the global pandemic challenge. We believe that both the breadth and diversity of the religious traditions reflected here as well as the various ways, politically speaking, that these traditions have been interpreted by their authors establishes this collection as a distinctive and compelling voice in emerging critical analyses and conversations. These essays serve as welcome occasions to appreciate how ubiquitous crises like the COVID-19 pandemic and other healthcare challenges should be appreciated and interpreted when the perspectives of various religious traditions and the transdisciplinary scholarly tools developed in the humanities and social sciences are embraced. In this world, it is rarely up to governmental entities alone, at their worst perceived as external Leviathans, to choose what people care about the most. It is our hope that in this respect these essays confront the reader as a welcome reality check.

Julia Brown interrogates the role that religion has played in communal identity-making during the pandemic in the United States, an identity-making, she argues, which in some cases has stymied public health efforts to stop, or at least significantly slow, the spread of COVID-19. Drawing from Gabriel Garcia Marquez's *Love in the Time of Cholera* as a historical case study, Brown uses Garcia Marquez's depiction of religion's identity-making power during the cholera pandemic depicted in his novel as a comparison by which to understand the reported experiences of white evangelical Christians in America. Among other things, Brown asks us to evaluate whether religion itself is inimical to public health objectives, or whether such a claim is perhaps too simplified.

Donald Heinz, likewise, takes up the directed responses of conservative religious expression which has often appeared in the form of right-wing political activism and individualism in the face of government regulation during health crises, straining, despite the temptation in his treatment to herald the virtues of compassionate legislation usually associated with leftist religious expression, to adopt the perspective of some of the biggest critics of public health efforts throughout the pandemic. Thus, he manages to do justice to the perspective of both the ideological right and left within a religious context and provide a useful overview of the American political landscape of the last three years, contributing a much-needed analysis rooted in sociological methods that inform a discussion about how COVID-19 has impacted religion and religious expression, and vice versa.

Andrew Lustig, in keeping with the caution not to be too quick to embrace convenient either/or constructions often imposed on secular versus sectarian responses to public health crises, addresses the Catholic perspective on health and health care that has crucially informed the language of both duties and rights of caretakers and sufferers during the COVID-19 era. Working from the body of knowledge comprising "Catholic Social Teaching" (CST), Lustig interprets the obligation of "good stewardship" to entail both individual health needs, which includes being sufficiently health-literate and informed, as well the flourishing of others. Among other insights, Lustig argues that if Catholic rights language is meaningful at all, then the implications of the Catholic case for expanding public health are decisively reformist and impactful on global health policy in their own right.

Efstathios Kessareas, assessing the Greek Orthodox tradition, takes a close look at the controversy surrounding the distribution of Holy Communion that surfaced during the COVID-19 pandemic, arguing that there is more than one way to assess the compatibility of taking the Eucharist with mitigation measures issued in response to the spread of SARS-CoV-2. He maintains that not only is the Church's Holy Communion controversy reflective of a familiar tension between religious and secular voices in the Greek Orthodoxy concerning what should have the most influence over daily ritual and practice during periods of societal upheaval, but also that religious norms are baked into the modern secular socio-political order itself.

Andrew Flescher addresses the applicability of religious exemptions to public health policies such as vaccine mandates, acknowledging the legitimacy of the category of such exemptions while arguing for the absence of any coherent basis for their invocation in resisting mandated workplace COVID-19 vaccines on traditionally accepted grounds of "sincerely held beliefs". Flescher argues that in the name of the principle of autonomy, or "medical freedom", those seeking exemptions to state issued health requirements in effect seek a "blank check" whereby they hope to become the sole determiners of the authority of their personal beliefs within the state. Flescher looks at recent Supreme Court cases in which this issue is currently being adjudicated, noting a recent trend whereby the system of checks and balances which had governed where the public good is supposed to give way to individual liberties (and vice versa) can no longer to be taken for granted. He observes that a consequence of how the authority of personally held beliefs is now being interpreted is that contested political position becomes deliberately disguised as a protected religious value, an outcome neither in the interests of those who care about public health outcomes, nor in the interests of religious leaders who care about promoting public health.

Aaron Quinn, like Flescher, is focused on what makes faith-based exemption requests for health-protective mandates like vaccines legitimate, but in Quinn's case the analysis is confined to the epistemic grounds for religious authorization to begin with from which the moral authority of their invocation presumably follows. Quinn argues that not all kinds of beliefs are supported by equally legitimate justifications, and furthermore, that one indication that a belief can be epistemically sustained is its demonstrable appeal to cross-cultural consensus about agreed-on facts about the world, facts which, he argues, rest in shared human experiences affirmed by empirically verifiable evidence or reliable testimony. Quinn maintains that due to the private character of religious belief, not inherently universalizable, appeals to it will not be convincing, particularly when a population's health is at stake. Positions that stake out rights to opt out of mandates based on such appeals, consequently, are at some level arbitrary.

Mahan Mirza, probing causes for vaccine resistance among Nigerian Muslims, discerns two general categories of reasons for non-compliance: theologically based reasons and worldly ones pertaining to a lack of trust in public institutions. He then goes on to demonstrate, systematically, that the latter, not the former, is the likely dominant explanation for the seeming reluctance among some to succumb, within a Muslim setting, to scientific authority. Theologically, Islam has as many resources to recommend scientific advance as it does to cast doubts upon it, but these resources are likely to be overlooked without concurrently establishing grounds for having faith in representatives of the state. Mirza recommends engagement with religious norms, rather than their dismissal, as the most encouraging way forward with regard to efforts to address vaccine resistance among local actors, especially in communities in which religious authority is likely to influence health and health care policy.

Tim Davies, Kenneth Matengu, and Judith Hall tackle the multi-dimensional phenomenon of vaccine refusal in sub-Saharan Africa, a problem they demonstrate became exacerbated during the pandemic when Western actors, some with the best intentions and pushing for a "science-based" approach to health policy formation, neglected to adopt an inclusive approach to involving native religious establishments in health protective efforts. Davies, Matengu, and Hall argue that Western and other aid agencies seeking to promote vaccination programs need to act less like their colonizing predecessors, and more collaboratively, in order to develop a dialogue with powerful local agencies otherwise resistant to implementing often complex initiatives which utilize several stakeholders and partners. To this end, the authors encourage more attention to and emulation of the ancient African philosophical tradition of "Ubuntu", which recommends interdependence and mutual trust as opposed to top-down directive as a way of achieving practical health goals.

Radhika Patel and Daniel Veidlinger probe the efficacy of the postures, breathing control techniques, and meditative states of Haṭha Yoga in promoting overall mental and physical health, asking whether this form of yoga could be effective in reducing serious illness during the COVID-19 pandemic. While exploring the considerable advantages of Hatha Yoga, they also take on a series of health-related counterclaims that ask whether its communal practice has the potential to create conditions that facilitate disease transmission due to heavy breathing in small, enclosed spaces. Thus, they seek comprehensively to work through an interesting tension within the religious practice that is their subject, weighing the health benefits of Hatha Yoga against concerns of engaging in it in the context of a health emergency known to be worsened by dense congregations of individuals in small spaces. Veidlinger and Patel conclude by introducing ways to resolve this tension, offering concrete recommendations for facilitating yoga practice in future pandemics.

Finally, Ellen Zhang looks at some of the unheralded advantages of the collectivist ethos intrinsic to the Confucian tradition for fighting a pandemic like COVID-19. To this end, she considers the normative justification for state intervention with respect to public health policies in the face of the health challenges precipitated by COVID-19 through the lens of Confucian paternalism. She distinguishes "Confucian exemplary paternalism" from the more criticized notions of paternalism understood in the West that are often used in contemporary political philosophy. Zhang argues that the former, "soft", notion of paternalism, and related paternalistic healthcare policies, are not only morally permissible, but also arguably preferable to, policies of thoroughgoing libertarianism in the face of a pandemic that threatens whole populations. Zhang's work, in essence, serves as a microcosm of the essays in this volume: Through an analysis of the collectivist norm of an eastern tradition in comparison with prized notions of individualism often featured in the West, she provides a balanced account of where it might make sense in any society for individual liberties, under dire health circumstances, to give way to a state regulation for the larger good.

Over the last three years, mistakes—which cost lives—were made when authorities promoting science and sound health care policy sought to have their advice heeded in local settings without making the extra effort to translate their often opaque public health message into language that would have been understood and appreciated by their target populations. Into the fourth year of the pandemic, most of the analysis on COVID-19 is expressed in the categories and assumptions of secular agents and, by extension, at the expense of a serious consideration of religious voices and responses. The claim of many of the contributors to these ten essays is that the scope and vision of such exclusively secular assumptions need to be expanded, first, in order to honor a commitment to openness and inclusiveness, and, second, by such inclusion, in order to expand the resources available for coordinating and implementing more effective public health policy (Erduran et al. 2019).

This volume is in part an effort to reflect on the lessons learned from some of these missed opportunities, which, if heeded, might have led to better health outcomes for many communities. In keeping with this ambition, each of the ten essays included here reflects a particular narrative account of an interplay between a local community and the global world order in the context of an unprecedented health crisis from which almost no one on the planet was spared. Each seeks to arrive at practical solutions as we continue to grapple with the issues raised by the COVID-19 pandemic. Each seeks concretely to recommend a set of best practices which might constitute good guidance for the next healthcare crisis that we will inevitably face. We do not believe that we will be able to leverage the knowledge and wisdom we have gained in this fight without a renewed appreciation of the ways that religious voices and scholarly insights can be more respectfully engaged and more fully integrated into well-coordinated public responses. Listening, critiquing, and debating with intellectual and faith communities not traditionally at the table will offer a better opportunity to attain greater success in facing the inevitable global challenges ahead.

Conflicts of Interest: The authors declare no conflict of interest.

References

American Public Media. 2023. APM Research Lab: COVID-19. Available online: https://www.apmresearchlab.org/covid (accessed on 15 May 2023).

Ammerman, Nancy Tatom. 2021. *Studying Lived Religion: Contexts and Practices*. New York: NYU Press.

Bartkowski, John P., Katherine Klee, Terence Hill, Ginny Garcia-Alexander, Christopher G. Ellison, and Amy M. Burdette. 2023. Fear God, Not COVID-19: Is Conservative Protestantism Associated with Risky Pandemic Lifestyles? *Healthcare* 11: 582. [CrossRef] [PubMed]

Blumczynski, Piotr, and Steven Wilson, eds. 2023. *The Languages of COVID-19: Translational and Multilingual Perspectives on Global Healthcare*. New York and London: Routledge, Taylor & Francis Group.

Centers for Disease Control and Prevention (CDC). 2023a. David J. Sencer CDC Museum: COVID-19 Timeline. Available online: https://www.cdc.gov/museum/timeline/covid19.html (accessed on 11 May 2023).

Centers for Disease Control and Prevention (CDC). 2023b. End of the Federal COVID-19 Public Health Emergency (PHE) Declaration. Updated May 5. Available online: https://www.cdc.gov/coronavirus/2019-ncov/your-health/end-of-phe.html#:~:text=The%20federal%20COVID%2D19%20PHE,share%20certain%20data%20will%20change (accessed on 12 May 2023).

Chang, Dianna, Xin Chang, Yu He, and Kelvin Jui Keng Tan. 2022. The determinants of COVID-19 morbidity and mortality across countries. *Scientific Reports* 12: 5888. [CrossRef] [PubMed]

Cortez, Michelle Fay. 2023. Covid Kills One Person Every Four Minutes as Vaccine Rates Fall. *Bloomberg*. May 23. Available online: https://www.bloomberg.com/news/articles/2023-05-23/covid-kills-one-every-4-minutes-as-vaccine-rates-fall-despite-end-of-emergency#xj4y7vzkg (accessed on 10 July 2023).

Covid Crisis Group. 2023. *Lessons from the Covid War: An Investigative Report*. New York: PublicAffairs.

COVID-19 Excess Mortality Collaborators. 2022. Estimating excess mortality due to the COVID-19 pandemic: A systematic analysis of COVID-19-related mortality, 2020–2021. *The Lancet* 399: 1513–36. [CrossRef]

Dartmouth College. 2023. Dartmouth Atlas Project. Available online: https://www.dartmouthatlas.org (accessed on 15 May 2023).

Ebi, Kristie L., Frances Harris, Giles B. Sioen, Chadia Wannous, Assaf Anyamba, Peng Bi, Melanie Boeckmann, Kathryn Bowen, Guéladio Cissé, Purnamita Dasgupta, and et al. 2020. Transdisciplinary Research Priorities for Human and Planetary Health in the Context of the 2030 Agenda for Sustainable Development. *International Journal of Environmental Research and Public Health* 17: 8890. [CrossRef]

Economist. 2021. Tracking COVID-19 Excess Deaths across Countries. October 20. Available online: https://www.economist.com/graphic-detail/coronavirus-excess-deaths-tracker (accessed on 12 May 2023).

Economist. 2023. The Pandemic's True Death Toll. October 25. Available online: https://www.economist.com/graphic-detail/coronavirus-excess-deaths-estimates (accessed on 12 May 2023).

Eisenberg, Joseph. 2020. How Scientists Quantify the Intensity of an Outbreak Like COVID-19. *Michigan Medicine*. March 17. Available online: https://www.michiganmedicine.org/health-lab/how-scientists-quantify-intensity-outbreak-covid-19 (accessed on 15 May 2023).

Erduran, Sibel, Liam Guilfoyle, Wonyong Park, Jessica Chan, and Nigel Fancourt. 2019. Argumentation and interdisciplinarity: Reflections from the Oxford Argumentation in Religion and Science Project. *Disciplinary and Interdiscriplinary Science Education Research* 1: 8. Available online: https://link.springer.com/article/10.1186/s43031-019-0006-9 (accessed on 30 June 2023). [CrossRef]

European Union. 2023. European Center for Disease Prevention and Control: COVID-19 Data Sets. Available online: https://www.ecdc.europa.eu/en/covid-19/data (accessed on 15 May 2023).

Georgetown University, Berkley Center for Religion, Peace & World Affairs. 2023a. Faith and COVID-19: Resource Repository. Available online: https://covidfaithrepository.georgetown.domains (accessed on 11 May 2023).

Georgetown University, Berkley Center for Religion, Peace & World Affairs. 2023b. Religious Responses to COVID-19. Available online: https://berkleycenter.georgetown.edu/subprojects/religious-responses-to-covid-19 (accessed on 11 May 2023).

Hartford Institute for Religion Research. 2021. Navigating the Pandemic: A First Look at Congregational Responses. November. Available online: https://www.covidreligionresearch.org/wp-content/uploads/2021/11/Navigating-the-Pandemic_A-First-Look-at-Congregational-Responses_Nov-2021.pdf (accessed on 13 May 2023).

Hartford Institute for Religion Research. 2023. Faith Communities Today: Research & Resources: U.S. Religion During COVID-19. Available online: https://faithcommunitiestoday.org/research-resources-religion-during-covid-19/ (accessed on 15 May 2023).

Harvard Global Health Institute. 2023. Projects: Coronavirus Response. Available online: https://globalhealth.harvard.edu/domains/pandemics/programs/project-1/ (accessed on 15 May 2023).

Idler, Ellen, John A. Bernau, and Dimitrios Zaras. 2022. Narratives and counter-narratives in religious responses to COVID-19: A computational text analysis. *PLoS ONE* 17: er0262905. [CrossRef] [PubMed]

Johns Hopkins Coronavirus Resource Center. 2023. Available online: https://coronavirus.jhu.edu (accessed on 15 May 2023).

Kantis, Caroline, Samantha Kernan, Jason S. Bardi, Lillian Posner, and Isabella Turilli. 2023. UPDATED: Timeline of the Coronavirus. *ThinkGlobalHealth*, May 12. Available online: https://www.thinkglobalhealth.org/article/updated-timeline-coronavirus (accessed on 11 May 2023).

Levin, Jeff. 2020. The Faith Community and the SARS-CoV-2 Outbreak: Part of the Problem or Part of the Solution? *Journal of Religion and Health* 59: 2215–28. [CrossRef] [PubMed]

Levin, Jeff, and Matt Bradshaw. 2022. Determinants of COVID-19 skepticism and SARS-CoV-2 vaccine hesitancy: Findings from a national population survey of U.S. adults. *BMC Public Health* 22: 1047. [CrossRef] [PubMed]

Levin, Jeff, Ellen L. Idler, and Tyler J. VanderWeele. 2022. Faith-Based Organizations and SARS-CoV-2 Vaccination: Challenges and Recommendations. *Public Health Reports* 137: 11–16. [CrossRef] [PubMed]

Majumdar, Samirah. 2022. How COVID-19 Restrictions Affected Religious Groups around the World in 2020. *Pew Research Center*. November 29. Available online: https://www.pewresearch.org/religion/2022/11/29/how-covid-19-restrictions-affected-religious-groups-around-the-world-in-2020/ (accessed on 11 May 2023).

Martens, Jason P., and Bastiaan T. Rutjens. 2022. Spirituality and religiosity contribute to ongoing COVID-19 vaccination rates: Comparing 195 regions around the world. *Vaccine: X* 12: 100241. [CrossRef] [PubMed]

New York Times. 2023. The COVID-19 Pandemic. Available online: https://www.nytimes.com/news-event/coronavirus (accessed on 15 May 2023).

Nortey, Justin. 2022. Americans skeptical about religious objections to COVID-19 vaccines, but oppose employer mandates. *Pew Research Center*. March 31. Available online: https://www.pewresearch.org/short-reads/2022/03/31/americans-skeptical-about-religious-objections-to-covid-19-vaccines-but-oppose-employer-mandates/ (accessed on 30 June 2023).

Our World in Data. 2023. Coronavirus Pandemic (COVID-19). Available online: https://ourworldindata.org/coronavirus (accessed on 30 June 2023).

Pankowski, Daniel, and Kinga Wytrychiewicz-Pankowska. 2023. Turning to Religion During COVID-19 (Part I): A Systematic Review, Meta-analysis and Meta-regression of Studies on the Relationship Between Religious Coping and Mental Health Throughout COVID-19. *Journal of Religion and Health* 62: 510–43. [CrossRef] [PubMed]

Pew Research Center. 2023. Search Results: COVID-19 and Religion. Available online: https://www.pewresearch.org/search/covid-19+and+religion (accessed on 15 May 2023).

Siddiqui, Sazada, Heba W. S. Alhamdi, and Huda Alghamdi. 2022. Recent Chronology of COVID-19 Pandemic. *Frontiers of Public Health* 10: 778037. [CrossRef] [PubMed]

Sisti, Leuconoe Grazia, Danilo Buonsenso, Umberto Moscato, Gianfranco Costanzo, and Walter Malorni. 2023. The Role of Religions in the COVID-19 Pandemic: A Narrative Review. *International Journal of Environmental Research and Public Health* 20: 1691. [CrossRef] [PubMed]

Stoto, Michael A, and Matthew K Wynia. 2020. Appendix C: Assessing Morbidity and Mortality Associated with the COVID-19 Pandemic: A Case Study Illustrating the Need for the Recommendations of This Report. In *A Framework for Assessing Mortality and Morbidity after Large-Scale Disasters*. Edited by Daniel L. Cork, Olivia C. Yost, Scott H. Wollek and Ellen J. MacKenzie. Washington, DC: National Academies Press.

Towards Science Data. 2023. COVID-19 Open Source Dashboard. Available online: https://towardsdatascience.com/covid-19-open-source-dashboard-fa1d2b4cd985 (accessed on 15 May 2023).

United Nations (UN). 2023a. United Nations Office for the Coordination of Humanitarian Affairs (OCHA) Humanitarian Data Exchange: European COVID-19: Subnational Cases. Available online: https://data.humdata.org/dataset/europe-covid-19-subnational-cases (accessed on 15 May 2023).

United Nations (UN). 2023b. WHO Chief Declares End to COVID-19 as a Global Health Emergency. May 5. Available online: https://news.un.org/en/story/2023/05/1136367#:~:text=The%20head%20of%20the%20UN,no%20longer%20a%20global%20threat (accessed on 15 May 2023).

Volet, Annie Kibongani, Cristina Scavone, Daniel Catalán-Matamaros, and Annalisa Capuano. 2022. Vaccine Hesitancy Among Religious Groups: Reasons Underlying this Phenomenon and Communication Strategies to Rebuild Trust. *Frontiers in Public Health* 10: 824560. [CrossRef] [PubMed]

Wallace-Wells, David. 2023. The Myth of Early Pandemic Polarization. *New York Times*, June 28. Available online: https://www.nytimes.com/2023/06/28/opinion/covid-pandemic-2020-or-covid-pandemic-politics.html?smid=nytcore-ios-share&referringSource=articleShare (accessed on 30 June 2023).

Washington Post. 2023. Coronavirus. Available online: https://www.washingtonpost.com/coronavirus/ (accessed on 15 May 2023).

Williams, Simon Nicholas. 2023. COVID-19 is no longer a global health emergency. Here's what it means. *World Economic Forum/The Conversation*. May 9. Available online: https://www.weforum.org/agenda/2023/05/who-covid-19-no-longer-global-health-emergency/ (accessed on 13 May 2023).

Witt-Swanson, Lindsey, Jennifer Benz, and Daniel Cox. 2023. Faith After the Pandemic: How COVID-19 Changed American Religion: Findings from the 2022 American Religious Benchmark Survey. Sponsored by the American Enterprise Institute's Survey Center on American Life. January 5. Available online: https://www.americansurveycenter.org/research/faith-after-the-pandemic-how-covid-19-changed-american-religion/ (accessed on 14 May 2023).

Woolf, Steven H., Derek A. Chapman, Roy T. Sabo, Daniel M. Weinberger, and Latoya Hill. 2020. Excess Deaths From COVID-19 and other Causes, March-April 2020. *JAMA: Journal of the American Medical Association* 324: 510–13. [CrossRef] [PubMed]

World Health Organization (WHO). 2023. Timeline: WHO's COVID-19 Response. Available online: https://www.who.int/emergencies/diseases/novel-coronavirus-2019/interactive-timeline#category-Leadership (accessed on 11 May 2023).

Wuthnow, Robert. 2010. *Be Very Afraid: The Cultural Response to Terror, Pandemics, Environmental Devastation, Nuclear Annihilation, and Other Threats*. Oxford: Oxford University Press.

Wuthnow, Robert. 2022. *Religion's Power: What Makes It Work*. Oxford: Oxford University Press.

religions

MDPI

Article

In God We Trust: Community and Immunity in American Religions during COVID-19

Julia Brown

English Department, Stony Brook University, Stony Brook, NY 11794, USA; julia.r.brown@stonybrook.edu

Abstract: From the systemic issues of race and class division to political partisanship and religious identity, the pandemic has affected many aspects of American social and political life. I interrogate the role that religions have played in communal identity-making during the pandemic, and how such identities shaped ideological responses, particularly in the US, stymying public health efforts to stop, or at least significantly slow, the spread of COVID-19. Drawing from Gabriel Garcia Marquez's *Love in the Time of Cholera* as a historical case study, I use Garcia Marquez's depiction of religion's identity-making power during the cholera pandemic depicted in the novel as a comparison by which to understand current experiences of white Evangelical Christians in America during the current COVID-19 pandemic, particularly those who reject risk-minimizing practices such as mask wearing, quarantining, and vaccination. Drawing both from representations of Roberto Esposito's theory of immunity and community, and from Lauren Berlant's concept of "cruel optimism", as well as sociological understandings of religion and identity, I argue that the boundary-making practices of religion and of communal and national identity are related to the complex and often contradictory set of moral practices that led many white Evangelicals to disregard public health policies surrounding COVID-19. A concurrent analysis of Garcia Marquez's novel and of current events will allow me to explore this phenomenon, as Lauren Berlant would put it, both through the historically affective aesthetic and through the affective present.

Keywords: COVID-19; white Evangelical Christianity; vaccines; religious identity; public health policy; community; immunity; *Love in the Time of Cholera*

Citation: Brown, Julia. 2023. In God We Trust: Community and Immunity in American Religions during COVID-19. *Religions* 14: 428. https://doi.org/10.3390/rel14030428

Academic Editors: Andrew Flescher and Joel Zimbelman

Received: 8 October 2022
Revised: 7 November 2022
Accepted: 17 March 2023
Published: 22 March 2023

1. Introduction

The COVID-19 pandemic has both highlighted and exacerbated the sharp divides in America that have been present since the country's foundation. From the systemic issues of race and class division to the urban/rural divide, political partisanship, and religious identity, the pandemic affected many aspects of American social and political life. Joining scholars such as Sandro Galea who have interrogated the social and systemic forces that shape health in America, I aim to question the role that religions played and continue to play in communal identity-making during the pandemic, and how such identities, particularly in the US, shaped both conscious and unconscious ideological responses, stymying public health efforts to significantly slow the spread of COVID-19. While individuals from the full range of representative belief systems and identities refused vaccination for myriad reasons, the group that did so most prevalently, as detailed later in this article, was that of white Evangelical Christians (Religious Identities and the Race Against the Virus: American Attitudes on Vaccination Mandates and Religious Exemptions (Wave 3) 2021). Many, but certainly not all, of the white Evangelical Christians who did receive vaccines remained silent about their vaccine status, while publicly espousing or passively assenting to anti-vax rhetoric. While of course white Evangelical Christianity is not a monolith, a significant percentage of the population of white Evangelical Christians did demonstrate anti-vax and anti-mask stances, and often refusing to socially distance. Not all white Evangelical Christians adopt an anti-vaccination stance, and many did, in fact, follow the public health guidelines put in place by the CDC (Religious Identities and the Race Against the Virus: American Attitudes on Vaccination Mandates and Religious Exemptions (Wave 3) 2021; The Coronavirus Pandemic's Impact on Religious Life n.d.), but they are not who I am writing about in this article.

By looking at both the sociological data collected across the pandemic and the multi-faceted nature of identity's role in decision making, this article identifies and ponders the power of religion as a cultural force. I posit that the boundary-making practices of religion and of communal and national identity created the complex and often contradictory set of moral practices that led many white Evangelicals to disregard public health policies surrounding COVID-19, despite the presence of radically different attitudes and responses from individuals who are representative of other strands of American Christianity and other religions. In particular, religions serve as the basis for a cultural community which in turn influences political views and enables in-group thinking. This groupish behavior as seen in white Evangelical Christians is then used to advance partisanship between religion and science as well as left- and right-wing political parties. It is this partisan thinking that led many to behaviors counter to reasonable health indicators.

Before exploring religious identity-making in relation to the pandemic, I would first like to account for the complex nature of a public health response and communicable disease. There is no one thing alone that caused the United States' devastating response to COVID-19 (Lewis 2021; Galea 2022; Simmons-Duffin 2022; Dias and Graham 2021; Religious Identities and the Race Against the Virus: American Attitudes on Vaccination Mandates and Religious Exemptions (Wave 3) 2021; The Coronavirus Pandemic's Impact on Religious Life n.d.). Rather, "health is the state of not being sick to begin with, and it is shaped by social, economic, environmental, and political forces" (Galea 2022, p. xvi). As public health scholar Sandro Galea (2022) points out, the American health care system has developed as a response to acute care illness, not as a preemptive public health system that seeks to ensure the health of Americans. Further, the decentralized nature of public health programs in the United States led to 50 states adopting as many approaches to stop the spread. America entered the pandemic with flawed systems that made health a commodity to be distributed unequally, with people of color and those of lower socioeconomic status least likely to have access to the resources necessary to live a healthy life. The pandemic, thus, struck those communities hardest.

Why then, one might ask, have I chosen to focus on white Evangelical Christians in this paper? Disease does not obey boundaries, class, or the color divide—public health means focusing on the health of all. If one group of people decides against following public health guidelines, especially in the case of a communicable disease such as COVID-19, it could put everyone at risk. While this is not unique to white Evangelical Christians, the fact remains that they were the most likely of any group to view COVID-19 as a non-threat, or worse, as not being real, and they were more likely to identify their faith as reasoning for these views (Dias and Graham 2021; Religious Identities and the Race Against the Virus: American Attitudes on Vaccination Mandates and Religious Exemptions (Wave 3) 2021). This noted, understanding why certain people choose to ignore these guidelines can further our knowledge on how to reach such communities and prevent the spread of future pandemics. Religion in America is positioned as both a social and a political force, and is therefore an especially rich area of study for COVID-19 response and public health.

As a complex and varied set of practices, religions have had both positive and negative effects for individuals during the pandemic. On the whole, individuals who prayed about COVID-19 were more likely to participate in risk-mitigating practices such as mask wearing—with the notable exception of white Evangelical Christians with belief in religious nationalism (Corcoran et al. 2022; Perry et al. 2020). Belonging to a community with a durable and tested shared religious identity provides a support system, with many individuals turning to religious leaders and other congregation members for guidance and care (Keshet and Liberman 2014; Krause et al. 2002). For example, in many Jewish communities, the sense of belonging provided by religion played an important role in building resiliency during quarantine (Frei-Landau 2020). Malaysian healthcare workers who practiced religion were less likely to exhibit symptoms of anxiety and depression throughout the pandemic (Chow et al. 2021). Likewise, research has shown that in America, religion has provided comfort in the face of growing anxiety throughout the pandemic. Yet, this same comfort also made a uniform public health response difficult in the United States, as many individuals and their communities were led to believe that COVID-19 might not be a threat or as great a threat as some surmised (Schnabel and Schieman 2022). Individuals with white Evangelical Christianity as an identity marker were significantly less likely to comply with public health policies (Funk and Gramlich 2021; Jackson 2021; Religious Identities and the Race Against the Virus: American Attitudes on Vaccination Mandates and Religious Exemptions (Wave 3) 2021; Schnabel and Schieman 2022; The Coronavirus Pandemic's Impact on Religious Life n.d.). Religious nationalism in the United States affected government policy to forgo mandated public health measures, with Evangelical Protestant officials more likely to be exposed to and align with religious nationalist ideals (Adler et al. 2021).

While much research has been done on the role of religions in shaping health practices during the COVID-19 pandemic, the primary methodology to study their response to the pandemic has been survey based with quantitative analysis of the results (Religious Identities and the Race Against the Virus: American Attitudes on Vaccination Mandates and Religious Exemptions (Wave 3) 2021; Chow et al. 2021). Though this research is helpful in determining the role of religious identity during COVID-19, it does not adequately address the potential reasoning or justifications behind these ideological responses, nor does it identify and explain different models of religious pandemic response. My exploration of pandemic response through the lenses of Lauren Berlant's concept of "cruel optimism" and Roberto Esposito's delineation of the relationship between community and immunity offers one explanation of the ideological responses, while my close reading of *Love in the Time of Cholera* provides a different response model.

Berlant's cruel optimism conceptually explains attachments, or objects of desire, to which the subject attributes a "cluster of promises" (Berlant 2011). The belief, or optimism, in the attachment is that it will make possible a dream or a goal the subject desires. The cruelty of such a bargain surfaces when the desire is either not fulfillable or, when fulfilled, is harmful to the subject (Berlant 2011). The communal identity associated with Evangelical Christianity became one such attachment.

To better understand how community affected immunity, and vice versa, I turn to Esposito. While I will be using Esposito's philosophy to discuss literal viral immunity, it is important to note that he is conceptualizing immunity in the abstract as a general term. Tracing the etymology of the words, Esposito suggests that community and immunity are related in that communities are bound by common laws, and immunity places individuals outside of that structure. To be immune, then, in an abstract sense, is to isolate oneself from a community. This concept can be seen not just in medical discourse, but in legal and political discourses as well. For example, the person who testifies in exchange for not being charged with a crime, or the person who holds a nationalist anti-immigrant stance, respectively. Esposito (2013) also posits a solution—a reframing of community as something that cannot exist without first achieving immunity—which I will return to in a close reading of *Love in the Time of Cholera*, immunity being the key that reopens the borders of the individual.

To better reach a multiplicity of populations in the responses to health crises, we must understand the roles religions play in individual and group decision making. Drawing from Gabriel Garcia Marquez's *Love in the Time of Cholera* as a historical case study, I compare Garcia Marquez's depiction of religion's identity-making power during the cholera pandemic at the end of the 19th century to current experiences of white Evangelical Christians in America during COVID-19, particularly those who refused to mask up, quarantine, and/or receive vaccination. Because the focus of *Love in the Time of Cholera* is, as the title suggests, on interpersonal relationships with the cholera pandemic as a backdrop, it gives unique insight into religious identity, community, and health. Garcia Marquez's novel suggests the possibility of a less partisan relationship between science and religion and allows us to envision what might be if we can highlight shared sets of values rather than focusing on difference.

2. American Identity and Religions in COVID-19

In the era of COVID-19, religious identity has taken the fore in public debates on risk-minimizing practices surrounding the pandemic. This stems from the paradoxical relationship between community and immunity that emerged from overlapping national, political, and religious identities. In America, the overwhelming view is that political decisions are made secularly and are empirically grounded, established by listening to the data points provided by scientists and responding to them appropriately. However, not every American citizen has the same relationship with scientific information, as many distrust science whether due to religious belief or other cultural ideologies. This complication is exacerbated by the reality that science communication is constantly providing us with new data—data which can be difficult to decipher for the layperson (Chan 2018; Dias and Graham 2021; Glass 2019; Olagoke et al. 2021; Payir et al. 2021). As Esposito, paraphrasing philosopher-anthropologist Arnold Gehlen, states, "In a situation of excessive environmental impact and pressures, institutions are charged with exonerating man from the weight with which the contingency of events saddles him. This requires a kind of 'plasticity,' or a capacity to adapt to a given situation so as not to expose the individual to an unbearable conflict" (Esposito 2013, p. 40). If one institution—say, one of science or reason-based political policy—fails to adapt, and an individual finds the divide between lived experience and policy (or belief and policy) too great, they will turn to an institution that better protects them from conflict. In the United States, we see this turn away from science and toward religion in the behavior of white Evangelical Christians (Plohl and Musil 2021). Such a response, very much a symptom of an ongoing distrust of the scientific community due to an in-group mentality and differing value systems, one that has essentially placed science and religion at odds with one another, dates back as far as the Scopes Trial in the 1920s (Evans 2013). The public trial pitted science against religion, sparking speeches such as "The Bible and its Enemies", and resulted in a decades-long debate about whether the Tennessee law banning the teaching of evolution in public schools was constitutional (Adams 2005). This ongoing moral debate regarding the history of evolution and current iterations around stem cell research and human cloning laid the groundwork for the evangelical response to COVID-19 by, as some believe, engraining distrust of science in the identity of Evangelical Christianity (Dias and Graham 2021). Further, as nation and religion are tightly bound in terms of identity, in-group members demonstrate political behaviors they perceive to match their own religious values—values which the current Republican party touts as foundational to their platform and traditionally "American" in nature (Glass 2019).

American national identity is founded, as many history textbooks would tell us, on religious freedom (or, perhaps more accurately, freedom for the particular religion of Puritanism). The first amendment of the Constitution expressly legalizes freedom of religion in the free exercise clause, and arguably the separation of church and state in the establishment clause, yet historically, these have been unevenly addressed by the Supreme Court. However, the upshot of both the constitutional recognition and establishment, as well as the attention to their construal over two and a half centuries, is that religious belief and cultural expressions have solidified themselves in the fabric of American culture to a degree not matched by other existing democracies or industrialized societies. The tie between religion and American identity is also evidenced in more recent history. For example, in the 1950s the Census Bureau debated for nearly a decade on whether religious affiliation should be included as a census question (Schultz 2006). On one side of the census debate was the recognition of the evolving presence of religious pluralism in the culture; on the other, a number of Protestant Christians who feared plurality was a façade—that the real agenda was to de-Protestantize America (Schultz 2006).

In the mind of these Christians, the fear of pluralism was justified, and highlights a similar concern that exists among various groups today, in that religious identity and national identity, alike, are concerned with the formation (or disintegration) of boundaries. These boundaries play a role in the formation of communities, and "Members of a community are such if and because they are bound by a common law" (Esposito 2013, p. 14). For a nation, such boundaries are drawn on maps, and by the laws instituted through political regimes. In the case of religions, this "common law" is that of their particular belief set defined as a shared "method of valuing" (Pecorino 2001). However, religion as an identity-making practice is not as simple as volitional membership in a group. As anthropologist Clifford Geertz argues, religion is a cultural system; it "provides a blueprint" by which individuals can shape their lives. In other words, religion provides structure and meaning through which individuals shape their reality, contributing to the structure of religions reciprocally (Geertz 1993, pp. 92–93). Religion's status as a cultural system makes religion a powerful factor in other aspects of identity, particularly political ideology. In a call to attend to Western religions' role in sociological phenomenon, Glass states, "As a social "glue" that allowed diverse individuals to see common purpose and affiliation, religion both defined a set of social values to be realized through social life and norms to be followed to achieve those values. The downside, however, of any bonding ideology is the in-group mentality it creates and the prejudice it incites against other value systems and behaviors, producing conflict both internally and externally with other social groups" (Glass 2019, p. 10). In the United States, as previously mentioned, religion and national identity are historically bound to one another. The in-groups created often run along these identity lines, and the values, or "common laws", which define them. Yet, researchers such as Glass show that political identity should also be factored into this equation. Rather than secularity determining political law, religions play a major factor in political ideology.

As debates about mask and vaccine mandates arose, COVID-19 became not just an issue of public health, but a political issue steeped in religious and nationalist ideals. Religion often influenced the pandemic response, not just of the American people, but of government officials (Adler et al. 2021). It is difficult to separate the threads of politics, nation, and religions in behavior, as identity is a complex formation of many facets of an individual's life. Whereas previous debates between Evangelical Christians and scientific reasoning have been relatively harmless in terms of immediate and widespread health outcomes, the pandemic posed a different kind of problem, one with direct consequences both inside and outside the religious community. Despite the scientific data that show the efficacy of quarantine, vaccination, and mask wearing in preventing the spread of COVID-19, white Evangelical Christians have been resistant to comply with these risk minimizing practices.

We can see this resistance in the reported numbers of vaccine refusers across identity groups. Data collected from November of 2021 by PRRI show that, at 25%, the percentage of white Evangelical Christians who refuse to get vaccinated again COVID-19 was higher than that of any other religion (Religious Identities and the Race Against the Virus: American Attitudes on Vaccination Mandates and Religious Exemptions (Wave 3) 2021). Other research has shown the difference to be even greater, with the percentage of vaccine refusers among white Evangelical Christians as high as 40% (Funk and Gramlich 2021). Moreover, only 63% of white Evangelical Christians reported that they always wear a mask—significantly less than other religious identity groups in the United States—while 75% believed that churches should be allowed to hold in-person services (The Coronavirus Pandemic's Impact on Religious Life n.d.). While mask-wearing policies have lifted as the vaccine proves effective and COVID-19 becomes endemic rather than a pandemic, a lack of mask wearing during in-person events at the time this data was collected turned every service into a potential super-spreader event. In the crisis time of COVID-19, such actions had dire consequences, the repercussions of which are still felt today. Many of the areas that experienced the highest infection rates also had a higher population of Evangelical

Christians, most likely due to the refusal to follow public health guidelines (Jenkins 2021; Gonzalez et al. 2021).

3. The Cruel Optimism of Religious Attachments: Immunity of Community

With the dangers presented by COVID-19, why then do white Evangelical Christians, in particular, continue to resist vaccination as a matter of principle? Lauren Berlant's idea of cruel optimism and Roberto Esposito's ideas on community and immunity are helpful in formulating a provisional and insightful response to this phenomenon. Religious identity in itself is not harmful, and in fact, is often beneficial in its community building. Rather, it is when religious identity cannot adapt in the face of crisis that the attachment becomes cruel. Embracing an identity that requires one to expose themselves to harmful situations, such as the increased potential of contracting a communicable and severe disease such as COVID-19, is clinging to an optimism that is cruel. In white Evangelical Christians, such attachment is rooted in, and exacerbated by, sociohistorical clashes between their theology and scientific findings. The presumed loss of the community in exchange for immunity is what thwarted many Evangelical Christians from following the risk-minimizing guidelines put forth by the CDC. This common behavior was propagated by two different means, or two different shared laws. First, the allegiance to a respected leader such as a pastor may result in the decision to respect the relationship and prescriptions given at the expense of other potential choices. In the case of the COVID-19 pandemic, spiritual leaders became role models in behaviors that extend beyond faith. Second, an enactment of shared and specific religious beliefs motivated the rejection of masking and social distancing, and in the second and third years of the pandemic, the use of vaccines. The optimistic promises attributed to being an in-member of the white Evangelical Christian group, for many, led to the turn from science, which could arguably be explained by science's (and its spokespersons') failure to adapt and appeal to these shared values.

Let me turn to a hypothetical case study posed by Sandro Galea in his book, *The Contagion Next Time*, to further illustrate the turn from scientific to religious institutions. Galea presents the story of Jean, who grew up in an abusive home and found church to be a place of refuge—a place that spread a message of harmony and shared purpose among people. When COVID-19 struck, Jean continued to attend church with much of her congregation. Galea frames this story in terms of a hierarchy of perceived health needs of an individual; in Jean's case, the communal nature of church held more importance for her mental and spiritual health than the threat of COVID-19 held for her physical health (Galea 2022). While Galea's explanation of Jean's decision to continue going to church is certainly part of the story, the motivation to attend goes beyond a weighing of health needs. It also entails cruel optimism. While mental and spiritual health are indeed important, achieving this spiritual health did not need to come at the expense of incurring the potential risks to physical health. The attachment to the church as a life-changing space becomes cruel when risking a life-threatening communicable disease becomes the real cost of attending. Mental and, to an extent, spiritual health are moot points if one is dead. In Galea's case study, as well as in many actual churches, masking was uneven and social distancing guidelines were not followed. Rather than attempt to strike a balance between the new circumstances of COVID-19 and mental/spiritual health, many churches and white Evangelical Christians refused to adapt to meet both sets of needs.

They also used their religion as the justification for not taking risk-mitigating measures against the virus. In one New York Times interview, "Lauri Armstrong, a Bible-believing nutritionist outside of Dallas, said she did not need the vaccine because God designed the body to heal itself, if given the right nutrients. More than that, she said, 'It would be God's will if I am here or if I am not here'" (Dias and Graham 2021). The logic behind Armstrong's assertion is that God determines all, and would ultimately decide the fate of those exposed to COVID-19. Following this reasoning to its extreme conclusion, supporting and participating in risk-mitigating behaviors would go against God's will. It is worth noting that there are a number of white Evangelical Christians who were hospitalized with

COVID-19 and are now advocating publicly for the vaccine, with the argument that if God made COVID-19 he also made the vaccine. At the same time, those from this cohort who are not vocal about their beliefs maintain a low profile in public forums so as not to attract ridicule or engage in public debates. Yet, many espouse beliefs like Armstrong's, finding (or remaining a member of) a community of like-minded religious people. Yes, individuals who get vaccinated and wear a mask are one step closer to immunity, but in doing so they are "break[ing] the circuit of social circulation by placing himself or herself outside of it" (Esposito 2013, p. 59); in essence, they are trading their community for immunity. They are not just betraying their religious beliefs, but in doing so are also removing themselves from the community that shares their religious identity, a community to which they are attached, and which can fulfill the desire of redemption and eternal life. Though such individuals would be at less risk of losing their life to COVID-19, they often feel they are at a higher risk of losing the life they built within their community and the promises which they believe that community makes possible. While loss of community is not the language that many anti-vax and anti-maskers use when expressing their reasoning for their actions, which is often rather complex, we can trace back these behaviors to a base of in-group reasoning that stems from their religious affiliation.

Ironically, in avoiding the immunity that comes with preventive measures against COVID-19, white Evangelical Christians were simultaneously and inadvertently stymying the potential for community in the long term. Esposito suggests that for these individuals "The idea of immunity, which is needed for protecting our life, if carried past a certain threshold, winds up negating life. That is, immunity encages life such that not only is our freedom but also the very meaning of our individual and collective existence lost" (Esposito 2013, p. 61). This sentiment is reminiscent of the arguments against vaccination and mask wearing, along with the belief that mandating such behaviors is a violation of personal freedom which, for many who espouse this logic, is analogous to the integrity of their community and relationship to God. In the case of white Evangelical Christians, the threshold for determining which steps to take to increase safety or establish herd immunity, steps which would have the consequences of negating life-as-normal in evangelical communities during the COVID-19 pandemic, was lower than in many other religious communities, such as Catholicism.

Why might this be so? Stemming in part from the overlap between political and religious identity groups, many of the arguments for the WEC position are made in the name of religion, but mask a deep and abiding allegiance to a political ideology that may have little to do—historically or substantively—to commitments to Christian faith and morals. As an example, loving thy neighbor has been used since the earliest decades of Christianity as a nonnegotiable touchstone and framework to encourage actions on behalf of the neighbor. During COVID-19, getting vaccinated was often framed as an act of care for those who are at greatest risk of the disease. While loving thy neighbor is a Christian ideal, statistically evangelicals are the least likely of any denomination to appeal to this reasoning when it comes to vaccines (Religious Identities and the Race Against the Virus: American Attitudes on Vaccination Mandates and Religious Exemptions (Wave 3) 2021), and white Evangelical Republicans even more so (Jackson 2021). Yet, not masking or vaccinating and continuing to hold large in-person gatherings in prayer settings puts the entire community at risk. Without preventive measures, COVID-19 can quickly spread through a community and have serious consequences, including death. Paradoxically, in focusing on immunity rather than community in an unbalanced way, the community is endangered.

Yet, such paradoxical beliefs are not unusual in partisan thinking. As social psychologist Johnathan Haidt (2013) points out, humans are both selfish, focused on what benefits the individual, and groupish, focused on what benefits groups to which they belong. Decisions are made not based on reason alone, but on an emotional level as well. When groupish thought becomes polarized and partisan—as with religion and science, or with left and right political parties—it is our emotional response that kicks in first, especially when receiving information contradictory or harmful to the group. Rationalizing such information releases dopamine, and as Haidt points out, "Like rats that cannot stop pressing a button, partisans may simply be unable to stop believing weird things. The partisan brain has been reinforced so many times for performing mental contortions that free it from unwanted beliefs" (Haidt 2013, p. 88). The rhetoric used in anti-mask debates is especially, and sometimes aggressively, partisan, positioning individual freedom to not mask against the tyranny of an oppressive government. Further, much of the rhetoric draws not just on political identity, but also on a Christian identity appealing to individual freedom as "God given rights" and holding politico-religious festivals such as Bards Fest, which featured several prominent Evangelical Christian speakers. It becomes easy for white Evangelical Christians to react groupishly, and justify not wearing masks as protecting collective existence, rather than interpreting this as a way to protect that very same ideal.

The imbalance and paradox in the COVID-19 response is not the fault of religion alone. Rather, white Evangelic Christians are caught in a double bind of neither religious nor scientific institutions adapting fully, as Esposito and Gehlen suggest is necessary, to relieve the burden placed on the individual. In the debate over vaccination, many Evangelical Christians cite the use of fetal stem cells acquired from an elective abortion as the reason they refuse vaccination. The development of the Johnson & Johnson vaccine did, in fact, use a cell line derived from a fetus aborted in 1985, while Moderna and Pfizer used the same cell line to confirm the viability of their vaccines (Schimelpfening 2021). Fetal cell lines are lab-developed stem cells that originated in fetal tissue, but do not contain actual fetal tissue. These cell lines are used in laboratory testing of the viability of many drugs, including common over-the-counter drugs, the usage of which is not opposed by white Evangelical Christians. Catholicism, whose teachings also oppose abortion, has, in contrast, adapted to the COVID-19 pandemic. Catholic religious leaders have publicly advocated for the vaccine, stating that it is morally sound to use any of the three vaccines approved by the FDA for use in the United States. Yet, leaders of the Evangelical Christian community continue to push back against vaccination and mask wearing on social media and television, while research has suggested that members of a religious community have a higher trust in such informal media sources (Olagoke et al. 2021). Even white Evangelical leaders who support vaccination are hesitant to speak out regarding the matter due to fear of alienating members of their congregation (Dias and Graham 2021).

On the other hand, clear communication of scientific concepts coupled with outreach and representation towards religious identity is where public health scientists were (and still are) lacking. From the Trump administration's downplaying of the seriousness of COVID-19, to the inconsistencies in messaging and personal compromises in integrity made by some health officials in order to maintain jobs and stability, to the decrease in CDC telebriefings during the Biden administration, public health officials, save for a couple of familiar faces, have not connected with the public, communicating primarily via text on the internet (Simmons-Duffin 2022). Rather than establishing a basis of trust between those most often in the public eye, (i.e., the professionals researching and acting on such research), and the peoples affected by those reactions (the population sheltering in place, glued to the television for any new information), those on whom we depended to fortify public trust dropped the ball. The nation was bombarded with conflicting messages and left to sift through dispassionate data and bureaucratic guidelines. Indeed, during COVID-19, science communication was marked by the speed at which circumstances changed. With rapidly unfolding new information regarding the spread of COVID-19, scientists took to Twitter to share data and information. Still, much of the communication regarding public health guidelines was too focused on data, and not enough on acknowledging the needs of the citizens that those guidelines affected (Galea 2022; Nabi 2021). For individuals who already have a distrust in scientific findings, sharing data alone is likely not going to suffice when asking them to make major lifestyle changes, even for a limited time. While scientific communication did adapt to the speed of the changing circumstances, and to the shift to social media as a major outlet for spreading awareness, it did not adapt enough to persuade those Evangelical Christians who were most likely to disregard risk-mitigating practices. How can public health officials and scientists be more effective at reaching such individuals?

4. The Affective Present and the Historically Affective Aesthetic

To better understand the present pandemic situation, we need to look to the past. As Michael Lewis reveals in his interviews, scientists and public health officials woefully neglected historical research conducted on pandemic response in formulating public policy strategies in 2020 and beyond. Instead, the response to COVID-19 was slow, and the fear of a public shut-down delayed quarantine measures (Lewis 2021). It is clear from Lewis' presentation that a wealth of pandemic modeling and scientific research had been performed in the fields of epidemiology and public health. Despite showing efficacy in slowing or stopping the spread of past contagions, these insights and tools were ignored as options in the current crisis. Along with Lewis's anecdotal material, as well as studies on previous public health crises such as polio and AIDS to highlight the roles played by vigilance and intransigence in the face of epidemics, I suggest a turn toward literature as a means to ascertaining why such attitudes exist and how to effectively respond to them.

As a supplement to looking at scientific data and biographical accounts which do not always or readily address cultural factors that play into a public health response, we might also consult fictional narrative accounts as prospective entry points into how human beings might cope with pandemics, or indeed have coped with them in the past. An exemplification of this approach occurs with Gabriel Garcia Marquez's *Love in the Time of Cholera*, a novel which details both the woe and the response attendant to such a delicate navigation that is precipitated by a historic and disruptive health crisis. As I write this article, cases are spiking yet again in New York City, even as vaccines and boosters have been rolled out, the city has reopened, and COVID-19 is well on its way to becoming endemic rather than a pandemic. Any analysis I write, though removed from the constant sirens and high death tolls that marked the height of the pandemic, is therefore situated in what Lauren Berlant deems the affective present. She writes: "everyone lives the present intensely, from within a sense that their time, this time, is crisis time" (Berlant 2011, p. 57). Yet, the crisis we are facing and the challenges that accompany it are not new. They are historically situated and can thus be explored both historically and presently. It is for this reason that Garcia Marquez's novel becomes a key piece of my analysis. As Berlant points out, "all genres are distinguished by the affective contract they promise: by claiming that certain affects embed the historical in persons and persons in the historical in ways that only the aesthetic situation could really capture" (ibid., p. 66). Rather than exploring strictly sociological inquiries into pandemic response, by incorporating the fictional novel I can explore the atmosphere of the historical moment of the cholera pandemic to further understand the role that religious identity played then and now. Like Berlant, I will be interrogating this text for "patterns of adjustment" in order to illuminate collective action in the time of the pandemic (Berlant 2011, p. 9), which can then be used as a comparative tool into the present—a mediation of this crisis time.

Garcia Marquez paints a picture of Colombia during and after the fourth and fifth cholera pandemics. The novel, set in an unnamed Colombian city (presumed to be Cartagena) across the span of the 1870s to 1930s, tells the story of Florentino Ariza, Fermina Daza, and Dr. Juvenal Urbino as they navigate love, illness, and a changing world. Florentino and Fermina were young and in love, though Fermina's father disapproved, seeking a more illustrious name for his daughter than marrying the son of a freed slave born out of wedlock. After being forbidden to communicate with Florentino and taken on a trip to her mother's homeland by her father, Fermina begins to see love in a different light. Upon her return, she rejects Florentino, only later to fall in love with and marry the doctor Juvenal Urbino while Florentino waits for his true love to be widowed. In weaving the narrative of this love story, Garcia Marquez illustrates the intricate web of identities in the city, revealing how varied conceptualizations of the world, especially regarding health and medicine, are crashing into one another. However, in the novel, the varied views co-exist with less tension than those regarding the COVID-19 pandemic. In fact, Dr. Urbino is able to reconcile the differences between religion and science and is thus accepted by the citizens and able to eliminate cholera outbreaks in the city.

Dr. Urbino's identity and how it is understood by those in the city he serves is key to his success in stopping the spread of cholera. Early on in the novel, regarding Urbino's differing view on the value of old age, the narrator states, "If he had not been what he was—in essence an old-style Christian—perhaps he would have agreed with Jeremiah de Saint-Amour" (Garcia Marquez 1988, p. 40). Even when serving in his role as doctor and friend to Saint-Amour, Urbino's religion is described at the fore of his identity. Importantly, here, Urbino is not just Christian, but described as "old-style", suggesting that he holds more traditional beliefs than others around him. Yet, unlike the rift between white Evangelical Christianity and modern science, his traditional beliefs do not interfere with his career as a medical professional, or vice versa. Instead, he is able to use his identity as a means to connect with the community and eventually institute life-saving public health policies and begin initiatives to transform the city into a safer space—one that does not readily breed and spread the cholera bacterium.

Still, Dr. Urbino's ideas were not accepted at first, neither by lay citizens nor by the doctors in the city. Having been trained in Europe, Urbino's suggestions to create more sanitary conditions were viewed as foreign intrusions that clashed with the traditional way of life in the city, and his way of thinking was scoffed at by fellow doctors, old and young alike. This tension comes to a head regarding the safety of the city's water supply. Locals believe that the mosquito larvae in the drinking cisterns were animes that cause inguinal hernias. Though Dr. Urbino was "aware of the scientific fallacy in these beliefs ... they were so rooted in local superstition that many people opposed the mineral enrichment of the water in the cisterns for fear of destroying its ability to cause an honorable hernia" (Garcia Marquez 1988, p. 110). The local beliefs are established as a key aspect of the identity of those who live in the city. Though Urbino is bringing knowledge from Europe that can help prevent ill health in numerous ways, the belief that a scrotal hernia was a mark of honor outweighed the up-to-date foreign scientific knowledge brought home by the doctor. Local identity and belief systems trumped scientific knowledge and Urbino was judged harshly and viewed as an outsider, rather than part of the in-group.

Despite this initial setback, Dr. Urbino is able to overcome the division between his views and the beliefs of the other citizens when cholera threatens the city yet another time in the pandemic's long history. During the earlier pandemic, the city had enough bodies to fill the church crypts and close off church attendance. Rather than allow the pandemic to spread, Urbino, a cholera expert, implemented quarantine and minimized the outbreak. It was this success that led the community to believe "the sanitary rigor of Dr. Juvenal Urbino, more than the efficacy of his pronouncements, had made the miracle possible. From that time on ... cholera was endemic not only in the city but along most of the Caribbean coast and the valley of the Magdalena, but it never again flared into an epidemic" (Garcia Marquez 1988, p. 115). The institutional flexibility that arose during the initial outbreak is what prevented a pandemic. Rather than stubbornly disregarding Urbino's suggestions, the institutions of medicine and military government adapted and abandoned outdated beliefs such as firing a canon to purify the air, and yet, religion still plays a role in the interpretation of events. The prevention of the pandemic is viewed as both a success for Urbino, but also as a miracle. The science-based policy making that Urbino instated is folded in with the belief systems that dominate the city.

During the outbreak of cholera, the damage of which Dr. Urbino did his best to minimize, mortality rates were kept in reasonable check and the city was able to go on with its daily routines mostly as usual, with the exception of some quarantines. Unlike previously when, "The air in the Cathedral grew thin with the vapors of badly sealed crypts, and its doors did not open again until three years later" (Garcia Marquez 1988, p. 111), the religious community was able to attend mass regularly and without pause. Without the immunity, or at least the risk-mitigating factors put in place by Dr. Urbino, the religious community could not have congregated, at least not in the way that it had previously. The health of the community was put first, and arguably at a greater interruption than today when technology such as Zoom has risen to the challenge of maintaining a semblance of community while still sheltering in place. Thinking back to Esposito, reframing our understanding of immunity from something that separates individuals from the community to something that allows community to exist safely and uninterrupted is key to more effectively preventing the spread of communicable diseases. Not adapting to the circumstances that diseases such as cholera or COVID-19 present only puts community at risk for the long term, whereas immediate adjustments that protect individuals enable the ongoing existence of the community. As we see evidenced for Catholicism in *Love in the Time of Cholera*, the medical science that informs public health policies is not *necessarily* a threat to the religious beliefs of evangelicals but rather something that could help preserve that community.

Even when the text echoes the arguments of white Evangelical Christians today, Garcia Marquez creates a sense of coexistence between religion and science rather than opposition. Like Lauri Armstrong, who believes that God's will is playing out with COVID-19, in Garcia Marquez's narrative cholera was also viewed by some as an act of God. While on a trip, after her husband all but eliminated cholera in her city, Fermina sees the bodies of people who died of cholera and remarks that they appear different than those she had seen in the past. An officer responds, "That is true ... Even God improves his methods" (Garcia Marquez 1988, p. 252). The speed and efficiency with which cholera killed was viewed as an act of God. However, scientific approaches to containing outbreaks were able to be implemented, including quarantining infected individuals. Rather than viewing necessary preventive measures as antithetical to their religion—as many white Evangelical Christians did—the characters in the novel saw them as miraculous, as though God's will worked through Dr. Urbino's new approaches to medicine and public health.

Furthermore, medical and religious habits are often described together through the character of Urbino, suggesting that the two are inseparable pieces of his identity. Early in the novel, his routine is described as the following: "He would spend an hour in his study preparing for the class in general clinical medicine that he taught at the Medical School every morning, Monday through Saturday, at eight o'clock, until the day before his death ... After class it was rare for him not to have an appointment related to his civic initiatives, or his Catholic service" (Garcia Marquez 1988, pp. 8–9). The nearness regarding the discussion of Urbino's Catholic religion with his medical career and his duty to the city in which he lives suggests that the strong ties he holds with both religion and science are not an anomaly, but rather something that permeates the rest of the local culture. As Berlant might suggest, Garcia Marquez is building a sense of unity between religion and science, a unity that may seem entirely alien to someone living in the present-day United States where the two are positioned as opposing forces. Dr. Urbino's routine is not a private affair, but rather something publicly known and related to his work in the community. He hides neither his medical training nor his faith, and as such, is not ostracized for either.

5. Unity Protects Community

Unity in public health response and the buy-in of the community are both needed to protect that community. In the present situation in which we find ourselves in the US, it is necessary to work creatively, like Urbino in the novel does, in order to bridge the divide between the communities of white Evangelical Christians who continue to reject the efficacy of policies and tools for fighting COVID-19 and the growing public who work with scientific tools and public health policy to reduce risk and death. As religion and science are so often framed as opposing systems in the United States, it may seem daunting, or even impossible, to reconcile the two. Some may argue that by increasing the visibility of religious identity in science, policy makers will turn to religious mores more often than scientific reasoning as the basis for their policy choices. Others may be concerned that scientists who affiliate themselves publicly with a religion would lose credibility, despite research that has shown that highlighting medical professionals' religious identities increases trust by religious individuals least likely to get vaccinated (Chu et al. 2021). This is not to suggest that science pander to religious belief, or vice versa. Rather, by acknowledging the presence and effect of both institutions upon each other and finding common ground through honest and open dialogue without the interference of partisan politics, both might be able to adapt and better serve the general population.

Appealing to general religious values such as loving thy neighbor may not be enough to sway some individuals, including large swaths of WECs, toward vaccination. The change in communication needs to be more holistic. If the institution that is appealing to a value is perceived as not sharing that value, such an appeal will ultimately fall short. Instead, a shared set of values needs to be established and shared at both a public and individual level. A 2005 survey found that 89.5% of American doctors identify as religious, or with a particular religion, 38.8% of them identifying as Protestant. Furthermore, 58% of those doctors who identified themselves as religious said their religious beliefs inform their treatment of patients (Curlin et al. 2005). While increasing transparency is a long and difficult process and not without potential drawbacks, it is most likely to help us attain our short terms goals of containing COVID-19 and our aspiration of bridging the divide between public health policy informed by science and religious groups such as white Evangelic Christians. Health practitioners and officials who practice minoritized religions in the United States—religions that do not have as prominent a voice in contemporary American political discourse—may feel less comfortable in disclosing their religious identity. For members of already stigmatized communities within academia, science, and the nation, self-disclosure poses the risk of further discrimination, though further research would have to be done on outing oneself as a believer in a minority faith. In the case of white Evangelical Christians, whose beliefs are represented in mainstream political movements, transparency of health care professionals who identify as such could help to bolster the response of their religious community and encourage them to follow guidelines.

Beyond the self-identification of individual doctors, public health campaigns that feature experts with a variety of identities, including various faiths, will reach a wider public. This will also normalize a relationship between science and religion and bolster support of religious leaders who might also encourage behaviors beneficial to public health. The divide between religion and science in the United States is not as polarized as the current COVID-19 crisis and its politicization might lead us to believe. However, the communication of the connection between the two institutions is lacking, and when considering the overlap and interplay of additional facets of identity, such as political affiliation, the divide seems even greater. If public health campaigns shift from the tactic of targeting segmented portions of the population and focus on depicting common values between health, science and religious institutions, it could lead to less polarization, encouraging more of the American population to follow public health guidelines (Chittamuru et al. 2020).

6. Conclusions

Religious identity is an influential piece of culture knit inextricably into the fabric of national identity, which itself is indelibly tied to religious identity. As such, the cultural system of religions holds sway over much of American life. Thus, it has historically and continues to influence the behaviors of Americans currently. The communal identity of white Evangelical Christians proved to hinder their adoption of risk-mitigating behaviors during the COVID-19 pandemic. Currently, while much quantitative research has been done in the form of surveys that identify white Evangelical Christians as the group least likely to receive the COVID-19 vaccine, there does not seem to be a critical mass of primarily qualitative research that compiles their narratives regarding resistance. My inspiration draws from news interviews of such individuals. Furthermore, while there has been research on anti-vax rhetoric, the focus tends to be on the messages targeting specific groups, rather than on the beliefs and responses of those groups' members (Billauer 2022). It would be fruitful, as others have suggested, to explore the reasons and discourse behind the resistance of white Evangelic Christian individuals to risking minimizing public health practices during COVID-19 in a wider variety of ways (Mylan and Hardman 2021). While Esposito's philosophy and Berlant's concept of cruel optimism are not the only lenses through which this phenomenon can be understood, they do provide insights that can be applied not just to religious identity, but other aspects of identity as well, reflecting the complex cultural systems that influence individual beliefs. Berlant's theory also provides a framework through which analysis can move from the present into the past through cultural texts such as Garcia Marquez's novel. It is this historic turn that gives cultural and behavioral insight beyond the quantitative analysis of a survey response. Yet, historical insight can only go so far, and future inquiry should continue to think through current and future pandemic responses in light of the past.

Despite the risk to their own well-being, as the pandemic became politicized, many white Evangelical Christians drew on their communal identity as an exclusive source of motivation and knowledge and thus rejected the recommendations of public health scientists and doctors to mask up and get vaccinated. However, health science and religious identity do not necessarily need to be at odds, and examining how tensions between the two have been resolved in the past can provide us a hopeful model for the future. As Garcia Marquez depicted and as is reflected in my analysis of *Love in the Time of Cholera*, the focus should be on the commonalities between medicine and religion rather than on the differences. As evidenced in the character of Dr. Urbino, medicine and religions can coexist in harmony and even strengthen each other. If we find a way to tamp down the partisanship and create a space for open dialogue between the scientific community and those skeptical because of their faith, perhaps then we will be ready for, to channel Galea, the contagion next time.

Funding: This research received no external funding.

Institutional Review Board Statement: Not applicable.

Informed Consent Statement: Not applicable.

Data Availability Statement: No new data were created or analyzed in this study. Data sharing is not applicable to this article.

Conflicts of Interest: The author declares no conflict of interest.

References

Adams, Noah. 2005. Timeline: Remembering the Scopes Monkey Trial. *NPR*, July 5. Available online: https://www.npr.org/2005/07/05/4723956/timeline-remembering-the-scopes-monkey-trial (accessed on 11 September 2022).

Adler, Gary J., Jr., Selena E. Ortiz, Eric Plutzer, Damon Mayrl, Jonathan S. Coley, and Rebecca Sager. 2021. Religion at the Frontline: How Religion Influenced the Response of Local Government Officials to the COVID-19 Pandemic. *Sociology of Religion* 82: 397–425. [CrossRef]

Berlant, Lauren Gail. 2011. *Cruel Optimism*. Durham: Duke University Press.

Billauer, Barbara Pfeffer. 2022. Anti-Vax Fear Speech: A Public-Health-Driven Policy Initiative When Counter-Speech Won't Work. *Health Matrix* 32: 215–309.

Chan, Esther. 2018. Are the religious suspicious of science? Investigating religiosity, religious context, and orientations towards science. *Public Understanding of Science* 27: 967–84. [CrossRef] [PubMed]

Chittamuru, Deepti, Ryane Daniels, Urmimala Sarkar, and Dean Schillinger. 2020. Evaluating values-based message frames for type 2 diabetes prevention among Facebook audiences: Divergent values or common ground? *Patient Education and Counseling* 103: 2420–29. [CrossRef] [PubMed]

Chow, Soon Ken, Benedict Francis, Yit Han Ng, Najmi Naim, Hooi Chin Beh, Mohammad Aizuddin Azizah Ariffin, Mohd Hafyzuddin Yusuf, Jia Wen Lee, and Ahmad Hatim Sulaiman. 2021. Religious Coping, Depression and Anxiety among Healthcare Workers during the COVID-19 Pandemic: A Malaysian Perspective. *Healthcare* 9: 79. [CrossRef] [PubMed]

Chu, James, Sophia L. Pink, and Robb Willer. 2021. Religious Identity Cues Increase Vaccination Intentions and Trust in Medical Experts among American Christians. *Proceedings of the National Academy of Sciences* 118: e2106481118. [CrossRef] [PubMed]

Corcoran, Katie E., Christopher P. Scheitle, and Bernard D. DiGregorio. 2022. Individuals' Use of Religion in Response to the COVID-19 Pandemic as Complementary to Their Use of Medically Recommended Responses. *Journal for the Scientific Study of Religion* 61: 293–313. [CrossRef] [PubMed]

Curlin, Farr A., John D. Lantos, Chad J. Roach, Sarah A. Sellergren, and Marshall H. Chin. 2005. Religious Characteristics of U.S. Physicians. *Journal of General Internal Medicine* 20: 629–34. [CrossRef] [PubMed]

Dias, Elizabeth, and Ruth Graham. 2021. White Evangelical Resistance Is Obstacle in Vaccination Effort. *The New York Times*, April 5. Available online: https://www.nytimes.com/2021/04/05/us/covid-vaccine-evangelicals.html (accessed on 9 August 2022).

Esposito, Roberto. 2013. *Terms of the Political: Community, Immunity, Biopolitics*. New York: Fordham University Press.

Evans, John H. 2013. The Growing Social and Moral Conflict Between Conservative Protestantism and Science. *Journal for the Scientific Study of Religion* 52: 368–85. [CrossRef]

Frei-Landau, R. 2020. "When the going gets tough, the tough get—Creative": Israeli Jewish religious leaders find religiously innovative ways to preserve community members' sense of belonging and resilience during the COVID-19 pandemic. *Psychological Trauma: Theory, Research, Practice, and Policy* 12: S258–S260. [CrossRef] [PubMed]

Funk, Cary, and John Gramlich. 2021. 10 Facts about Americans and Coronavirus Vaccines. *Pew Research Center (Blog)*, September 20. Available online: https://www.pewresearch.org/fact-tank/2021/09/20/10-facts-about-americans-and-coronavirus-vaccines/ (accessed on 9 August 2022).

Galea, Sandro. 2022. *The Contagion Next Time*. New York: Oxford University Press.

Garcia Marquez, Gabriel. 1988. *Love in the Time of Cholera*. New York: Vintage International.

Geertz, Clifford. 1993. *The Interpretation of Cultures: Selected Essays*. London: Fontana Press.

Glass, Jennifer. 2019. Why Aren't We Paying Attention? Religion and Politics in Everyday Life. *Sociology of Religion* 80: 9–27. [CrossRef]

Gonzalez, Kelsey E., Rina James, Eric T. Bjorklund, and Terrence D. Hill. 2021. Conservatism and Infrequent Mask Usage: A Study of US Counties During the Novel Coronavirus (COVID-19) Pandemic. *Social Science Quarterly* 102: 2368–82. [CrossRef] [PubMed]

Haidt, Jonathan, ed. 2013. *The Righteous Mind: Why Good People Are Divided by Politics and Religion*. New York: Vintage Books.

Jackson, Natalie. 2021. Why Some White Evangelical Republicans Are So Opposed to The COVID-19 Vaccine. *FiveThirtyEight (Blog)*, August 26. Available online: https://fivethirtyeight.com/features/why-some-white-evangelical-republicans-are-so-opposed-to-the-covid-19-vaccine/ (accessed on 9 August 2022).

Jenkins, Jack. 2021. In Many COVID Hot Spots, a Pattern: High Concentrations of White Evangelicals. July 15. Available online: https://religionnews.com/2021/07/15/in-covid-hot-spots-a-pattern-high-concentrations-of-white-evangelicals/ (accessed on 12 August 2022).

Keshet, Yael, and Ido Liberman. 2014. Coping with Illness and Threat: Why Non-religious Jews Choose to Consult Rabbis on Healthcare Issues. *Journal of Religion and Health* 53: 1146–60. [CrossRef] [PubMed]

Krause, Neal, Christopher G. Ellison, Benjamin A. Shaw, John P. Marcum, and Jason D. Boardman. 2002. Church-Based Social Support and Religious Coping. *Journal for the Scientific Study of Religion* 40: 637–56. [CrossRef]

Lewis, Michael. 2021. *The Premonition: A Pandemic Story*. New York: W.W. Norton & Company.

Mylan, Sophie, and Charlotte Hardman. 2021. COVID-19, Cults, and the Anti-Vax Movement. *The Lancet* 397: 1181. [CrossRef] [PubMed]

Nabi, Junaid. 2021. What the Pandemic Has Taught Us about Science Communication. *World Economic Forum*. Available online: https://www.weforum.org/agenda/2021/06/lessons-for-science-communication-from-the-covid-19-pandemic/ (accessed on 12 August 2022).

Olagoke, Ayokunle A., Olakanmi O. Olagoke, and Ashley M. Hughes. 2021. Intention to Vaccinate Against the Novel 2019 Coronavirus Disease: The Role of Health Locus of Control and Religiosity. *Journal of Religion and Health* 60: 65–80. [CrossRef] [PubMed]

Payir, Ayse, Telli Davoodi, Kelly Yixin Cui, Jennifer M. Clegg, Paul L. Harris, and Kathleen Corriveau. 2021. Are high levels of religiosity inconsistent with a high valuation of science? Evidence from the United States, China and Iran. *International Journal of Psychology* 56: 216–27. [CrossRef]

Pecorino, Philip. 2001. What Is Religion? In Philosophy of Religion. Available online: https://www.qcc.cuny.edu/socialsciences/ppecorino/phil_of_religion_text/CHAPTER_1_OVERVIEW/What_is_religion.htm (accessed on 9 August 2022).

Perry, Samuel L., Andrew L. Whitehead, and Joshua B. Grubbs. 2020. Culture Wars and COVID-19 Conduct: Christian Nationalism, Religiosity, and Americans' Behavior During the Coronavirus Pandemic. *Journal for the Scientific Study of Religion* 59: 405–16. [CrossRef]

Plohl, Nejc, and Bojan Musil. 2021. Modeling compliance with COVID-19 prevention guidelines: The critical role of trust in science. *Psychology, Health & Medicine* 26: 1–12. [CrossRef]

Religious Identities and the Race Against the Virus: American Attitudes on Vaccination Mandates and Religious Exemptions (Wave 3). 2021. PRRI (Blog). Available online: https://www.prri.org/research/religious-identities-and-the-race-against-the-virus-american-attitudes-on-vaccination-mandates-and-religious-exemptions/ (accessed on 9 August 2022).

Schimelpfening, Nancy. 2021. Fetal Tissue Wasn't Used to Create J&J COVID-19 Vaccine. *Healthline*, March 18. Available online: https://www.healthline.com/health-news/no-fetal-tissue-wasnt-used-to-create-the-jj-covid-19-vaccine (accessed on 11 September 2022).

Schnabel, Landon, and Scott Schieman. 2022. Religion Protected Mental Health but Constrained Crisis Response During Crucial Early Days of the COVID-19 Pandemic. *Journal for the Scientific Study of Religion* 61: 530–43. [CrossRef]

Schultz, Kevin M. 2006. Religion as Identity in Postwar America: The Last Serious Attempt to Put a Question on Religion in the United States Census. *Journal of American History* 93: 359–84. [CrossRef]

Simmons-Duffin, Selena. 2022. CDC Is Criticized for Failing to Communicate, Promises to Do Better. *NPR*, January 7. Available online: https://www.npr.org/sections/health-shots/2022/01/07/1071449137/cdc-is-criticized-for-failing-to-communicate-promises-to-do-better (accessed on 11 September 2022).
The Coronavirus Pandemic's Impact on Religious Life. n.d. PRRI (Blog). Available online: https://www.prri.org/research/the-coronavirus-pandemics-impact-on-religious-life/ (accessed on 9 August 2022).

religions MDPI

Article

COVID-19 and Religion

Donald Heinz

Department of Comparative Religion and Humanities, California State University, Chico, CA 95929-0740, USA; dheinz@csuchico.edu

Abstract: The COVID-19 pandemic has produced a social drama in which churches, government, and individual actors have played prominent roles. While neo-conservative evangelicals have resisted governmental and scientific overreach in the name of "faith over fear", liberal religious groups have joined in government and medical efforts for the good of the commons, offered comfort and assurance to those suffering, and called for support of the poor at home and abroad. Religions have turned right and left, from apocalyptic "resets" of global order to new calls for social justice. In this context, the root metaphor of the *epidemic* has been called up as a historical construct that helps to conceptualize, analyze, and act upon the COVID-19 crisis. Searching the past helps us see that not everything about COVID-19 as a social drama is a new or unheard-of challenge. For example, there are new evocations of the black death of 14th-century Europe that became a crisis in the church, as well as the great Lisbon earthquake in 1755, which upended the confidence of the European Enlightenment. Another way to appraise the dimensions of the COVID-19 outbreak is to call on the varied approaches characteristic of the sociology of religion, that is, to consider how ideology and belief are socially constructed in order to account for new intellectual responses to societal challenges. Does religion always produce the "collective effervescence" Durkheim posited? Does religious change always arrive downstream of cultural change, or can it also become an independent variable? This article attends primarily to the sharp responses of conservative religious expression in the face of attention-getting upheaval, which has readily translated into right-wing political action and electioneering. But the social uplift and altruism of liberal religion is not neglected either. Thus, this article provides an account of how science and governmental action have both been challenged and embraced in response to COVID-19. As such, it is not an empirical study stemming from new Pew-like social polling. Rather, it is a wide overview rooted in sociological methods and theory for tracking religion historically and presently in America in a manner that aims to inform a discussion of how COVID-19 has impacted religion and religious expression, and vice versa.

Keywords: Christian nationalism; apocalyptic; ideology; conspiracy theories; libertarianism; religious exemptions; social justice; social drama

Citation: Heinz, Donald. 2023. COVID-19 and Religion. *Religions* 14: 478. https://doi.org/10.3390/rel14040478

Academic Editors: Andrew Flescher and Joel Zimbelman

Received: 10 August 2022
Revised: 21 March 2023
Accepted: 21 March 2023
Published: 3 April 2023

1. Introduction: The Moment of the Epidemic

In *The Anthropology of Performance*, Victor Turner defines *social drama* as "a sequence of social interactions of a conflictive, competitive, or agonistic type" (Turner 1988), and he delineates stages of the breach, crisis, redress, and reintegration or schism. This essay is an invitation to see the play, analyze the actors and their settings, and inquire about the final acts. We are witnessing a drama on the national stage in which the COVID-19 pandemic and American religion are mightily engaged, just as all epidemics or natural disasters in history have produced social dramas in which religious and national cultures go up against cataclysmic disruptions and sometimes against each other.

A simple google search leads to a wide array of newspapers, journals, books, and government documents reporting on COVID-19 and religion interaction. A notable actor is conservative evangelical religion, but there are also surprises in the wings. In August 2022, Sheera Frenkel of the New York Times reported that a wealthy, liberal, upper-class population in the Bay Area suburb of Orinda, CA, gathered to proclaim "No Vaccines, Protect our kids, and "Our kids, our choice" (Frenkel 2022). Of course, requests for religious exemptions to vaccinations, masks, and restrictions to public gatherings are far more common on the evangelical right. Misinformation driven by anti-science, anti-elitist, and anti-government instincts gives rise to conspiracy theories. Ideological intensity disguised as religion reveals a Christian nationalism that sanctifies America as God's country, which exempts conservative religion from cultural norms and hallows conservative ideologies with a patriotic obligation.

But religion can also produce cooperation among government, culture, and churches in times of crisis. Cooperation may be rooted in many admired religious instincts, such as the sense of obligation to the whole human family; serving one's neighbor and the common good; charitable obligations to the poor; the religious support of institutions that aspire to serve the community; the increase in religious sensibility in times of common distress; appeals of faith to the support of vaccination; and even new discussions of Bishop Tutu's African ideal of *ubuntu*, "I am who I am because we are who we are" (Battle 2009). Both conservative and liberal religions struggle for space in the plot.

Lest we think of COVID-19 as a de novo occurrence, and in order to learn from the past, I turn to the concept of an epidemic as a widespread occurrence of infectious disease in a community at a particular time. The term "epidemic" evokes all the ways in which societies have responded to the catastrophic spread of disease. These responses represent challenges to religion and society, and the radical changes they sometimes produce have a long history. Epidemic becomes a signal for what we might expect today in the current moment of our own pandemic and a paradigm for coaching and cautioning church and society during the present crisis. In this respect, as Randy Shilts has noted, an epidemic is both a litmus test for learning what society currently values, as well as an indication of what power various actors have in the public space for shaping social values (Shilts 2007).

At least until now, the great influenza of 1918 was regarded as the greatest pandemic in American history (Barry 2005). But the most famous example of this model in Western history is the civilizational crisis of the plague in 14th-century Europe. Not an epidemic (or pandemic), but a natural disaster was the great Lisbon earthquake of 1755, which shook the easy conscience of the European Enlightenment and required fundamental re-imaginations of religion and culture.

Epidemics do not appear in a social vacuum. Problems and themes already pressing now make an accelerated appearance. One of these is government regulation and the administrative state. Indeed, it is now possible to suggest that the after-effects of COVID-19 may lie less for religion itself than for emerging political action through movements driven in part by an awakened conservative evangelicalism.

The drama is not over, but it may be abating as the infection rate and level of virulence of COVID-19 begin to oscillate. At its height, however, over a hundred books were written about "religion and epidemic". These ranged from angry volumes (Lugeons 2020) that curse the church for obstructing society's well-meaning response to the COVID-19 pandemic and ruining worthy efforts to equally angry responses, to government and science posing as all-encompassing religious-like worldviews (Habakus and Holland 2012; LeRoy 2022), to many volumes that picture the challenges of an epidemic, to the churches as opportunities for self-transformation, "reset", and modernization in its ministries.

2. COVID-19 and Religion as Social Drama

The COVID-19 pandemic and religion have collided to produce a social drama in which all of us are implicated as actors, and government, society, culture, and religion are the platform and wings of the stage. According to Victor Turner's theory (Turner 1988), we can expect "a sequence of social interactions of a conflictive, competitive, or agonistic type" and stages of the breach, crisis, redress, and reintegration or schism. In such circumstances, it is not unusual to discover that the emperor has no clothes. In Hans Christian Anderson's tale, the weavers play on the emperor's vanity by saying the suit is only visible to people who are clever and competent. In our time of COVID-19, a different game may be in play. When Dr. Fauci appears on the stage, not many are willing to acknowledge the clothes he is, in fact, wearing.

Social dramas occur within groups sharing common values and interests and a common history. Public reflexivity takes the form of a performance—not theatrical but political, cultural, and religious. The languages through which a group communicates within itself are not just talk, they are political action, graphic representation, symbols, and rituals. All are stepping into "liminality", Turner's term for threshold experiences, betwixt-and-between (Turner 1969). Turner's anthropology of performance has taken the play off the stage and centered it in the commons. The performance is the making of culture, that is, the reinventing of new ways of being in the world, where power often changes hands. Rituals are staged actions in which individuals or groups perform themselves, as when the public health officials who rose to recognized prominence over the last three years appeared weekly to declare what was what, announcing a new order in which the masses chose to participate or not. Turner's theory invites us to keep our eye on the interplay of event, spectacle, culture, religious ritual, and audience so that we can see and not miss how we are performing the social drama in which we are involved.

The deployment of the idea of an epidemic serves as a challenge to religion and society, and is at the root of radical changes in culture and belief with a long history (Snowden 2019). Recent works follow the epidemic paradigm in coaching and cautioning the church on pastoral responses to the COVID-19 crisis (Danielson and Whyte 2021; Pless and Corzine 2020; Wright 2020). In *The World the Plague Made: The Black Death and the Rise of Europe*, James Belich traces how the Black Death unleashed revolutionary change across the medieval world and ushered in the modern age (Belich 2022). In 1346, a catastrophic plague beset Europe and its neighbors. The Black Death was a human tragedy that abruptly halved entire populations and caused untold suffering but also brought about a cultural and economic renewal on a scale never before witnessed. Belich's book is a panoramic history of how the bubonic plague revolutionized labor, trade, and technology and set the stage for Europe's global expansion.

Belich takes readers across centuries and continents to shed new light on one of history's greatest paradoxes. Why did Europe's dramatic rise begin in the wake of the Black Death? He shows how the plague doubled the per capita endowment of everything even as it decimated the population. Many more people had disposable incomes. Demand grew for silks, sugar, spices, furs, gold, and slaves. Europe expanded to satisfy that demand—and plague provided the means. Labor scarcity drove more use of wind power and gunpowder. Technologies such as water-powered blast furnaces, heavily gunned galleons, and musketry were fast-tracked by plague. A new "crew culture" of "disposable males" emerged to man the guns and galleons. Setting the rise of Western Europe in a global context, Belich demonstrates how the mighty empires of the Middle East and Russia also flourished after the plague and how European expansion was deeply entangled with the Chinese and other peoples throughout the world. Who knew epidemics could be generative rather than degenerative?

Although Belich does not take up the question of how European Christianity responded to the Black Death, there is much information available elsewhere. An Honors Thesis by Mclaurine Zentner, "The Black Death and its impact on the church and popular religion" (Zentner 2015), nicely summarizes three issues: the severely weakened and compromised status of the church, the rise of traveling flagellants as an alternative (and heretical) religious response, and the persecution of Jews who were blamed for bringing on the plague. Of course, the official church's position was that the plague came as God's punishment for sins. People were admonished to pray, repent, and plead with God to stop the pestilence. But an increasingly secular church, and then one whose manpower was decimated by the plague, was not up to the task. The plague fully exposed the vulnerability of a Christian society. The black death contributed to the decline in confidence and faith of the laity towards the church. A church that had been turning towards wealth and political power was now overwhelmed by the needs of the populace. A Christian society no longer seemed coherent. The clergy proved unprepared, and so a flagellant movement arose. Groups of men and women publicly flogged their bodies while they traveled to and from European cities, preaching their version of Christianity without the permission of the Church. When all else failed, Jews were attacked for having spread the plague. Nothing approaching this is present today.

A natural disaster is not unlike an epidemic in its effects. A famous disaster that similarly challenged the religious and social order of the day was the great Lisbon Earthquake of 1755 (Gibbons 2010; Molesky 2016; Paice 2009; Shrady 2009). It struck a land that was economically busy and deeply religious—with 40 churches, 90 convents, and a population with 10% of its members in religious orders. The earthquake struck on November 1, All Saints Day. Ten percent of the population died, and every important church was destroyed. But the European Enlightenment of the time had confidently posited a well-ordered universe. Its philosophers observed nature and used reason to deduce a clockmaker God. The German polymath Leibniz famously produced a theodicy in which we find ourselves in *the best of all possible worlds* (von Leibniz 1985). In his *Essay on Man,* Alexander Pope wrote: "One truth is clear: Whatever is, is right." All that crashed with the great earthquake in Portugal.

The *ars moriendi*, an elaborately ritualized art of dying, had been an important tradition in preparing for the ultimate journey of death. Now the clergy who coached this art were in disarray or absent without leave. Confessions were not heard. Boccaccio wrote that plagued bodies lay around like dead goats with no proper burial (Boccaccio 1995). Rituals failed the living and the dying, who no longer experienced the sacramental overlay of the church. Many parish priests fled, leaving no one to offer services, deliver last rites, and comfort the sick. Flight might have been intellectually explicable, but it was morally inexcusable. One dubious response was the provision of new papal indulgences, more expensive now and providing time off from purgatory. COVID-19 does not provoke quite this dramatic a civilizational crisis.

Since epidemics do not happen in a vacuum, it may be expected that latent themes in religion and society will now come to the fore. Before COVID-19 appeared, there was a simmering debate over government regulation and the administrative state. Contemporary government regulation, or government and science posing as the new gods, came forth as the triggers of conservative religion protesting masks, vaccination, and external controls over when and where religious groups could gather. Resistance to the big government was not a unique issue but had become a rallying cry ever since the Reagan revolution made a call for small government a theme.

We may consider another example in response to climate change, which also engages the debate over the role of government control and the administrative state in furthering the good of society—or spoiling it. Indeed, there is a significant argument on both the left and the right regarding this. Global warming, a catastrophe on the horizon, has been declared a hoax by some conservatives, while liberals advocate drastic government controls in response to the service of social justice and equity (Merrill 2022). In "Federalist Society: The Conservative Pipeline to the Supreme Court", Jeffrey Toobin has documented the history of the Federalist Society and its grooming of judges certain to assert small government and a deregulated capitalist economy (Toobin 2017). With this political backdrop, crises were bound to become triggering events. Upheaval, inevitably surfacing from time to time, gives way to a new round of societal decision making about governmental intervention, with the corresponding convictions of proponents and detractors there to determine the shape of the social drama.

3. The Discipline of Sociology as a Way into Religion

Beyond the utility of the epidemic as an interpretive concept and the latent themes which may underlie it, I turn now to the role of *sociological* understanding and to the entire enterprise of the sociology of religion, which promises to be a view into the interaction of

COVID-19 and religion. Sociology is not a new partner in understanding religion. For the last fifty years, sociological methods have played a significant role in Biblical interpretation, becoming a key variable in historical-critical approaches and, more recently, in feminist biblical studies. For example, in *A Home for the Homeless: A Social-Scientific Criticism of 1 Peter, Its Situation and Strategy* 2005, John H. Elliott (2005) discusses at length the role of the sociological method in his commentary on and grasp of the situation in the late 1st century when the letter appeared. Another example is the well-regarded work of Elizabeth Schussler Fiorenza, *In Memory of Her: Feminist Theological Reconstruction of Christian Origins* (Schussler Fiorenza 1994). After its promising origins in the late 19th century, the sociology of religion came into its own in the middle of the 20th century as a distinctive discipline and flourished in many universities, such as Berkeley, Chicago, and Columbia. Charles Glock and Rodney Stark were early practitioners of survey research (as now also practiced by the Pew Research Center), in which an issue is carefully defined, standardized questionnaires or interviews are constructed, and a statistically formulated sample size ("n") is identified—in order to gain a macro impression of the social-cultural landscape by carefully interviewing, or collecting surveys, about people and their preferences, thoughts, and behaviors in a systematic manner. In *Religion and Society in Tension* Glock and Stark studied religions' place in society (Glock and Stark 1965). In *American Piety: The Nature of Religious Commitment*, the first of three volumes in "Patterns of Religious Commitment", Glock and Stark startle their readers with the contrasts in beliefs, practice, and experiences revealed among eleven major Christian denominations that are compared (Stark and Glock 1968).

In this setting, American civil religion has become a much-developed and argued phenomenon rooted in sociology. Jean-Jacques Rousseau had already coined the term in chapter 8, book 4, of *The Social Contract* (Rousseau 2019). The concept of "civil religion" built bridges between sociology and religion and referred to the implicit values of a nation, as expressed through public rituals, symbols, and ceremonies on sacred days and at sacred places. But much more recent and influential was Robert Bellah's 1967 essay "Civil Religion in America" (Bellah 1967). Bellah saw civil religion as an institutionalized collection of sacred beliefs about the American nation. But Bellah wanted to raise the prophetic role of civil religion which challenged "national self-worship", calling for the subordination of the nation to ethical principles that transcend it in terms of which it should be judged.

Bellah considered the significance and possibilities of civil religion, to which he kept looking for its best example. Relying on the requirements of "virtue ethics", Bellah wrote *Habits of the Heart: Middle America Observed* (Bellah et al. 1988). This is a longing for a democratic community that draws on our diverse civic and religious traditions. Later he returned to civil religion in *Varieties of Civil Religion* (Bellah and Hammond 1982), in which he once again examined the force of religion in politics and society. But he was always a realist and a prophet. Along the way he kept picking into a too easy going civil religion and wrote his anguished *The Broken Covenant: American Civil Religion in Time of Trial* (Bellah 1992). This was a caution about the encroachment of a secular world order and a plea that the religious dimensions of American society, as distinct from its churches, must also have their own integrity and the same care in understanding that any religion requires. This would suggest that in a time of epidemic, it is not just a vigorous churchly presence which is called for, but the constructive presence of religion in the national psyche. From the powerhouse at Berkeley of Glock and Bellah came their most distinguished student, Robert Wuthnow, who examined the human response to existential threats—once a matter for theology but now looming before us in multiple forms (Wuthnow 2010). Nuclear weapons, pandemics, global warming: each threatened to destroy the planet, or at least to annihilate our species. Freud, he notes, famously taught that the standard psychological response to an overwhelming danger is denial. In fact, Wuthnow writes that the opposite is true: we seek ways of positively meeting the threat, of doing something—*anything*—even if it is wasteful and time-consuming.

Wuthnow began to turn to small community life, as in *Small Town America: Finding Community, Shaping the Future*, in which he showed the fragility of community in small towns (Wuthnow 2013). Almost anticipating the fractures in society this pandemic would open, he wrote *The Left Behind: Decline and Rage in Small-Town America* (Wuthnow 2018). What is fueling rural America's outrage toward the federal government? Why did rural Americans vote overwhelmingly for Donald Trump? And is there a more nuanced explanation for the growing rural-urban divide? Wuthnow shows that rural America's fury stems less from economic concerns than from the perception that Washington is distant from and yet threatening to the social fabric of small towns. In the rituals and public performances of COVID-19, where was small-town America? Protesting vaccinations and masks? Wuthnow would come to argue, in *What Happens When We Practice Religion? Textures of Devotion in Everyday Life,* that throughout the past few decades, the study of religion has shifted away from essentialist arguments that grandly purport to explain what religion is and why it exists (Wuthnow 2020). Instead, using methods from anthropology, psychology, religious studies, and sociology, scholars now focus on what people do and say: their daily religious habits, routines, improvisations, and adaptations.

By 2020 Robert Putnam was producing a revised addition to his highly influential *Bowling Alone: The Collapse and Revival of American Community* (Putnam 2000) to address social media and the internet. Simply put, everyone once bowled in leagues, but no longer. Now we live disconnected from family, friends, neighbors, and social structures. Our shrinking access to the social capital that is the reward of communal activity and community sharing poses a serious threat to our civic and personal health. One might add that there is insufficient social capital to be spent on COVID-19. Between his two editions, Putnam wrote *American Grace: How Religion Divides and Unites Us* (Putnam 2012). Based on vast survey research, this is a sweeping look at contemporary American religion and assesses its sociological causes. Unique among nations, America is deeply religious and religiously diverse, but in 2012, it was already undergoing seismic shocks. Today, and not only because of COVID-19 but possibly accelerated by it, the deep and sharp divisions between neo-conservative evangelicalism (with aspirations to become a political movement) and mainstream Catholicism and Protestantism are most noticeable in the American drama.

This was all in keeping with the classical preoccupation present in Peter Berger and Thomas Luckmann's 1966 (Berger and Luckmann 1966) major treatise on the sociology of knowledge, *The Social Construction of Reality*. Berger and Luckmann posited three stages in social construction: *Externalization* posits society as a human product. *Objectivation* sees society as an objective reality. *Internalization* finds humans to be a social product. Many conclusions arise: Society is a habit. If we define certain situations as real, they become real in their consequences. Religion could be thought of as successive definitions of a situation. Concepts do not have an independent reality.

One can see how rich the background detailed above is as an interpretive backdrop for thinking about the interface of plague and religion. From the seminal works just mentioned, we might pause to reflect: The Bible itself originated amidst defining social circumstances, and its interpretation is aided by the insights and approaches of sociology. Questions characteristic of the sociological approach emerge. How is reality itself, and therefore also religion, a social construction, and is it the case that once we define certain situations as real, they become real in their consequences? The original scholarship of survey research, now a mainstay of the Pew Research Center, opened up access to endless data and reflection about the role of religion in American life as well as called to attention American civil religion as the conceptualization of how religion may clothe American society and nation with ultimate meaning, and vice versa. Will our practice of "bowling alone" continue to shrink our access to the social capital that is the reward of communal activity and community sharing?

4. Ideology and Belief as Social Construction and the Social Construction of Apocalypse

The social construction of belief or ideology may therefore be seen through the lens of the sociology of religion—and the social construction of religion. Many religious people see theology as deriving from sacred texts. Many see religious assertions and practices as constructions emerging from social situations. Some look for a combination of the two. An ideology seems to be a person's or group's set of beliefs or assertions as a social construction to serve a theory or practice for the times. Religious tenets may be a combination of revealed theology and the social constructions of religious communities.

A theodicy is a religious account of good and evil that wants to offer a vindication of divine ways. Some ideologies, functioning like theodicies, want to account for difficult realities amidst massive uncertainty in a bewildered age. Recently some ideologies have morphed into conspiracy theories that explain events or situations by invoking sinister and powerful groups bent on evil. To some, these transpositions are no more than outrageous self-serving inventions out of nothing, while to others, they are satisfying explanations of evil and what to do about it, functioning as unifying, if bizarre, grand narratives.

Not every belief arrives as a virgin birth from religion itself. Social construction alludes to constructed beliefs and religious claims from materials at hand that amount to responses to secular ideology, cultural and economic norms, and political actions and processes in a sustained and systematic way. A religious ideology can refer to an entire system of belief or an ephemeral spiritual mood that arises from the times. To call it religious is to claim that it has ultimate grounding or that it participates in an apocalyptic movement—often alluding to what may ensue before Christ returns. Already in the Berkeley 1970s, a common bumper sticker was "Jesus is back, and he's pissed.".

Common themes in conspiracy theories are anti-science, anti-elites, anti-establishment, and anti-globalism. All these may arise during a pandemic to challenge old or new orthodoxies. These narratives are typically stoked by right-wing, often white supremacist political figures. The dictates of science, which are viewed as unreliable or authoritarian, are contrasted with one's own spiritual devotion for providing unseen, and therefore miraculous, protection. Science is seen by some as part of an intellectual elitism that also embraces critical race theory, LGBTQ, and trans movements and is, therefore, to be ignored and denounced. Survey after survey, for example, shows that religious believers identify with Q'Anon somewhat more than others (Cox 2021). The core Q'Anon theory is that of a cabal of Satanic, cannibalistic sexual abusers of children operating a global child sex trafficking ring conspired against former U.S. President Donald Trump. Such a stark narrative is at once totally constructed based on prior convictions about a sense of a world in disrepair and, once constructed, further reifies just this worldview.

We may think about some of these recent phenomena that arise as apocalyptic responses to the times from within an increasingly politicized conservative evangelicalism. Reverend Tony Spell, a pastor of Life Tabernacle Church, a Oneness Pentecostal congregation in Baton Rouge, explained his defiance of the Louisiana Governor's order banning meetings of more than fifty people. He said: "It's not a concern. *The virus, we believe, is politically motivated.* We hold our religious rights dear and we are going to assemble no matter what someone says" (Vowell and Foster 2022). About three hundred people gathered on the Tuesday after the ban and over a thousand on the following Sunday. Reverend Spell handed out anointed handkerchiefs, preached against fear, and told his people, who are mostly bussed in from poor regions all around the city, that this was an extreme test of faithfulness brought on by the spirit of the antichrist. While this pastor saw himself as championing "faith over fear", he also provoked a petition calling for his arrest and prosecution for reckless endangerment, signed by over 7000 people. Some found this flirting with endangerment reminiscent of earlier Christian practices in Appalachia, in which members of some Holiness churches saw themselves as proving their faith and celebrating divine love and care by taking poisonous snakes out of their cages and handling them in an ecstatic trance-like state, thereby taking a serious health risk to demonstrate God's protection.

Likewise, in the June 2022 issue of the *Atlantic*, Tim Alberta wrote about "How politics poisoned the church" (Alberta 2022). Pastor Bill Bolin of Flood Gate Church in Brighton, Michigan, fills each Sunday's worship with 40 minutes of praise music, 40 minutes of preaching, and in-between those two activities, 40 minutes of what he calls his *diatribe*. For a decade, Bolin preached to a crowd of about 100 congregants on a typical Sunday. Then came Easter 2020, when Bolin announced he would hold indoor worship services in defiance of Michigan's emergency shutdown orders. As word spread around the conservative suburbs of Detroit, Bolin became a minor celebrity. Local politicians and activists borrowed his pulpit to promote right-wing interests. Flood Gates' attendance soared as members of other congregations defected to this small roadside church—becoming a community of 1500 people. His themes are the election stolen from Trump and, ominously, hone in on how the left has made a power grab to systematically dismantle religion and banish God from the minds and hearts of believers.

This posture grew from apocalyptic concerns about the rise of secularism and the decline of religion. It was characterized by a faith affiliation that rose in light of politics, concerns about the next election perhaps triggering the nation's demise, with more and more Trumpers self-identifying as evangelicals (rather than the other way around). These movements had already arisen in part from profound distrust of Obama, which took the form of both questioning whether he was American-born and of the spreading rumor that he wore a secret Islamic ring. In response to all this, Pastor Bolin saw himself as the rock star who disobeyed the government. For good and for evil, Pastor Bolin saw the nation moving *from pandemic to endemic*. Radical change, God-pleasing or not, was on the way.

Apocalyptic thought, with a reach back into the Old Testament and continuing into the New Testament, is certainly an attempt to find God amidst the ways of the current perilous times, providing a nomos by delineating for God's people what to expect and how to respond. But both religious and secular observers are likely to see apocalyptic as a social construction in the face of disaster. If the world may be coming to an end or heading for disaster for God's people, then the idea of a *global reset* makes sense. A drastic religious response to COVID-19, or other disasters, is the projected coming of the anti-Christ and a self-conscious call for a complete change of view in the Christian worldview (Hitchcock and Kinley 2022). The apocalyptic preoccupation opens believers' eyes and alerts them to how world leaders are using their own concept of global reset to seize pandemics, natural disasters and catastrophes, civil disorder, political unrest, and other current events to reshape every facet of life—all pointing toward the universal economy and godless global government of the Antichrist. Some look back and wonder if COVID-19 is equivalent to the Biblical Flood (Hever 2021). Others imagine a future with the coming apocalypse (Hitchcock 2020). "After the rapture" is the keynote of others (Jeremiah 2022). Religion, in this respect, poses its own reset to counter an all-embracing secular reset—to keep the secular world from getting away with anything—as when science, and not God, is where one looks in responding to a disaster. COVID-19 is seen as unleashing a cascade of consequences that are now reaching far beyond the pandemic itself. Governments are seen as leveraging the coronavirus and even the vaccine as a power grab, setting the stage for further intrusions in the future. These accelerants are driving the world to the precipice of fundamental, irreversible transformation. The winds of change are blowing. Tectonic shifts are underway at every level.

To the apocalyptic eye, these realities are alarming by themselves. And yet, there remains a still deeper, more sinister agenda embedded within. According to prophecies found in the Bible, a one-world government will indeed emerge in the end times. According to a dominant interpretation of the book of Revelation among evangelical conservatives, a future unified government will encompass the whole earth, and Satan himself will be behind it for the ultimate purpose of ruling over all the earth and being worshipped by its inhabitants. While we are not yet in the end times, we are on the edge of the precipice. In the ideology of "global reset" readers will discover not only the setting for the end-time scenario prophesied in Scripture but also the cosmic setting for the return of Christ.

To many on the right, being unable by government decree to practice corporate worship seemed catastrophic. Locking church doors meant that religious ritual and online worshippers were not happening in the same space, at the same time, in a way that evoked a sense of community—the very contravention of the *collective effervescence* Durkheim thought was the origin and heart of religion, necessarily including the emotional arousal resulting from an intense form of communal sharing that empowers us and touches us in deep, often implicit ways. Collective effervescence is the basis for Durkheim's theory of religion, as posited in his seminal work *Elementary Forms of Religious Life* (Durkheim 1912). When an entire group gathers together, they can become sacred and experience the transformation through the ritual of the present into the sacred beyond.

From the perspective of the one accustomed to this form of religious expression, forced isolation risks this essential dimension of religion. Although zoom technology arrived in time to meet the new challenge of access, churches found online services a little different from styles of worship with featured performers, particularly those that are heavily sacramental or emphasized an Orthodox physicality in daily ritual. Congregants had cause to ask: could the government be allowed to tamper with such basic religious freedom as coming together regularly? Can science and government constrain what Durkheim thought was the very inner dynamic of religion?

5. Are Religious Representatives Permitted to Be Actors with Something to Say about COVID-19?

We have seen how the discipline of sociology opens up our understanding of religion, particularly with the idea of the "social construction" of religion. This concept does not weaken or negate the spokesperson for religion as an imaginative actor or one who takes the initiative, interrupts the flow, or is driven into new space by its theological motivations. Yet we may have to grant that such a figure can be an independent, imaginative actor—with a theological agenda.

But what if that person is all dressed up but not allowed to go anywhere? What if they are quarantined in homes or church buildings? What if they are denied room to be present and active in public life? Richard John Neuhaus takes up this question in *The naked public square: Religion and democracy in America* (Neuhaus 1984). He describes the empty and uncomely condition of today's public space doctrine, which has been developed without consideration of religion and religious values. In the face of a secularism which disdained religion, Neuhaus calls for an activist religion that acts out its values and aspirations precisely in the public square and not just in the confines of church buildings. Admittedly, he made this argument in light of neoconservative Christianity, as seen in the years he edited the journal *First Things*. But that is not the only direction to go in Christianity, as becomes evident if we pay attention to the social justice characteristic of the Sojourners movement, a vigorous example of an Anabaptist movement as well as the leftist or social gospel which actively contends with the state (Heinz 2020, 2022).

So illuminative was the term "the naked public square" that religion's forced isolation from the public square as a result of the latter's domination by the religion of secularism became a major trope. The earlier prominence of concern over church and state issues and the fear of religious establishment gave way to vigorous assertions of the free exercise of religion as just one of the "discourse communities" contending for public space in post-modern times. The decline or elimination of the God hypothesis had seemed to become the default worldview of science, modernism, the Enlightenment, higher education, and even government. Religion would have no role in shaping the public conversation and public policy. But then changes ensued. A telling historical example is the silencing of church bells following the French Revolution. This became a contest for presence in the "aural landscape". Eventually, the sound of church bells returned, and religion was no longer silenced. It could be heard again.

In the post-modern world of multiple discourse communities, religion is one of them—both left and right. In *A Secular Age* (Taylor 2007), Charles Taylor argued that both secularism and religion are more fluid concepts than lately acknowledged. According to Taylor, postmodernism is both post-religious and post-secular. Secularism is not the absolute assertion of nothing but just another competing something. Taylor's challenge to the concept of "immanent frame" protested that all the available windows permit only one way of seeing. Loss of transcendence became another dimension of modern life.

The secularization thesis in the social sciences had been based on a single global idea of religion, a definition of secularity as the absence of religion, and then the triumph of instrumental reason. To this extent, it became the subtraction of religion from the public square. This is the understandable key to conservative evangelicalism's feeling of displacement and loss of heritage. Religion seeking its place may feel it is coming upon a total secular occupation of the public square. Secularism as an all-embracing meaning system escapes the Establishment Clause because it claims to be no religion while, in fact, functioning as an absolute claim-making religion. Thus, as Stanley Hauerwas and William Willimon note, the church must contest for the right to speak its own language, in its own dialect, to tell and be its own story—in public (Hauerwas and Willimon 2014). Religion is one of the stories jostling for acceptance in a post-modern age, one of the master narratives. In this context, many religious studies scholars suggest that religion, and other worldviews, be tested by their "adequacy to the human condition". Bold religious leaders insist they, too, have something to say when it comes to subjects, including the subject of COVID-19.

A world disenchanted may become disenchanting. A world without the depth of the sacred can become superficial, without ultimate comfort. If late capitalism is the only ideology left standing, how well does it pass the test of responding to a pandemic? Is economics all anyone has to say? How adequate to the human condition is it? A reduced social imaginary is secularism's result in the Western Master Narrative. Matter minus spirit. When religion returns to the public square, it questions this hermeneutic and exposes its inadequacy and challenges its sufficiency for human meaning.

What if a dissenting church is the only meaning system left standing to offer a counter-story to that of late capitalism or scientism and the challenges of the epidemic? In this context, the Roman Catholic Declaration of Religious Freedom in 1965 argues not merely for courts to be neutral toward religious freedom, but nurturing and enabling (but without privileging one particular religion). Religion would like to be the yeast that leavens the commons. It does not concede that only politics, not religion, is the realm of cultural power.

So religion claims the right to be a social movement in the public square. St. Francis and the current Pope Francis saw that you have to see something and be something and do something—if you are to be a disciple of Christ (Pope Francis 2020). But the religious may lose their nerve. Consider the "God-gap among Democrats", fearful of being too assertive but perhaps catching up, as depicted by Amy Sullivan in *The Party Faithful: How and Why Democrats are Closing the God-Gap* (Sullivan 2008). Or the hopeful prodding of Brian McClaren, in *The Great Spiritual Migration: How the World's Largest Religion Is Seeking a Better Way to Be Christian* (McClaren 2017), which wants to display better ways to be Christian (and become the Church 2:0!).

When churches or individual religious actors decide they have something they must say or do, they may remain individual prophets called by and responding to sacred *texts*. But it may have been perilous contexts that called them forth. (These are sometimes called "Bonhoeffer moments" to refer to the Lutheran theologian and martyr who felt called forth by Nazi Germany to form the "pastors' emergency league" and become the "confessing church".) When I wrote my dissertation on the Bay Area Jesus Movement in the 1970s, I practiced participant-observation in a Jesus Movement in Berkeley that sassily called itself the Christian World Liberation Front (Heinz 1976). Although its early leadership originated in the conservative evangelical student ministry Campus Crusade for Christ (now called CRU), it quickly moved leftward, certainly in its style, but also soon enough in its political and religious message. It was a good example of how well-sighted individuals can turn themselves into movements that bring new blood into a Christianity in need of cultural transfusion and radically new religious vision and of how re-discovered Biblical texts achieve relevance in new contexts. They become what the times require. There is a "history of effects" (*Wirkungsgeschichte*) going far back into the Hebrew Bible, picking up again in the New Testament, and then persistently breaking through in new ways throughout the history of Christianity. Sociological analysis cannot miss how new religious movements rise up at opportune moments and change the course of religious traditions, equipping them for radical change as a new and necessary environmental response, thereby changing the course of society and culture as well. The Christian World Liberation Front moved to Berkeley from California beaches, introduced guitars to worship, appointed themselves to preach on the Berkeley campus, and could have petered out there. But they transformed much of American evangelicalism and became a yeast in American Protestantism. They became pastors and professors and college presidents, and even Orthodox bishops. Last year they met in Berkeley to celebrate their 50th anniversary.

And yet American history displays a series of "great awakenings", periodic revivals that stirred individual hearts and refreshed the commonwealth. These did not necessarily call for resistance to government but may have implied stirring the government—and especially tens of thousands of camp followers—to religious values. The more "individual religion" was expressed, and this was typical of the several awakenings, the less likely such hearts were to resist the government or challenge social norms.

6. Turning Right or Left?

Therefore, when actors and movements are born, when the religious feel called to respond to a crisis like COVID-19, do they turn right or left? To take an extraordinary individual, Martin Luther King, Jr. began as a black evangelical, practiced moving to the center, and ultimately moved to the left—both calling for radical social justice for the poor and then, when he saw the connection, opposing the Vietnam War. To the outside observer, of course, religion may turn right or left. While many, like Bishop Tutu, or social gospelers, would expect religion to be communal, constructive of societies that become commonwealths in which much "social capital" is traded and committed to building up a community, in some other religious communalism libertarianism rings the bells.

Once, it was thought that Ayn Rand's philosophy, for example, was inimical to religion and its commitment to the community. Religion would stand up in favor of social construction for the good of all. Meanwhile, Rand's hero in *The Fountainhead*, Howard Roark, seemingly expressed a worldview opposite to religion: "I do not recognize anyone's right to one minute of my life. Nor to any part of my energy. Nor to any achievement of mine. No matter who makes the claim, how large their number or how great their need" (Rand 1996). Rand's world is defined as a battle between *creators and parasites*. The creator is self-sufficient, self-motivated, and self-generated. He lives for himself. The parasite lives second-hand and depends on others.

A principled conservative religion that instinctively resists government encroachment on the commons and believes social justice is a leftist cause may resemble the libertarianism of Ayn Rand. When Paul Ryan, whose hero was Ayn Rand, was still the Speaker of the House, the Georgetown Jesuit faculty admonished him that his social and economic philosophy was in clear opposition to the social theology of the Catholicism he also claimed. The welfare of the commons far exceeds the claims of the individual entrepreneur. A common trope one sees on Facebook depicts two libertarians looking out their window during a severe blizzard and pronouncing, "Here comes that socialist snowplow again."

On the other hand, perhaps it is a government that has recently come to be libertarian in denying its responsibility to serve the commonwealth. The legacy of economic theorist Milton Friedman, and every "rational actor" following in his train, declares that the only responsibility of a capitalist economic system is to achieve maximum profits for its shareholders and renounce all claims from so-called "stakeholders", which is to say the entire commons. An epidemic is likely to surface debates about the meaning and demands of the commons. Both conservative evangelical religion and Republican politics may share a libertarian view (Heinz 2020).

A piece of good humor in recent decades is the counselor who says she would not do "marriage counseling" because marriage is an abstract construct devoid of personal or social reality. She only does "individual counseling"—meeting men and women who happen to be married separately. Indeed, the very word *social* has become suspicious, as in neo-conservative religion's certainty that "social gospel" must imply "cultural Marxism". Conservative evangelicals commonly denounce social justice as a possible Christian aspiration. Religion as a source of spiritual and psychological comfort remains a major theme, both to the left and the right, and evangelicals are often leaders in "world relief" organizations such as Franklin Graham's *Samaritan's Purse.* But religion as a source and motivation for public benevolence and building community may split the right from the left, despite that almost all world relief organizations, liberal or conservative, enthusiastically apply for and accept government funds allocated to worldwide economic and famine and medical relief organizations, which have long appeared on the right and the left, among evangelicals and social gospelers.

7. Do *Religious Exemptions* Lean Right or Left?

A response that seems unlike the above and has caused consternation in the body politic is the request for religious exemptions from vaccinations and masks and prohibitions of public gatherings. The shepherd of the flock grants exemptions! To many, this seems more like resistance to the government, but it is a churchly response when the stakes are high, and there is considerable public pressure. Such exemptions on church letterhead are rarely offered by mainstream churches, nearly unanimous in support of vaccinations and masking, and willing to experiment with zoomed worship. Two-thirds of U.S. adults say that most people who claim religious objections to a COVID-19 vaccine are "just using religion as an excuse to avoid the vaccine" (Nortey 2022). Only 10% of the public seem to believe that pandemic policies conflict with their religious beliefs, but they manage to garner much attention. And yet requests to accommodate individual consciences are typically made and answered among conservative Christians.

Conservative clergy have offered exemption letters to those in their own flocks, often emphasizing freedom of conscience rather than specific dangers of the vaccine itself. In rural Hudson, Iowa, Sam Jones informed his small congregation at Faith Baptist Church that he is willing to provide them with a four-paragraph letter stating that "a Christian has no responsibility to obey any government outside of the scope that has been designated by God". Jones's stories are told on the website, *The Gatekeepers: Church, culture, politics*, available by googling. Online, a loose web of largely independent faith leaders has volunteered to provide exemption letters to those who request them. An independent evangelist in Texas is offering letters online in exchange for a donation. In California, a megachurch pastor is offering a letter to anyone who checks a box confirming the person is a "practicing Evangelical that adheres to the religious and moral principles outlined in the Holy Bible". The letters are not necessary, experts say, but they can help bolster claims that religious objections to the vaccine are sincere. Generally, such exemptions are not offered by Catholics or mainstream Protestants.

Of course, groups outside the churches can capitalize on what some churches do. Indeed, one of the most noticed phenomena in the US is with regard to Trump-voting Christians, who voted 80% for him in 2016, or neo-evangelicals and neo-conservatives looking roughly the same. Indeed, there is a debate about whether conservative Republicans have taken over evangelicalism or vice versa. It is true that religion-fueled action can turn into political movements or that conservative Republicans can capitalize on the religion-based pandemic backlash. And it may be that conservative Republicanism has capitalized on the pandemic backlash as a further argument for small government. If political backlash were to shift elections to conservatives, this could become the biggest theme in the social drama, not whether Christianity is "liberal" or "conservative".

But even as neo-conservative evangelicals may imagine they are a decisive religious-political movement, partly as an after-effect of COVID-19, liberal Christians may dream that a global pandemic could become the call for a new holistic era of mutual cooperation and concern for a world family in which the wealthy and privileged—and effective government aid—must arise to sustain the needy. There is evidence from polls (Pew Research Center 2020) that spirituality can aid people with the everyday comfort of faith and mental relaxation in times of crisis and dangerous diseases. Religion can hold up images of the entire community, of society as a commonwealth, and seek the good of the whole. Religion can assist health professionals by urging and encouraging people to wear masks and get vaccinated. Religion has urged governments of wealthy countries to be generous with their COVID-19 aid to poor countries. One of the traditional roles of religious individuals and religious communities has been to serve a positive, integrative, charitable function in crisis situations.

At the same time, evangelical nationalism can be seen as its own kind of armed civil religion, the unquestioned assertion of America as God's favorite country. The use of force, with the AR-15 as its icon, is aimed at defending white supremacy and other values coming into vogue. Possibly the chief angle driving conservative evangelicals into anti-vax postures is that they want to be non-conforming nationalists with their own agenda, as we saw above in the stories of small churches chasing larger memberships. If they have also been pushed around by the state regarding when and how they can worship, that is an additional impetus. But mostly, they are out to build a national movement, and they can see the kinds of people already becoming activists in the anti-mask and ant-vax mode. They are likely to accept free market and free choice fundamentalism as an expression of God's right hand and connect without reservation conservative small government/unregulated capitalism/extreme caution about social constructions like "justice" or "firearms".

By contrast, a Christian social gospel would seem to imply that church and government achieve together a just society, building social programs for the unhoused, the hungry, the sick, the hungry, and the imprisoned—among whom Christians are to see Jesus, according to Jesus' last judgment story in Matthew 25 (Heinz 2022). In this move, however, conservative Christians see not a Christian ethic but a "cultural Marxism" buttressed by tired leftwing slogans. They might assert this as a way to protect the authenticity of their own understanding of religion, or they may resist a social gospel mentality in the name of their own libertarianism or in a political conservatism disguised as conservative religion. The social gospel, once regarded in the early 20th century as America's distinctive contribution to world Christianity in response to the late 19th century Gilded Age, has been derided by American fundamentalists and many evangelicals as a false delusion that leads Christians away from salvation in the hereafter that is their destiny and calling, relieving the expected behaviors of sanctified selves by displacing them onto the government. To such religious conservatives, Christianity is about individualist freedom and redemption. Any new deal is never to use the word *social*, especially if it is twinned with justice.

8. Pastoral Action

A less political label than left or right, conservative or liberal, is to conceive of religious leaders' responses as pastoral action, borrowing from the New Testament the concept of Jesus and Christian leaders as shepherds. *Pastoral* is a mellow word in Christianity, evoking a shepherd tending the flock, giving spiritual guidance to the community, or urging believers to stay the course.

"Intervention", that is, resistance in a social system, may be a religious concept, and it can certainly be of high value in Christianity. A pastoral approach, by slight contrast, is deeply caring but not always gentle. It could be coaching for resistance to government encroachment, as often in the New Testament. I see this in a story that unfolded in an evangelical Christian day school on the East Coast. Friends whose children attend that private Christian school asked me for advice as they faced a vaccination and mask dilemma. The "teaching pastor" at this large church issued a long and carefully argued manifesto about why the school should not accept masking or vaccination mandates from the government. What struck me was his deliberate clarification that he was *not* objecting to the science or public health issues surrounding vaccinations and masks. As I studied the pastor's position statement, I came to see something I had not observed in discussions on this topic. I think it may be more common to evangelical resistance than most people thought.

This pastor saw the individualizing nuclear family as the first and last, and often only, carrier of Christian values in the public arena, the first and indispensable unit of resistance to society, culture, and government whose practices are often likely to run counter to Christian teaching and the practice of Christ himself. Government overreach is likely to impose, with sanctions, cultural values that concern the church. If Christian families (typically with the father as head) did not constantly exercise vigilance against external moral forces, if they did not hold the line, they might lose their well-practiced habit of principled resistance to contemporary (and often *au currant*) public values, including, without mentioning them, legal legitimation of gay marriage, LGBTQ, trans recognition, and abortion. A compliant church accustomed to an agreement with government and cultural trends might gradually lose its instincts for resistance, and indeed its right to resist under the freedom of religion clause of the Constitution, much fought before the Supreme Court in the last fifty years. If the science and medical authority of vaccinations and masks were not the problem, the outside force of the government's ability to bind the Christian conscience was. The government's recent and unexpected establishment of new sets of hitherto objectionable values had further delegitimized government, in the eyes of the church, as a force for the public good and rang the alarm bell calling for religious resistance. The teaching pastor saw it as his mission to train his congregation in the habit of instinctive resistance and protest to fortify the church against overpowering government and social institutions as carriers and champions of non-Christian values. Of course, the forced closing of churches or governmental directions regarding what could or could not be done when Christian communities gathered were often marked as particularly egregious.

I was not immediately prepared to interrogate these conservative oppositions to government further until I reflected on the unending calls for resistance and non-conformity in my own Christian leftism. In my book *After Trump: Achieving a New Social Gospel* (Heinz 2020), I call precisely for a social gospel that extends the church's reach, in part as a community of Christians lobbying the government into society on behalf of the poor. Indeed, I saw the social gospel as a form of resistance to and overcoming of Trumpism that dates back to Reagan's ideology of small government and almost complete neglect of those in need (imagine a government unwilling to offer vaccinations for COVID-19). I wanted Christian movements that opposed not only governmental policies of gross inequality but also invoked ambitious new government policies on behalf of the common good, especially pleading the cause of "the least of these". In my book *Matthew 25 Christianity: Redeeming Church and Society* (Heinz 2022), I call for a leftist Christianity that would regain the ability to see the presence of Jesus amidst the "least of these". A good deal of that book built on compelling observations and critiques of Max Weber more than a century earlier and was devoted to vigorous critiques of deregulated American capitalism as the government's default position and, in response, to vigorous opposition to the government (Weber 1905). The legacy of the Chicago School of economics had been responsibility only to *shareholders (economic stockholders)* but never to *stakeholders (citizens of the commons)*. With great regret, I note that neo-conservative evangelicals are much more effective at saying "don't" than liberal Christians are at saying "do". Was I in the same boat as the conservative *resistance* to the government, but from the left, not the right? This raises the obvious issue that resistance to the government can come from the left as well as the right. Indeed, the phrase "non-conforming resistance movement" that periodically describes Christianity in different ages is more likely to derive from the left than the right.

A well-known test case occurs to me. It is not uncommon in Christian ethics classes to assign the book *Lest Innocent Blood be Shed* (Hallie 1984), which tells the story of how a historic Huguenot community in the French village of Le Chambon resisted the Nazi Vichy government and managed to save the lives of four to five thousand Jews who were hidden from deportation. How did this come about? The Huguenots were French Protestants following the 16th century Reformation, who had a long history of persecution and expulsion from Catholic France, but over time some were allowed to remain under a posture of separatism. Philip Hallie argues that these Protestants, over time, developed the posture of resistance as natural to their lives, to their moral fiber. If the government forbade the ringing of the church bell, they rang it. If the government said to raise the Nazi flag, they refused to run it up the pole. When Vichy ordered them to identify and turn over the Jews in hiding, they were fully prepared to bear real risks and resist.

The irony of these resistance comparisons is not lost on me. Comparing modern evangelicals with a Le Chambon persecuted community raises a new question: How would you decide Le Chambon as right and American conservative evangelicals as wrong? Granted, it must be the issues, not the practice of resistance itself, one might reply, but the formal comparison itself raises two questions: Does Le Chambon, in fact, appeal to a Biblical ethic, while American evangelicals, in fact, appeal to political conservatism (e.g., Reagan's notion that big government is always wrong)? And when liberal Christians oppose the government, is it because the government fails to produce justice across the land? Does the left, then, oppose the government in order to get the government to do good, to cooperate with the churches in practicing a social gospel, while evangelicals are determined to keep the government from doing bad?

But do not conservative Christians resist the government in order to avoid being forced by government to surrender *Christian* obedience to *political* obedience? Is the evangelical nuclear family not being called on to practice a steady line of defense and non-surrender that is, in many ways, admirable? We saw above that epidemics, natural disasters, and upheaval can become test cases of whether and when religious cooperation or resistance is called for. Pandemics such as the one through which we are currently living can reveal the emperor has no clothes. If these historical moments of crisis have historically brought about social change, or at least revealed cracks in the system, what role does the prevailing national culture, whether libertarian conservatism, deregulated capitalism, or a New Deal-like social gospel, play in the probabilities of religious resistance to, or cooperation with, government?

9. Conclusions

COVID-19 has inaugurated a social drama in which pandemic, government, science, religion, and churches all play significant roles. All of these actors may undergo change, wanted or unwanted, as the play unfolds. As in Biblical religion, both Hebrew Bible and Christian New Testament, powerful upheavals in the world can produce apocalyptic postures. What new revelations are on the way? Or is the crisis all over—a featherweight compared to the Black Death? What challenges will traditional religion undergo as it keeps evolving? What movements of God will be uncovered? What prophets will hear calls? On what fronts will the opposition between sacred texts and contemporary contexts be felt? What God seems to be calling for can seem to arrive from the left or the right. Did God not turn left after the Exodus? When COVID-19 departs, what will society and religion look like in its wake? For what new challenges will we have to be prepared?

The epidemic is a historic medium for understanding society and religion in perilous times. Epidemics have the power to expose strengths and weaknesses. The European Black Death was the quintessential epidemic. The Lisbon Earthquake was a natural disaster not unlike a pandemic. But an unexpected comparison to responses to an epidemic is the continuing argument over whether climate change or global warming or worldwide poverty or, even in the United States, completely inadequate healthcare are fundamental and undeniable facts and how big government should be authorized to mobilize in response. The notion of *global reset* is useful in estimating the religious and social change likely to respond to either.

Finally, the COVID-19 pandemic could be a useful and concrete way of cataloging for university classes the whole range of topics involved in the sociology of religion or in the history of American religion. Years ago, I began sub-titling my sociology of religion class, "religious contests for public space". COVID-19 discussions could bring these issues to life, make test cases of them, and inquire whether the historic disciplines involved in the sociology of religion and the histories of Christian thought are sufficient to understand the times in which we live.

Funding: This research received no external funding.

Data Availability Statement: No survey research was involved in preparing this article. Research was in books and journals mentioned in bibliography. Analysis was rooted in the public availability of the intellectual disciplines of sociology of religion and history of religions and Christian theology.

Conflicts of Interest: The author declares no conflict of interest.

References

Alberta, Tim. 2022. How politics poisoned the Church. *Atlantic* 329: 28–42.

Barry, John M. 2005. *The Great Influenza: The Story of the Deadliest Pandemic in History*. New York: Penguin Books.

Battle, Michael. 2009. *Reconciliation: The Ubuntu Theology of Desmond Tutu*, rev. ed. Foreward by Desmond Tutu. New York: Pilgrim Press.

Belich, James. 2022. *The World the Plague Made: The Black Death and the Rise of Europe*. Princeton: Princeton University Press.

Bellah, Robert N. 1967. Civil religion in America. *Daedalus: Journal of the American Academy of Arts and Sciences* 96: 1–21, Special Issue Entitled "Religion in America".

Bellah, Robert N. 1992. *The Broken Covenant: American Civil Religion in Time of Trial*. Chicago: University of Chicago Press.

Bellah, Robert N., and Phillip E. Hammond. 1982. *Varieties of Civil Religion*. San Francisco: Harper San Francisco.

Bellah, Robert N., Richard Madsen, William M. Sullivan, Ann Swidler, and Steven M. Tipton. 1988. *TiptonHabits of the Heart: Middle America Observed*. New York: Harper Collins Publishers.

Berger, Peter, and Thomas Luckmann. 1966. *The Social Construction of Reality: A Treatise in the Sociology of Knowledge*. New York: Anchor.

Boccaccio, Giovanni. 1995. *1313–1375, Author The Decameron*, 2nd ed. London and New York: Penguin Books.

Cox, Daniel A. 2021. After the Ballots are Counted: Conspiracies, Political Violence, and American Exceptionalism. *Survey Center on American Life*, February 11. Available online: https://www.americansurveycenter.org/research/after-the-ballots-are-counted-conspiracies-political-violence-and-american-exceptionalism/ (accessed on 27 January 2023).

Danielson, Robert Alden, and Greg S. Whyte. 2021. *The Church's Response to COVID-19*. Wilmore: First Fruits Press.

Durkheim, Émile. 1912. *The Elementary Forms of Religious Life*. Translated by Carol Cosman. Abridged with an Introduction and Notes by Mark S. Cladis. Oxford: Oxford University Press.

Elliott, John H. 2005. *A Home for the Homeless: A Social-Scientific Criticism of 1 Peter, Its Situation and Strategy*. Eugene: Wipf and Stock.

Frenkel, Sheera. 2022. Pandemic Made Some Parents Fervent Anti-Mandate voters. *New York Times*, August 1, p. A1.

Gibbons, Thomas. 2010. *A Sermon Preached at Haberdashers-Hall, November 30th, On Occasion of The Tremendous Earthquake At Lisbon, November 1, 1755 (1756)*. Whitefish: Kessinger Publishing, LLC(1756).

Glock, Charles Y., and Rodney Stark. 1965. *Religion and Society in Tension*. Chicago: Rand McNally.

Habakus, Louise Kuo, and Mary Holland. 2012. *Vaccine Epidemic: How Corporate Greed, Biased Science, and Coercive Government Threaten Our Human Rights, Our Health, and Our Children*, rev. ed. New York: Skyhorse.

Hallie, Phillip P. 1984. *Lest Innocent Blood Be Shed: The Story of the Village of Le Chambon and How Goodness Happened There*. New York: HarperPerennial.

Hauerwas, Stanley, and William H. Willimon. 2014. *Resident Aliens: Life in the Christian Colony*, expanded, 25th anniversary ed. Nashville: Abingdon Press.

Heinz, Donald. 1976. Jesus in Berkeley. Dissertation Presented to The Graduate Theological Union. Available online: https://archive.org/stream/jesusinberkeley01heinrich/jesusinberkeley01heinrich_djvu.txt (accessed on 25 January 2023).

Heinz, Donald. 2020. *After Trump: Achieving a New Social Gospel*. Eugene: Cascade Books.

Heinz, Donald. 2022. *Matthew 25: Redeeming Church and Society*. Eugene: Cascade Books.

Hever, Amnon. 2021. *Is COVID 19 the Flood 2.0?—The Biblical Explanation for the Roots of Coronavirus*. Independently Published. ISBN 9798769620928.

Hitchcock, Mark, and Jeff Kinley. 2022. *Global Reset: Do Curren Events Point to the Antichrist and His Worldwide Empire?* Nashville: Thomas Nelson.

Hitchcock, Mark. 2020. *Corona Crisis: Plagues, Pandemics, and the Coming Apocalypse*. Nashville: Thomas Nelson.

Jeremiah, David. 2022. *After the Rapture: An End Times Guide to Survival*. Nashville: Thomas Nelson.

LeRoy, A. 2022. *The Covid Protocols: Upholding Your Rights in Authoritarian Times*. Seattle: Independently Published. ISBN 979-8404956078.

Lugeons, Noah. 2020. *Outbreak: A Crisis of Faith: How Religion Ruined Our Global Pandemic*. Independently Published. ISBN 979-8695028560.

McClaren, Brian. 2017. *The Great Spiritual Migration: How the World's Largest Religion Is Seeking a Better Way to Be Christian*. Colorado Springs: Convergent Books.

Merrill, Thomas W. 2022. *The Chevron Doctrine: Its Rise and Fall and the Future of the Administrative State*. Cambridge: Harvard University Press.

Molesky, Mark. 2016. *This Gulf of Fire: The Great Lisbon Earthquake, or Apocalypse in the Age of Science and Reason*, reprint ed. Visalia: Vintage.

Neuhaus, Richard John. 1984. *The Naked Public Square: Religion and Democracy in America*. Grand Rapids: W. B. Eerdmans.

Nortey, Justin. 2022. Americans Skeptical about Religious Objections to COVID-19 Vaccines, but Oppose Employer Mandates. *Pew Research Center*, March 31. Available online: https://www.pewresearch.org/fact-tank/2022/03/31/americans-skeptical-about-religious-objections-to-covid-19-vaccines-but-oppose-employer-mandates/ (accessed on 27 January 2023).

Paice, Edward. 2009. *Wrath of God: The Great Lisbon Earthquake of 1755*. London: Quercus Publishing.

Pless, John T., and Jacob Corzine. 2020. *Faith in the Shadow of a Pandemic*. St Louis: Concordia Publishing.

Pope Francis. 2020. *Christ in the Storm: An Extraordinary Blessing for a Suffering World*. Notre Dame: Ave Maria Press.

Putnam, Robert. 2000. *Bowling Alone: The Collapse and Revival of American Community*, rev. ed. New York: Simon & Schuster.

Putnam, Robert. 2012. *American Grace: How Religion Divides and Unites Us*. New York: Simon & Schuster.

Rand, Ayn. 1996. *The Fountainhead*. New York: Signet Book.

Rousseau, Jean-Jacques. 2019. *On the Social Contract*, 2nd ed. Translated by Donald A. Cress. Introduction and New Annotation by David Wootton. Indianapolis: Hackett Publishing Company.

Schussler Fiorenza, Elizabeth. 1994. *In Memory of Her: Feminist Theological Reconstruction of Christian Origins*, 10th ed. New York: Crossroad Publishing Company.

Shilts, Randy. 2007. *And the Band Played On: Politics, People, and the AIDS Epidemic*, 20th-anniversary ed. New York: St. Martin's Griffin.

Shrady, Nicholas. 2009. *The Last Day: Wrath, Ruin, and Reason in the Great Lisbon Earthquake of 1755*, reprint ed. New York: Penguin Books.

Snowden, Frank M. 2019. *Epidemics and Society: From the Black Death to the Present*. The Open Yale Courses Series; New Haven: Yale University Press.

Stark, Rodney, and Charles Glock. 1968. *American Piety: The Nature of Religious Commitment*. Berkeley: University of California Press.

Sullivan, Amy. 2008. *The Party Faithful. How and Why Democrats Are Closing the God Gap*. New York: Scribner.

Taylor, Charles. 2007. *A Secular Age*, 2018 reprint ed. Cambridge: Belknap Press.

Toobin, Jeffrey. 2017. The Conservative Pipeline to the Supreme Court. *The New Yorker*, April 10. Available online: https://www.newyorker.com/magazine/2017/04/17/the-conservative-pipeline-to-the-supreme-court (accessed on 27 January 2023).

Turner, Victor. 1969. *The Ritual Process: Structure and Anti-Structure*. Chicago: Aldine Publishing Co.

Turner, Victor. 1988. *The Anthropology of Performance*. New York: PAJ Publications.

von Leibniz, Gottfried Wilhelm Freiherr. 1985. *Theodicy: Essays on the Goodness of God, the Freedom of Man, and the Origin of Evil*. Edited and an Introduction by Austin Farrer. Translated by Huggard E. M.. Lasalle: Open Court.

Vowell, Elizabeth, and Kevin Foster. 2022. La. Pandemic Restrictions Violated Religious Rights, Court Rules; Pastor Tony Spell Takes Victory Lap. *Pastor Tony Spell Wins against Governor, WVUE-TV Channel 8, New Orleans, LA*, May 13. Available online: https://www.fox8live.com/2022/05/13/la-covid-emergency-orders-violated-tony-spells-rights-state-supreme-court-rules/ (accessed on 27 January 2023).

Weber, Max. 1905. *The Protestant Ethic and the Spirit of Capitalism: The Coplete Text-Inclusive of Notes, January 1905*. Translated by Talcott Parsons. Cambridge: Pantianos Classics.

Wright, N. T. 2020. *God and the Pandemic: A Christian Reflection on the Coronavirus and Its Aftermath*. Grand Rapids: Zondervan.

Wuthnow, Robert. 2010. *Be Very Afraid: The Cultural Response to Terror, Pandemics, Environmental Devastation, Nuclear Annihilation, and Other Threats*. New York and Oxford: Oxford University Press.

Wuthnow, Robert. 2013. *Small Town America: Finding Community, Shaping the Future*. Princeton: Princeton University Press.

Wuthnow, Robert. 2018. *The Left Behind: Decline and Rage in Small-Town America*. Princeton and Oxford: Princeton University Press.

Wuthnow, Robert. 2020. *What Happens When We Practice Religion?: Textures of Devotion in Everyday Life*. Princeton: Princeton University Press.

Zentner, McLaurine H. 2015. The Black Death and Its Impact on the Church and Popular Religion. Honors Thesis, The University of Mississippi, Sally McDonnell Barksdale Honors College, Oxford, MS, USA. Available online: https://egrove.olemiss.edu/hon_thesis/682/ (accessed on 27 January 2023).

religions

MDPI

Article

Fostering the Global Common Good: The Relevance of Catholic Social Teaching to Public Health Debates

Andrew Lustig

Holmes Rolston III Professor of Religion and Science Emeritus Department of Religious Studies, Davidson College, Davidson, NC 28036, USA; anlustig@davidson.edu

Abstract: Given the scope and intensity of its impact, the COVID-19 pandemic proves instructive as an example of the shortfall in regnant legal and policy approaches to global health issues. Secular discussions of such issues tend to rely on a perspective best described as "policy realism", with current international arrangements and institutions viewed as the acceptable context for future reform. Much of recent Catholic social teaching (hereinafter, CST) has challenged such realism in fundamental ways. While CST is often dismissed as merely prophetic in its tone, I defend its salience by assessing several aspects of its distinctive perspective: (1) the broad theological and anthropological vision reflected in the Catholic framework of basic norms, especially the norm of solidarity; (2) issues that arise in identifying different modes of moral discourse in modern CST; and (3) an effort to resolve such apparent tensions that unifies a distinctively Catholic approach to global health even as it suggests a series of "talking points" between the Catholic theological vision and various secular philosophical and political perspectives.

Keywords: Catholic social teaching; common good; COVID-19; globalization; personalism; public health; right to heath care; solidarity

Citation: Lustig, Andrew. 2023. Fostering the Global Common Good: The Relevance of Catholic Social Teaching to Public Health Debates. *Religions* 14: 504. https://doi.org/10.3390/rel14040504

Academic Editors: Andrew Flescher and Joel Zimbelman

Received: 23 November 2022
Revised: 16 January 2023
Accepted: 30 March 2023
Published: 6 April 2023

1. Introduction

The tradition of modern CST, since the papacy of Leo XIII (1878–1903) offers a distinctive set of lenses through which to assess and justify the basic goods of human flourishing, which include both individual health and the communal good of public health. Catholic natural law reasoning is both axiological and deontological: moral imperatives are generated by reflection on the basic goods that contribute to human flourishing, and such reflection generates both duties and rights concerning health. There are virtue-based duties of all persons to act, to the extent they can, as responsible stewards for their own health. There are also the rights of persons to adequate health care, with entitlements to basic care to be guaranteed by social institutions as concomitants of human dignity. In addition, there are the requirements of the common good that provide the larger context that both justifies and constrains the claims of individuals to pursue their own ends within society. The latter point is especially relevant to the COVID-19 context, in which some have resisted wide-scale vaccination efforts in the name of individual "liberty". As I will discuss, such claims to unfettered individual freedom have no basis in Catholic thought. Individuals have duties to protect and promote their own health and the health of others. Persons also have rights to such protection and promotion as individuals and as members of the larger society. At the same time, the common good provides the appropriate framework for understanding persons as necessarily social, with rights and duties both justified and constrained by that foundational awareness.

In what is perhaps the most comprehensive recent overview of the fundamental values invoked by CST, Anthony Annett identifies a range of basic norms that he describes as "concrete principles" of CST (Annett 2022a, pp. 42–66). While each of the principles Annett identifies might serve to inform an analysis of collective obligations in response to the

COVID-19 pandemic, my focus here will be CST's recent emphasis on solidarity as a virtue that should animate both individual and social morality, especially its relevance to the functions of multilateral institutions in the context of ever-greater global interdependence. In the context of the COVID-19 pandemic, I will argue that the appeal to solidarity supports both the global right to vaccination and the general duty of persons to avail themselves of the vaccine as a necessary contribution to the common good. The warrants at work in CST's arguments for a right to basic health care, ordinarily discussed within the context of individual care, *a fortiori* justify the provision of the goods of public health, where the Catholic understanding of individual claims as necessarily situated in the context of larger society is especially obvious in its implications and application. The Catholic case for a global responsibility to provide effective vaccines to all persons at risk, as well as the duty of individuals to be vaccinated, follow directly from the moral and theological warrants for CST's distinctive understanding of the rights of persons *vis-a-vis* the requirements of the common good. Moreover, the norm of solidarity helps to resolve certain tensions that may arise in interpreting the relevance of the Catholic vision to the global discussion of public health. Especially as developed in the writings of John Paul II (but also invoked regularly by his two successors, Benedict XVI and Francis), solidarity emerges as a virtue that should animate both individuals and institutions, especially the institutions of government.

My discussion will also engage two aspects of the vaccine discussion raised by certain "dissenting" Catholic voices: first, the charge of "moral complicity" in the evil of abortion insofar as the recent vaccines, as well as earlier ones, have relied on decades-old research that included the use of cell lines initially derived from abortions; and second, the issue of whether and to what extent various policy "restrictions" on personal behavior (e.g., mask mandates, limits on or refusals of public access, required quarantine) are justified or challenged by a distinctively Catholic understanding of personal liberty of conscience. In each instance, I judge the "dissenting" voices to be in error. In addition, while the Catholic literature on the second topic—that of justified restrictions during the pandemic—is not extensive, I conclude that the answers follow straightforwardly from a distinctively Catholic understanding of individual rights as necessarily exercised within and constrained by the requirements of the common good.

2. CST: The General Background

While Catholic reflections on issues of justice and social ethics have long drawn on a scholastic tradition of natural-law reasoning and, more recently, on scriptural themes, CST generally refers to papal and episcopal documents beginning with Leo XIII's encyclical *Rerum Novarum* in 1891. The so-called "social encyclicals" continue to the present, with later popes sometimes using the anniversary dates of the publication of *Rerum Novarum* to issue encyclicals that draw upon, even as they extend, key elements of Leo's analysis. Such celebratory encyclicals include Pius XI's 1931 *Quadragesimo Anno* on the fortieth anniversary of *Rerum Novarum*, Paul VI's 1971 *Octogesima adveniens* on its eightieth anniversary, and John Paul II's 1991 *Centesimus Annus* on its one-hundredth anniversary. In overview, CST reveals both continuity and development, with three aspects especially prominent. First, CST self-consciously brings the Catholic theological tradition to an engagement with the political and socio-economic conditions of modernity that, depending on the historical circumstances at the time of publication, will offer different emphases. Thus, Leo XIII was especially concerned with the rights of workers in an era of largely unfettered capitalism. Forty years later, Pius XI, amidst the rise of communism and fascism, highlighted the dignity of persons in the context of intermediate institutions and voluntary associations with an appeal to the principle of subsidiarity. Paul VI, drawing from the writings of his predecessor, John XXIII, emphasized the global dimensions of human rights claims. John Paul II criticized the inadequacies of both collectivist economic systems and unregulated market approaches, emphasizing the need for both perspectives to offer safeguards to protect the dignity of persons, with particular attention paid to the needs of the poor.

Second, the social encyclicals illustrate the varied theological and philosophical warrants at work in Catholic teaching. Appeals to natural law reasoning, drawing on traditional Thomistic understandings, are significant. At the same time, and increasingly since the papacy of John XXIII, one finds the language of individual rights based on the dignity of persons, including civil, political, and economic rights. Moreover, especially since the papacy of John Paul II (1978–2005) and continuing in the social encyclicals of Pope Benedict XVI (2005–2013) and Pope Francis (2013–), one finds appeals to human solidarity as a central theme, an emphasis that reflects an increasingly global perspective on such issues as poverty, immigration, and environmental devastation.

Third, the range of warrants at work in CST reflects the broad audience for such documents: persons for whom expressly theological and scriptural themes will resonate, as well as others of "good will" for whom natural law and humanistic appeals may prove persuasive. While these different warrants may at times generate tensions, especially in the context of social and religious pluralism, there are ways to view Catholic social teaching as there are ways to view Catholic social teaching as distinctive in its own right while also often intersecting with other perspectives in political and social ethics.

3. The Norm of Solidarity

In CST since Vatican II, access to health care, including the ready availability of vaccines in the context of the COVID-19 pandemic, has been deemed a positive right, i.e., a justified entitlement claimable by individuals from society. The warrants for this understanding are expressly theological, involving a number of themes and principles that, while interconnected, can be analyzed separately. I have analyzed most of those themes extensively elsewhere and will not review the first six of them here beyond listing them again as norms central to the Catholic conversation (Lustig 1990, 1993, 1996, 2012). The first six of these themes are (1) the dignity of persons, (2) the common good, (3) subsidiarity, (4) social justice, (5) distributive justice, and (6) the so-called "preferential option for the poor". However, a seventh theme, that of solidarity, has emerged as a core emphasis in the encyclical literature since the papacy of John Paul II. Herein, I analyze its development as a unifying norm in recent CST, one that helps to illuminate the responsibilities of individuals and institutions in the context of the current pandemic.

In the social encyclicals of the last three papacies, solidarity has emerged as perhaps the central value invoked in the ongoing tradition. To be sure, solidarity as a political concept long predates its use in Catholic discussion. It first appeared in Napoleon's 1804 *code civil* and was invoked as a principle for reordering society by various political and social theorists during the nineteenth and early twentieth centuries, especially in the writings of French socialist Charles Fourier (1772–1837). The term first appeared in Catholic teaching in Germany in the late nineteenth century in the writings of social reformer Franz Hitze (1851–1921) and the Jesuit Heinrich Pesche (1854–1921). In the modern encyclical literature, cognates of solidarity are invoked in other explicit appeals from the earlier decades of CST. It seems clear that the value of solidarity was at least foreshadowed in the two major encyclicals of John XXIII, *Mater et Magistra* in 1961 and *Pacem in Terris* in 1963, in Paul VI's 1967 *Populorum Progressio*, as well as in *Gaudium et Spes* in 1965, a core document of Vatican II. However, solidarity appears in full-blooded fashion only in the social encyclicals of John Paul II and continues to be cited regularly in the writings of his successors (Doran 1996).

To appreciate the importance of solidarity in John Paul II's thought, it is helpful to situate it within the larger context of personalism, the theologically informed philosophy that shapes his approach to ethical issues at both the personal and institutional levels. As a priest and cardinal archbishop before becoming Pope John Paul II, Karol Wojtyla was a serious scholar and author, with particular interest in exploring the phenomenology of the person as the most appropriate focus for understanding the nature of human freedom and responsibility. While a professor of ethics at the Catholic University of Lublin in Poland, Wojtyla authored two significant books on personalism (Wojtyla 2013, 1979). In *Love and Responsibility* (Wojtyla 2013) and *The Acting Person* (Wojtyla 1979), he synthesized traditional scholastic understandings of human nature with insights from phenomenology. In his writings, he emphasized the inviolable and transcendent worth of each human being as the necessary safeguard against the dangers of materialistic and reductionist views. By underscoring the transcendent worth of persons as the necessary starting point for ethical reflection, Pope John Paul's personalism seeks to avoid perspectives that would view persons as isolated individuals pursuing "consumerist" ends or as "units" of a larger collectivity. Instead, personalism insists upon the irreducibility of persons in their freedom. However, in that affirmation, the "liberty" central to the personalist account is not that of the atomistic individual, but of the socially situated self, with direct implications for understanding the appropriate relations between self and society.

At the same time, this personalism is expressed in terms of an anthropology that maintains a fairly traditional understanding of an objective moral order. It is that combination of commitments—to the inviolable dignity of the person as a subject who freely pursues the shared and definable goods of human flourishing—that leads to John Paul's emphasis on solidarity as a norm. Viewed theologically, solidarity is best construed as a holistic virtue of both individuals and institutions that serves to integrate the more focused emphases of other theological norms (e.g., distributive justice, the preferential option for the poor, specific rights claims). In its integrating function, it has significant theoretical and practical promise as a value that both unifies CST and reinforces its growing call for international mechanisms to support personal rights and to enforce collective obligations in pursuit of the global common good.

While there are etymological precedents in CST for solidarity as an ethical norm, earlier terms (e.g., relationship, agreement, cooperation, interdependence) often appeared primarily in descriptive fashion, i.e., as features of the increasing complexity of modern socioeconomic circumstances. In an illuminating analysis of John Paul's explicit use of "solidarity" as a norm in its own right, Constance Nielsen observes the decided shift in terminology one finds in John Paul. While earlier encyclicals had noted the facts of modern interdependence, John Paul speaks in *Sollicitudo Rei Socialis* about how solidarity, as an effective virtue based in fraternal love, can *transform* interdependence:

> ... in a world divided and beset by every type of conflict, the conviction is growing of a radical interdependence and consequently of the need for a solidarity which will take up interdependence and transfer it to the moral plane ... [T]he idea is slowly emerging that the good to which we are called and the happiness to which we aspire cannot be obtained without an effort and commitment on the part of all, nobody excluded, and the consequent renouncing of personal selfishness (Pope John Paul II 1987, #26).

Nielsen comments that, for John Paul, "[s]olidarity does not replace interdependence, it transforms it. It elevates human unity to a higher moral dimension" (Nielsen 2007, p. 321). This transformation has implications for both individuals and institutions. As John Paul continues,

> I have wished to introduce this type of analysis ... in order to point out the true *nature* of the evil which faces us with respect to the development of peoples: it is a question of a *moral evil*, the fruit of *many sins* which lead to "structures of sin". To diagnose the evil in this way is to identify precisely, on the level of human conduct, *the path to be followed* in order *to overcome it* (Pope John Paul II 1987, #37).

What, then, constitutes the aforementioned "path to be followed"? Here, John Paul is quite explicit:

> ... it is the virtue of solidarity: This then is not a feeling of vague compassion or shallow distress at the misfortunes of so many people, both near and far. On the contrary, it is *a firm and persevering determination* to commit oneself to the *common good;* that is to say, to the good of all and of each person, because we are *all* really responsible *for all* (Pope John Paul II 1987, #38).

In her analysis, Nielsen draws together a number of earlier notions in CST that serve as precedents for John Paul's explicit formulation of solidarity. There are two important aspects to John Paul's discussion of the term. As a norm, it has extensive implications for both individuals and institutions. On the one hand,

> while the earlier tradition rested primarily upon the twin categories of justice and charity, there was another animating love that went beyond the individual act of charity in the giving of superfluous wealth—a love that had social impact and worked for the common good ... It is a love that promotes justice, goes beyond justice, seeks to perfect the structures of society, and is willing to go beyond self for the sake of others. Solidarity springs from this discussion of love. Yet, if the term solidarity is truly to be a development, it cannot simply be another term for the love already described. It goes beyond charity (Nielsen 2007, p. 336).

How, then, does solidarity "go beyond" charity? Unlike both charity and justice, which "can always be reduced to individual acts or personal dispositions that may or may not affect the common good" (Nielsen 2007, p. 337), John Paul draws out the necessarily social implications of solidarity at the level of *culture*, which is even "more fundamental to the ordering of society than either State or market" (Nielsen 2007, p. 341). Most profoundly, in Nielsen's judgment,

> Solidarity is neither a political nor an economic concept. It is a Christian virtue for the formation of people who will then go on to transform culture. They will naturally use the State and the market for the purposes for which they are intended. Their solidarity will motivate struggles for justice, and great acts of charity. In all they will be dedicated to the development of each and every human person (Nielsen 2007, p. 342).

Lest one confuse matters, while solidarity is "neither a political nor an economic concept", it provides a rich context of reflection that has powerful implications in the analysis and critique of current global issues, including that of effective access to the basic goods of health care. As Anna Rowlands observes, the power of solidarity as a norm is that it integrates the sometimes more restricted emphases of other principles in three ways: "as an anthropological fact and theological reality; as an ethical principle or moral outlook; and ... as a structural and institutional imperative" (Rowlands 2021, p. 265).

Each of these functions helps to provide a useful lens through which to consider the nature and scope of personal and social responsibilities during a pandemic. As an anthropological and theological reality, the pandemic serves as a stark reminder that we are inevitably interconnected, and that we are, in fact, both our own and our brothers' (and sisters') keepers. As an ethical principle or moral outlook, solidarity invites us, indeed challenges us, to understand our necessary interdependence as both a fact and a value. We become ever more fully ourselves in cooperation and, ultimately, in communion with others. As a structural and institutional imperative, solidarity offers a perspective on persons and institutions that views them as necessary partners rather than as antagonists in pursuit of the common good.

In light of solidarity, one can rather straightforwardly make the Catholic case for global basic rights within the context of what is called "the universal destination of earthly goods" (Second Vatican Council 1965, #69). John Paul II calls that concept "the first principle of the social order" (Pope John Paul II 1981, #19). The dignity of persons is affirmed as fundamental even as it is justified and constrained by the requirements of the common good. Thus, the "universal destination" remains a general norm for regulating the excesses of both an unfettered libertarianism and an unrestrained collectivism. It has served to both justify and limit property holding since the time of Aquinas. While private property is recognized as a legitimate feature of economic life, it is ultimately assessed in light of its contributions to the common good and regulated as necessary. According to Annett, the practical implications of the "universal destination" include both the taxation of excessive profits and the redistribution of overly concentrated wealth. In the context of

COVID-19, he concludes that it justifies overriding the intellectual property protections of pharmaceutical companies by making inexpensive generic versions of the vaccine widely available (Annett 2022b).

When linked to the virtue of solidarity, "the universal destination" principle generates a powerful critique of current global realities. This critique points to the need for significant reform of current international approaches to ameliorating issues of global import, including climate change, hunger, lack of access to basic medical care, and inequities of access to the goods of public health. Central to that reform will be a recognition of the inadequacy of continuing to engage large-scale problems in piece-meal fashion, especially when one acknowledges the links between and among putatively separate issues. The more that such "systemic discernment" is encouraged, the more that integrated solutions will need to be sought as the necessary and compelling implications of recent Catholic discussion.

4. Two Misunderstandings among Catholic Commentators on COVID-19

There are two aspects of the recent discussion of COVID-19 in Catholic circles that merit further scrutiny here. First, some Catholic voices have cautioned against using any forms of the COVID-19-vaccine that relied, in their development, on earlier cell lines generated from the tissue of aborted fetuses. That charge has been raised before with the use of other vaccines, most notably the vaccine for rubella, and it is useful to summarize briefly the recent position paper of the United States Conference of Catholic Bishops that offers general approval of vaccine use (United States Conference of Catholic Bishops 2020). As David Cloutier observes, "the vaccine controversy raises the larger question of how to evaluate the present use of benefits derived from past evils" (Cloutier 2021, p. 20). To their credit, the bishops draw useful distinctions in response to the charge of moral complicity. They focus on the question of receiving a vaccine whose development employed the use of cell lines initially generated from tissues of an act of abortion, which Catholic moral theology deems intrinsically evil. The bishops are not reconsidering the licitness of abortion, nor the question of using cells taken directly from fetal tissue, but the use of vaccines whose "process of production or testing includes the use of cells taken from a cell line (HEK-293) that is virtually ubiquitous in basic medical research" (Cloutier 2021, p. 21). Cloutier cites the important analysis offered by Catholic scholar Cathleen Kaveny, who challenges the appropriateness of the charge of "cooperation" by critics of vaccine use. Kaveny distinguishes cases of "cooperation", which involve judgments about direct and indirect complicity, from cases of "appropriation", which involve the use of the "fruits of an initially evil act" (Kaveny 2000, p. 281). In light of Kaveny's detailed analysis, Cloutier concludes that efforts to analyze at least some cases of appropriation according to categories of cooperation are, in effect, mirror images of that concept: "in cases of appropriation, you are not helping the evildoer; it is the evildoer who is (unintentionally) helping you" (Cloutier 2021, p. 21).

A second document from the Vatican raises another seeming confusion. The document states that vaccination "is not, as a rule, morally obligatory" and "must be voluntary", and that those who "for reasons of conscience, refuse vaccines" must avail themselves of alternative measures (e.g., masking) to serve the common good (Congregation for the Doctrine of the Faith 2020). Here, as Cloutier observes, the document seems to suggest that such objectors to vaccination are praiseworthy, a judgment seemingly at odds with the subsequent statement of Pope Francis that receiving the vaccine is "the most reasonable solution for the prevention of the disease" (Pope Francis 2022). Numerous politically conservative voices have interpreted policy "restrictions" on personal behavior (e.g., mask mandates, limits on or refusals of public access, required quarantine) as infringements upon personal conscience or violations of freedom of religious practice. As noted above, some Catholics may mistakenly interpret their opposition to vaccines as a refusal to cooperate materially with abortion. That judgment, as the bishops' letter indicates, is erroneous; as Kaveny persuasively argues, "appropriation" rather than "cooperation" is the preferable framework of moral analysis. However, independent of that potential concern with cooperation, some Catholics may claim such an unfettered "freedom of conscience" in refusing public health restrictive measures. That judgment is equally mistaken. Traditional Catholic moral theology makes clear that, in service to a proclaimed "right of conscience," there is the prior duty to "rightly inform" one's conscience (Lustig 2012). As should be abundantly clear from my earlier review of solidarity, it is unjustified to equate the Catholic understanding of personal freedom with a libertarian commitment to unfettered individualism. From first to last, the Catholic tradition is, as Charles Curran defines it, a "both/and" tradition: persons and community as well as persons in community (Curran 2002). To show indifference to the health of one's neighbors by rejecting basic public health measures amidst a pandemic in the name of individual "liberty" is to fundamentally misread CST.

5. The Relevance of CST in the Public Square

Given the political context of pluralism in most of the developed world, one might ask how a distinctively Catholic conversation can contribute to an analysis of our collective obligations in response to the current pandemic. A more full-blooded reading of pluralism would likely celebrate, rather than discourage, the vibrancy of various voices in the public square about complex issues, which may be expressed in distinctive fashion. James Gustafson has reminded us that moral discourse, whether theologically inspired or not, may function in several ways. He discusses four "modes" of moral discourse—ethical, prophetic, narrative, and policy discourse. Each mode, Gustafson suggests, functions in the moral deliberations of particular communities and society at large, but none, as a singular emphasis, is sufficient (Gustafson 1990). Ethical discourse may be the mode most familiar to us—the language of basic norms, rules and principles, rights and duties, and the vocabularies of consequentialism and deontology. Ethics frames our reflections as we justify choices in a pluralistic society where a common narrative cannot be assumed. However, ethics tends to work within the status quo of current moral, legal, and political theory, and seems far less engaged with the larger anthropological or sociocultural picture. Prophetic discourse, by contrast, is often passionate in its sweeping indictments of larger cultural trends and social sins. It highlights those large-scale background features that the ethical mode in the foreground tends to underplay, but it seldom offers fine-grained analysis of particular issues. Narrative discourse is the language of story rather than argument. Before all else, narrative is about inspiration, about the ways that character is shaped by the stories we tell. Finally, there is the policy mode of moral discourse, which tends to work with the values already embedded in the choices we have made. Seldom if ever prophetic, it asks not "What is the good or the right choice?" but, within a range of alternatives, "What is the reasonably good and feasible choice?".

In light of Gustafson's distinctions, it is helpful to consider which mode or modes function most prominently in applying CST to the recent pandemic. As ethical discourse, Catholic thought challenges us to achieve a better balance between the language of rights and that of duties. Persons have basic rights, both negative and positive, but the language of the common good offers a useful corrective to the not-uncommon stridency of rights language. Neither utilitarian average outcomes nor unfettered individualism will survive the scrutiny of common good considerations. As prophetic discourse, CST affirms the necessary limits on private property in order to fulfill the requirements of solidarity and the common good. In that light, it emphasizes the necessity of a robust social safety net, including access to basic public health. So too, CST, by emphasizing certain themes in the Christian story, especially the universalizing tendency of Christian love, invites broader reflection about global responsibilities for the meeting of basic human needs. As a result, CST increasingly discusses the rights of persons and the scope of the common good in global terms. What might have once been dismissed by policy "realists" as largely utopian notions formulated at a fairly general level have taken on a new and practical urgency in light of COVID-19 and its aftermath. In this regard, the pandemic is a stark reminder of the quite literally global consequences that have challenged the sufficiency of Westphalian commitments to the primacy of the nation-state on a range of global issues.

The encyclicals, as well as numerous episcopal statements by Catholic bishops addressed to their national constituencies, have targeted such issues with an appeal to the universalizing impulse of CST. An earlier language of natural law already espoused certain basic norms as foundationally social in their implications and bindingness. The language of human rights based on personal dignity, while drawing on the legacy of that earlier methodological emphasis on natural law, has increasingly spoken of the full panoply of rights—civil, political, and socioeconomic—in universal terms. *All* persons have claimable entitlements to the concomitants of human dignity. That assertion, sometimes dismissed as either wishful thinking or, at best, as a promissory note for its realization in some distant future, is decidedly "realistic" as a Catholic commitment *precisely* because of the theological perspective that informs it. If we are equal members of the human community, equally deserving of dignity, then remediable inequities in the creation and distribution of the basic goods of human flourishing *must* be addressed. The force of the normative logic at work in the theological claim is clear in two basic respects. First, systemic indifference to global needs that rest on outmoded conceptions of "balance of power" politics must be challenged as violations of the rights of those excluded from such calculations. Second, in light of the first conclusion, there are duties increasingly incumbent on global alliances and institutions to address remediable inequities in meeting basic human needs (in the current case, access to vaccines).

To this point, I have considered the general Catholic case for a right to basic health care, one that moves along a steadily globalizing vector. At the same time, we must acknowledge certain tensions that arise when seeking to interpret and apply CST, because, at times, it employs Gustafson's different modes of moral discourse in ways that defy easy integration. For example, as prophetic discourse, CST emphasizes access to basic health care as a universal right, while understanding, according to the principle of subsidiarity, that the scope of that right will often be contextualized in ways that make universal guarantees difficult to specify with precision, much less to implement fully. So long as current patterns of resource distribution are determined primarily at the regional or national levels, how professedly universal rights are to be instantiated raises fundamental challenges to their provision. However, if one seeks to interpret CST as something closer to a policy mode of discourse, that would appear to temper, if not undercut, the universalizing impulse reflected in the prophetic language of human rights, especially in view of the variable local and regional contexts to which considerations of subsidiarity will apply. Indeed, looking though a policy lens might well lead to a judgment similar to that offered by Joel Feinberg about global claims of basic positive entitlements. According to Feinberg, while such claims should not be dismissed as nonsensical, given current realities, they should be construed as what he calls "manifesto rights," i.e., statements that offer visionary perspectives on ideals toward which we should aim but which cannot be implemented at present (Feinberg 1970).

A careful reader of modern CST will not be indifferent to such tensions among modes of discourse, nor of the need for further specification of their implications for particular issues. Nonetheless, whatever the cautions appropriate in distinguishing prophetic from policy discourse, the Catholic arguments, if they are to illuminate a path forward, will exhibit a form of what might be called a "hopeful realism", i.e., a commitment to expanding health care access as widely as possible, precisely because the primary theological warrant undergirding that impulse is that of the dignity of all persons made in the image of God. Seen in that light, fundamental failures to expand access are to be judged not simply as unfortunate consequences of the genetic and social lotteries, but as failures to honor the requirements of personal dignity, distributive justice, the common good, and solidarity. Each of these norms is fully justified in CST as a *moral* claim; the challenge remains to instantiate them as legal and political realities. The complexities of that "translation" of rights—from moral claims to global political realities—cannot be denied, nor can the power of the "Catholic case" for such progress to be realized.

6. Public Health and the Global Common Good

In light of CST's recent emphasis on solidarity, which I reviewed in Part III, I turn now to the specific context of public health and the development and provision of vaccinations in a pandemic situation. The argument here is a straightforward one. The Catholic perspective on health and health care involves the language of both duties and rights. Each person, insofar as possible, has a duty of good stewardship for his or her own health as God's gift. In a time of pandemic, a key aspect of that duty is to educate oneself about the COVID-19 vaccine as a contributor to one's own flourishing, despite the prevalence of extreme public misinformation and disinformation. The correlative of that individual duty is the right of access to vaccination by all persons as a necessary prophylactic in the defense of one's own health. However, the Catholic duty to oneself is amplified by the duty to contribute to the common good—in this instance, the overall benefits of universal vaccination to the population at large. The Catholic case that justifies both the duty of one's own health stewardship and the right to basic health care is cogent and persuasive as a general claim about ordinary medical care involving individual patients. It justifies, with equal or even greater force, the duties and rights involved in public health measures, where the focus, while involving access by individuals, is preeminently concerned with population health. Granted, persons comprise communities; thus, "public health rights" entail individual claims. However, as we have seen, the Catholic vision of personal dignity as situated in and fulfilled by participation in the larger community is especially relevant to matters of public health. A libertarian notion of individuals unencumbered by larger social obligations makes no sense regarding either the science underlying the pandemic or the need for community-based rather than merely individual measures of prevention, protection, and mitigation.

In his final two chapters of *Cathonomics*, Annett draws specific global implications of the Catholic social vision, offering a lengthy list of specific but interlinked recommendations on a range of topics, including international tax policy, sustainable development goals, debt relief, and trade and subsidy policies (Annett 2022a, pp. 249–85). It is important to acknowledge the complex synergies between and among the many ostensibly "separate" policy concerns that he reviews. It is also worth emphasizing yet again that CST has increasingly emphasized the global dimensions of solidarity as a norm: first, a recognition that the world is ever more characterized by interdependence, and second, in light of that interdependence, an ever-greater need for effective international mechanisms, especially a reformed and strengthened United Nations.

Pope Francis has placed particular emphasis on the importance of reforming the current world order through a more robust commitment to a global vision of solidarity. In his most recent encyclical, *Fratelli Tutti*, written after the outbreak of the pandemic, Francis stresses the urgency of moving beyond what he deems both outmoded and ineffective earlier perspectives on global problems (Pope Francis 2020, #172, #173). In addition, in an address to the United Nations General Assembly, he describes the sweeping nature of the choice we face:

> We are faced, then with a choice between two possible paths. One path leads to the consolidation of multilateralism as the expression of a renewed sense of global co-responsibility, a solidarity grounded in justice and the attainment of peace and unity within the human family, which is God's plan for our world. The other path emphasizes self-sufficiency, nationalism, protectionism, individualism, and isolation; it excludes the poor, the vulnerable, and those dwelling on the peripheries of life. That path would certainly be detrimental to the whole community, causing self-inflicted wounds on everyone. It must not prevail (Pope Francis 2020).

Notice the moral vision at work in Francis's words: global co-responsibility and solidarity within the human family, understood in universal terms as the foundational virtues for both persons and the institutions acting on their behalf. Such virtues, Francis observes, stand in clear contrast to the cramped visions of nationalism and individualism often voiced in current political discussions.

The starkness of the choice Pope Francis presents underscores the urgency of the decisions we face. Since the time of Leo XIII, CST has been especially concerned with the inequities generated by the effects of modernization on the dignity of persons and the common good. CST affirms both subsidiarity and solidarity. On that joint basis, it critiques the excesses of both capitalism and socialism, depending on the historical context within which a particular encyclical is written. However, especially now, in light of the increased interdependence and global nature of many of our most pressing problems, the "society" within which persons live requires a broader framework of analysis and application than in earlier times. The "national interests" of states should therefore include, as a necessary feature of their reckoning, meeting the remediable basic needs of all, both citizens and "foreigners". How those needs are to be met may be accomplished through a variety of institutional mechanisms, depending on circumstances—direct governmental aid, public–private partnerships, and incentivization of market distributive patterns. However, *that* basic human needs should be met is not in dispute, and global institutions should be held accountable on that basis. Such personal rights and collective obligations are well-developed moral claims in CST. The challenge remains to make them legally and politically binding.

For all the difficulties of integrating the various modes of discourse in CST, in this pandemic situation, there is merit in viewing the prophetic and policy modes of discourse as more complementary than opposed. The Catholic conversation is not merely prophetic in the often dismissive sense its critics intend. The power of the prophetic voice in the context of global issues is also to challenge the adequacy of a relatively complacent realism. Several such challenges come readily to mind. As I close, I offer several points by way of summary emphasis.

First, if the goods of health care, including public health goods, are the necessary concomitants of personal dignity, they are entitlements to be honored and provided for all persons, not merely as utilitarian "average" outcomes. Either Catholic rights language is meaningful or it is not. If the former is true, then the implications of the Catholic case for expanding public health guarantees on a universal scale are decidedly reformist in tone. Indeed, if taken more seriously at the policy level, such "prophetic" discourse about a morally justified universal right of access to basic health care carries implications for broadly systemic restructuring and reform of current global political institutions.

Second, while the goods of health care, including public health goods, are personal entitlements justified on theological grounds, Catholic natural law theology offers a series of "interim norms" (especially of social and distributive justice) that find areas of overlap and affinity with other moral perspectives that are not theologically grounded. A few examples will suffice here. "Revised natural law" approaches affirm that certain fundamental "truths" about human flourishing are rationally available to all persons engaged in practical reasoning without appeal to particular theological or philosophical premises (e.g., Finnis 2011). Appeals to the "common morality" are central to the dominant theory of "principlism" in biomedical ethics developed by Tom Beauchamp and James Childress (Beauchamp and Childress 2019). In political ethics, Michael Walzer (2019) and Peter Singer (2016) appeal to certain broadly shared intuitions that undergird global appeals to basic justice. Amitai Etzioni and other proponents of communitarian theory speak of the crucial function of social commitments in the flourishing of persons (Etzioni 2004). In such instances, and many others, a workable consensus can be accomplished even without convergence at the level of fundamental theoretical commitments. Granted, all such comparisons would require significant and rigorous exploration to be fully persuasive, but rather than the usual "straining of gnats" among various camps of theorists, I simply affirm, by way of summary here, the powerful plausibility of achievable consensus among different perspectives at the level of policy choice and crafting.

Third, if the goods of health care, including public health goods, are necessary concomitants of human dignity, and if, in fact, global welfare guarantees are now achievable (see, e.g., Sachs 2006; Thurow and Kilman 2009), then, in light of plausible policy consensus, what *can* now be accomplished (e.g., eradication of hunger, basic health care as a global right) *should* be accomplished. In a reversal of the usual Kantian dictum, in this situation, "can implies ought". Past incapacities may have left the claims of positive entitlements, including the goods of public health, as more akin to Joel Feinberg's "manifesto rights" (Feinberg 1970). Our current capacities shift the burden of moral proof immediately, and the burden of legal proof must be shifted as quickly as resources and institutions can be reconfigured to make such claim rights both legally and morally binding.

Fourth, the nation-state framework is no longer fully adequate (if it ever was), given the urgency of the moral and political tasks at hand. "Balance of power" politics is increasingly ineffective, both in its squandering of available resources and in its tendency to deny or ignore the universal positive rights of persons. Therefore, new multilateral mechanisms should be developed and implemented, including (according to principles of subsidiarity, social and distributive justice, and solidarity) a mix of international, global, and public/private partnerships to meet the needs of persons irrespective of the former constraints of national borders.

Finally, in keeping with Annett's emphasis on the interlinkage of global issues, strategies of coordination and prioritization should be emphasized in order to overcome piecemeal bureaucratic "solutions" that fail to integrate the often competing tactics at work on putatively "single" issues (Annett 2022a, pp. 249–85). As Annett's analysis clarifies, such bureaucratic silos too often tend to define targets for policy intervention in an unduly restrictive fashion. By so doing, they undercut the effectiveness of larger strategies of response and limit the vision required to actualize universal human rights within the context of the global common good.

Funding: This research received no external funding.

Institutional Review Board Statement: Not applicable.

Informed Consent Statement: Not applicable.

Data Availability Statement: Not applicable.

Conflicts of Interest: The author declares no conflict of interest.

References

Annett, Anthony. 2022a. *Cathonomics*. Washington, DC: Georgetown University Press.

Annett, Anthony. 2022b. The Universal Destination of Goods and the Contemporary World. Available online: https://wherepeteris.com/the-universal-destination-of-goods-and-the-contemporary-world (accessed on 14 March 2023).

Beauchamp, Tom, and James Childress. 2019. *Principles of Biomedical Ethics*, 8th ed. New York: Oxford University Press.

Cloutier, David. 2021. A Dangerous Confusion. *Commonweal* 148: 20–23.

Congregation for the Doctrine of the Faith. 2020. Note on the Morality of Using Some Anti-COVID-19 Vaccines. Available online: https://www.vatican.va/roman_curia/congregations/cfaith/documents/rc_con_cfaith_doc_20201221_nota-vaccini-anticovid_en.html (accessed on 14 March 2023).

Curran, Charles. 2002. *Catholic Social Teaching, 1891–Present*. Washington: Georgetown University Press.

Doran, Kevin. 1996. *Solidarity: A Synthesis of Personalism and Communalism in the Thought of Karol Wojtyla/Pope John Paul II*. New York: Peter Lang Publishers.

Etzioni, Amitai. 2004. *The Common Good*, 1st ed. New York: Polity Press.

Feinberg, Joel. 1970. The Nature and Value of Rights. *The Journal of Value Inquiry* 4: 245–7. [CrossRef]

Finnis, John. 2011. *Natural Law and Natural Rights*. New York: Oxford University Press.

Gustafson, James. 1990. Moral Discourse About Medicine: A Variety of Forms. *The Journal of Medicine and Philosophy* 15: 125–42. [CrossRef] [PubMed]

Kaveny, M. Cathleen. 2000. Appropriation of Evil: Cooperation's Mirror Image. *Theological Studies* 61: 280–313. [CrossRef]

Lustig, Andrew. 2012. Conscience, Professionalism, and Pluralism. *Christian Bioethics* 18: 72–92. [CrossRef]

Lustig, B. Andrew. 1990. Property and Justice in the Modern Encyclical Literature. *Harvard Theological Review* 83: 415–46. [CrossRef]

Lustig, B. Andrew. 1993. The Common Good in a Secular Society: The Relevance of a Roman Catholic Notion to the Health Care Allocation Debate. *The Journal of Medicine and Philosophy* 18: 569–87. [CrossRef] [PubMed]

Lustig, B. Andrew. 1996. Reform and Rationing: Reflections on Health Care in Light of Catholic Social Teaching. In *Secular Bioethics in Theological Perspective*. Edited by Earl Shelp. Dordrecht: Springer, pp. 31–50, Reprinted in *Moral Medicine: Theological Perspectives on Medical Ethics*, 3rd ed. Edited by M. Therese Lysaught, Joseph Kotva, Stephen Lammers and Allen Verhey. 2012. pp. 201–10.

Nielsen, Constance. 2007. *The Harmony Between the Right to Private Property and the Call to Solidarity in Modern Catholic Social Teaching*. Ann Arbor: ProQuest LLC.

Pope Francis. 2020. *Fratelli Tutti*. Available online: https://www.vatican.va/content/francesco/en/encyclicals/documents/papa-francesco_20201003_enciclica-fratelli-tutti.html (accessed on 14 March 2023).

Pope Francis. 2022. Address to the Members of the Diplomatic Corps Accredited to the Holy See. Available online: https://www.vatican.va/content/francesco/en/speeches/2022/january/documents/20220110-corpo-diplomatico.html (accessed on 14 March 2023).

Pope John Paul II. 1981. *Laborem Exercens*. Available online: https://www.vatican.va/content/john-paul-ii/en/encyclicals/documents/hf_jp-ii_enc_14091981_laborem-exercens.html (accessed on 14 March 2023).

Pope John Paul II. 1987. *Sollicitudo Rei Socialis*. Available online: https://www.vatican.va/content/john-paul-ii/en/encyclicals/documents/hf_jp-ii_enc_30121987_sollicitudo-rei-socialis.html (accessed on 14 March 2023).

Rowlands, Anna. 2021. *Towards a Politics of Communion*. London: T&T Clark.

Sachs, Jeffrey. 2006. *The End of Poverty*. New York: Penguin.

Second Vatican Council. 1965. *Gaudium et Spes*. Available online: https://www.vatican.va/archive/hist_councils/ii_vatican_council/documents/vat-ii_const_19651207_gaudium-et-spes_en.html (accessed on 14 March 2023).

Singer, Peter. 2016. *One World Now: The Ethics of Globalization*. New Haven: Yale University Press.

Thurow, Roger, and Scott Kilman. 2009. *Enough: Why the World's Poorest Starve in an Age of Plenty*. New York: Public Affairs Press.

United States Conference of Catholic Bishops. 2020. Chairmen of the Committee on Doctrine and the Committee on Pro-Life Activities. Moral Considerations Regarding the New COVID-19 Vaccines. December 11. Available online: https://www.usccb.org/moral-considerations-covid-vaccines (accessed on 14 March 2023).

Walzer, Michael. 2019. *Thick and Thin: Moral Argument at Home and Abroad*. South Bend: University of Notre Dame Press.

Wojtyla, Karol. 1979. *The Acting Person*. Dordrecht: D. Reidel.

Wojtyla, Karol. 2013. *Love and Responsibility*. New York: Pauline Books.

religions MDPI

Article

Holy Communion in Greek Orthodoxy in the Time of Coronavirus: Ideological Perspectives in Conflict

Efstathios Kessareas

Department of Religious Studies, Faculty of Philosophy, University of Erfurt, 99089 Erfurt, Germany; efstathios.kessareas@uni-erfurt.de

Abstract: This article examines the controversy over the mode of distribution of Holy Communion that surfaced during the COVID-19 pandemic, with a focus on debates that took place in the Greek Orthodox community. After describing and evaluating the role of secular and religious experts in the context of the pandemic, the paper analyzes three main perspectives on the issue of the Eucharist: (1) the secularist-rationalist viewpoint; (2) the religious–traditionalist outlook; and (3) the "Third Way" perspective. The paper argues that the Church's Holy Communion controversy is indicative of a deeper struggle between religious and secular thinkers and among various voices in the Greek Orthodox Church concerning the latter's place in, and influence over, the modern secular socio-political order.

Keywords: Greek Orthodoxy; Holy Communion; COVID-19; ideology; tradition; modernity; secularization

Citation: Kessareas, Efstathios. 2023. Holy Communion in Greek Orthodoxy in the Time of Coronavirus: Ideological Perspectives in Conflict. *Religions* 14: 647. https://doi.org/10.3390/rel14050647

Academic Editors: Andrew Flescher and Joel Zimbelman

Received: 30 November 2022
Revised: 27 December 2022
Accepted: 21 February 2023
Published: 12 May 2023

1. Introduction

The COVID-19 pandemic has affected many spheres of human life, including individual and community religious belief and practice. In the early days and for reasons of public health, a number of restrictions were imposed on religious life, ranging from strict social distancing and masking measures to the closure of places of worship. Given its complexity—competing traditions and theological perspectives, as well as different policy responses to the virus globally—there has been little agreement among religious voices on the necessity, scope, and implications of these measures. In Greek Orthodox communities, encompassing the hierarchy, theologians, and the laity, the debate in the early days of the pandemic focused on the mode of distribution of Holy Communion. Various religious and secular actors participated in the public discussion, either in favor of or against the existing practice of giving Communion from the same spoon. The issue acquired the character of an ideological struggle between the proponents of "scientific reason" and the guardians of the "genuine" Greek Orthodox tradition. Various religious agents and voices sought to overcome this polarization by forging a middle path framed in terms of a necessary reconciliation between tradition and modernity.

There is diverse and still-growing literature on the responses of the disparate voices in the Greek Orthodox churches on the conditions of the COVID-19 pandemic. Kosmidis was one of the first to discuss, from a theological perspective, the impact of the pandemic on Greek Orthodoxy's ecclesiastical life, highlighting what he saw as the spread and affirmation of irrational religiosity in confronting the virus (Kosmidis 2020). Mitrofanova analyzed the attitude of the Russian Orthodox Church and of various fundamentalist groups that exist within its ranks during the pandemic (Mitrofanova 2021). Hovorun demonstrated that the distribution of the Eucharist during the viral pandemic provoked an intense polarization between fundamentalists and "*Eucharist realists*", particularly (but not exclusively) in the Russian Orthodox Church (Hovorun 2021). Various publications of collected essays were produced (e.g., Vassiliadis 2020; Asproulis and Wood 2020; Zorbas 2021), rich in theological and pastoral perspectives, which explored the effects of the pandemic on ecclesiastical life. While they ably analyzed and critiqued opposing perspectives, they were less attentive to contextualizing their own theological points of view and the important place and established voice that they occupy within the Greek Orthodox Community (Bourdieu 1977, 1991).

Theological analysis is important to this debate, but it is not an exclusive or sufficient perspective that can shed light on the issues of concern to this faith community. My efforts in this article might best be understood as interpretive sociology. It is a position that attempts to examine, in a systematic way, the ideological struggle that takes place among different groups within Greek Orthodoxy. What I hope to accomplish is to present in a Weberian ideal-typical manner modes of thought that represent these different ideological orientations. To this end, my work critically and comparatively analyzes three conflicting perspectives on a specific concrete issue, namely, the distribution of Holy Communion during the pandemic: (a) the secularist–rationalist viewpoint, (b) the religious–traditionalist outlook, and (c) what I call the "Third Way" perspective. The voices that represent these three perspectives envision the positions and roles of the Greek Orthodox Church in the context of secular modernity quite differently, not only with regard to issues surrounding Holy Communion during a pandemic, but around other controversial and contested issues that sporadically occupy believers and others in the public sphere.

The fierce debate surrounding the praxis of Holy Communion that emerged during the COVID-19 pandemic offers fertile ground both for an ideological confrontation and for deeper analysis. From a strictly scientific and public health perspective, viruses can be potentially transmitted between individuals via contact with contaminated objects, such as communion utensils. However, from the standpoint of those who perceive Holy Communion *literally* as "medicine of immortality," it is impossible for the liturgical spoon to transmit an illness (see Section 3.2 below). The Eucharist stands unequivocally at the heart of Greek Orthodox Christianity, carrying deep but also competing and conflicting meanings for its adherents. By engaging in the sort of comparative and interpretive sociological analysis I am suggesting, I try to show that we can better comprehend the deeper reasons and justifications for these various positions and gain a deeper appreciation of why the Church as an institution and so many individual religious actors are hesitant or refuse to change established beliefs and ritual practices.

My study focuses on primary sources of the most varied kinds produced by Greek Orthodox clerics and lay persons during the COVID-19 pandemic, including encyclicals, announcements, articles, interviews, and sermons. My focus lies on Greek Orthodoxy, and particularly on the Church of Greece, the Patriarchate of Constantinople, and on the Orthodox diaspora. For comparative reasons, I also provide an elaboration of the views of the Serbian Orthodox Church, the Orthodox Church in America, and of various other Orthodox intellectuals, without claiming to give a complete picture of the complex Orthodox world.[1] Since the material is vast, I selected discourses that reveal the distinctive character and orientation of these three perspectives. Additionally, I examined actors who hold different positions within and outside the organized religious community (e.g., bishops, priests, monks, lay theologians, journalists, health professionals). Methodologically, I applied a multi-dimensional discourse analysis (Thompson 1984). First, I comparatively analyzed the content of the primary sources. In doing so, it was possible to distinguish subtle differences concerning the perception of the Holy Communion and corresponding proposals about the method of its distribution in the age of COVID-19. Additionally, borrowing theoretical insights from framing analysis (Benford and Snow 2000), I gave attention to the symbolic vocabulary and framing strategies that these actors employed in an attempt to justify their arguments and delegitimize antagonistic ones. Finally, I attempted to associate the different viewpoints with the institutional position and ideological preferences of their promoters, taking into consideration the various social contexts in which the pandemic crisis arose.

Weber rightly observes that real life is much more chaotic than ideal-types (Weber 2012, p. 125). Frequently, the ideal-typical categories that the researcher constructs manifest in complex, overlapping, and contradictory ways in a given individual or institution. This tendency is evident in the subject under discussion here. A progressive religious actor, who, for instance, might support a new method of giving of Holy Communion, might simultaneously agree on other church issues with individuals who are characterized by a conservative mindset.[2]

2. Secular and Religious Specialists: Scientific versus Sacred Knowledge

In the contemporary world of health, medicine, and increasing public policy development, the value, priority, and decisiveness of scientific knowledge is axiomatic. This principle is elaborated in systems of practical and functional reasoning, which affirm that the ultimate criterion for evaluating the various socio-political and economic proposals is whether they are capable of producing practical, enduring solutions to existing problems. Proposals that do not comply with the criterion of effectiveness are rejected, often after being defamed as ideologically informed, metaphysically asserted with no empirically verifiable justification, or as just "magical thinking".

Even the purveyors of positions based on science and pragmatism, specialists who hold privileged status as problem solvers for various professions and who serve an important role in the public sphere as representatives of their fields, often come under similar criticism and disapprobation. To take an example, in the ongoing COVID-19 crisis, it was initially epidemiologists globally who held the public's attention, as their research findings were translated into concrete policy measures that were taken to be the best chance of stemming the spread of the virus. Historically, epidemiologists have enjoyed significant public acceptance because of the perceived objectivity of medical science and their willingness to pursue their research in an "objective" and unbiased way. As the pandemic crisis deepened, however, the public role and expert knowledge of the epidemiologist, and that of public health professionals who were dependent on epidemiology as the baseline for their policy decisions, grew to be contested. This reality invites a situation where multiple authorities simultaneously bear on policy-making.

In addition to these secular experts, in the context of the pandemic traditional specialists in religious communities exert influence on believers' schemes of thought. The Greek Orthodox priest is one such figure, standing at the center of the community's religious life. Not only does that figure have a great knowledge of theological issues, but also possesses technical expertise on the so-called salvific rituals of the church. Bishops have supreme power within the religious field legitimized by reference to the special identity and role that occupies "in the place" and as a "type" of Christ (Zizioulas 1997, p. 229). Still, because the clergy must also be preoccupied with the "mundane", various worldly, administrative, and pastoral concerns, the community's ultimate ideal type of religious expertise is the *saint*. The latter comes close to God through charismatic experience, not through the intellect nor the physical performance of either ritual or other responsibilities. It is not accidental that spiritual elders who have acquired reputations as holy men and women are often idolized in a manner that cultivates attitudes of radicalism, especially in monastic milieus (Kessareas 2022a). Lay theologians form another influential group within the constellation of religious professionals and experts, since they formulate and disseminate schemes of thought and practical proposals, legitimizing them as the product of deep theological knowledge ratified by the tradition.

The various and incommensurable secular and religious values do not, in principle, need to lead to conflict and confrontation as long as the representative actors or experts from each remains and functions within the walls or limitations of their own field. However, the social world, though complex, differentiated, specialized, and dispersed, is hyperconnected. The possibility of conflict on many levels, and between arenas of knowledge and expertise, arises during periods of crises, when issues of individual, broader social interests, and national identities are at stake. Specialists readily engage in public controversies justifying or delegitimizing proposals that have an *ideological* or *utopian* character, namely proposals that aim either to preserve or transform established social relations (Mannheim 2015).

To understand the prestige and appeal of religious actors in the context of the pandemic, we should also take into account the traditional connection that has been established over centuries, even millennia, between religion, sickness, care, and healing (Larchet 2002). Significant religious rituals emerged that were deeply connected to the experience and trauma of human suffering and the care of the sick and dying, even before the efficacy of much medical care became a reality in the modern period. For instance, prophets became famous for their healing skills (Weber 1978, p. 441), the pastor playing a significant role over time in keeping with the needs of local communities dealing with the challenges of illness and infirmity, while the provision of hospital and other medical services by religious organizations themselves evolved as central activities of ministry. The coming of modernity has not diminished the impetus for medical and spiritual intervention by religious organizations on behalf of those who suffer. The Greek Orthodox faith, in this way, does not oppose or underestimate the efficacy of science (Knight 2020). Seeking the care of a physician is fully compatible with the teachings of the church. But the point is that this religious tradition retains a strong sense of mystery, which in certain circumstances can bring the believer into conflict with the tenets, claims, and aspirations of scientific rationality. In the eyes of the faithful, church rituals are both real and useful, even in situations where the interventions of modern medicine are accepted. However, when modern medicine fails to provide therapy, then the road to miraculous salvation opens more broadly as an avenue to be explored and embraced by the believer.

3. Holy Communion: Ideological Perspectives in Conflict

Having considered the important role of secular and religious specialists in the public sphere, I want now to explore the narrow issue of how Holy Communion is viewed and practiced in the Greek Orthodox Church in the context of the pressures brought on religious communities during the COVID-19 pandemic. The analysis of various primary sources allows us to establish and elaborate in a quasi ideal-typical manner three distinct perspectives that appear in the emerging literature and the life of Greek Orthodox communities and the larger societies of which they are a part.

3.1. The Secularist–Rationalist Viewpoint: Holy Communion as "Religious Obscurantism"

Speaking in ideal-typical terms, social agents who hold to a secular, rational morality and a liberal or progressive political orientation are critical towards religious values and practices, especially when the latter exert influence in the public, secular sphere. This perspective is driven in large part by an attitude shared by these agents that considers religion as a private issue that must concern only the existential–spiritual needs of the believers and avoid incursions into the public affairs of the culture in domains, such as politics, education, law, or, in the case at hand, health policy. It is hardly surprising, therefore, that on the issue of Holy Communion, secular–rationalists establish a clear line of demarcation between faith and science, urging the Church to restrict its sphere of activity to the care of the human soul and leave the treatment of body and related public policy decisions to science (Tountas 2020). By extension, they call for a broader scope of justified health policy interventions into religious communities with the argument that the common good (public health) must precede the particular commitments and ritual practices of the religious subsystem. With respect to the current pandemic crisis and the challenge of viral transmission, secularists have argued that with respect to social policy implementation, there are no "exceptions for religious, liturgical or metaphysical reasons"[3] (Federation of Hospital Unions Doctors of Greece 2020).

In this context, the use of a common liturgical spoon during the pandemic was presented as a public health threat. Labeling opposing views as "unacceptable, obscurantist, and DANGEROUS!" (Imerodromos 2020), the secularists framed the issue as a battle between the proponents of "scientific truth" and the forces of "obscurantism" and "metaphysics" (Federation of Hospital Unions Doctors of Greece 2020; Imerodromos 2020). At the same time, they urged scientific associations to take a clear position against the current method of Holy Communion. The implication is that the state must, for reasons of public health, impose restrictions over this religious practice as long as such practice is construed as a pandemic risk, or until Church officials opt for safer modes of distributing Holy Communion.

The case in point concerns the imposition by The Federal Republic of Germany of a temporary ban on the distribution of Holy Communion from a common spoon. Greek Orthodox Metropolitan Augoustinos of Germany abided by this measure, albeit stating that this was the "most painful and difficult decision" he has ever taken (Augoustinos 2020). Patriarch of Constantinople Bartholomew's response on this issue appeals to a classic balance of power to set limits. Drawing on Jesus' famous saying: "Render therefore unto Caesar the things which are Caesar's, and unto God the things that are God's", the Patriarch recognized the authority of the state to regulate its own affairs, but at the same time, he highlighted the "holy and indestructible right" of the Church to "organize its ecclesiastical life and to celebrate the Holy Sacraments (Mysteries) according to its canonical and ecclesiological tradition" (Augoustinos 2020). In various respects, the modern, secular state has the power to impose restrictions, even on core aspects of religious life, as this ban clearly proves. However, in predominantly Orthodox majority countries, such as Greece, such strict restrictions were not entertained by the church leadership and not pushed unflinchingly by the government because of competing religious commitments of the majority of its population and the high political cost such a position would have exacted on politicians and church leaders.

3.2. The Religious–Traditionalist Outlook: Holy Communion as the "Medicine of Immortality"

The official ecclesiastical hierarchies largely complied with the preponderance of temporal restrictions on religious life and practice, issuing statements in favor of medical protective measures and public health restrictions, including on worship life. However, nearly all hesitated or even categorically refused to alter the method of receiving Communion from a common spoon. For instance, the Holy Synod of the Serbian Orthodox Church claimed that "well-known anti-church and anti-Serbian circles" question its "most important and sacred" ritual. It thus depicted secular and critical voices within the Church as being a threat not only to religion but also to the nation itself. At the same time, it stressed the historic practice of long duration of this method of Communion ("two thousand years"). This reference had a specific aim: historical time adds more weight and prestige to ritual, for it is implied that it is not something ephemeral that can or should be changed according to the spirit of the times. The Holy Synod deployed two types of argument in this regard. First, it asserted that the state has no right to "deal with the content and manner of conducting the Divine Liturgy", for it is a "sole matter of internal or autonomous church order and legislation". Second, it framed the issue decisively in terms of individual freedom by invoking the voluntary character of the Eucharist (Holy Synod of the Serbian Orthodox Church 2020).

The Holy Synod of the Greek Orthodox Church also categorically rejected any change in the administration of Holy Communion, declaring that the latter "certainly cannot become a source of transmission of diseases", because the "Body and Blood of Christ becomes the 'medicine of immortality'" (Holy Synod 2020a). The former Metropolitan of Kalavryta depicted the Church as a "hospital for both soul and body ... [which] heals and does not make one sick!" (Amvrosios 2020). The use of such medical metaphors justified the continuation of the ritual during the pandemic and, additionally, highlighted the special role of the priests who offer the precious medicine of immortality to the faithful. This medicine is asserted to be superior to the various drugs of science developed against illnesses. Framed in this way, a restriction or temporary ban of this ritual endangers the ultimate goal of people's eternal salvation. The threat of the COVID-19 pandemic and the importance of public health are not ignored, but they are ranked hierarchically: at the very top of the hierarchy stands the holistic—and for this reason more important—value of eternal life, which encompasses that of human health (for the concept of hierarchy, see Dumont 1980). From the standpoint of modern secular thought, such a way of thinking is irrational. However, from within the community of faith, believers orient their action according to a reframed rationality that facilitates the achievement of ultimate religious ends (Weber 1978, pp. 85–86). Keeping this in mind, it comes as no surprise that bishops offered the following explanation as self-evident: "the Body and the Blood of Christ cannot become a bearer of infection and death, *because* the Lord of Life cannot bequeath decay and death" (Hierotheos 2020, p. 9, my emphasis).

In order to appeal to the skeptics, members of the hierarchy invoked the additional authoritative source of the "experience of centuries", which was used to establish the non-contagious character of Holy Communion (Hierotheos 2020, p. 1; Holy Synod 2020a). The challenge of addressing infections among believers of course persists and creates significant challenges. If a believer gets infected, will that endanger the whole system of belief? To prevent this, religious intellectuals implicitly leave open the possibility of an infection, attributing it either to a lack of appropriate preparation or to weak belief on behalf of the believer. For instance, the hieromonk Koutloumousianos emphasized that "the Lord's body becomes a 'safeguard', 'for strength, healing and health of soul and body'", adding the caveat, "to those that receive communion with faith and true repentance" (Koutloumousianos 2020). Similarly, he highlighted that "although immortality is an eschatological condition . . . yet 'doses' of incorruption are given in this mortal life according to the measure of each one's faith, longing, godly fear and love" (Koutloumousianos 2020). We notice, therefore, a transfer of causal responsibility for infection to the individual believer. In any case, the latter is advised not to be preoccupied with such a "totally dead-end scholastic preciosity", behaving like a "deeply neurotic and compulsive person obsessed with germs in front of the biggest miracle of creation" (Hierotheos 2020). Since "everything is in the hands of God", the faithful are advised to "carry out God's will and trust all the rest to the absolute goodness of Lord, who works everyone's salvation with the best possible way" (Hierotheos 2020).

Such arguments cannot appeal to secular-minded actors. Church officials denounced the criticism of the latter as "blasphemy" that "brutally offend[s] the sacred and the holy, the dogmas and the holy canons of our faith" (Holy Synod 2020b). By contrast, they portrayed themselves as "vigilant guardians of the boundaries set by the Holy Spirit through the Apostles, the Fathers and the Holy Synods", reassuring the faithful that the "red lines neither have been nor will be surpassed" (Holy Synod 2020c; Gabriel 2020; Athenagoras 2020). Further, they labeled adversarial and critical voices as advancing a discourse of "division" that aims at "torpedoing the national consensus and unanimity needed by our homeland at these moments" (Ieronymos 2020). The frequent references to the nation reveal a specific perception of the Church as an "ark" that preserves national identity in the context of our globalized world.

Orthodox fundamentalists who are drawn to conspiracy theories, ethno-religious nationalism, and dualistic thinking (Kessareas 2018; Makrides 2016), expressed this point more explicitly. They cast restrictive COVID-19 policy measures as a threat to religion and nation, using not only a pre-modern religious discourse but also a modern, secular one. Specifically, they depicted the public health mandates and measures as works of the devil and as a violation of the constitutional rights of religious freedom and freedom of assembly (e.g., see Amvrosios 2020; Neophytos 2020; Stylianakis 2020). For instance, former Metropolitan Amvrosios in his letter to the current Prime Minister of Greece, Kyriakos Mitsotakis, stressed that the "dark, demonic organizations of globalization" manufactured COVID-19 and that the Church and the Greek nation are under attack. A member of the church hierarchy, he acquires here the role of a prophet who warns the evil collaborators that "God's curse" will fall upon them, exclaiming: "Hands off the Orthodox Church, the Mother and wet nurse of the Greek Nation" (Amvrosios 2020). Likewise, Metropolitan Neophytos of Morphou in Cyprus attacked the earthly "representatives of devil", those "secretive men of the New Order of Things", who promote the "vaccines of Bill Gates", but hinder the salvific practice of Holy Communion. In his public speeches, churches are equated with hospitals; however, their own medicine is considered to be more precious: "the best medicine, both for this illness and for the other that is coming, is the Body and Blood of Christ ... when we close the churches and we restrict the Holy Communion ... it is like we close the hospitals, like we shut down the pharmacies" (Neophytos 2020).

One should not conclude that only Church leaders, and particularly ultra-conservative ones, believe that Holy Communion is the "medicine of immortality." No doubt, clerics have legitimate interest in the dissemination of this belief. The laity, too, shares this fundamental conviction. Otherwise, they would not have continued to receive Holy Communion during the pandemic. One Greek priest praised his congregation for continuing to receive Holy Communion, admitting that after the end of the liturgy, he provided Communion to infected persons. He portrayed his own negative corona test as a "proof that the Holy Communion does not transmit [illnesses], because it is Christ" (Kantanis 2021). Such beliefs even appeal to professionals, whose specialization in medicine one might have expected to inculcate in them a secular habitus, to use Bourdieu's (1977) term. The public interventions of well-known Greek epidemiologists in favor of the mystical effect of Holy Communion are illustrative cases. For instance, Eleni Giamarellou, Professor of Internal Medicine and an infectious disease specialist, specified her viewpoint on the issue as follows:

> The Holy Communion is a sacrament ... you do not receive it out of habit [but] ... because it is the Body and Blood of Christ. Either you believe it and you receive Holy Communion in the normal manner, or you do not believe it. There are no compromise solutions, spoons, etc. ... If I believe that this can infect me, then I do not believe in the greatest mystery. People who want to receive communion must not be afraid that bacteria can ever be transmitted via the Holy Communion. (Giamarellou 2020)

Similarly, Athina Linou, Professor of Epidemiology, declared in the Greek state-operated television station:

> I am a faithful Orthodox Christian ... there is no epidemiological study that proves that the disease is transmitted through ingestion not only of saliva but also of the virus itself ... We cannot solve issues of spirituality and Orthodox faith with logic; the metaphysical ... is not proven [question by journalist: 'would you receive Holy Communion at this time in the usual way?']. Of course! Of course! (Linou 2020)

Such cases demonstrate the penetration and appropriation of traditional religious ideas into broader segments of advanced secular societies, including Greece, in which Orthodoxy is a strong cultural force that contributes to the formation of people's identity. This tendency appears frequently among contemporary medical experts who have strong conservative religious commitments. They accept, without hesitation, the existing method of Communion, disdaining "compromise solutions" as a lack of genuine belief.

3.3. A "Third Way": Reconciliation between Tradition and Modernity

Between the secularists and the traditionalists, there are those who seek a compromise or middle ground between faith and science, between "receiving Christ in the Eucharist and taking a reasonable and 'worldly' precaution", as they put it (Cohen 2020). These actors, mostly of a younger generation of theologians, possess significant intellectual capital evidenced in academic titles, positions in universities, and publications in well-regarded journals. They hold progressive positions on various theological and church issues, motivated by a desire to bring Orthodoxy into a constructive relationship with the multicultural, global, and democratic contexts of modernity (Kessareas 2022b, pp. 133–37; Makrides 2020). As Pantelis Kalaitzidis, Director of the Volos Academy for Theological Studies in Greece and representative of this current, describes it, they seek to "contextualize the message of the Gospel in our time, to ensure the constructive role of Orthodoxy in the public sphere, and to highlight the prophetic and eschatological dynamic of the Orthodox Christian tradition in the dialogue with the anthropological, political, and other parameters of (Western) modernity" (Kalaitzidis 2022). These religious actors reject both the so-called "ethnodoxy" (Karpov et al. 2012) that is the identification of religion with a particular nation, and the equation of secularization with the privatization of religion; for them, the Church can play a productive role in civil society by supporting core values of Christianity and of liberal democracy (e.g., justice, freedom) without violating the alterity of the "Other" (Kessareas 2022c).

On the controversy over the method of distribution of Holy Communion during the pandemic, individuals representative of "the third way" attempted to offer a compromise solution between the traditional "medicine of immortality" perspective and the medical logic underlying the imposition of health measures. More precisely, they distinguished between the inner essence and the external method of the Holy Communion ritual. The first component is construed as sacred and unchangeable, functioning as "medicine of immortality". The second is perceived as an historical element and event that can be changed. To justify this interpretation, these thinkers employed a set of arguments from theology, physics, and history. Specifically, they argued that since both the bread and the wine continue to retain their material qualities in the Eucharist, they could become pathways of transmission for pathogenic bacteria (Hovorun 2020; Cohen 2020). They refuted opposing viewpoints by labeling them as "distortions/heresies", "myth and superstition", "idolatry", "magical understandings of religious life", and "Manichaeism" (Arida 2020; Papathanasiou 2020; Hovorun 2020). Advocates of "the Third Way" thus accused their opponents of transforming religion into pure magic by spiritualizing the Eucharist. In sharp contrast, they invoked core values of modern thought, including "freedom of choice" and the physical "laws of nature" to ground their claims (Hovorun 2020).

From the standpoint of the traditionalists, the real heretics are the liberal theologians who downgrade the mystical meaning of the Eucharist. Although the bread and wine retain their physical qualities—as the traditional argument goes—their "mode of being" changes during the Mystery, becoming the actual Body and Blood of Christ (Koutloumousianos 2020; Hierotheos 2020). The fear is that the denial of this fundamental axiom of faith calls into question the saving power of Christ and so must be emphatically condemned as a "blasphemous theological virus" (Hierotheos 2020, p. 2). To conservative traditionalists, religious reformers pose a more serious threat than secularists, because they attribute to their ends the same theological concepts that are recognized by and can appeal to the faithful. Speaking sociologically, they are direct antagonists within the religious field.

The proponents of "the third way" also employed church history and historical practices as useful resources in constructing their position, highlighting the "dynamic nature of historical Eucharistic practices", namely, various ways of offering Communion throughout history, and the evidence of embracing "flexibility and adaptability" during times of crisis (Armanios 2020). For these moderates, the non-core elements of tradition can change according to historical conditions and contextual needs of the faithful. The call is for a method of Holy Communion that respects its theological integrity but is consistent as well with the medical instructions and the basic hygienic rules of modern society. In order to rebut charges of implementing changes under pressure from secular modernity, they framed their proposals in overtly theological language. For instance, they presented the use of disposable bamboo spoons or even the deprivation of Holy Communion during the pandemic as serving the most fundamental Christian values of "sacrifice" and of "love" for the fellow Christian, who will thereby be able to participate without any fear in or risk from the Eucharist (Roosien 2020; Cohen 2020).

The question must then be asked: does this middle-ground or "Third Way" approach manage to balance the commitments and interests of the two opposing sides? No doubt, it combines elements from both sides. Still, the basic aim of these moderating actors, which is to bring the Orthodox Church into a constructive relationship with modernity, moves the terms of the debate towards the side of secular-minded agents, even though these church moderates do not share with the secularists the vision of a privatized faith. This is also the reason why religious hardliners oppose liberal theologians so strongly. Liberal theologians critically reflect on tradition, embracing fundamental values and structural transformations of the modern world (e.g., human rights, civil society, multiculturalism). Of course, when they also hold an ecclesiastical office in the Church, the tensions between traditional beliefs and the spirit of intellectualist criticism inherent in any reform agenda increases significantly. Overall, therefore, we can interpret the middle way identified here as an attempt at reaching a compromise between the competing views and goals of the two opposing sides.

4. Sacred Tradition vs. Profane Worldliness

Despite the seriousness of the pandemic, which resulted in significant deaths among clerics and monks, Church authorities were hesitant to implement changes in the procedure for the reception of Holy Communion. As noted earlier, the Orthodox Church of Greece excluded *a priori* the possibility of any change by declaring the issue a "red line". The Orthodox Church of Serbia even banned a priest and theologian from speaking publicly after his critical remarks on the current mode of distribution (Kubat 2020). Yet, there were a few exceptions, mostly by Churches that operate in multicultural environments, where the pressure for a change in the existing practice of Holy Communion seems to have been significant. Even in such cases, however, the relevant decision was taken very carefully and in an ambiguous manner. Let me give some examples.

The Greek Orthodox Metropolis of Austria decided, for a "limited period", to offer the Eucharistic bread in the hand of the believers. It framed this decision as an act of "philanthropy" towards the "expectations of the outsiders" who have weak faith. Moreover, it presented this change to be within the boundaries of tradition, for it follows the old liturgical tradition of Saint James (Greek Orthodox Metropolis of Austria 2020). Archbishop Melchisedek of Pittsburgh of the Orthodox Church in America offered a double justification for the use of individual spoons: first, there was the need to avoid accusations "from those outside of the church" who do not understand the holy character of its rituals. Second, it was important to be able to "ease the conscience of those in the church" who are anxious about receiving Holy Communion from a common spoon during a pandemic. He, too, was cautious enough to highlight that this change was "not to be understood as a declaration about the possibility of the Body and Blood of Christ spreading disease" (Melchisedek 2020).

Archbishop Elpidophoros of the Greek Orthodox Archdiocese of America justified the implementation in the Church of various public health measures against the COVID-19 with reference to "science and our God-given reason" as well as to theology: "the same material elements that can convey the blessings of God are also subject to the broken nature of our fallen world". In an attempt to rebut accusations of modernism, he stressed that the protective measures are "temporary precautions" that "do not change the traditions of the church" (Elpidophoros 2020a). The restrictive COVID-19 measures were presented as an "act of love and responsibility" and not as "a sin" (Holy Eparchial Synod 2020). Despite Elpidophoros' emphasis on exercising the "rational, scientific knowledge that we possess through our God-given intelligence" (Elpidophoros 2020b), the clergy were instructed to distribute the Eucharist in the usual way (Greek Orthodox Archdiocese of America 2020). The theological argument was that the "sacrament of sacraments, the Holy Eucharist, is not simply a material element but the very body and blood of our Lord Jesus Christ" (Elpidophoros 2020a).

How can we best understand the difficulty faced by Orthodox Churches to accept changes to how the Eucharist is administered in the face of the risks manifest in the COVID-19? The answer to this question must account for the central position and role of tradition in Greek Orthodox Christianity, in which the Church has developed a strong tradition-bound culture through its centuries of existence. It is a product of history that, when perceived in an essentialist and static manner, provides fertile ground for attitudes of traditionalism and invariant liturgical practices (Makrides 2012a). Tradition consists both of dogmatic beliefs and practices, whose alleged sacred origin and repetition in the lifetime of the faithful makes them appear as unchanging entities. For the traditionalists, the institutional Church has legitimate responsibility to observe the adherence to the "right" beliefs (orthodoxy) and "correct" practices (orthopraxy) that shape its identity. However, you cannot have "orthodoxy" without "heresy", and vice versa. Since Orthodoxy is equated with the maintenance of tradition, any change runs the risk of being considered as heterodoxy or heresy. This attitude characterizes especially zealotic monastic circles who believe in the absolute and timeless essence of tradition: "the dogmas, the holy canons and traditions of the church ... by no means change with the passing of time, but they remain valid and unchanged until the end of the ages" (*Agios Agathaggelos Esfigmenitis* 2003, p. 4).

Of course, renewal and innovation are not unknown within the Greek Orthodox tradition (Willert and Molokotos-Liederman 2012; Makrides 2012a). The evolving economic activities and modernization of the Greek Orthodox churches currently taking place in even the most important symbolic contexts of the tradition, including among monastic communities of Mount Athos, are prime examples of this trend. However, in religious environments customarily characterized by dogma and repetition of the familiar, change occurs in a slower rhythm and always must be framed in the language of tradition in order to avoid the specter of heresy. Moreover, in this community, changes are more easily accepted when they concern external matters (e.g., technological ones) rather than issues of religious belief and practice.

The Eucharist is one such fundamental ritual. It remains "the sacrament of sacraments" for most Greek Orthodox Christians, a pivotal moment during which the individual believers *become* a community, experiencing "here and now" the relational essence of God (Elpidophoros 2020a; Zizioulas 1997, p. 115). From this perspective, the congregation does not merely come in contact "with the supreme source of its spiritual life" (Durkheim 1995, p. 30), but—by receiving the body and blood of Christ—it partakes of the sacred life that comes from the otherworld. Thus, in the critical moment of eucharistic celebration, the realms of "the immanent" and "the transcendent" meet but not on equal terms; it is transcendence that charismatically raises the elements of the mundane world to a higher level.

For conservative religious agents, the transformation of the common bread and wine into the Body and Blood of Christ is not merely a symbolic act, but a real event. It is considered to stand above reason, for it perceived as a product of miraculous action:

> It is clearly a matter of faith and metaphysical inductive proof [αναγωγής]. Is it possible to contract a psychosomatic disease from partaking of the Holy Communion? This is not possible. The believer, who comes to Holy Communion, believes that he/she comes to God, who has the power to heal, anticipate, and intervene miraculously. There is no need for someone to receive communion if s/he has not the faith that this is the blood and body of Christ. This cannot be a cause of disease and transmit any microbe! (Seraphim 2020)

This mode of religious thought classifies the various microbes and diseases as part of a profane realm. We occupy a world of decay, corruption, and death. By complete contrast, the sacred realm is believed to be the source of eternal life. Any extraordinary action that brings the two realms into contact with each other—a divine intervention into the profane world that transfigures its natural laws, including the conditions of human existence (illnesses etc.)—is recognized to be a miracle. Recognizing such miracles when they present themselves presupposes human faith *and* participation in the ecclesiastical life. The church thus emerges as the *locus* of the manifestation of the divine itself, the place where miracles, healing, and salvation happen. For this reason, it is difficult for deeply traditional Greek Orthodox believers to accept that their churches can be sources of infection, particularly during the eucharistic ritual. For them, such transmission can certainly occur "outside", in the profane space of everyday life, but not "inside" the temple of God, which is consecrated ground and where the faithful participate in the eternal life of God. Metropolitan of Aitolia and Akarnania Kosmas, who died in early January 2022 from COVID-19, declared in a sermon: "My fellow men, God does not permit you to be infected within the church. God does not infect! . . . [The church] is a holy place; 'the church is sky', says saint Kosmas Aitolos. It is God's sanctuary" (Kosmas 2020). Likewise, a Greek archimandrite-psychiatrist expressed this spatial demarcation in his own sermon:

> Our people are imprisoned *outside* the church [building] . . . We even put disinfectants *inside* the church . . . There are priests who offer Holy Communion *out of* the church, the antidoron [blessed bread] *outside* the church. We have exiled the blessings of the church, namely we have taken them *out of* the church as if the church is a dangerous and contaminated place . . . We reached a point where in our country, in Greece, our belief, our religion is persecuted. This is not a coronavirus; it is a devil-virus . . . The person who is talking to you at the moment is a doctor; we also know something about medicine. (Stylianakis 2020, italics mine)

This last reference would not have seemed at all odd to Stylianakis's religious audience, even if the priest had not studied medicine. Just as the church is considered to be a "hospital" for the soul and for the body, providing the "medicine of immortality", the priest is a "doctor" and an agent of God's spiritual healing. For the religious conservatives, even wearing a mask inside the church is inevitably construed as a sinful act; it signifies a lack of trust in the sacredness of the church's space. It is only through religious means (e.g., faith, prayer, sacraments), and not through human created technologies such as masks, that genuine protection is assured:

> It is wrong and a lie what some people say: 'wear the mask, because you have to protect others'. I pray for others to protect them. When a person enters the church and does not respect the holy things of the church, then s/he is not protected no matter how many masks s/he wears. When you come and fear the Holy Communion, [or] you are afraid of the spoon, when you go to worship the icon and you are afraid of getting infected, it is then that you get infected. (Stylianakis 2020)

For conservatives, it is God and the saints, as bearers of authentic charisma, who define this space, not specialists of other fields, such as politicians or doctors. Thus, the real power of the priests is concealed behind the mantle of God and the saints. Since, following Weber, the prophetic charisma is transformed into office charisma it is the priest who defines and controls the sacred space (Weber 1978, pp. 1139–41, 1164–66):

> Specialists of all kinds can provide an opinion only for the narrow domain of their specialization. As to the existential matters of human vindication and salvation, only the saints are competent to respond. Due to their personal struggle, they enjoy already from this life the eternity through the communion and unity with Christ. (Damaskinos 2021)

It is important to note that for these religious actors, faith and science are not viewed in opposition to each other. Rather, the two are related hierarchically. Faith is the broader category (for it leads to eternal life), *encompassing* the truth claims of human science. The principles and axioms of the latter are accepted *as long as* they do not attempt to usurp or question the fundamental assumptions of faith. Any attempt of reversing this hierarchy is condemned as blasphemy, for the partiality and imperfectness of human knowledge (science) cannot replace the catholicity of the sacred (mystical revelation). This is perceived as a "red line", a sacred prohibition.

The proponents of the middle-path have elaborated an alternative proposal based on the distinction between the inner essence and the external form of the ritual. In this way, they have attempted to reconcile faith with modernity, which historically has been a point of grave difficulty for Orthodox Christianity (Makrides 2012b). Their proposal is in accordance with what they perceive to be the demands of contemporary life. Casting such contemporary claims as a necessary guide for shaping the religious life of the Orthodox communion is also its weak point, and one that hinders its acceptance by the traditionalists. This is mainly because the proposed middle way is itself a product of modernity, asserting a licit version of Orthodoxy that has already come to terms with western modernity (e.g., functional differentiation, pluralism, individualism). However, Orthodoxy's constructive engagement with modernity has not yet been fully achieved. Many religious actors view the Greek Orthodox tradition at once as holistic and a reality in which there is an organic unity between nation and faith and between form and content. By contrast, secularists and religious reformers criticize the nationalization of religion as a heresy and the mechanistic adherence to the existing method of distributing Holy Communion as a mere formalism that fails to respond to the anxieties—and the authentic needs—of modern believers. To strengthen their attack against an essentialist perception of tradition, these actors highlight that, historically, there have been various ways of receiving Communion approved by the traditional Church. But from the perspective of the religious conservatives, any alteration of this "religious formalism" would endanger the "efficacy" of the ceremony (Durkheim 1995, p. 33). While conceding that historically there may have been alternative traditional practices, their counter-argument is that what matters most in the present situation is adherence to the mode that has prevailed as holy tradition in the collective conscience of the faithful.

Church leaders at many levels reject a change in the method of distributing Holy Communion because they fear that it will destabilize the essential and nonnegotiable belief in the divine presence during the ritual. Speaking sociologically, the fear is that such a change will destroy the "absolute heterogeneity" between the sacred and the profane in favor of the second realm (Durkheim 1995, p. 36). The rational spirit of this worldly life will impose its logic even upon the "sacrament of the sacraments", restricting in this way the "Lebensraum" of the sacred. The mystical character of the sacred will thus be accepted *only* as a general religious belief under the presupposition that its mode of practice does not contradict the dominant scientific logic and assertions of modernity. Allow for such changes, and the hierarchy of values is thus reversed with allegedly fatal consequences: such a change would function as a "kerkoporta" (backdoor) of worldliness that will inevitably cause the fall of "genuine" Orthodoxy.[4] The fear is that Orthodoxy will lose its distinctive identity transformed into an Orthodox version of Protestantism.

5. Conclusions

The Greek Orthodox Church is not monolithic or uniform. It is comprised of various agents (e.g., bishops, priests, monks, lay theologians) who hold different positions in the church community and who engage in different and, at times, contradictory ways in the process of (re)interpreting common dogmatic beliefs and ritual practices in an attempt either to preserve or adjust them in the narrow contemporary context in which they find themselves, or to a broader rapprochement with secular modernity. In this process, these believers must contend with the presence and pressures of competing secular intellectuals, all bearers of different, often antithetical, political ideologies and practical proposals. The result is a plurality of perspectives, which dialogue and compete with one another and frequently assume conflicting postures, particularly during times of crisis such as the one that we face now with the COVID-19 pandemic.

The challenges and fatal consequences of the pandemic ignited a lively and contentious public and church dialogue surrounding the method of distributing Holy Communion from a common spoon. Although the official ecclesiastical authorities supported various preventive measures against COVID-19, they hesitated or categorically refused to alter this method. As Patriarch Bartholomew noted: "We have obeyed the exhortations of the health and political authorities, and as is natural, we obey, to the point, however, where the essence and the center of our faith is not touched" (Bartholomew 2020).

Such public statements, which highlighted the church's close collaboration with secular authorities but also sought to set a red line to safeguard its own interests, were not enough to prevent the outbreak of a fierce ideological battle between the proponents of scientific reason and the traditional guardians of Greek Orthodoxy. The first camp sheltered behind claims of objectivity in the medical sciences embodied in the expertise of epidemiologists. The traditional voices in the Church held fast to centuries-old dogmas and rituals of the sacred tradition, and to the charisma of saints. Theologians seeking to stake out viable positions between these camps tried to find a compromise solution in the distinction between the external form and inner essence of the ritual. All sides employed their own de-legitimization strategies. The conservatives were cast as advocates of obscurantism, who transform Christianity into pure magic, putting people at risk of getting infected. Conversely, the reformers were portrayed as heretics who distorted the charismatic essence of Greek Orthodoxy in their attempt to adjust it to secular modernity, jeopardizing people's eternal salvation in this way. Religious reformers and secular-minded actors openly discussed the possibility of changes, but without managing to develop a working alliance that could put pressure on the church authorities to adopt a new method of distributing Holy Communion, their aspirations went largely unrealized. Even when some temporary changes were implemented, these were accompanied by a vocabulary framing that reinforced more than challenged the prevailing practice of giving Communion from the same spoon.

Since the Greek Orthodox hierarchy is invested with the obligation to preserve the essentials of the sacred tradition, changes in theology and practice are easily and frequently condemned as blasphemous and as dangerous heterodoxies. For this camp, such changes can only be accepted within a framework of tradition and as long as they do not compromise the core elements of ecclesiastical life. Otherwise, the identity of Orthodoxy is perceived as being threatened by the spirit of the world, which desecrates the sacred. To avoid this danger, more progressive church officials seek a balance between, on the one hand, the pragmatism that stems from their administrative position in the church and from their close relationship with the secular spheres of life (e.g., politics), and, on the other hand, the need to maintain an identity boundary for their community within the context of secular society. By presenting themselves as guardians of tradition, they attempt to allay fears and tame the ultra-conservatives, but as a rule with no success, because the latter claim for themselves this title and role.

The controversy over the method of distributing Holy Communion just outlined is really just the tip of the iceberg of a deeper conflict that concerns the position and role of the Orthodox Church in the modern secular socio-political order. The secularists support the tendency to embrace the privatization of religion, attributing to the institutional Church only the mere role of a spiritual organization that addresses the metaphysical anxieties of its members. In their opinion, the Church should have a limited presence and restricted voice in matters related to the public sphere. By no means is the Church justified in defying the state, even when the latter imposes restrictions on religious practices and even when such impositions are justified in terms of public safety, risk reduction, and communal solidarity. By contrast, the religious ultra-conservatives aspire to the "Orthodoxization" of all spheres of human life, for they perceive the Church as the "ark of the nation" that encompasses and shapes all the other particular identities and organizations, including the state. In their opinion, the Church should always submit to its sacred tradition, rejecting any changes to its beliefs and practices in response to the ephemeral needs of the secular culture and its political agents. Situated delicately between these two extremes are those who reject both the nationalization and the privatization of the Orthodox faith. These actors support the Church's active role in civil society in the direction of recognition and respect of the alterity of the "other", rejecting any claims of religious or cultural hegemony. In their eyes, the much needed reconciliation of tradition and modernity passes through the rejection of all forms of dogmatism and through the cultivation of a *habitus* of honest dialogue in the interest of the well-being of all members of the society. The outcome of this ideological struggle remains open and offers new possibilities for reaction and counter-reaction to the transformations of its ecclesiastical, cultural, economic, and political conditions.

Funding: This paper is an output of the research project 'The Challenge of Worldliness to Contemporary Christianity: Orthodox Christian Perspectives in Dialogue with Western Christianity' at the University of Erfurt, Germany. Available online: https://www.uni-erfurt.de/philosophische-fakultaet/seminare-professuren/religionswissenschaft/professuren/kulturgeschichte-des-orthodoxen-christentums/research-project-the-challenge-of-worldliness-to-contemporary-christianity-orthodox-christian-perspectives-in-dialogue-with-western-christianity (accessed on 4 February 2023).

Acknowledgments: I would like to thank Andrew Flescher and Joel Zimbelman for their careful editing work and the anonymous reviewers for their feedback. I also wish to thank Vasilios N. Makrides for useful comments on an earlier version of this paper.

Conflicts of Interest: The author declares no conflict of interest.

Notes

1. For the attitude of the Russian Orthodox Church during the pandemic, the reader is advised to consult (Mitrofanova 2021; Hovorun 2021).
2. I use the labels "conservatives" and "traditionalists" interchangeably to designate religious actors who have an essentialist perception of tradition, rejecting *a priori* any change in the method of Communion. I use the terms "reformist", "progressive" or "liberal" theologians for agents who tend to be more open to change as they critically reflect on traditional beliefs and practices. Finally, I use the terms "secularists" or "secular-minded" agents to designate those who reject the metaphysical way of thinking, understanding human life within the immanent order.
3. All translations from Greek by the author.
4. Tradition says that the Ottoman army managed to invade the city of Constantinople in 1453 through a small gate called Kerkoporta, which was intentionally left open. Thus, in the Greek Orthodox collective consciousness the term signifies betrayal and severe disaster.

References

Agios Agathaggelos Esfigmenitis. 2003. *Agios Agathaggelos Esfigmenitis, Martyria Agonizomenis Orthodoxias Agioriton Monachon*, Issue 196, 4.

Amvrosios, Metropolitan of Kalavryta. 2020. Επιστολή Αμβροσίου σε Μητσοτάκη. *Tempo24*, March 2. Available online: https://tempo24.news/eidisi/281344/epistoli-amvrosioy-se-mitsotaki-den-ehete-dikaioma-na-diataxte-to-sfragisma-ton-naon (accessed on 11 July 2022).

Arida, Robert M. 2020. Faith, Reason, and the Eucharist: A Reflection in Light of the Coronavirus Crisis. *Public Orthodoxy Blog*, May 13. Available online: https://publicorthodoxy.org/2020/05/13/faith-reason-and-the-eucharist/# (accessed on 24 August 2022).

Armanios, Febe. 2020. Coptic Orthodox Communion in the Age of COVID-19. *Public Orthodoxy Blog*, March 10. Available online: https://publicorthodoxy.org/2020/03/10/coptic-orthodox-communion-in-the-age-of-covid-19/# (accessed on 25 June 2022).

Asproulis, Nikolaos, and Nathaniel Wood, eds. 2020. *Καιρός του Ποιήσαι: Η Ορθοδοξία ενώπιον της πανδημίας του κορωνοϊού*. Volos: Volos Academy.

Athenagoras, Metropolitan of Ilion, Acharnes and Petroupolis. 2020. Συνέντευξη στη Μάριον Μιχελιδάκη. *ERTFLIX*, November 14. Available online: https://www.ertflix.gr/ert1/kati-trechei-me-tin-marion/14noe2020-kati-trechei-me-tin-marion/ (accessed on 14 November 2020).

Augoustinos, Metropolitan of Germany. 2020. Hirtenbrief an den Klerus und das Kirchenvolk der Griechisch-Orthodoxen Metropolie von Deutschland. *Website of the Greek Orthodox Metropolis of Germany*, May 13. Available online: https://www.orthodoxie.net/post/hirtenbrief-an-den-klerus-und-das-kirchenvolkder-griechisch-orthodoxen-metropolie-von-deutschland (accessed on 4 March 2021).

Bartholomew, Ecumenical Patriarch. 2020. Correspondence of the Ecumenical Patriarch with Primates of Other Local Orthodox Churches Regarding the Way of Distribution of the Eucharist. *Website of the Ecumenical Patriarchate Permanent Delegation to the World Council of Churches*, June 2. Available online: https://www.ecupatria.org/2020/06/02/correspondence-of-the-ecumenical-patriarch-with-primates-of-other-local-orthodox-churches-regarding-the-way-of-distribution-of-the-eucharist/ (accessed on 5 April 2021).

Benford, Robert D., and David A. Snow. 2000. Framing Processes and Social Movements: An Overview and Assessment. *Annual Review of Sociology* 26: 611–39. [CrossRef]

Bourdieu, Pierre. 1977. *Outline of a Theory of Practice*. Cambridge: Cambridge University Press.

Bourdieu, Pierre. 1991. Genesis and Structure of the Religious Field. *Comparative Social Research* 13: 1–44.

Cohen, Will. 2020. Coronavirus and Communion. *Public Orthodoxy Blog*, March 14. Available online: https://publicorthodoxy.org/2020/03/14/coronavirus-and-communion/# (accessed on 25 June 2022).

Damaskinos, Metropolitan of Didymoteicho. 2021. Διδυμοτείχου: Οι πάσης φύσεως ειδικοί μπορούν να γνωματεύουν μόνο για το στενό τομέα της ειδικότητάς τους. *orthodoxia.info*, March 28. Available online: https://orthodoxia.info/news/didymoteichoy-oi-pasis-fyseos-eidikoi/ (accessed on 30 March 2022).

Dumont, Louis. 1980. Postface: Toward a Theory of Hierarchy. In *Homo Hierarchicus: The Caste System and Its Implications*. Chicago: University of Chicago, pp. 239–45.

Durkheim, Émile. 1995. *The Elementary Forms of Religious Life*. New York: The Free Press.

Elpidophoros, Archbishop of America. 2020a. Encyclical of His Eminence Archbishop Elpidophoros of America and the Eparchial Synod on the COVID-19 Pandemic (Coronavirus). *Website of the Greek Orthodox Archdiocese of America*, March 6. Available online: https://www.goarch.org/news/archbishop/encyclicals/-/asset_publisher/TS6kMZY0ZfXF/content/encyclical-covid-19-pandemic (accessed on 22 March 2022).

Elpidophoros, Archbishop of America. 2020b. Archbishop Elpidophoros Announces Further Measures to Protect the Faithful. *Website of the Greek Orthodox Archdiocese of America*, March 16. Available online: https://www.goarch.org/-/further-measures-to-protect-the-faithful (accessed on 22 March 2022).

Federation of Hospital Unions Doctors of Greece. 2020. Ομοσπονδία νοσοκομειακών γιατρών: Οι συστάσεις για κορωνοϊό δεν εξαιρούν τη Θεία Κοινωνία. *iefimerida.gr*, March 6. Available online: https://www.iefimerida.gr/ygeia/omospondia-nosokomeiakon-giatron-oi-systaseis-gia-koronoio-den-exairoyn-ti-theia-koinonia (accessed on 10 September 2022).

Gabriel, Metropolitan of Nea Ionia and Philadelphia. 2020. Διαδικτυακή συνάντηση με νέους της Ιεράς Μητροπόλεως. *Facebook of the Metropolis of Nea Ionia*, November 11. Available online: https://m.facebook.com/mitropoliNif/?__tn__=C-R (accessed on 13 November 2020).

Giamarellou, Eleni. 2020. Κορονοϊός: Λοιμωξιολόγος καλεί τους πολίτες να κοινωνήσουν παρά τον ιό. in.gr, March 6. Available online: https://www.in.gr/2020/03/06/greece/koronaios-loimoksiologos-kalei-tous-polites-na-koinonisoun-para-ton-io/ (accessed on 7 April 2022).

Greek Orthodox Archdiocese of America. 2020. Directives to be followed by the Clergy dealing with COVID-19 (Coronavirus). *Website of the Greek Orthodox Archdiocese of America*. Available online: https://www.goarch.org/-/directives-covid-19 (accessed on 22 March 2022).

Greek Orthodox Metropolis of Austria. 2020. Hygienevorschriften für Gottesdienste ab dem 15. Mai 2020. *Website of the Metropolis of Austria*, May 11. Available online: https://www.metropolisvonaustria.at/index.php/de/lebenslauf/stellungnahmen/1876-200515corona (accessed on 4 March 2021).

Hierotheos, Metropolitan of Nafpaktos and Agios Vlasios. 2020. Η μαρτυρία της Ορθόδοξης Εκκλησίας για την Θεία Κοινωνία. *Parembasis.gr*. Available online: https://parembasis.gr/images/2020/284/MARTYRIA_GIA_THN_KOINWNIA.pdf (accessed on 11 September 2022).

Holy Eparchial Synod. 2020. Further Guidance from the Holy Eparchial Synod. *Website of the Greek Orthodox Archdiocese of America*, March 14. Available online: https://www.goarch.org/-/further-guidance-coronavirus-2020-03-14 (accessed on 22 March 2022).

Holy Synod of the Greek Orthodox Church. 2020a. Ενημέρωσις του Χριστεπωνύμου Πληρώματος περί του νέου κορωνοϊού, Εγκύκλιος 3013. *Website of the Greek Orthodox Church*, March 10. Available online: http://www.ecclesia.gr/greek/holysynod/egyklioi.asp?id=2631&what_sub=egyklioi (accessed on 11 June 2022).

Holy Synod of the Greek Orthodox Church. 2020b. Αποφάσεις της Διαρκούς Ιεράς Συνόδου της 12.5.2020, Εγκύκλιος 3021. *Website of the Greek Orthodox Church*, May 13. Available online: http://www.ecclesia.gr/greek/holysynod/egyklioi.asp?id=2661&what_sub=egyklioi (accessed on 11 June 2022).

Holy Synod of the Greek Orthodox Church. 2020c. Συνοδικός ευχαριστήριος λόγος, Εγκύκλιος 3023. *Website of the Greek Orthodox Church*, May 15. Available online: http://www.ecclesia.gr/greek/holysynod/egyklioi.asp?id=2663&what_sub=egyklioi (accessed on 11 September 2022).

Holy Synod of the Serbian Orthodox Church. 2020. Communique of the Holy Synod of Bishops. *Website of the Serbian Orthodox Church*, March 23. Available online: http://spc.rs/eng/communique_holy_synod_bishops_0 (accessed on 11 June 2020).

Hovorun, Cyril. 2020. COVID-19 and Christian (?) Dualism. *Public Orthodoxy Blog*, March 23. Available online: https://publicorthodoxy.org/2020/03/23/covid-19-and-dualism/# (accessed on 24 January 2022).

Hovorun, Cyril. 2021. Covid Theology" or the "Significant Storm" of the Coronavirus Pandemic. *State, Religion and Church* 8: 20–33. [CrossRef]

Ieronymos, Archbishop of Athens and All Greece. 2020. Το μήνυμα Ιερώνυμου για τον κορωνοϊό. *enikos.gr*, March 13. Available online: https://www.enikos.gr/society/707448/to-minyma-ieronymou-gia-ton-koronoio-i-ekklisia-efarmozei-tis-odi (accessed on 11 August 2022).

Imerodromos. 2020. Διαδώστε: Ο 'ιός' του σκοταδισμού βλάπτει σοβαρά την υγεία. *Imerodromos*, March 6. Available online: https://www.imerodromos.gr/diadoste-o-ios-toy-skotadismoy-vlaptei-sovara-tin-ygeia/ (accessed on 7 March 2022).

Kalaitzidis, Pantelis. 2022. An Interview with Dr. Pantelis Kalaitzidis. November 2. Available online: https://www.uni-erfurt.de/fileadmin/fakultaet/philosophische/Seminar_Religionswissenschaft/Orthodoxes_Christentum/The_Challenge_of_Worldliness_to_Contemporary_Christianity_Projektseite/Interviews/Interview_with_Dr._Kalaitzidis.pdf (accessed on 21 December 2022).

Kantanis, Konstantinos. 2021. Κήρυγμα π. Κ. Καντάνη για τη Θεία Λειτουργία και τον κορωνοϊό. *YouTube Agrinio TV*, January 12. Available online: https://youtu.be/xc4NcTY3LT8 (accessed on 13 August 2022).

Karpov, Vyacheslav, Elena Lisovskaya, and David Barry. 2012. Ethnodoxy: How Popular Ideologies Fuse Religious and Ethnic Identities. *Journal for the Scientific Study of Religion* 51: 638–55. [CrossRef]

Kessareas, Efstathios. 2018. The Greek Debt Crisis as Theodicy: Religious Fundamentalism and Socio-political Conservatism. *The Sociological Review* 66: 122–37. [CrossRef]

Kessareas, Efstathios. 2022a. Geistliche Väter und ihre Idolisierung im orthodoxen Christentum. *Religion & Gesellschaft in Ost und West* 11: 3–5.

Kessareas, Efstathios. 2022b. *Εκκλησία, Ιδεολογία και Πολιτική στην Ελλάδα της Μεταπολίτευσης. Κοινωνιολογική Προσέγγιση*. Athens: Papazisi.

Kessareas, Efstathios. 2022c. Saints, Heroes, and the 'Other': Value Orientations of Contemporary Greek Orthodoxy. *Religions* 13: 360. [CrossRef]

Knight, Christopher C. 2020. *Science and the Christian Faith: A Guide for the Perplexed*. Yonkers: St Vladimir's Seminary Press.

Kosmas, Metropolitan of Aitolia and Akarnania. 2020. *Δεν αφήνει ο Θεός μέσα στον ναό να μολυνθείς*. *pelop.gr*, September 10. Available online: http://www.pelop.gr/?page=article&DocID=592221 (accessed on 26 January 2022).

Kosmidis, Nikos. 2020. A Search for a Theology of Life: The Challenge of COVID-19 for Orthodox Ecclesiology and Religious Practices. *The Ecumenical Review* 72: 624–35. [CrossRef]

Koutloumousianos, Chrysostom. 2020. The Bread, the Wine, and the Mode of Being. *Public Orthodoxy Blog*, April 28. Available online: https://publicorthodoxy.org/2020/04/28/bread-wine-and-mode-of-being/# (accessed on 25 January 2022).

Kubat, Rodoljub. 2020. Silencing Theologians in Serbia: An Interview with R. *Kubat*. *Public Orthodoxy Blog*, May 7. Available online: https://publicorthodoxy.org/2020/05/07/silencing-theologians-in-serbia/# (accessed on 30 September 2022).

Larchet, Jean-Claude. 2002. *The Theology of Illness*. Crestwood: ST Vladimir's Seminary Press.

Linou, Athina. 2020. Συνέντευξη στη Μάριον Μιχελιδάκη. *ERTFLIX*, November 14. Available online: https://www.ertflix.gr/ert1/kati-trechei-me-tin-marion/14noe2020-kati-trechei-me-tin-marion/ (accessed on 14 November 2020).

Makrides, Vasilios N. 2012a. Orthodox Christianity, Change, Innovation: Contradictions in Terms? In *Innovation in the Orthodox Christian Tradition? The Question of Change in Greek Orthodox Thought and Practice*. Edited by Trine Stauning Willert and Lina Molokotos-Liederman. Farnham: Ashgate, pp. 19–50.

Makrides, Vasilios N. 2012b. Orthodox Christianity, Modernity, and Postmodernity: Overview, Analysis, and Assessment. *Religion, State, and Society* 40: 248–85. [CrossRef]

Makrides, Vasilios N. 2016. Orthodox Christian Rigorism: Attempting to Delineate a Multifaceted Phenomenon. *Interdisciplinary Journal for Religion and Transformation in Contemporary Society* 2: 216–52. [CrossRef]

Makrides, Vasilios N. 2020. Le nouveau document social de l'Église orthodoxe: Son orientation, son élaboration, son contexte et son importance. *ISTINA* 65: 387–413.

Mannheim, Karl. 2015. *Ideologie und Utopie*. Frankfurt: Klostermann.

Melchisedek, Archbishop of Pittsburgh, and Western Pennsylvania. 2020. Hierarchical Instructions: Holy Week/Pascha 2020. *Website of the Archdiocese of Pittsburg*, April 3. Available online: https://www.ocadwpa.org/files/Official%20Letters/Letter-MELCHISEDEK-Holy-Week-Instructions.pdf (accessed on 4 March 2022).

Mitrofanova, Anastasia. 2021. The Impact of COVID-19 on Orthodox Groups and Believers in Russia. In *Religious Fundamentalism in the Age of Pandemic*. Edited by Nina Käsehage. Bielefeld: transcript Verlag, pp. 48–81.

Neophytos, Metropolitan of Morphou. 2020. Ο εκφοβισμός των πιστών το Πάσχα του 2020. *YouTube*, April 12. Available online: https://www.youtube.com/watch?v=cV3mHks1qcM&t=467s (accessed on 3 March 2022).

Papathanasiou, Thanasis. 2020. Πανδημία και Εκκλησία. *Epohi*, November 29. Available online: https://www.epohi.gr/article/37650/pandhmia-kai-ekklhsia (accessed on 26 January 2022).

Roosien, Mark. 2020. Fasting from Communion in a Pandemic. *Public Orthodoxy Blog*. March 17. Available online: https://publicorthodoxy.org/2020/03/17/fasting-from-communion-in-a-pandemic/# (accessed on 25 January 2022).

Seraphim, Metropolitan of Piraeus. 2020. Κινδυνεύουν μόνο όσοι κοινωνούν χωρίς να πιστεύουν πραγματικά. *Alfavita.gr*, March 6. Available online: https://www.alfavita.gr/koinonia/314517_mitropolitis-serafeim-kindyneyoyn-mono-osoi-koinonoyn-horis-na-pisteyoyn-pragmatika (accessed on 20 October 2022).

Stylianakis, Antonios. 2020. Virus vs Church—father Antonios Stylianakis. *YouTube Synaxaria*, November 1. Available online: https://www.youtube.com/watch?v=wvMJPc5nnlw&t=0s (accessed on 2 April 2022).

Thompson, John B. 1984. *Studies in the Theory of Ideology*. Berkeley: University of California Press.

Tountas, Giannis. 2020. Ο κορωνοϊός μπορεί να μεταδοθεί με τη Θεία Κοινωνία. *Iefimerida*, December 16. Available online: https://www.iefimerida.gr/ellada/toyntas-ekpa-koronoios-mporei-na-metadothei-me-theia-koinonia (accessed on 5 April 2022).

Vassiliadis, Petros, ed. 2020. *The Church in a Period of Pandemic: Can the Present Pandemic Crisis Become a Meaningful Storm for Renewal in Our Churches?* Thessaloniki: CEMES Publications.

Weber, Max. 1978. *Economy and Society: An Outline of Interpretive Sociology*. Edited by Guenther Roth and Claus Wittich. Berkeley: University of California Press.

Weber, Max. 2012. The 'Objectivity' of Knowledge in Social Science and Social Policy. In *Max Weber: Collected Methodological Writings*. Edited by Hans Henrik Bruun and Sam Whimster. London: Routledge, pp. 100–38.

Willert, Trine Stauning, and Lina Molokotos-Liederman, eds. 2012. *Innovation in the Orthodox Christian Tradition? The Question of Change in Greek Orthodox Thought and Practice*. Farnham: Ashgate.

Zizioulas, John. 1997. *Being as Communion: Studies in Personhood and the Church*. Crestwood: St. Vladimir's Seminary Press.
Zorbas, Konstantinos, ed. 2021. *Κοινωνική κρίση και πανδημία. Μελετώντας τα Κείμενα της Αγίας και Μεγάλης Συνόδου: Προβληματισμοί για την κοινωνική κρίση και την πανδημία του COVID-19*. Athens: Akritas.

religions MDPI

Article

How Well Do Religious Exemptions Apply to Mandates for COVID-19 Vaccines?

Andrew Flescher [1,2]

1 Department of Family, Population, and Preventive Medicine, Core Faculty in Public Health, State University of New York, Stony Brook, NY 11794-8338, USA; andrew.flescher@stonybrookmedicine.edu
2 Department of English, State University of New York, Stony Brook, NY 11794-8338, USA

Abstract: In the United States, religious exemptions to health-driven mandates enjoy, and should enjoy, protected status in medical ethics and healthcare law. Religious exemptions are defined as seriously professed exceptions to state or federal laws, which appeal to Title VII of the Civil Rights Act of 1964, allowing workers to request an exception to a job requirement, including a health-protective mandate, if it "conflicts with their sincerely held religious beliefs, practices, or observances". In medical ethics, such religious exceptions are usually justified on the basis of the principle of autonomy, where personally held convictions, reflected in scripture or established religious norms, are safeguarded on the basis of the first amendment, thereby constituting an important area in which societal good must yield to individual liberty. Acknowledging the longstanding category of "religious exemptions", and referencing some examples that adhere to its parameters in good faith (e.g., objections made by some institutions to HPV vaccines), I argue that, to date, no coherent basis for religious exemptions to COVID-19 vaccines has been offered through appeal to the principle of autonomy, or, in a healthcare context, to "medical freedom". Indeed, proponents of characterizing these exemptions as legitimate misconstrue autonomy and abuse the reputation of the religious traditions they invoke in defense of their endeavors to opt out. The upshot is not only an error in interpreting the principle of autonomy, whereby it is issued a "blank check", but also a dishonesty in itself whereby a contested political position becomes deliberately disguised as a protected religious value. "Sincerely held beliefs", I conclude, appear no longer to constitute the standard for religious accommodation in the era of COVID-19. Individual declaration, seemingly free of any reasonable constraint, does. This is a shift that has serious consequences for public health and, more broadly, the public good.

Keywords: religious liberty; autonomy; "sincerely held beliefs"; vaccine mandates; religious exemptions; Title VII of the Civil Rights Act; COVID-19

Citation: Flescher, Andrew. 2023. How Well Do Religious Exemptions Apply to Mandates for COVID-19 Vaccines? *Religions* 14: 569. https://doi.org/10.3390/rel14050569

Academic Editor: Katarzyna Skrzypińska

Received: 26 December 2022
Revised: 7 March 2023
Accepted: 27 March 2023
Published: 24 April 2023

1. Introduction: A New Sort of Religious Exemption to a Well-Established Mandate

In the United States, religious exemptions to health-driven mandates in the workplace and, under exigent circumstances, even in the public square, enjoy, and should enjoy, protected status in medical ethics and healthcare law. Religious exemptions are defined as seriously professed exceptions to state or federal laws that appeal to Title VII of the Civil Rights Act of 1964, allowing workers to request an exemption to a job requirement, including a health-protective mandate, if it "conflicts with their sincerely held religious beliefs, practices, or observances" (US Department of Labor 2014). In the context of labor law, religious ethics, and medical ethics, religious exemptions are justified on the basis of the principle of *autonomy*, whereby one's personally held convictions, often reflected in the scriptures or established norms of the religious traditions of which they are a member, are safeguarded on the basis of the first amendment. The invocation of autonomy in this respect constitutes an important area in which the societal good must yield to individual liberty. According to the principle of autonomy, one should have the freedom to make decisions about one's body for oneself, as a result of which one cannot be forced against one's will to undertake any proposed medical therapy (Beauchamp and Childress 2001, pp. 176–77). In its strongest versions, autonomy presupposes that patients should be free to override their caretakers when the latter paternalistically propose a course of action that, in good faith, is in the patient's medical interests. (Glover 1977, pp. 80–81; Buchanan and Brock 1990, pp. 38–39; Gillon 2003, p. 310).

Notably, what is *not* entailed in this understanding, neither here nor in any other standard definition of the term in medical or legal ethics, is that autonomy should be considered an absolute claim, not required to be in balance with the other principles with which it stands in tension. More important, while autonomy implies one's stewardship over one's body, it does not give license to put others in danger. While there is a burden on employers and public officials to *accommodate* individuals claiming exemptions reasonably, this does not imply unrestricted prerogative in the public square or the workplace. The critical question before us is what happens when a pandemic arrives and public health officials, with the state's backing, have determined that the safety of the population under their jurisdiction requires adherence to a health-mandated vaccination, which, given the stakes, cannot be worked around through a "reasonable accommodation"?

Until recently, the answer in our country has been that while one is not required to be forced to stick one's arm out to receive an injection—there is no *direct* bodily coercion—it is within the state's jurisdiction to decide to refuse entry of vaccine-refusers into shared spaces. Specifically, this precedent had been set in Jacobson v. Massachusetts, where the majority ruled: "The liberty secured by the constitution of the United States to every person within its jurisdiction does not import an absolute right in each person to be, at all times and in all circumstances, wholly freed from restraint. There are manifold restraints to which every person is *necessarily* subject for the common good". (Jacobson v. Massachusetts 1905). Religious exemptions are real and must be respected, but not at the expense of the "life and liberty" of everyone who lives in society, not just privileged or exempted groups.

Acknowledging the longstanding category of "religious exemptions", and referencing a controversial example that does adhere to its parameters in good faith (namely, that of objections made by some institutions to HPV vaccines), I set out to argue that, to date, no coherent basis of religious exemptions to COVID-19 vaccines has been offered, particularly through appeal to the principle of autonomy, or, in a health care context, to "medical freedom". Indeed, proponents who characterize *these* exemptions as legitimate misconstrue autonomy and even abuse the reputation of the religious traditions they invoke in support of their endeavors to opt out. While in what follows I address recent developments in how "religious exemptions" are being interpreted in the workplace, as this is where labor law applies, the conclusions I draw about policy are applicable also to the public square, more broadly. In both settings, at work no less than in a grocery store or at a motor vehicles department, there is a group of people who constitute a captive audience insofar as they cannot perform functions necessary for basic daily living without convening in these shared spaces. This noted, the scope of this effort is neither to affirm nor to undo legal grounds for abstention. The law about what the state can do to impose vaccine mandates is changing so rapidly, in some instances being overturned at the appellate level only to be re-overturned by the Supreme Court, that at this time it is anyone's guess to say where things land (Council on Foreign Relations 2021). What I do hope to present, if not prescriptively then descriptively, is that the checks and balances customarily in effect when individuals object to public health mandates issued in response to exigent crises, alarmingly, appear to be no longer.

Traditionally, one would have had to justify a claim of a violation of individual rights within the context of a coherent belief system to which one had showed evidence of adhering over time. A sharp shift in the way in which "religious belief" itself is now understood, however, as a strictly *subjective* conviction, makes it an unchecked prerogative. This historical shift, in essence, awards a blank check to prospective believers claiming exemptions to not be compelled to justify their choice. One may simply assert that one's personal interests trump the public good when the two come into conflict. In this manner, a believer exempting oneself from a health-protective vaccine mandate is afforded an opportunity to cloak ideological objections under the guise of religious rationale. The burden shifts to the state to demonstrate that *it* is not violating individual freedoms, thereby allowing for a strategic exploitation of religion that promotes political activism.

Thus, what I present here is neither a legal argument nor an argument about the threat we collectively face when we do not respond to a pandemic such as COVID-19 on a population level (which is an empirical argument), nor even an argument about the normative justification for collective action, e.g., that the threat entailed by the contagious and ubiquitous virus of SARS-CoV-2 is so compelling that individual beliefs ought not to take precedence over the public good, even if it is evident that that case can be made. Rather, it is an elucidation of what the consequences in fact are for a rampant subjectivism in the application of religious exemptions, particularly in the Abrahamic traditions, amidst a worldwide exigent health crisis. In such a state of affairs, not only does the traditional requirement of "sincerely held beliefs", a requirement for which there has been longstanding and historical respect, lose its power of distinction, but we inhabit a world in which public health—and the public good—is declared to be ancillary to political identity and self-interested action.

What are the options available to public health officials, and more broadly to policy makers, who want to promote safety and human flourishing, in a shifting legal landscape according to which personally held beliefs can likely no longer be checked by reasonable constraint? Is there a threshold beyond which claims of the sacrosanct nature of "bodily autonomy" lead to a harmful state of affairs from the perspective of shared health goals and policy initiatives? These questions become even more pointed in a legal and cultural environment in which religion and religious belief are increasingly fragmented, individualized, and divorced from traditional religious institutions and communities.[1] No doubt, there are ethical implications tied to these inquiries, particularly in light of the seeming tension this shift reveals between safety and individual expression in the public square. (What does an individual living through the pandemic owe to other individuals in the state? Conversely, what must the state tolerate for the sake of preserving individual liberty, a prized and precious good in our society?) However, the principal contribution of this article is descriptive. Specifically, it elucidates the consequences of modifying the longstanding framework for interpreting and adjudicating claims about individual belief in the public square, consequences for which, in the context of a pandemic, the stakes could not be higher.

2. Religious Belief as "Individually Authoritative"

In a seminal lecture clarifying the nature of mystical experiences, William James famously described the convictions about the believer's claim that such experiences were "true", as individually, but only individually, "authoritative" (James 1985, p. 422). In this judgment, James sought to convey both the power and fulfillment of a quintessential affirmation of faith while simultaneously recognizing that the content of such faith articles could not only vary, but possibly stand in contradiction from individual to individual. That is, James sought to preserve the believer's right to stand unflinchingly behind a worldview that furnished life with purpose and richness while recognizing as a matter of common sense and pragmatic justice that that believer was not alone in the world; should any belief result in action, it could affect more than that one believer. From this principle, James gave voice to a key principle of the First Amendment: Individuals ought to be free to explore and benefit from a religious expression that gives their lives meaning while not being issued carte blanche to prevent others from doing the same. This principle—or compromise—arguably became a tacit dictum for the setting of policy in instances in which individual liberties ran up against the public good. The former was given a proverbial vote, but not a veto, when the well-being and flourishing of many lives stood in the balance.

The implications of this compromise are critical for setting health policy. Until recently, for example, vaccines could be required by the state in exigent circumstances to protect the population at large. According to the American Bar Association, under the U.S. Constitution's 10th Amendment and nearly 200 years of Supreme Court decisions, state governments have had the primary authority to control the spread of dangerous diseases within their jurisdictions, allowing them to assume authority to take public health emergency actions, such as setting quarantines and business restrictions (American Bar Association 2022). This constraint historically has not pertained just to public health emergencies. In normal life, too, public health and safety historically have taken precedence over individual liberties in scenarios where the two conflict. In 1922, the Supreme Court held in Zucht v. King that making accessible public education conditional on standard vaccine compliance did not violate the Fourteenth Amendment (Shachar 2022). By 1980, all fifty states had laws requiring vaccines for children to attend public schools. Naturally, there are constraints on governmental authorities in a position to declare a state emergency. Under Section 319 of the Public Health Service Act of 1944, (Roosevelt 1944) establishing the government's quarantine jurisdiction, the Secretary of the Department of Health and Human Services was given the power to declare a public health emergency "after consulting with such public health officials as may be necessary", in the event that a disease, a separate public health disorder, or even a bioterrorist attack, presented an imminent health crisis (US Department of Health and Human Services 2019). To be sure, the burden of demonstrating an emergency was high, but that is the point. In the setting of policies that can entail emergency powers, until very recently, the thresholds have been transparently understood by all parties. Our nation's legal and medical history establish a public health precedent such that a balance is struck between individual liberties, to be held intact, all other things being equal, and the public good, which in an emergency can override the government's default "hands off" approach to the setting of health policy. Leaving aside the question of trusting the right authorities when empirical judgments must be made about assessing a public health emergency, when one is, in fact, declared, it is respected.

Public buy-in, in fact, heavily relies not only on public opinion but also on clerical figures who speak for their respective communities. When polled, representatives of a cross-section of the world faiths have tended to express no canonical disposition against vaccines and immunoglobulins, with the lone exception among major sects or denominations being Christian Science (Grabenstein 2013). This is not to say that sanction for vaccine hesitancy does not exist in some congregations of various denominations. Members from Pentecostal sects such as Endtime Ministries or groups such as Christ Church or General Assembly Church of the Firstborn believe in the primacy of prayer and that the human intervention in God's work is obstructive, from which it follows that the administering of a vaccine to prevent a health outbreak is for these believers at best futile, and more likely, seen as provocative. (Linnard-Palmer and Christiansen 2021). As many as 42 groups from the Christian tradition feature teachings that could be interpreted to support the refusal of medical treatment, including in the case of children (Linnard-Palmer and Christiansen 2021; Adams and Leverland 1986; Asser and Swan 1998). However, this attitude is not representative of mainstream Christianity, where a duty to preserve life can be inferred from Gospel sources. "Pro-life" usually means being anti-exemption. In deference to the First Amendment, and as an explicit specification of Title VII, religious exemptions have been available options in such historical moments as health-related public health mandates were deemed necessary. However, these have always been regarded as exceptions to a rule for which there was remarkable ground-level support among religious insiders, exceptions, by the reckoning of the clergy themselves, which are more likely to be abused than legitimately claimed (Reiss 2014). This is important to note, if only to demonstrate the establishment of presumed limits on individual claims that went against chosen representatives of a faith. That one's exemption is *defined* as an "exemption", as opposed to a subjective preference, maintains the historical balance between individual liberties and the public good on which American public health policy has been traditionally predicated.

This point is not just pragmatic from a public-policy-making standpoint, but also one about regard for religious traditions themselves. The compromise in play since 1905, as a result of the decision in Jacobson versus Massachusetts, had been that religious claims on the basis of which one sought to opt out of public policy could not be absolute; some emergencies afforded no exceptions. But another tacit constraint on claims of religious liberty was that they had to be pursued in good faith. Here, one might draw a contrast between reservations voiced by Catholics to their schools providing support for the administering of HPV vaccines (and to Catholic institutions in general providing resources for abortion or birth control), on the one hand, and clinicians seeking religious exemptions in health care settings to COVID-19 vaccines, on the other. In 2007, The Catholic Medical Association issued a position paper that, while acknowledging the safety and effectiveness of the HPV vaccine Gardasil, opposed any form of a mandate that girls be vaccinated against HPV. (Catholic Medical Association 2007). While the Catholic Medical Association found nothing in and of itself unethical about Gardasil, it did note that given "the importance of parental involvement for raising children, and particularly in forming their children in chastity, it would be counterproductive to override their ethical objections and negate their authority on this issue". Not denying that many Catholic women were bound to have pre-marital sex despite the teachings of their faith, the group found that condoning such a mandate, even for a worthy public health cause, was tantamount to inducing a subversion of one of the tradition's central pro-life tenets of discouraging pre-marital sex. To not stand against a regulation that would *impose* such a health-protective measure, the Catholic Medical Association found, would effectively be to ask faith-adherents to forego that which they saw to be a crux of their discipleship.

What is interesting about this response is that, whether or not one buys the argument on the basis of which the regulation is rejected, one has no problem seeing that the objection is issued in good faith: public health officials are being told the truth about the motivations for hesitancy among those who are being asked to sanction this preventive health measure. By contrast, there is mounting evidence during the pandemic that the opposite has taken place with regard to individuals seeking religious representatives to sign off on ad hoc requests for religious exemptions for vaccine mandates in healthcare settings, which are petitioned on the basis of no discernable or consistent grounds. As Michelle Mello notes, we are for the first time in our history seeing clergy not only not supporting COVID-19 mandates, but at odds with their flock:

> It's not that a person is failing to produce a letter from a clergy member saying, yes, I back them up on this claim. It's that clergy members have actively gone out in public and said: No, we don't bar COVID vaccination in our religion. Our religion either has nothing to say about this or we are going on record as saying in our church we want people to get COVID vaccines. It is acceptable. It's consistent with doctrine to get COVID vaccines. There is no bar here. And nevertheless, there is a person who identifies with that religious belief system who comes forward and says: Yes, but my interpretation of the Bible, of Catholic doctrine, is that I shouldn't get this vaccine. And it doesn't matter that the religious leader has said this. (Council on Foreign Relations)

Mello goes on to document the increased frequency of these contestations brought on behalf of individuals in the era of COVID-19, who, despite being at odds with official teaching on a narrow issue, are finding support among courts at all levels of appeal, up to the Supreme Court. (Council on Foreign Relations) According to Mello, the new precedent signals that something other than a "sincerely held" religious belief is being invoked, which "looks more ideological" than spiritual.

Mello's suggestion that the recent spate of religious objections to health-protective mandates in proposed legislation which are not on the basis of religious grounds is reminiscent of examples introduced by Dorit Rubenstein Reiss of individuals who strategically attended services held by denominations to which they did not belong in order to acquire sympathy they found lacking in their own congregations (Reiss 2014). The affiliations were almost always temporary, and in some cases, the faith surfers admitted their deception. (Reiss). Without the presumed burden to share one's reasons for objecting to health protecting measures introduced by the state, the stable compromise to which Jacobson versus Massachusetts had led—while in dire health crises vaccination laws do not violate due process or the 14th amendment, requiring enforcing parties to shoulder the burden of finding a "reasonable accommodation" if they can—falls away, and with it, any deference to a "common good". The upshot is a violation of the implied constraint on the believer as identified by William James in his reference to the faith-leaper who has license to maintain a religious conviction unflinchingly, for belief is now not *only* individually authoritative but also impacting others in society. Indeed, the public health consequences of this shift are undeniable. Given the nature of how "herd immunity" works, where thresholds of protection via vaccine immunity need to be established across a population, any individual decision on whether to vaccinate impacts the health and safety of everyone. (Flescher and Kabat 2018; Yeh 2022).

3. The Public Health Consequences of Jettisoning "Sincerely Held Beliefs"

One of the key concepts on the basis of which exemptions had been evaluated was whether they were "sincerely held", a standard formally introduced in Title VII of the Civil Rights Act of 1964 (Civil Rights Act 1964). Under federal law, as supported by several Supreme Court cases in the twentieth century, such as United States v. Ballard (1944), United States v. Seeger (1965), and Wisconsin v. Yoder (1972), an individual religious exemption from vaccines was deemed legitimate when it rested on *sincere*, i.e., longstanding and committed, beliefs grounded in one's religion, even if the nature of such beliefs themselves were not fully understood by the individual claiming an exemption (Anders 2020). The effect of this stipulation was to tether one's ability to opt out of health protective public policy to affiliation with a recognizable religious tradition. In such an understanding, exemptions do not qualify as religious if they are merely *personally* held beliefs, including social, political, or economic philosophies, for according to the Equal Employments Opportunity Commission's interpretation of Title VII, religion is "comprehensive in nature; it consists of a belief-system as opposed to an isolated teaching" (Africa v. Commonwealth of Pennsylvania 1981).

This is a standard upheld by ample juridical precedent. Burwell v. Hobby Lobby Stores, Inc. (Burwell v. Hobby Lobby Stores 2014) was a landmark decision where the Court acknowledged the claims of for-profit business owners to engage in discrimination on the basis of not violating their religious convictions. Justice Samuel Alito, writing for the majority, nevertheless concluded that the courts are quite capable of determining when insincere claims are put forward. Fraudulent or inappropriate attempts to skirt state regulation can be detected in instances in which an individual request is not consistent with demonstrated past action (Adams and Barmore 2014). While the impact of the majority's decision in this case was to strike down a requirement that the company's health insurance packages provide contraceptive options for their female employees, as had been directed by the enactment of the Affordable Health Care Act four years earlier and enforced by the US Department of Health and Human Services, the case did reinforce the importance in maintaining the distinction between sincerely and non-sincerely held beliefs. Not only could the two sorts of beliefs be meaningfully distinguished from one another, but there were also criteria for scrutinizing and evaluating a person's record:

> [C]ourts are best able to examine sincerity "where extrinsic evidence is evaluated" and objective factors dominate the analysis. First, courts look for any secular self-interest that might motivate an insincere claim. In [US v. Quaintance], for instance, the defendant's desire to avoid prison and continue selling drugs offered an obvious motive to fabricate religious belief. This factor is particularly probative where the purported religious belief arose only after the benefit of claiming such a belief became apparent. (Adams and Barmore)

While on the substantive issue Burwell v. Hobby Lobby Stores signaled a setback for governmental regulatory health initiatives, sincerity as a criterion itself became reinforced following the decision. As recently as 2014, self-interest, including acting on the basis of ideology, was re-determined to be insufficient grounds for rejecting health-protective policies. As Adams and Barmore concluded in their analysis of this case, while "the judiciary has no business evaluating the moral truth underlying religious claims", objective standards do and should continue to be applied by evaluating the "factual sincerity" of proposed exemptions based on demonstrated past behaviors of the claimant. This is far from an "anything goes" standard.

Nevertheless, although the vast majority of today's religious leaders do not object to medical vaccinations, questioning the legitimacy of "suddenly held" beliefs when they are claimed (Wojcik 2022), requests for such exemptions on the basis of religion are precipitously on the rise. This is the situation in which individuals, finding no authoritative sanction in their appeal to opt out, contend that their *interpretation* of doctrine instructs them not to get a mandated vaccine in the workplace for which it is appropriately designated. For the first time in recent history, breaking over a hundred years of court precedent, these individuals' arguments are in many instances (depending on the deciding court) allowed to sidestep the distinction between "sincerely held" and "suddenly held", finding merit because the courts, more politicized than during any time in recent American history, are split. Weighing in on this "constitutional moment" in American history, Michelle Mello explains: "The Second Court of Appeals, which is a fairly high-level court of appeals, just … joined at least one other district court, a lower-level federal court, in holding that a member of a religious denomination can assert their own interpretation of doctrine … cit[ing] a Supreme Court case that indeed seemed to suggest something along that line" (Council on Foreign Relations).

This sea change, giving more discretion to the individual in court decisions of this nature, is occurring in a context in which the standard of scrutiny applied to any law which allows for secular exemptions is now "strict". As such, it must allow the same flexibility for comparable religious exemptions, despite the fact that secular activities bear a public character while religious activities are significant only to those individuals engaging in them. Mello cites a recent case in which the Supreme Court refused to support public health officials in the State of California during mitigation efforts following a severe outbreak of COVID-19. (Council on Foreign Relations). In the decision, the Court offered injunctive dispensation against an issuance barring at-home or private-residence Bible studies and comparable settings by restricting the headcount of all congregants. Mello concludes that decisions such as this, combined with a surge in applications for exemptions, create a "potential catch-22" for any public health organization adopting a medically exigent mandate. "If you don't have a religious exemption, you might get strict scrutiny … because these medical contraindications are treated more favorably than the religious objections. But if you do have a religious exemption process, well, now you've got a problem because now you've got this process for considering individualized exemptions, and that could trigger strict scrutiny. So it seems like either way you turn, as a mandate designer, you might have a problem" (Council on Foreign Relations).

The implications of this new restraint on collective regulation during health emergencies are profound, especially in a context in which for vaccination campaigns to be effective they need to be adopted by a critical mass of individuals. This trend needs to be evaluated in a health policy-making environment in which, aside from COVID-19, we have also seen the resurgence of measles, and now polio, which had been absent for decades (Kuehn 2020). As critical as these cases are, it does not require a stretch of the imagination to envision worse; yet the new standard is uncompromising, not allowing for any emergency-thresholds that trigger a suspension of the norm of maximal deference to liberty.

There is an additional reason to be concerned that this shift in our traditional system of checks and balances will make a difference in population health. Historically, the link between legal barriers and nonmedical exemptions rates has long been established in public school systems in several states. States with fewer barriers to immunization exemption procedures have religious exemption rates more than twice as high as those states where it is legally harder to opt out, with predictable health consequences. (Blank et al. 2013; Rota et al. 2001) This finding suggests that if the Supreme Court decides to make the non-medical exemption process more convenient, more people will be likely to avail themselves of the option. The standard of "sincerely held", traditionally a rate-limiter, would no longer serve as the organic barrier it had been to reducing illegitimate exemption claims, since it would not matter whether one had demonstrated longevity of commitment to the religious tradition in whose name the exemption was being sought. Nor, moreover, would it matter what authoritative representatives of that invoked religious tradition would be likely to rule on the matter. Only the arbitrary and non-morally relevant factor of *where* such exemptions happened to be invoked would be decisive, additionally welcoming an instance in which individuals would only have to move to the state where their pattern of religious commitment would not be scrutinized. In a context in which a Supreme Court is likely to restrict governmental health regulation, we all become increasingly susceptible to public health emergencies whose containment a government is impotent to affect.

4. From Religion to Ideology

It bears reminding that I have not suggested that the *category* of religious exemptions should be eliminated or is not legitimate. Rather, I have called into question the manner in which exemptions are being invoked with unprecedented frequency in the context of the COVID-19 pandemic. I now, perhaps controversially, want to suggest that religious exemptions, insofar as they have been applied to vaccine mandates for COVID-19, are not even "religious", but ideological. To be sure, I want to argue that the debate about whether vaccine mandates should be enforced under exigent health emergencies is not being driven by religious considerations so much as by the realities of a highly polarized political environment fueled by the suspicion of governmental intrusion into the private sphere.

Shortly after COVID-19 vaccines became available to the public, a survey conducted in successive waves from the Public Religion Research Institute (PRRI) and the Interfaith Youth Core (IFCY), the largest conducted to date on the issue of the influence of religion on views of vaccination, revealed that over half of Americans who reported attending religious services regularly found their encouragement to get vaccinated in the faith-based approach to which they were exposed at those services (PRRI-IFYC November 2021). This survey affirmed that in the case of African-Americans, an initially vaccine-hesitant group, attending services had a resoundingly net-positive effect in encouraging participation (PRRI-IFYC April 2021). In terms of perceived compatibility with the ethos of one's religious teachings in America, exhortations considered in religious settings were found to be consistent with vaccine acceptance, particularly when injunctions to "love the neighbor", a cross-cultural value affirmed across traditions, was invoked. As the survey reports:

> A majority of Americans (53%) agree with the statement "Because getting vaccinated against COVID-19 helps protect everyone, it is a way to live out the religious principle of loving my neighbors", while 44% disagree with the statement. … With the notable exceptions of white evangelical Protestants (46%) and Hispanic Protestants (49%), majorities of all major religious groups agree that getting vaccinated is a way to live out the religious principle of loving their neighbors. More than six in ten Jewish Americans (69%), Mormons (66%), non-Christian religious Americans (64%), and other Christians (61%) agree with the statement. Majorities of other Protestants of color (58%), white Catholics (57%), Hispanic Catholics (55%), white mainline Protestants (55%), religiously unaffiliated Americans (53%), and Black Protestants (52%) agree. (PRRI-IFYC April 2021)

The survey supplied compelling evidence that religious leaders are regarded as sources of authority in providing sanction for taking a vaccine, and the majority of those polled

(71%) reflected confidence that the distribution of the COVID-19 vaccine took into account the needs of religious people, including one in five (20%) who were *very* confident that the needs of religious people were being taken into account (PRRI-IFYC April 2021). Significantly, across nearly every major group, fewer than two in ten people rejected the idea that the teachings of their religion prohibited vaccinations for childhood diseases, while even fewer reported that the COVID-19 vaccine stood in conflict with their personal religious beliefs (13%), or that the teachings of their religion prohibited them from getting vaccinated for COVID-19 (10%). The survey concluded that Americans by and large believe too many people use religion as an excuse to sidestep COVID-19 vaccine requirements, with 45% going so far as to assert that in general no one should be allowed to use religion as a basis for an anti-mandate platform (PRRI-IFYC November 2021).

What, then, accounts for the uptick in the percentage of people claiming "religious freedom" as the grounds for exemption status, if, when polled, religious insiders tend not to identify their religions as a source of hesitancy or refusal? The PRRI-IFYC survey was illuminating here as well: "Beyond Fox News, the rise of far-right media outlets dramatically affect vaccine hesitancy among Republicans", with Republicans (45%) less likely than independents (58%) and Democrats (73%) to be vaccine accepters. The survey reports that attitudes towards vaccination are strongly influenced by television news consumption, the highest rates of resistance occurring among Republicans who trust far-right news sources the most (42%) (PRRI-IFYC April 2021). It turns out that even the majority of Republicans who indicated that they trusted mainstream news sources (58%) or Fox News (54%) accept vaccines. By contrast, only about three in ten Republicans who reported trusting only far-right news (32%) or no television news (30%) do so (PRRI-IFYC November 2021). These findings suggest that while religion might serve as the *claimed* reason for vaccine hesitancy and refusal, politically biased media outlets were the real reason.

Notably, Title VII, under which religious exemptions are claimed, is not invoked in the comparable case of disabled individuals who are entitled to the same accommodations as refusers considered under religious grounds. The Americans with Disabilities Act of 1990 specifies that employers should offer the same "reasonable" accommodation to disabled Americans as they do for religious Americans, yet there is no evidence that this community is availing itself of the right to this accommodation with anywhere near the same frequency as individuals who claim religious exemption status. If anything, the opposite is so: Those with disabilities report difficulty obtaining vaccines relative to the general population to the vaccines they *do* want. In one prominent study, an analysis of the National Immunization Survey Adult COVID Module (NIS-ACM), researchers concluded that in comparison to adults without a disability, those with a disability were less likely to have received a vaccination, but not for want of trying but because of comparatively restricted access. (Ryerson et al. 2021).

This contrast between religious and disabled communities becomes even more conspicuous in light of new research that establishes the correlation between political orientation, susceptibility to conspiracy theorizing, and vaccine resistance, finding that conservative worldviews that uphold vaccine resistance do so as a symbol of the exercising of freedom in society overrun by big government (Albrecht 2022). In a well-publicized recent study, Don Albrecht found that counties across the US with a high proportion of Trump voters had more per capita cases and deaths from COVID-19 than those with fewer Trump voters (Albrecht 2021). This suggests that the discussion about vaccine refusal based on resistance emanating from religious doctrine or worldview would be different in an alternative political environment. That the sincerity of held religious beliefs is no longer required might account for the conflation between exemption status *claimed* on behalf of one's religion and that actually *based* on one's religious belief, a distinction that may have not been as relevant in a previous epoch of adjudication.

5. Religious Leaders on the COVID-19 Vaccines and "Love thy Neighbor"

This emerging hypothesis and claim that it is not religion itself which directly influences the opting out of public policy is given even more circumstantial credence by the support the majority of religious leaders have lent in their own voices to public and secular vaccine efforts. There is surprising and significant agreement among leaders of the world's major religious traditions that vaccines are not about oneself but the vulnerable "other", where great theological weight is placed on the preservation of a communal good in the form of the health and safety of a population. To the extent that there are deeply held cultural or individual justifications to be hesitant about vaccination mandates, these should be balanced against other reasons. Religious exemptions should not be regarded as a birthright, but something to be evaluated in a larger context, if only to ensure that religions and their leaders are not being exploited for ideological reasons. The analysis would be otherwise if religious leaders issued some statement about what is problematic about COVID-19 vaccines, as many did in the case of HPV vaccines for reasons relatable, if not convincing, to fellow religious insiders. But religious leaders have tended either to stay silent on COVID-19 vaccines or come out resoundingly in favor of them.

The PRRI-IFCY survey notes that one of the significant developments in the era of COVID-19 in religious communities in America has been the near consensus among religious leaders to lend support for vaccination efforts, support that is grounded in resources internal to their own traditions. Such arguments are both theological and ethical in nature, often referring to communal norms and shared understandings of scripture, in general featuring no standing objection to vaccines, with only occasional caveats to known dietary restrictions (Grabenstein 2013). With regard to COVID-19 specifically, the growing number of religious groups who have come out in favor of vaccination is impressive. For example, when the mRNA vaccines first became available, leaders in the Southern Baptist community comprising theologians and professors made the following public statement:

> It is not possible to properly love a person and act so as to unnecessarily jeopardize their health. If by the minimal burden of wearing a mask, we can potentially protect others from grave illness, then it seems we have a moral obligation to wear a mask. The same can be said for COVID-19 vaccinations. If by being vaccinated we can protect others from illness, then we have a corresponding obligation, given our Lord's command to love neighbors, to be vaccinated. Vaccinations not only protect me, but also protect other vulnerable members of society. (Arbo et al. 2020)

In the same vein, tying the exhortation to get vaccinated to injunctions to cultivate compassion and keep in mind the vulnerable, the Pope instructs Catholics: "Thanks to God's grace and the work of many, we now have vaccines to protect us against COVID-19 ... Getting the vaccines that are authorized by the respective authorities is an act of love" (Juffras 2021). Likewise, the Islamic Society of America and the National Black Muslim COVID Coalition have determined that even in the event vaccines might contain non-Halal ingredients, necessity overrides prohibition. Of utmost importance is preventing the spread of a highly contagious and deadly disease that could wreak havoc in Muslim and human communities (Juffras). As for Jewish communities across all denominations, the overriding normative value of *pikuach nefesh* (the "saving of lives") takes precedence:

> Jewish law is strongly and invariably supportive of vaccination, including mandatory vaccination with suspension of non-medical exemptions if the health of the surrounding community is at stake. *Halachic* views do not provide a deterrent for Jews to inoculate; rather, it would be "*halachically irresponsible*" to not vaccinate. (Muravsky et al. 2023)

The exhortation is again unequivocal and decisively rooted in communal care for the vulnerable neighbor. These examples, ecumenically reflected across traditions, are not meant to be exhaustive or not allowing for exceptions, but representative of attitudes among leaders in the Abrahamic faiths of the West. There are no specific disclaimers in any of these instances with regard to the mRNA COVID-19 vaccines. Even when usual concerns are reported, as in the case of dietary considerations in Muslim traditions, leaders have issued a specification that this consideration should not carry the day.

Importantly, faith leaders have proactively advised their congregants *not* to worry about usual sources of ambivalence when technology rubs up against science. For example, leaders of Christian and Catholic faiths go out of their way to make known that in contrast to prior vaccines, fetal cells are not used in the creation, development, and general production of the Pfizer and Moderna mRNA vaccines (Juffras). With regard to the Abrahamic traditions, we can readily point to the injunction in Protestant and Catholic traditions from Luke 10 to "love one's neighbor as oneself", or Rabbi Hillel's inspirational instruction "if I am only for myself, what am I?" in the Jewish tradition, or the observation issued by the canonical and revered ninth century Muslim Persian theologian and scholar, Saheeh Al-Bukhari: "None of you truly believes until he loves for his brother what he loves for himself". All three of these authoritative sentiments imply an obligation to participate in population protective action when the opportunity arises because, to reiterate what public health officials are often wont to say, "the vaccine is not about you".

The larger point here, however, is that when we pay attention to context and the larger picture, evidence of a misleading tactic among exempters under the banner of "religious freedom" begins to emerge. Not only are religious exemptions typically not "religious" in nature, but they are not representative of the religious traditions they invoke. More likely, their exemptions serve as a litmus test for political power in the public square and are not really about religion at all. The familiar mantra, "my body, my choice", a rallying cry against the intrusion of big government, is in this light more plausibly interpreted as an expression of political power than the advocacy of a religious norm. (Astor 2021).

Finally, such rhetoric raises critical questions about the deployment of the terms such as "liberty" or "autonomy" in the public square. The concept of liberty is taken to safeguard individual freedom, but in the context of a pandemic liberty, counterintuitively, becomes an expression of tyranny at the level of population. In keeping with the injunctions to "love the neighbor" we have seen featured in the Abrahamic traditions, the unchecked assertion of individual rights, given biological realities and the nature of herd immunity, becomes a kind of enslavement and imposition on those who are dependent on the actions of unknown others to assure their well-being. In such a context, the "medical liberty" of one becomes a medical oppression of many. It may be that liberty is emblematic of the "American way", a familiar and prized value for which there is historical precedent. However, *this* sort of invocation is not a justification for non-participation that we are likely to hear from our religious leaders, for whom by and large, and to their credit, the welfare of all everywhere is instead the driver of what is motivating their messaging on COVID-19.

6. Religious Autonomy as a Blank Check, Christian Nationalism, and a Tension within the First Amendment

The discussion to this point has not substantively engaged the juridical arguments for or against the permissibility of considering objections to public policy that are "religious" in nature as legitimate. I have not made a legal argument. Rather, I have focused on the shift in the way in which religious objections are *de facto* currently being deployed in contrast to the recent past. "Sincerely held beliefs" is no longer the standard for religious accommodation. Individual declaration, seemingly free of any reasonable constraint, is. My aim has been to look at the consequences of this shift. The issuance of a blank check based on personal liberty to public policy is the undermining of public policy itself, particularly during a public health crisis. Finally, the argument above has been intended as an examination of the nature of belief itself and what, technically, makes it "religious" to begin with. If religious *leaders* are themselves to serve as guides, we have grounds for concluding that exemptions claimed to necessary mandates in the name of religion during public health crises constitute not only a formidable obstacle to the state's efforts to keep people safe at the level of population, but also an abuse of religious rationale. To be sure, in terms of bodily autonomy, whatever grounds for *it* can be located in the first amendment, they are not synonymous with "religious liberty".

Or, rather, the shift reflects the ascension of a particular understanding of religious belief as the template for all others, namely, one that puts the interpretative authority of scripture solely in the hands of the individual believer while preferencing a sense of belief that concentrates on the fate of that believer at the hands of an infinite and all-powerful redeemer. In such an account, there is little allowance for deference to "population-level" concerns; the will of the individual trumps objections that potentially arise even from the community or congregation. John Fea identifies this "blank check" as a kind of "cherry-picking" of notions such as "my body is my temple" roughly expressed in verses such as Luke 17: "Jesus touched the leper and healed him, so I don't need a vaccine to be healed". (Council on Foreign Relations) This logic is part of a self-protective strategy in which no mortal has the prerogative to contravene God's will:

> The vaccine is a threat on my liberty and rights as an American, but my rights and liberties as an American come from God, right? So this is not just a constitutional or Declaration of Independence, right, endowed by our creator with certain inalienable rights kind of threat. This is also a threat to the kind of divine order, the kind of nation that the United States is supposed to be. And it's deeply embedded in these ideas of Christian nationalism, or the idea that America is somehow a Christian national, is a special nation, is blessed by God. And God has given us rights in an exceptional way no other nation has. (Council on Foreign Relations)

This interpretation of the explanation of the shift to individual authority in claims of religious exemption is a kind of exceptionalism that utilizes subjectivism for purposes of nationalistic preference. In this account, rules that come from the authority of the state, especially in heterogenous, pluralistic settings, take a back seat to the imperative of Christian, and "American", interest. According to Christian nationalism, no "outside" authority is empowered to supersede native representations of one's manifest density among God's favored. At once, a radically individualistic account of choice and freedom in society is also a tribalist one, bereft of concession and compromise.

This is the state of affairs in which the current Supreme Court is presently poised to deliberate on the issue of how to interpret claimed religious exemptions. How this issue has been decided in recent cases suggests the Court will support proponents of the strong individualist/nationalist view. With regard to mitigation efforts implemented at the state level early on in the pandemic, on November 2020, in Roman Catholic Diocese of Brooklyn v. Cuomo, the Court determined New York's order violated First Amendment free exercise principles despite clear demonstration of exigent public health circumstances justifying the order, while in February 2021, the Court deemed unconstitutional a similar ban on indoor religious gatherings in Southern Bay United Pentecostal Church v. Newsom (Hodge 2022). In April of the same year, the Court again restricted the state's right to impose mitigation efforts, granting an injunction in another key case against regulations limiting at-home Bible studies. What these recent cases suggest is that public health concerns, which are population-level considerations, shall not take precedence over individual religious prerogative.

While it remains to be seen what the Supreme Court ultimately does with regard to upholding mandates in the case of FDA approved vaccines shown to be highly effective against contagious and deadly diseases such as COVID-19, it should be noted that the deference in these recent cases given to unqualified assertion of individual religious belief signals a resolution to a tension manifest within the First Amendment. The "free exercise" clause of the First Amendment has long been interpreted to safeguard citizens' rights to practice their religion in their own way on the condition that such practicing is compliant with upholding compelling governmental interests (Religious Freedom Restoration Act 1993). This check on the basic liberty of religious freedom is no longer to be taken for granted. The "liberty" of the First Amendment is precisely that no one is to be subject to tyranny: *neither* religious minorities seeking to practice their faith in a society where most practice the majority faith, *nor* third parties environmentally enslaved by the exercise of harmful religious prerogatives. It is a fallacy to think that "my body, my choice", implemented as an unchallenged right without this standard internal check on the "free exercise" clause, will never lead to more harm than good. The rare mandate to keep the public safe during a pandemic defined by a deadly and contagious virus is meant to ensure the liberty of all, not just some. An analogy can here be drawn to the Second Amendment. The "freedom" entailed in the right to bear arms can, under tragic circumstances, can come to entail the deprivation of the very notion of liberty it is meant to uphold. Just ask parents who trusted the safety of their children in public spaces only to be informed after the fact, helplessly, that they lost their children in a mass shooting. In a "free" society they have become the victims of the tyranny of an environment unsafe for their children which they were powerless to alter. Full, unrestrained freedom can be the undoing of freedom.

7. Conclusion: Fractured Community, The Rise of Individualism, and the New Meaning of "Liberty" in Contemporary Society

In *Age of Fracture*, Daniel Rodgers argues that in the last three decades of the twentieth century the US experienced a key cultural paradigm shift during which we began to think less about populations and communal values and instead emphasized individual liberties. (Rodgers 2011) Classical liberal notions of "social justice" and "fairness" gave way to the prizing of the principle of autonomy and free choice, understood on the left to be a flexibility with which one could define one's own identity, and on the right to indicate a new preoccupation with unregulated markets, the promise of upward mobility, and the prioritization of the downsizing of the role of oversight in government. For the last half century, the ground has been made fertile for a broad and sweeping undermining of state-issued powers, even when exercised for the good of the people, for example, in the form of preventive, health-protective policy-making. It is in this context that the assertion of "religious rights" has come to be reinterpreted as an extension of this presumptive prerogative of autonomy and, correspondingly, as a challenge to a history of precedent-setting Supreme Court decisions over the previous century that had previously imposed checks and balances on the expression of religiosity and the importance of individual belief within the larger society. This development is not so much an overcoming of the "separation of church and state" as it is a holding at bay church *and* state in deference to the ideology of individualism and the unfettered expression of belief.

This historical context perhaps explains why there is no coherent basis, particularly in the Abrahamic traditions on display in the present examination, to reject policies in which COVID-19 vaccines come to be mandated. For, in such a social environment there *need* be no coherent basis. The first order assertion of one's claim to individual expression of belief is all one needs. The current pandemic, during which, for a time, in certain environments (e.g., health care settings in this country), mandates became a crucial part of the toolkit in the "mitigation effort", is just one case study. However, the thought experiment in which we consider how things might play out over the next pandemic, likely not another hundred years away this time around, is illuminating. Without a system of checks and balances where the assertion of exemption on the basis of individual belief is all one needs to opt out, no pandemic can be deemed to be too severe, nor the consequences of not contributing to herd immunity considered to be too grave, to deprive one of the autonomous right to assert dominion over one's body. This development would represent a total triumph of the ethos Rodgers describes emerging over the last twentieth century. If it lasts, it signals the death of communal action, shared values, civic policy-making, and ultimately public health itself.

In such a future, actions of "liberty" collectively risk being repurposed for an enduring state of tyranny, especially for the most vulnerable among us who depend on the taking of health-protective action among, and on behalf of, strangers. Such an attitude could not have helped us to overcome the spread of cholera in the 19th century when, with the revelation of the contaminated Broad Street water pump in London, it was quickly understood that clean water is something in which we all have a common interest (Smith 2002). The brainchild of dot maps, because of which the contaminated pump could in the first place be located, is itself an innovation of collective action. The basic tools of public health, not just vaccines or compulsory policies, depend on a notion of the individual that is reliant on, and to an extent deferential to, the society of which it is a part.

I have also tried to argue, however, that it is not just policymaking and the concerted efforts of public health leaders that are weakened by the unnuanced and ultimately poorly understood interpretation of the unchecked right to religious expression as reflected in the First Amendment. Religion itself, and in particular the significance of the longevity and congregation-forming aspects of religious community, also hang in the balance. When religious leaders go out of their way to endorse the COVID-19 vaccines as safe and effective instruments against a plague, they do so not merely out of love of their flock, but also from a position of authority as ambassadors of their respective traditions. Among other things, *as* religious leaders, they are presumably depending on the good historical influence that religion has many times over had on the secular affairs in the society where that tradition is prevalent. In other words, their authority is legitimate because, again to return to a notion popularized by William James, of the fruits (they are in the best position to show) their religion has borne over time (James 1985, p. 19). Religion and religious expression are meant to work with the world, not apart from, and certainly not against, it. All the more reason the standard criterion of "sincerely held beliefs" makes sense. The alternative, ideological assertion, is a shortcut as well as a failure to embrace the authority of religious communities and the legal conventions of the nation.

Funding: This research received no external funding.

Conflicts of Interest: The author declares no conflict of interest.

Note

1 I thank an anonymous reviewer of Religions for calling my attention to this exacerbating nuance about the fragmentation of religious experience in the American context.

References

Adams, Ben, and Cynthia Barmore. 2014. "The Role of the Courts After Hobby Lobby", 67 STAN. L. REV. ONLINE 59. November 7. Available online: http://www.stanfordlawreview.org/wp-content/uploads/sites/3/2014/11/67_Stan_L_Rev_Online_59_AdamsBarmore.pdf (accessed on 21 December 2022).

Adams, Carolyn E., and Michael B. Leverland. 1986. The Effects of Religious Beliefs on the Health Care Practices of the Amish. *The Nurse Practitioner* 11: 58–67. [CrossRef] [PubMed]

Africa v. Commonwealth of Pennsylvania. 1981. 662 F.2d 1025. Available online: https://law.resource.org/pub/us/case/reporter/F2/662/662.F2d.1025.81-2325.html (accessed on 21 December 2022).

Albrecht, Don E. 2021. COVID-19 in rural America: Impacts of politics and disadvantage. *Rural Sociology* 86: 1–25. [CrossRef] [PubMed]

Albrecht, Don E. 2022. Vaccination, politics and COVID-19 impacts. *BMC Public Health* 22: 96. [CrossRef] [PubMed]

American Bar Association. 2022. Two Centuries of Law Guide Legal Approach to Modern Pandemic April 2022. Available online: https://www.americanbar.org/news/abanews/publications/youraba/2020/youraba-april-2020/law-guides-legal-approach-to-pandemic/ (accessed on 21 December 2022).

Anders, Cameo C. 2020. Individual and Institutional Religious Exemptions from Vaccines. *The National Catholic Bioethics Quarterly* 20: 501–23. [CrossRef]

Arbo, Matthew, Ben Mitchell, and Andrew Walker. 2020. Why We Plan to get Vaccinated: A Christian Moral Perspective. *The Journal of Witherspoon Institute*. December 8. Available online: https://www.thepublicdiscourse.com/2020/12/73110/ (accessed on 21 December 2022).

Asser, Seth M., and Rita Swan. 1998. Child fatalities from religion-motivated medical neglect. *Pediatrics* 101, Pt 1: 625–29. [CrossRef] [PubMed]

Astor, Maggie. 2021. Vaccination mandates are an American Tradition. So is the Backlash. Available online: https://www.nytimes.com/2021/09/09/us/politics/vaccine-mandates-history.html (accessed on 21 December 2022).

Beauchamp, Tom L., and James F. Childress. 2001. *Principles of Biomedical Ethics*, 5th ed. New York: Oxford University Press.

Blank, Nina R., Arthur Caplan, and Catherine Constable. 2013. Exempting Schoolchildren from Immunizations: States with Few Barriers Had Highest Rates of Nonmedical Exemptions. *Health Affairs* 32: 1282–90. Available online: https://www.healthaffairs.org/doi/10.1377/hlthaff.2013.0239 (accessed on 21 December 2022). [CrossRef] [PubMed]

Buchanan, Allen E., and Dan W. Brock. 1990. *Deciding for Others: The Ethics of Surrogate Decision Making*. New York: Cambridge University Press.

Burwell v. Hobby Lobby Stores. 2014. 573 U.S. 682. Available online: https://supreme.justia.com/cases/federal/us/573/682/#:~:text=Hobby%20Lobby%20Stores%2C%20Inc.%2C%20573%20U.S.%20682%20 (accessed on 21 December 2022).

Catholic Medical Association. 2007. Catholic Medical Association Position Paper on HPV Immunization. Available online: https://www.cathmed.org/assets/files/Position%20Paper%20on%20HPV%20Immunization.pdf (accessed on 21 December 2022).

Civil Rights Act. 1964. Available online: https://www.archives.gov/milestone-documents/civil-rights-act (accessed on 21 December 2022).

Council on Foreign Relations. 2021. COVID-19 Vaccines and Religious Exemptions (Tuesday, November 30th) | Council on Foreign Relations. Available online: https://www.cfr.org/event/covid-19-vaccines-and-religious-exemptions (accessed on 21 December 2022).

Flescher, Andrew, and Geoffrey Kabat. 2018. 'Heard Immunity': In an Age of Skepticism, it is Critical to Understand Heard Immunity. *Forbes*. February 16. Available online: https://www.forbes.com/sites/geoffreykabat/2018/02/26/heard-immunity/?sh=42bedecf1399 (accessed on 21 December 2022).

Gillon, Raanan. 2003. Ethics Needs Principles–Four Can Encompass the Rest—And Respect for Autonomy Should be "First Among Equals". *Journal of Medical Ethics* 29: 307–12. [CrossRef] [PubMed]

Glover, Jonathan. 1977. *Causing Death and Saving Lives*. Harmondsworth: Penguin.

Grabenstein, John D. 2013. What the World's religions teach, applied to vaccines and immune globulins. *Vaccine* 31: 2011–23. [CrossRef] [PubMed]

Hodge, James G., Jr. 2022. Constitutional Recognition of Religious Exemptions to Vaccination Requirements. *Canopy Forum*, June 10. Available online: https://canopyforum.org/2022/06/08/constitutional-recognition-of-religious-exemptions-to-vaccination-requirements/ (accessed on 21 December 2022).

Jacobson v. Massachusetts. 1905. 197 US. 11. Available online: https://tile.loc.gov/storage-services/service/ll/usrep/usrep197/usrep197011/usrep197011.pdf (accessed on 21 December 2022).

James, William. 1985. *The Varieties of Religious Experience*. New York: Penguin.

Juffras, Diane. 2021. An in Depth Look at Religious Exemptions from COVID-19 Vaccine Mandates. (Blog). Available online: https://canons.sog.unc.edu/2021/10/an-in-depth-look-at-religious-exemptions-from-covid-19-vaccine-mandates/ (accessed on 21 December 2022).

Kuehn, Bridget M. 2020. Urgent Action Needed to Prevent Measles, Polio Resurgence. *JAMA* 324: 2356. [CrossRef] [PubMed]

Linnard-Palmer, Luanne, and Ellen Christiansen. 2021. *Against Medical Advice*, 2nd ed. Sigma Theta Tau Honors Society of Nursing. Chapter 9: "Overview of Religious Doctrines". Indianapolis: Sigma Theta Tau International.

Muravsky, Nicole L., Grace M. Betesh, and Rozalina G. McCoy. 2023. Religious Doctrine and Attitudes Toward Vaccination in Jewish Law. *Journal of Religion and Health* 62: 373–88. [CrossRef] [PubMed]

PRRI-IFYC April. 2021. Faith-Based Approaches Can Positively Impact COVID-19 Vaccination Efforts: Religious Identities and the Race Against the Virus (April 22). Available online: www.prri.org/research/prri-ifyc-covid-vaccine-religion-report/ (accessed on 21 December 2022).

PRRI-IFYC November. 2021. Religious Identities and the Race Against the Virus: Successes and Opportunities for Engaging Faith Communities on COVID-19 Vaccination (November 28). Available online: https://www.prri.org/research/religious-identities-and-the-race-against-the-virus-american-attitudes-on-vaccination-mandates-and-religious-exemptions/ (accessed on 21 December 2022).

Reiss, Dorit Rubinstein. 2014. Thou Shalt Not Take the Name of the Lord Thy God in Vain: Use and Abuse of Religious Exemptions from School Immunization Requirements. 65 Hastings L.J. 1551. Available online: https://repository.uchastings.edu/hastings_law_journal/vol65/iss6/5 (accessed on 21 December 2022).

Religious Freedom Restoration Act. 1993. Public Law 141, 103rd Cong., 1st Sess. (November 16). STATUTE-107-Pg1488.pdf. Available online: https://www.govinfo.gov/ (accessed on 21 December 2022).

Rodgers, Daniel T. 2011. *Age of Fracture*. Cambridge: Belknap Press.

Roosevelt, Franklin D. 1944. *Statement of the President on Signing the Public Health Service Act-July 1944*. Internet Archive. Washington, DC: National Archives and Records Service, pp. 191–93.

Rota, Jennifer S., Daniel A. Salmon, Lance E. Rodewald, Robert T. Chen, Beth F. Hibbs, and Eugene J. Gangarosa. 2001. Processes for obtaining nonmedical exemptions to state immunization laws. *American Journal of Public Health* 91: 645–48. [CrossRef] [PubMed]

Ryerson, A. Blythe, Catherine E. Rice, Mei-Chuan Hung, Suchita A. Patel, Julie D. Weeks, Jennifer L. Kriss, Georgina Peacock, Peng-Jun Lu, Amimah F. Asif, Hannah L. Jackson, and et al. 2021. Disparities in COVID-19 Vaccination Status, Intent, and Perceived Access for Noninstitutionalized Adults, by Disability Status—National Immunization Survey Adult COVID Module, United States, May 30–June 26, 2021. *Morbidity and Mortality Weekly Report* 70: 1365–71. [CrossRef] [PubMed]

Shachar, Carmel. 2022. Understanding Vaccine Hesitancy and Refusal Through Rights-Based Framework. *American Journal of Public Health* 122: 229–31. [CrossRef] [PubMed]

Smith, George Davey. 2002. Commentary: Behind the Broad Street pump: Aetiology, epidemiology and prevention of cholera in mid-19th century Britain. *International Epidemiology Association* 31: 920–32. Available online: http://ije.oxfordjournals.org/content/31/5/920.full.pdf (accessed on 21 December 2022). [CrossRef] [PubMed]

United States v. Ballard. 1944. 322 U.S. 78. Available online: https://supreme.justia.com/cases/federal/us/322/78/ (accessed on 21 December 2022).

United States v. Seeger. 1965. 380 U.S. 163. Available online: https://supreme.justia.com/cases/federal/us/380/163/ (accessed on 21 December 2022).

US Department of Health and Human Services. 2019. Public Health Emergency: Public Health and Medical Emergency Support for a Nation Prepared. Last Updated. Available online: Phe.gov/Preparedness/legal/Pages/phe-qa.aspx#:~:text=Under%20section%20319%20of%20the,%2C%20or%202)%20a%20PHE%2C (accessed on 21 December 2022).

US Department of Labor. 2014. Religious Discrimination and Accommodation in the Federal Workplace. Available online: https://www.dol.gov/agencies/oasam/civil-rights-center/internal/policies/religious-discrimination-accommodation (accessed on 21 December 2022).

Wisconsin v. Yoder. 1972. 406 U.S. Available online: https://supreme.justia.com/cases/federal/us/406/205/ (accessed on 21 December 2022).

Wojcik, Mark E. 2022. Sincerely Held or Suddenly Held Religious Exemptions to Vaccination? 47 Hum. Rts. 20. Available online: https://www.americanbar.org/groups/crsj/publications/human_rights_magazine_home/intersection-of-lgbtq-rights-and-religious-freedom/sincerely-held-or-suddenly-held/ (accessed on 21 December 2022).

Yeh, Ming-Jui. 2022. Solidarity in Pandemics, Mandatory Vaccination, and Public Health Ethics. *American Journal of Public Health* 112: 255–61. [CrossRef] [PubMed]

religions MDPI

Article

The Arbitrariness of Faith-Based Medical Exemptions

Aaron Quinn

Department of Journalism & Public Relations, California State University Chico, Chico, CA 95929, USA; amquinn@csuchico.edu

Abstract: There are a variety of reasons for which one might claim an exemption from a public health mandate such as a required COVID-19 vaccine. Good-faith exemption requests—for medical, religious, or other reasons—are generally recognized as legitimate and granted to individuals when the imposition of the mandate on the requestor is perceived to outweigh the corresponding risk their lack of vaccination poses to the health and rights of others. This paper develops a method of analysis rooted in Western analytic philosophy designed to examine these issues and arrive at a framework for assessing the scientific, moral, and religious claims for exemptions from COVID-19 vaccinations. I argue that some empirical and moral beliefs are epistemically superior to others when they have a correspondence with agreed-upon facts about the world, are grounded in shared human experience, employ strong and substantive reasons for their claims, and embrace common convictions evidenced in the character of moral agents. Such facts must be demonstrable in the form of observably verifiable evidence and reliable testimony. Only then should a request for an exemption to an otherwise-required public health mandate (including a vaccine) be recognized. The alternative creates various difficulties, including the problem of moral arbitrariness.

Keywords: COVID-19; vaccine exemption; virtue theory; epistemology; empiricism; skepticism; religious faith; belief; vaccine mandates; moral decision-making

Citation: Quinn, Aaron. 2023. The Arbitrariness of Faith-Based Medical Exemptions. *Religions* 14: 934. https://doi.org/10.3390/rel14070934

Academic Editors: Andrew Flescher and Joel Zimbelman

Received: 30 January 2023
Revised: 31 March 2023
Accepted: 6 April 2023
Published: 19 July 2023

1. Introduction

This essay asks whether, in the context of making public health policy, claims for, and the granting of, religious exemptions for COVID-19 vaccinations meet *prima facie* ethical and epistemological standards for such requests insofar as such exemptions are recognized as "reasonable," that is, justifiable, legitimate, compelling, and authoritative. To explore this issue, I employ two distinct though synergistic philosophical fields, namely (1) epistemology (the study of knowledge) and its grounding in an empiricist scientific methodology; and (2) normative ethics and its instantiation in virtue theory. I use this approach to analyze various claims for medical and religious exemptions to COVID-19 vaccines, particularly because medical and scientific reasoning, as well as analytic philosophical reasoning, are both committed to the scientific method of inquiry.

Many scholars exploring cultural or spiritual rationales for impactful and policy-forming beliefs advance or examine various versions of reason-giving and moral justification provided by various religious traditions. While members of a given religious community might be moved by the arguments advanced by their own tradition on the issues under consideration, there is no guarantee that they will find compelling the descriptive or normative claims of those in other—including various secular—traditions. I seek to provide a non-religiously grounded entry into this debate, and one that commends to religious and non-religious thinkers, alike, a set of presuppositions and starting points for critical reflection and policy development around the myriad of issues related to COVID-19 and public health. While secular and employing the analytic tools of philosophy, the empirical method I favor, which legitimates modern science and advances a theory of morality that links judgements of specific acts and practices to the consistent character of the individuals who advance such normative claims, should be seen itself as one voice in the conversation among diverse traditions. Unlike the parochial and partial perspectives of various religious voices, however, it has more to commend it, strategically and practically speaking. I hope to show how Western analytic epistemology and one version of a normative secular virtue ethic inform beliefs and justifications that can be morally compelling for secular thinkers, even for individuals from various global religious and cultural traditions. The ethico-epistemic methodology I embrace suggests that in order to make good moral decisions one needs to be properly informed regarding the facts tantamount to moral decision-making, particularly in complex cases in which moral intuitions are unable to provide adequate guidance in making such decisions. Additionally, it asserts that specific ways of reasoning from such facts, and what those facts imply about the sorts of humans we are, must be accounted for in our moral judgments, decisions, and even in the shaping of our public health policies.

This paper will evaluate and assess three sorts of claims for and against vaccine exemptions: (1) those advanced by people with medical claims to exemptions; (2) those advanced by people with religious claims to exemptions; and (3) claims advanced by a broader population of agents whose well-being might be compromised by the spread of COVID-19 through those who are granted vaccine exemptions for whatever reason. These foci serve as the basis for formulating and exploring three questions:

(1) Can select medical diagnoses establish an ethico-epistemic standard upon which to support the request for COVID-19 vaccination exemptions in light of current public health standards and practices?
(2) Can religious beliefs establish an ethico-epistemic standard upon which to grant COVID-19 vaccination exemptions in light of current public health standards and practices?
(3) Can at-large members of society establish an ethico-epistemic standard that can successfully ground a normative claim that would require other members of the society to submit to appropriate COVID-19 vaccination mandates even against their will?

In what follows, I acknowledge that there are diverse forms of religious reasoning and that those who are religious, or who at least tend to find reasoning which proceeds from religious premises to be the most persuasive, might naturally object to what they see as a favoritism displayed on my part towards a non-sectarian methodology. While fully respecting the *de facto* nature of different means of arriving at "truth" in the process of policy-making, I nevertheless argue that a secular approach, while not totally free from making errors, represents our best chance of approximating accuracy, accommodating inevitably divergent perspectives in pluralistic, non-homogeneous settings like the ones reflected in our society, and, as such, is the one which is most commensurate with pursuing the ideal of objectivity.

2. Epistemology and the Basis for Believing

Epistemology—or the study of knowledge—is a branch of Western philosophy that, among other things, focuses on whether or how we can come to know facts about the world as a way to attain, in the words of Steup and Ram, "cognitive success" (Steup and Ram 2020). The term derives from the Greek word *episteme*, meaning "knowledge," or "understanding." One of the most common definitions of knowledge is a "justified, true belief," (hereafter JTB) that is grounded in a tripartite analysis of knowledge (Gettier 1963; Ichikawa and Steup 2017), structured as follows:

S knows that *p* if and only if:

- *p* is true
- *S* believes that *p*
- *S* is justified in believing that *p*

Here is an example of how such justified belief arises. I can claim with high confidence that the statement "Sacramento is the current capital of California" is a justified true belief (JTB) of mine, because it is true; I believe it; and I am justified in believing it. I can argue the claim is true because of a decision made by state leaders long ago. I believe it is true because of my experience of what it means for a city to be a capital. Additionally, I have only encountered assertions that Sacramento is the current capital of California and I have never encountered an assertion that claims a different current capital of California. All of these experiences provide me with an empirical basis for the establishment of my belief. No existing text or person has ever contradicted this experience. Finally, and because of the truth claim, the nature of the evidence, and the way I have come to believe that truth, I am justified in believing the status of Sacramento as California's capital.

While this logic seems basic enough, it is crucially relevant to any analysis of what circumstances there are, if any, which warrant exempting oneself from the law of the land when that law is meant to safeguard the well-being and health of a population. Can private beliefs which do not accommodate universalization ever be authoritatively cited as a means of legitimately not adhering to laws intended to apply to everyone for the sake of the good of everyone? I argue that the final conclusion of the tripartite—justified belief—can be a useful tool for validating many of our assertions in various practical contexts, including the key example from public health of vaccine exemption this essay considers. At the same time, the tripartite analysis of knowledge as the means of arriving at JTBs is not without challenges, problems, and limitations. To demonstrate challenges with the JTB tripartite theory let me raise two additional issues.

First, if I have established that an assertion is true and that I believe it, why should there be a need for a justification beyond that it's true? In other words, when it comes to what I will refer to as *simple claims of knowledge*, the fact that a statement is true itself should be enough justification for one's belief, because steps two and three of the tripartite are redundant. Thus, one could argue that simply establishing "true belief" is sufficient to justifying that belief, again, when this involves simple claims such as the one asserting Sacramento as California's capital. What happens, however, when the claims being advanced are what might be called "complex claims to knowledge"? A 1963 paper by Edmund Gettier titled "Is Justified True Belief Knowledge" offered cases in which justified true belief was derived from a false, but apparently justified, belief (Gettier 1963). Dreyfus (1997, p. 292) offered one such case when he described someone searching for water on a hot day. The water-seeker suddenly sees what she believes is water in the distance. In fact, what she observes is a mirage. However, when she follows the mirage, there just happens to be water there. For Gettier and Dreyfus, both, the case in question reveals that the JTB may establish the set of necessary though not sufficient conditions for knowledge. It is likely a necessary set of conditions, but what more is necessary still seems unsettled in the literature (Dreyfus 1997).

Let me offer another example of such a challenge from the early days of the COVID-19 pandemic in 2020. At that time, many independent physicians and public health officials proposed that shoppers wash or sterilize food, the bags in which the food was transported, and the surfaces that they might have touched before sanitization. What these officials generally knew was that many or most viruses are killed on contact with certain sterilizing agents. What they did not know was whether (armed with little evidence to support their assertions and policy recommendations) those sterilizing agents could be applied effectively to COVID-19 in the way they suggested. As more and better empirical evidence became available, such recommendations were eventually found to be excessively cautious or unproductively ineffective, not efficacious for slowing the spread of the virus. Were these individuals wrong in initially asserting their recommendations and policies regarding such precautions? Given the range of unknowns concerning the natural history of COVID-19, the virus's initial risk to some individuals and groups, and the lack of society's preparation in addressing the emerging pandemic, it seemed clear to many that the beliefs, concerns, cost-benefit analysis, and precautions that undergirded these early and provisional public health practices were initially justified. Similarly, recommendations for broad public masking, social distancing, isolating, and quarantining were also proposed in several contexts in response to the best construal of the data and out of a similar abundance of caution. In hindsight these appear to have been part of an overall life-saving strategy, even if not yet fully justified at the time they were implemented. Both recommendations were made without complete empirical data or scientific certainty, and not all of them turned out to be fully accurate. Taken together, however, they were arguably justified in the context of an early-stage pandemic and in a manner consistent with the fundamental methodological principles of public health based on empirical evidence. Still, there was a public trust cost with regard to treating these health measures as beyond questioning (Frieden 2022).

A second limitation with claims of the necessity and sufficiency of JTB's tripartite structure and components surfaces when we note that most of our concerns in applied or practical epistemology and ethics are not simple, definitional truth claims like "Sacramento is the capital of California". The city's status was simply asserted and legally decreed once a set of procedural and material criteria were met and agreed to. As a result, it serves as a facile example to test the adequacy of the theory of JTB. Employing such an example to establish an epistemic theory fails to appreciate the complexity of how we come to justify more complex truth claims.

In contrast, a more interesting epistemic challenge arises from an assertion such as the statement: "Sacramento is the *right* city to be the capital of California." This formulation raises a range of practical questions that puts significant pressure on the sufficiency of the tripartite structure of arriving at JTB. In this formulation, there is room for debate, empirical error, divergent judgements, various readings of the facts, and even a recognition that miscalculations of several aspects of what hierarchy of needs might be best for a capital city are likely. One could assume an evolving debate about whether a particular placement of the capital is justified, with that decision ultimately based on how well informed decision-makers were in the past, and what anticipated or unanticipated new information might surface over time. What should a capital city be like? What aspects of those criteria are held by Sacramento and other competing cities? How might the construal of facts (and the way we apprehend such facts) inform our belief about the truth claims made on behalf of the city, and what would it mean to justify such a claim in ways that meet our provisional definition of JTB? Finally, how might cultural, political, and ethical considerations shape our evolving sense of what the "right" choice might be?

It appears as if the establishment of any JTB will have to factor in many, potentially opposing, value-laden moral considerations in some way. Even the basic example above raises a host of concerns about employing exclusively the tripartite establishment of JTP as the basis for all of our claims to legitimate judgement and action. Indeed, a straightforward example like this, complicated only a bit beyond its "facile" formulation, serves to exemplify how tricky it might be ever to arrive at "true, justified belief", and thus calls into question the prospect of agreeing upon rules to live by "universally". More will have to be established if we are to place special faith in regulatory health guidelines intended for a *population* of individuals.

3. Augmenting Epistemic Claims with Moral Commitment and Virtue Theory

These limitations noted, I maintain that JTB is nevertheless essential to our ability to publicly and coherently justify the choices that we make for ourselves, and in our capacity as moral agents who sometimes critique, interrogate, or uphold society's actions, choices, and mandates. Science and empiricism are non-negotiable bases of the claims of medicine and public health. Their epistemic assertions are essential for assessing the legitimacy of beliefs about COVID-19 and responses to it. At the same time, if a large part of our lives is composed of encounters with truth claims and counterclaims that cannot be demonstrated in unambiguous and straightforward ways that employ the tripartite structure of arriving at JTB, and if we cannot always establish a certain ground for our truth claims, then we must shift our task away from a narrow focus on establishing simple JTBs and augment such commitments with additional tools that can help us justify our beliefs in the absence of a fully demonstrable truth. This realization is nothing new. Many concerns of practical epistemology involve accounting for moral values and ethical commitments, and these debates must go forward regardless of whether we can attain the complete and coherent knowledge of the truth that we need. What additional considerations and tools might assist us in this endeavor?

Making the right decision is hard, and public health decisions in times of crisis reveal how intractable that process can be. Justified beliefs and actions require recourse to logic, but also consideration of our shared values that we claim are essential to life in community. Given the complexity of many decisions made in the medical and public health professions, I want to argue for a need—beyond the knowledge generated by the JTP—of moral commitments as the practical foundation for the normative claims made in the fields of ethics and public health.

There are a range of approaches to morality that might be considered for this task. Most pervasive in the literature of medicine and public health is principlism, popularized in the work of Tom Beauchamp and Jim Childress (Beauchamp and Childress 2019). Principlism judges the moral rightness or wrongness of an action by whether or not that action can be justified using one of a number of discreet and well defined substantial moral principles that possess broad appeal across various cultures and traditions. In this approach to morality, the rightness or wrongness of an action is a function not of the character of the moral actor *per se*, but of whether or not the action under analysis can be justified in a compelling way in terms of a given moral principle. Beauchamp and Childress identify four critical principles: non-maleficence, respect for autonomy, beneficence, and justice (ibid).

In spite of its comprehensiveness, coherence, relative simplicity, compatibility with our moral experience and considered intuitions, and provisional compatibility with much of the moral teaching of various religious and secular communities, principlism is an inadequate method of ethics for the project we are developing. Its weakness is that it fails to explicitly account for the need of moral actors to instantiate in their own person the substance of morality. This is particularly true in the context of public health, where the credibility of spokespersons, policy developers, agencies, and governments are crucial in establishing the trust needed in a complex, sometimes ambiguous, and politically inflected context. Because of this, we must explore an approach to ethics that can account for the considered values that we hold as important, captured in the substance of critical moral principles, but one that also informs both our view of the importance of moral agents and allows a means legitimately to assess those agents as viable and trustworthy in dealing with the important health aspects of our individual and corporate lives. In other words, we need to explore the viability of a virtue theory of morality, one that centers moral decision-making on agents and inculcates in them the characters, dispositions, motivations, and commitments needed to act effectively and in a manner in which they can establish trust and lead to good action.

Aristotle's *Nicomachean Ethics* is a good place to begin this process of exploration because of Aristotle's concurrent commitments to establishing an empirically grounded, agent-centered, psychologically aware, critically astute, and politically and culturally sensitive appreciation of how morality functions in complex situations in life. These elements are precisely the attributes that are most important as we think about what regulations or guidelines could be universalized in response to COVID-19. Aristotle developed what has become known as the *ergon* argument, which states: "[e]very art and every inquiry, and similarly every action and pursuit, is thought to aim at some good; and for this reason the good has rightly been declared to be that at which all things aim ... the end of the medical art is health, that of shipbuilding a vessel, that of strategy victory, that of economics wealth" (Aristotle 2009, Book I, chap. 1). For something to become a rule that is meant to be binding on the individuals in a population, it has to demonstrably lead to the flourishing good of that population. Applied to our current situation, the research, production, and distribution of COVID-19 vaccines fits well in this mold of the "art" of medicine, which is to bring about good health. From the perspective of an Aristotelian construal of right action, the moral role of public health practitioners—consistent with the declared ends of public health—is to determine what steps regarding vaccine use will reduce harm and enhance individual and community health based on our knowledge and our justified beliefs (Oakley and Cocking 2001). Public health professionals, then, are called upon to embrace the specific epistemic principles that will guide that moral function of harm reduction and health enhancement by integrating their reading of the facts of the situation, gathered data, and the best justification for their moral commitments.

Aristotle provides the rudimentary impetus for this move, and Aristotelian virtue theory, which hinges on the "ergon," or *function* of any action in pursuance of the human good, has been widely assessed and elaborated in contemporary scholarship by philosophers as various and influential as Philippa Foot (1978), Gertrude Elizabeth Margaret Anscombe (1958), Bernard Williams (1985), Alisdair MacIntyre (1985), Michael Slote (1992), and Christine Swanton (2003), all of whom help to construct the bridge between our epistemic commitments to provisional JTB and the virtue theory of role-related morality. What constitutes flourishing, including healthful flourishing, is not an *arbitrary* construct, but rather a refined assessment of the particular animal a human being is and judgment about what that being requires to participate in the good. In Aristotelian virtue ethics, opt-outs are not easily tolerated when the individual who is opting out negatively impacts the pursuit of these humanly flourishing ends in others.

If we accept the power of the Aristotelian construction of morality in role-related virtue theory and embrace our earlier commitment to empirical scientific reasoning as the basis for establishing truth claims, the task before us is to determine how best to bring these two elements together in a functional model of research, public health, and policy. The insights of three contemporary epistemologists can be invoked to elucidate the point. In *Science as Social Knowledge*, Helen Longino argues that belief justifications ought to be made based on sound scientific reasoning, even in the absence of empirical certainty (Longino 1990). "[T]o say that a theory or hypothesis was accepted on the basis of objective methods does not guarantee that it is true, but it does–if anything does–justify us in asserting that it is true" (p. 268). C.A.J. Coady's work in social epistemology grapples with the enduring dilemma that we have when faced with individuals or institutions that claim to be asserting the truth or suggesting that their pronouncements should serve as the basis for justified truth claims (Coady 1992). Coady provides various reasons for why one might or might not believe—or not be justified in believing—a person's testimony. For Coady, the trustworthiness of a testifier is supported by several conditions, including one's expertise in a given matter, whether that person has been historically reliable in truth-telling, and whether that person exhibits other traits that make someone epistemically reliable. Finally, in his insightful and synthetic *A Virtue Epistemology*, Ernest Sosa blends epistemic and normative principles to establish a functional and complex foundation for the justification of true belief (Sosa 2007). Sosa likens ethico-epistemic judgments to a skilled archer's shooting in three distinct ways. First, there is the judgment of whether the arrow hits the target—its *accuracy*. Second, there is the question of whether the archer's accurate shot makes use of his skill. This skill is what Sosa calls *adroitness*. Third, Sosa asks whether a successful shot from the archer resulted from his adroitness or mere luck. If it is skill that led to the accurate shot, this is called *aptness*.

According to all three of these thinkers, in lieu of deductive certainty, which real-world situations rarely, if ever, make available, we have a duty of intellectual honesty to tether justificatory warrants to the wealth of information that can be gleaned from past experience, often relayed through the meaningful testimony of established authorities. Experience matters a great deal in terms of establishing trust of authorities. Sosa's three principles of accuracy, adroitness, and aptness, for example, are essential to establishing and providing a test for judgment of the beliefs that we form in response to our interactions with people, facts, and events in our daily lives. To claim a belief is justified in this model, any epistemic successes must arise by way of adroitness, yet the theory also accounts for practitioners who, despite their general skill (adroitness), don't always hit the target. For example, a public health practitioner in early-stage COVID-19 might have recommended that people wear masks in public gatherings, even in airy outdoor areas with ample sunlight when gatherings were only brief. It's reasonable that, with limited information and inadequate data, the practitioner did not possess perfect knowledge of the efficacy of the normative claims on which recommendations of provisional public policy were based. The person, generally speaking, is apt to make accurate judgments, but in that instance, missed the mark for lack of accuracy. Nonetheless, given the complexity of the task before them, they performed reasonably well and acted in a manner justified by the competing claims of epistemic coherence and moral commitment to which they are committed.

According to the functional ethico-epistemic model elaborated by Longino, Coady, and Sosa, to lay a legitimate foundation for the attainment of knowledge one must commit to scientific reasoning consistent with the scientific method, which is presumably what constitutes *scientific objectivity*. This requires one to observe, form a negative hypothesis, venture a provisional prediction, engage in experimentation, and then analyze the results either to confirm the hypothesis or advance a new testable negative hypothesis. At the same time—because many sources of prospective knowledge related to pandemic concerns are public health professionals—it is essential that any proffered testimony be trustworthy. In this context, one is typically judged trustworthy based on a track record of adroitness, but, as discussed above, with some tolerance for error in respect to accuracy. Additionally, public health officials must be correct in their judgments, but in the absence of certainty they must be adequately qualified to have made an imperfect or even flawed policy decision, and to have shown sincerity throughout the process by acknowledging the admission of failure when failure occurs. These three attributes, taken together, offer a substantive moral and epistemic groundwork for analyzing public health decisions.

4. Applying the Ethico-Epistemic Framework to Public Health and COVID-19 Vaccine Policy

To attain an exceptional level of certainty in many practical areas of life, including public health, is rare. Certainty is relatively attainable with regard to the sorts of simple claims mentioned earlier in this paper (e.g., Sacramento's status as California's current capital), but such certainty quickly deteriorates in a world of greater complexity, continuous discovery, reformulated theories, and considerations of moral, political, cultural and psychological realities and differences. Many things once thought of as fact, even in science, are now known to be false or inscrutable. Deliberately bleeding patients to stimulate recovery from disease was once commonplace but has been abandoned because other medical practices proved superior after experimentation. On this model, and with a firm commitment to the epistemic assumptions that we have discussed, medical and public health errors and inferior methods can be overcome and continuously improved upon.

A great challenge to current public health policy development, messaging, and instantiation of recommendations in social practices is accounting for this nearly continuous process of aiming for aptness but dealing with imperfect and incomplete knowledge, while simultaneously honing the skills elaborated by Sosa. To err, and err publicly, opens one's reputation to public scrutiny, and makes one vulnerable to the assaults of those who are often least adroit at scrutinizing the reasons and justifications for those errors or oversights. Whether such scrutiny stems from simple antagonism, a lack of information, a polluted public arena and media environment populated by self-styled political and social influencers, or results from honest disagreements on how facts are read and moral values are instantiated, the loss of public trust and social stability undermines public well-being. As with most imperfect ventures, the most successful long-term antidote appears to be systemic efforts to learn the truth and compellingly communicate justifiable true beliefs using historically sincere and accurate messengers who are seen as credible because of their typical accuracy, adroitness and general aptness. Experience counts. There is, unfortunately, no easy means for overcoming reputational damage from errors, other than to continue to ground one's empirical claims more firmly in a rigorous scientific method and to analyze and adjust one's recommendations consistent with new knowledge and our evolving sense of our obligations to our community. Error, and the responsible manner of dealing with error when it inevitably comes to pass, in this respect, is not tantamount to the "anything goes" policy of a post-truth society. Rather, such a process is the alternative to a policy of rampant and vulgar subjectivism.

In light of the foregoing discussion, how might we assess the claims made by various groups and individuals for a COVID-19 vaccine exemption? Anticipation of an efficacious vaccine was present in most of 2020, as various companies designed, put through trials, and rolled out vaccines to great fanfare in December 2021 with full deployment in early 2022. But the speed of their development, the use of new mRNA technologies, concerns about drug trials, and accompanying public health, political, and cultural turmoil complicated the process. In much of the world, the most pressing issue was how to obtain clinically tested vaccines for ravaged populations, and issues related to the logistics and financing of vaccine rollout and determination of vaccine priority were decisive considerations. In the United States those concerns occupied the public health infrastructures of all fifty states as well. However, in this context one of the most important issues that needed to be addressed was whether and on what basis to permit COVID-19 vaccine exemptions, given the assumed need for widespread vaccination to reduce the spread of the disease and unrelenting pressure on the public health system and economy.

A first case in which our epistemic and normative tools can be used in action is the situation in which the presence of specific allergies are advanced as medical justifications for a public health exemption from the COVID-19 vaccine. The Centers for Disease Control and Prevention (CDC) and the World Health Organization (WHO) suspected rare allergies to at least two compounds in the four major COVID-19 vaccines. It appeared that polyethylene glycol (PEG) in the Pfizer and Moderna vaccines might provoke severe allergic reactions in a small portion of the population. A similar suspicion applied to polysorbate present in the Novavax and J&J vaccines (De Vrieze 2020). Individuals who had real or suspected adverse anaphylactic reactions to either of those compounds in actual vaccines or in other common products such as shampoo and toothpaste seemed *prima facie* to be likely candidates for a justified medical exemption. Still, a lack of certainty about the causal relationship between those compounds and anaphylaxis also prompted the CDC to recommend that those who had experienced a severe reaction to any vaccine or injectable medication consider avoiding the COVID-19 vaccines.

With respect to standards of evidence, an assertion of a JTB requires that these compounds have been shown to likely cause a severe allergic reaction in some potential vaccine recipients. There is evidence these two compounds are known to be allergic irritants to some people, and though few recipients have severe reactions, the reactions occur at a consistent frequency across the monitored US population. The US Department of Health and Human Services (HHS) database tracking adverse reactions (HHS 2022) was designed systemically to display how frequently these reactions occurred with a best hypothesis as to the cause. Although this was an imperfect diagnostic tool, it conformed to a systemic means of identification and determination of symptoms accompanied by a reasonable hypothesis as to the cause of allergic reactions.

The cited evidence offers a reasonably strong justification to allow medical exemptions based on CDC guidelines. It uses scientific objectivity insofar as data is available, and it is consistent with the application of Sosa's three-pronged approach: It is accurate insofar as the allergies are systemic. It is adroit with respect to using skill (data) to avoid harming. And it is apt to the degree that it prevents unnecessary harm. At the same time, the CDC has been criticized for poor and infrequent communication regarding a number of factors, including confusing messaging about quarantine and return-to-work guidelines (Simmons-Duffin 2022). With the reputation of the CDC's data-gathering function undermined by flawed messaging and poor communication, a waning credibility of its testimony, and in some high-profile instances unfortunate presentation of data, the successful fulfillment of its role and task eroded. Though the CDC employs some of the foremost global experts in immunology, sincerity—as judged by the public—is a matter of perception, and the perception of the CDC was quickly compromised because the public was not sufficiently familiar with any prior good reputation associated with the agency, something exacerbated by the rapid onset of the COVID-19 pandemic. Given these factors in their totality, it is a reasonable conclusion that at the height of the pandemic the CDC offered the public at best a weak justification for believing its sincerity, if not its accuracy, when it came to recommendations for any action, including medical vaccine exemptions specifically. As mentioned by Coady (1992), much of what makes a person or organization appear sincere is a consistent, truthful message, but with very little prior experience with the CDC among most of the public, there was little to no history from which to develop trust-based judgments. Only time and improved messaging can repair this harm. All of this creates significant failure with respect to the justificatory value of testimony.

5. Epistemology and Religious Exemptions

If challenges surface with respect to justifying vaccine exemptions for health reasons, they are even more complicated for public health professionals and others when they are based on religious claims. One definition of religion derives from Latin and describes the act of venerating God or the gods (Smith 2009; Noss and Grangaard 2017). A more culturally inflected and expansive definition of religion comes from Grabenstein: "religions are fundamentally sets of beliefs about God or spirituality held by groups of people. Like all groups, religious groups develop their own systems of culture ... [however] behaviors of like-minded individuals are not necessarily related to the theological basis of their religions. 'Religious' differs from 'theological,' in part, as social differs from scholarly" (Grabenstein 2013, p. 2012). These definitions of religion give rise to divergent justifications that individuals and groups put forward for their religious beliefs, the truth claims they assert, and the self-understandings and identities as religious adherents that they embrace.

Following scholars working in the field of the comparative study of religion, we can distinguish two common categories with respect to believers' justifications for their belief. First, justification for belief can be seen in individuals and religious groups that affirm an axiomatic belief in God; the authority of specific religious scriptures, dogma, official teachings and interpretations of authoritative texts; and theological doctrines and the pronouncements of religious leaders as either absolutely true or inspired in some way based on faith. Second, a recognized social construct that generates reasons for religious belief and justifications for related choices is what Neil Van Leeuwen argues is an *identity-constituting role* (Van Leeuwen 2014, 2018). In this expression of religious belief, the believer's position among a like-minded community committed to specific values, roles, world-construal, and normative ways of being in the world is the basis for religious truth claims. Adherence to and recourse to religious doctrines as the basis for truth claims and motivation for normative choices are of secondary importance. Here, I examine these two modes of religious reasoning in greater detail.

5.1. *Thomist and Kalam Cosmologist Arguments for Faith Belief*

Two of the most common arguments developed in the Western theological literature for the reasonableness or truth of faith are inspired by Medieval Catholic theologian Thomas Aquinas and Contemporary philosopher Richard Swinburne, who developed Aquinas's views. Neither Aquinas nor Swinburne claim to establish absolute certainty that they or anyone has knowledge of theistic truths that are derived from their assertions and the resulting embrace of faith. In what Swinburne calls the Thomist view, "The person of religious faith is the person who has the theoretical conviction that there is a God: a sincere belief that God exists and is the cause of the universe which then animates a range of subsidiary and reasonable conclusions that inform the religious perspective" (Swinburne 2005, p. 138). For Swinburne, the reasonableness of the belief is based on a probabilistic argument—if there is reason to think it is more probable than not that there is a God, then there is a justified belief in God.

Swinburne's disciple William Craig articulates a standard version of the Kalam Cosmological Argument—Thomistic in nature—as such:

The classic Thomistic assertions (1–3)

- Everything that begins to exist has a cause.
- The universe began to exist.
- Therefore, the universe has a cause
- Craig adds additional conclusions that follow from Swinburne's insights (4–5)
- If the universe has a cause, then an uncaused, personal Creator of the universe exists who *sans (without)* the universe is beginningless, changeless, immaterial, timeless, spaceless, and enormously powerful.
- Therefore, an uncaused, personal Creator of the universe exists, who *sans* the universe is beginningless, changeless, immaterial, timeless, spaceless and enormously powerful (Craig 1997).

Numerous analytic philosophers and logicians have pointed out the misconceptions, erroneous presumptions, and inconsistencies under which cosmological arguments for the existence of God labor. A focus simply on the first premise, which need not be embraced as true in the absence of any supporting empirical evidence, illustrates the challenges. As philosopher Graham Oppy, observes:

> One Kalām cosmological argument relies on the premise that it is impossible for there to be physically instantiated infinities (e.g., infinite temporal sequences, hotels with infinitely many rooms, Thomson lamps, etc.). Professor Craig claims that, even though such things are narrowly logically possible--as is shown by the (apparent) consistency of Cantorian set theory--nonetheless, they are not broadly logically (or metaphysically) possible. On the other hand, I see no reason to say that it is broadly logically impossible for there to be physically instantiated infinities. That is, I am not prepared to rule out the suggestion that it is broadly logically possible for there to be physically instantiated infinities. And that is enough to allow me to reasonably refuse to be moved by this Kalām cosmological argument. (Oppy 1995, p. 17)

In Oppy's view, the cosmological proposition presents two problems: First, there is no reason to believe it is true; but, second, if it were true, it seemingly embraces the reality of an infinite regression of causation, undercutting the claims of a first cause. The failure of the first premise renders the full argument suspect.

Aquinas lived in the 13th Century and, though deeply indebted to Aristotle, had no experience of the changing insights and perspectives of the 17th century scientific revolution that would grip the West. Independent of this fact, his conception of the divine is construed as a strictly mental, revelatory, or imaginative construction, inviting confusion about who or what is in control of God's existence (and by extension God's relevance to issues of religious belief and practice). Aquinas' argument about faith as a "justified reasonable belief", much like the Kalam argument that attempts to probabilize the existence of God, does not assert that the divine should be assumed as a fact about the world. Instead, Aquinas argues that faith is "the theoretical conviction that God exists and is "midway between knowledge and opinion" (*Summa Theologiae* 2a2ae 1, 2) (Aquinas 2006, p. 11). Aquinas further describes faith as "assent" which is understood as a mental state or inner will that if not blocked allows God to reveal the truths behind faith and of God (*Summa Theologiae*, 2a2ae, 2, 1 (Aquinas 2006, pp. 59–65)). Based on this argument, the truth about the existence and nature of God is dependent upon a person's willingness to believe, but it does not appear to establish a strictly logical foundation for that belief. It is a "believe and you will see" rather than a "see and you will believe" proposition.

The Kalam cosmological formulation and Aquinas' assessment of the power but limited nature of what it is able to claim presents a clear challenge for believers who are dependent on this belief to support their theism and derivative religious worldview. A more practical and concrete problem inevitably emerges from this situation. Individuals who assume the role of witness to, or asserter of, the truth claims of belief in God fail in nearly all important ways to meet the ethico-epistemic tests of accuracy, adroitness, and aptness introduced earlier by Sosa. Though individuals who speak as the voices of this tradition might be sincere in their expressed beliefs, their assertions fail the tests of accuracy as established by empiricists' claims of miracles like raising individuals from the dead, bearing witness to visitations by celestial beings, assertions of divinity to human beings, and so forth. All such claims suggest a failure of the standard of "reliable testimony" that serves as a functional tool of everyday human life. The empiricist criticism against believers in God and in the religious worldview that is generated by this belief is not so much that such believers are inept or weak in their execution of accuracy, adroitness, or aptness. It is rather that by embracing their faith and beliefs, these terms cease to have any meaning in even referring to their endeavor. They are, in a real sense, functioning outside of a reality where such terms can even be used meaningfully. Abandoned, in this logic, is Aristotle's argument based on *ergon*, supplanted by subjectivist claims of the improbable that lack what could constitute verifiable or falsifiable, evidence. While the scientific method welcomes the possibility of uncertainty, and even error, faith-based claims on the part of those who "bear witness" do not so easily do so.

5.2. Identity-Constituting Religious Adherents and Derived Affirmations of Faith

A second sort of religious justification proffered by ones who want to step outside of ethico-epistemic standards in pluralistic settings is more cultural than theological. Van Leeuwen distinguishes "epistemic confidence" from "identity centrality" (Van Leeuwen 2022, p. 2). *Epistemic confidence* refers to "[T]he degree to which someone feels a belief state approximates knowledge," while *identity centrality* refers to "{T}he degree to which someone experiences a belief state as part of their social identity" (ibid). Social identity is defined as a "cluster of psychological states and behavioral dispositions that constitute someone as a member of an actual or potential in-group, or that an individual uses to achieve a desired social position" (ibid). This view correlates with Grabenstein's aforementioned reference to religious culture, which signals the potential for variation in the expression of religious belief. Van Leeuwen posits that the majority of those who identify as religious understand this association in terms of the "identity-centrality" category. This observation is supported by documented incongruities between the professed theological or doctrinal religious beliefs and actual behavior in a given religious group. For example, recent empirical social science research has revealed that followers from well-known religions are more likely to act according to religious tenets when such behavior is cued by a like-minded community's expressions rather than by deeply held personal religious convictions. One concrete example that illustrates this is the "Sunday Effect": Christians are more likely to engage in altruistic behavior on Sundays than other days (Malhotra 2010).

How does recent research on vaccine acceptance or vaccine hesitancy or refusal among these sorts of individuals and communities support or undercut the theoretical claims regarding the identity-constituting paradigm advanced by Van Leeuwen? For example, if a particular religion's doctrine—or even culture—eschews vaccination, is it also the case that a member who might wish to vaccinate defer vaccination for fear of ostracism or some other social penalty? With some notable exceptions, few religious groups in the United States prohibit COVID-19 vaccination among their adherents as a matter of policy. However, research conducted among religious communities that do not explicitly reject vaccines for their members has revealed individual members of these communities who are vaccine hesitant and who may individually attribute a posture of vaccine rejection to specific theological or doctrinal beliefs of their community. Grabenstein notices that "[i]n multiple cases, ostensibly religious reasons to decline immunization actually reflected concerns about vaccine safety or personal beliefs among a social network of people organized around a faith community, rather than theologically based objections per se" (Grabenstein 2013, p. 2011). In such situations, "identity-centrality" drives behaviors that may not even correspond to beliefs about a specific matter (e.g., whether to vaccinate). Instead, larger commitment to faith belief and its social penalties inform these choices.

It is possible to appreciate this complicated mechanism better if we examine the context in the US in which it is seen most consistently to play out and which has been the subject of significant research over the course of the pandemic. A preponderance of White evangelical Christians in the United States has been resistant to COVID-19 vaccination. Recent studies suggest a premium on in-group values like purity and liberty, which reinforce vaccine hesitancy (Amin et al. 2017). A number of pastors and religious organizations such as Shane Vaughan—a Pentecostal minister in Mississippi—have created networks to spread form letters that they hope will be effective in securing vaccine exemptions (Hals 2021). The form letter aims to convince employment attorneys that the requesting employee embraces a "sincerely held" religious belief—a legal bar for exemptions at the federal level. Vaughn claimed in late 2021 that his form letter had been downloaded from his website more than 40,000 times. Clearly, the in-group pressure to establish recognized justifications for religious exemptions has fueled a grassroots movement that can undermine vaccination mandates and risk the health of the broader public by doing so.

However, a study that spanned fall 2020 and spring 2021 showed that a certain type of public health messaging was more effective than others in persuading evangelicals to vaccinate (Bokemper et al. 2021). It concluded that White evangelicals were most likely to vaccinate if they were presented with a public health message that highlighted community interest and emphasized reciprocity in addition to including a shaming component in cases where one chose to eschew vaccination. This mixture of a pro-social message with the expectation of reciprocity and a nudge to avoid the shame that would come if one were to infect a fellow group member led to a thirty percent increase in participants' intent to vaccinate over the placebo, including a thirty-eight percent increase in negative evaluations of a non-vaccinators (ibid). These findings seem supportive, in many ways, of the characteristics and thinking that one would be likely to find in identity-constituting belief systems. And though the outcome of the pro-social study may be considered a success (i.e., increased vaccination acceptance among members of a reticent group), it also points to the vulnerability of group pressures that can be equally effective in promoting anti-social behaviors.

It is clear that some evangelical Americans who are opposed to vaccination are under pressure to form or retain beliefs that originate in their group identity. Though they might have been moved to some degree to vaccinate for the sake of helping others in their group, they tend to be receptive to reasons appealing only to their in-group. Empirical data reveals their response to public health messaging about non-vaccinators threaten their identity. To the extent it informs their choices, it does so against, not in favor of, the interests of population health (Chu et al. 2021). In other words, their reasons are not only not universalizable, but epistemically outside of the kind of "refinement of knowledge" in response to revealed errors which we determined earlier was reflective of an intellectually virtuous approach to supporting justified belief. So, whether one is a religious absolutist with respect to belief in the divine, scripture, or doctrine, or an individual whose religious identity is constituted by belonging to a religious group, the potential to put others at risk does great harm to the majority outside their group. In any case, no proffered objective or inclusive reasons will be put forward to motivate such religious insiders to vaccinate.

6. Conclusions

I have argued that knowledge and justified beliefs as established in this paper's ethico-epistemic argument give significant and necessary consideration to both empirically-verified facts about the world as well as to moral judgments regarding decisions about what constitutes a just policy for vaccination exemptions. I have also argued that some specific medical exemptions—and the general approach to justifying medical exemptions—are morally justified because they have at least *prima facie* evidence-based reasons and competent voices behind them. Though this does not guarantee the prevention of human and methodological error—nor its reputational fallout—it does offer the best-available means of assessing a fair way of determining vaccine exemptions. At the same time, I have argued that two forms of belief justification typical of religious reasoning, namely, belief in the divine and canonical based beliefs as well as identity-constituting beliefs, fall short with respect to empirical and justifiable evidence offered in support of their claims and therefore fail the test of attaining acceptable justifications for belief.

On first blush, there appears to be greater promise for vaccination acceptance in the identity-forming groups for at least two reasons. First, within such groups, there are people who appear to personally desire vaccination, but hesitate because of fear of social fallout. In such cases, their lesser reasons (desire to avoid negative group pressure) arguably override their better reasons (judgements about the efficacy of vaccination). Among such individuals, it might only take a nudge to change their avoidance posture to one of acceptance, although what that nudge must be is as of yet unclear. Second, there are instances in which religious believers who are prominent and do vaccinate have a motivational effect on vaccine hesitant religious adherents, as illustrated by the persuasive power that US National Institute for Health Director Francis Collins—a well-regarded evangelical Christian—has had on these debates in various evangelical churches (Chu et al. 2021; Bokemper et al. 2021).

Though it might be tempting to allow public health policy to accommodate the arguments of various contrarian religious thinkers and individuals by incorporating their choices into policy, this strategy ultimately does a disservice to the larger society. Some—probably most—humans embrace religious beliefs at some level. Some will refuse vaccines for the reasons explored in this paper. But it is not the obligation of the secular society, the scientific community, and the public health agents to whom we have entrusted our public health to embrace unjustified, unverified, even harmful consequences of beliefs without significant empirical and reasonable evidence to the contrary. To do so invites an arbitrariness and a posture that in the end is arguably unethical in its failure to advance the interests of others.

Funding: This research received no external funding.

Informed Consent Statement: Not applicable.

Data Availability Statement: No data available.

Conflicts of Interest: The author declares no conflict of interest.

References

Amin, Avnika B., Robert A. Bednarczyk, Cara E. Ray, Kala J. Melchiori, Jesse Graham, Jeffrey R. Huntsinger, and Saad B. Omer. 2017. Association of moral values with vaccine hesitancy. *Nature Human Behavior* 1: 873–80. [CrossRef]

Anscombe, Gertrude Elizabeth Margaret. 1958. Modern Moral Philosophy. *Philosophy* 33: 1–19. [CrossRef]

Aquinas, Thomas. 2006. *St. Thomas Aquinas's Summa Theologiae, Vol 31, Faith (2a2ae. 1–7)*. Latin text and English Translation. Translated by T. C. O'Brien. Cambridge: Cambridge University Press.

Aristotle. 2009. *The Nicomachean Ethics*. Translated by David Ross. Edited by Lesley Brown. Oxford World Classics. Oxford and New York: Oxford University Press, ISBN 9780199213610.

Beauchamp, Tom L., and James F. Childress. 2019. *Principles of Biomedical Ethics*, 8th ed. New York: Oxford University Press.

Bokemper, Scott E., Alan S. Gerber, Saad B. Omer, and Gregory Huber. 2021. Persuading US White evangelicals to vaccinate for COVID-19: Testing message effectiveness in fall 2020 and spring 2021. *Proceedings of the National Academy of Sciences of the United States of America* 7: 118. [CrossRef]

Chu, James, Sophia L. Pink, and Robb Willer. 2021. Religious identity cues increase vaccination intentions and trust in medical experts among American Christians. *Proceedings of the National Academy of Sciences of the United States of America* 118: e2106481118. [CrossRef] [PubMed]

Coady, Cecil Anthony John. 1992. *Testimony*. Oxford: Oxford University Press.

Craig, William Lane. 1997. In Defense of the Kalam Cosmological Argument. *Faith and Philosophy: Journal of the Society of Christian Philosophers* 14: 236–47. [CrossRef]

De Vrieze, Jop. 2020. Suspicions grow that nanoparticles in Pfizer's COVID-19 vaccine trigger rare allergic reactions. *Science* 10. Available online: https://www.science.org/content/article/suspicions-grow-nanoparticles-pfizer-s-covid-19-vaccine-trigger-rare-allergic-reactions (accessed on 5 April 2023).

Dreyfus, George B. J. 1997. *Recognizing Reality: Dharmakirti's Philosophy and Its Tibetan Interpretations*. Suny Series in Buddhist Studies; Albany: SUNY Press.

Foot, Philippa. 1978. *Virtues and Vices*. Berkeley: University of California Press.

Frieden, Tom. 2022. Three Solutions for Public Health—And One Dangerous Idea. *The Atlantic*, August 31. Available online: https://www.theatlantic.com/ideas/archive/2022/08/cdc-reform-covid/671296/ (accessed on 21 March 2023).

Gettier, Edmund L. 1963. Is Justified True Belief Knowledge? *Analysis* 23: 121–123. [CrossRef]
Grabenstein, John D. 2013. What the world's religions teach, applied to vaccines and immune globulins. *Vaccine* 31: 2011–23. [CrossRef] [PubMed]
Hals, Tom. 2021. U.S. pastors, advocacy groups mobilise against COVID-19 vaccine mandates. *Reuters.com*, October 14. Available online: https://www.reuters.com/world/us/us-pastors-advocacy-groups-mobilize-against-covid-19-vaccine-mandates-2021-10-14/ (accessed on 5 April 2023).
Ichikawa, Jonathan Jenkins, and Matthias Steup. 2017. The Analysis of Knowledge. *The Stanford Encyclopedia of Philosopy*. Edited by E. N. Zalta. Available online: https://plato.stanford.edu/entries/knowledge-analysis/ (accessed on 5 October 2022).
Longino, Helen E. 1990. *Science as Social Knowledge: Values and Objectivity in Scientific Inquiry*. Princeton: Princeton University Press.
MacIntyre, Alasdaire. 1985. *After Virtue*. London: Duckworth.
Malhotra, Deepak. 2010. (When) are religious people nicer? Religious salience and the 'Sunday Effect' on pro-social behavior. *Judgment and Decision Making* 5: 138–43. [CrossRef]
Noss, David S., and Blake R. Grangaard. 2017. *A History of the World's Religions*, 4th ed. London: Routledge.
Oakley, Justin, and Dean Cocking. 2001. *Virtue Ethics and Professional Roles*. London: Cambridge University Press.
Oppy, Graham. 1995. Kalām cosmological arguments: Reply to professor Craig. *Sophia* 34: 15–29. [CrossRef]
Simmons-Duffin, Selena. 2022. CDC is criticized for failing to communicate, promises to do better. *NPR.org*, January 7. Available online: https://www.npr.org/sections/health-shots/2022/01/07/1071449137/cdc-is-criticized-for-failing-to-communicate-promises-to-do-better (accessed on 5 May 2023).
Slote, Michael. 1992. *From Morality to Virtue*. New York: Oxford University Press.
Smith, Huston. 2009. *The World's Religions*, 50th Anniversary ed. New York: HarperOne.
Sosa, Ernest. 2007. *A Virtue Epistemology: Apt Belief and Reflective Knowledge*. Oxford: Clarendon Press, vol. I.
Steup, Matthias, and Neta Ram. 2020. Epistemology. *The Stanford Encyclopedia of Philosophy*. Edited by Edward N. Zalta. Available online: https://plato.stanford.edu/archives/fall2020/entries/epistemology (accessed on 5 May 2023).
Swanton, Christine. 2003. *Virtue Ethics: A Pluralistic View*. New York: Oxford University Press.
Swinburne, Richard. 2005. *Faith and Reason*, 2nd ed. Oxford: Clarendon Press.
United States Department of Health and Human Services (HHS). 2022. Vaccine Adverse Event Reporting System (VAERS). Available online: https://vaers.hhs.gov/ (accessed on 5 May 2023).
Van Leeuwen, Neil. 2014. Religious credence is not factual belief. *Cognition* 133: 698–715. [CrossRef] [PubMed]
Van Leeuwen, Neil. 2018. The factual belief fallacy. *Contemporary Pragmatism* 15: 319–43. [CrossRef]
Van Leeuwen, Neil. 2022. Two Concepts of Belief Strength: Epistemic Confidence and Identity Centrality. *Frontiers of Psychology* 13: 939–49. [CrossRef] [PubMed]
Williams, Bernard. 1985. *Ethics and the Limits of Philosophy*. Cambridge: Harvard University Press.

religions

MDPI

Article

Between Tyranny and Anarchy: Islam, COVID-19, and Public Policy

Mahan Mirza

Keough School of Global Affairs, University of Notre Dame, Notre Dame, IN 46556, USA; mmirza@nd.edu

Abstract: Research on the causes for vaccine resistance among Nigerian Muslims reveals what the philosopher Žižek terms a "heaven in disorder:" lack of trust in public institutions, conspiracy theories, ignorance of basic science, individual apathy, and faith in "Allah as the only protector." Other social contexts demonstrate far greater compliance. How can governments improve outcomes in vaccine resistant communities amidst such complexity, especially in instances where theology provides a right to dissent? Alongside a right to dissent, "obedience to authority" for the sake of social and political harmony is also an important principle of Islamic thought. It has the ability to enhance widespread compliance to public health guidelines by obligating the setting aside of private convictions in favor of collective cooperation. Religious literacy is an important element for responding effectively to pandemics, and by extension, other global emergencies. While policymakers must tailor their outreach to incommensurable worldviews in society, the human family must also imagine effective political models for cooperation despite divergence in worldviews. Otherwise, societies may need to choose between tyranny and anarchy. This article adds to efforts already underway which aim to demonstrate that engagement with religious norms, rather than their dismissal, represents the most promising path towards tackling vaccine resistance, especially in communities in which religious authority significantly informs social practice.

Keywords: COVID-19; Islam; authority; science; governance; Nigeria; vaccination policy; political theology

Citation: Mirza, Mahan. 2023. Between Tyranny and Anarchy: Islam, COVID-19, and Public Policy. *Religions* 14: 737. https://doi.org/10.3390/rel14060737

Academic Editors: James Carr, Andrew Flescher and Joel Zimbelman

Received: 14 December 2022
Revised: 18 April 2023
Accepted: 23 April 2023
Published: 2 June 2023

1. Introduction

Research on COVID-19 in Nigeria reveals a wide array of reasons for the country's notorious vaccine resistance (Da'wah Institute 2023). Africa's most populous nation, Nigeria became the last country on the continent to become polio-free because of its skepticism of global health regulations (JICA 2020). As such, Nigeria is an excellent site for a case study on the causes and potential remedies for COVID-19 vaccine resistance. This paper classifies twenty-one distinct claims presented in a significant recent study under two broader causes for vaccine resistance: (1) lack of trust in public intuitions and (2) complete trust in God. It then looks at these two categories analytically, as launch points for integrating awareness of religious belief and expression into efforts to promote compliance with government health initiatives responsive to crises like pandemics.

The problem of compliance with good public health guidelines is not something theologically specific to the religion of Islam. To be sure, in contrast to the diverse religious landscape of Nigeria covered in the aforementioned study, many Muslim-majority countries or social groups with established or legitimate authority figures have by and large enjoyed widespread compliance with public health guidelines, "obedience to authority" being a generally accepted principle of Islamic political theology. A "right to dissent," the placing of complete "trust in God," the "acceptance of science," and "obedience to authority" are each, in their own right, theologically well-grounded in scripture and tradition. The Quran, for example, commands believers to "obey God and obey the Messenger and those in authority among you" (Nasr 2015, 4:13). It is also well known that the natural sciences flourished in medieval Islamic societies (Al-Khalili 2011). The Quran commands believers to "reflect upon the creation of the heavens and the earth," and it considers every aspect of the natural world an āyah, "a sign of God" (Nasr 2015, 3:191). The prophet Muhammad is also reported to have said that God "has appointed a cure for every disease" (Al-Tabrīzī n.d., 4538). Theology thus invites reflection on, if not the systematic study of, the natural world.

The independent spirit of inquiry that science fosters is not altogether absent in other domains of intellectual life, including politics. Islamic thought and practice, thus, developed a robust tradition of both defending political authority to preserve order and a right to dissent from authority in order, in turn, to uphold the independence of human conscience and agency. This tradition is grounded as much on reason as it is on revelation, identified in part by the imperative to "command what is right" and "forbid what is wrong" (Cook 2001). Above all, every aspect of our lives as Muslims lies under the sovereignty of God. God created us, just as he created the virus. Only God can give life and take life. Accepting God's decree and God's power over all things is part of faith. "No misfortune befalls the earth nor yourselves," proclaims the Quran, "save that it is in a Book before We bring it forth—truly that is easy for God—that you not despair over what has passed you by, nor exult in that which He has given unto you. And God loves not any vainglorious boaster" (Nasr 2015, 57:22–23).

It is evident that the four "ideal-type" approaches do not exist in isolation. "Obedience to authority," "acceptance of science," "right to dissent," and "trust in God" interact with each other in unpredictable and subtle ways. The primary mode of justification for each is rooted in a unique set of arguments that has theological validity in normative Islam. At the same time, the nonlinear overlap between them results in human behavior that is not easy to regulate in public policy. Attitudes toward mask-wearing, social distancing, fulfilling communal rites, and vaccines vary widely, and this variation, when blended with new technologies in evolving global cultures, has generated fresh perspectives on faith and practice in the midst of COVID-19. (Taragin-Zeller and Kessler 2021).

Differences of opinion among believers within Islam—believers who sincerely desire faithful submission to God in reference to the very same scripture delivered to them by the very same prophet—are not uniquely a Muslim problem. It is the human condition writ large, a fact that is painfully on display in the global response to the pandemic at several sites. Even societies that claim to rely on science alone for determining their public health policies have not agreed on what to do. Whereas China insisted on a "zero-Covid" policy, Sweden opted to remain fully open (Bergman and Lindström 2023). Meanwhile, the different U.S. municipalities and states adopted diametrically opposed policies, depending on whether they were "red states" or "blue states" (Mitropoulos 2022).

Societies comprised of Muslims practicing Islam, just like societies in which science is utilized to make sense of the world, manifest internal differences for similar reasons. People, even when they inhabit the same intellectual tradition, privilege different modes of reasoning and have different conceptions of how the world works. At times, people with similar modes of reasoning in two different traditions will be more likely to get along with each other than people who think differently while following the very same tradition (Quraishi-Landes 2006). People arrange facts within narratives, and the narratives, what some call worldviews, are the primary lenses that drive the interpretive process (Gottschall 2012; DeWitt 2018). In the second book of his bestselling trilogy, *Homo Deus*, Yuval Noah Harari suggests that humans are able to engage pandemics today in ways that break completely from the past, allowing us to set "new human agendas" unfettered by existential concerns (Harari 2017). Whereas our inability to adequately cooperate to meet climate goals has already demonstrated the difficulty of setting shared human agendas, COVID-19 has demonstrated its near impossibility. The philosopher Žižek describes this reality of competing agendas as a "heaven in disorder" (Žižek 2021). He remains pessimistic about our future, absent a revolutionary political solution. Bracketing Žižek's proposed solution for a "wartime communism" to save humanity from itself, his fundamental insight may be on the mark: we should look not to unify the heavens, but rather, we should attempt to unify our politics.

Islamic political theology provides a framework for obeying authority while recognizing the right for individuals to hold dissenting views, offering valuable theological resources for effective public policy. Research into humanitarian ways of dealing with public health crises recognizes the characteristic "secular" nature of such well-intended responses, often reluctant to engage "messy" religious and cultural dynamics (Wilkinson 2020). This paper adds to the growing body of evidence arguing in favor of engagement with religion in order to better tackle global problems.

2. Survey Data

The Nigerian study helps to illuminate the impact of trust deficit in Muslim society and culture, a decidedly different explanation for vaccine resistance than one that is directly theological, or, indeed, essential about Islam. Research conducted by the Da'wah Academy captures twenty-one distinct "claims" for vaccine resistance with the help of 3127 survey responses and 4749 interviews. (Da'wah Institute 2023). The research targets primarily Muslim faith leaders and members of faith-based institutions across over seventy organizations. The study, which provides "Islamic responses to vaccine hesitancy", systematically addresses each claim on its own terms by drawing on science, scripture, and plain fact-checking to counter misinformation. The study then categorizes the various claims under six thematic areas: conspiracy theory, ignorance of basic biology, concerns about the effectiveness of the vaccine, trust-related issues, concerns about side effects, and "miscellaneous". This paper further abstracts these six thematic areas under the two headings of "trust in God" versus "trust deficit". Pandering in misinformation and conspiracy theories is merely a manifestation of the "trust deficit". Whereas "trust in God" comes straight from theology, a "trust deficit" is grounded in a lack of trust in public institutions. The trust deficit, nevertheless, enables a "right to dissent," which is not just a right but, under proper conditions, an obligation. In other words, there are valid religious reasons for vaccine resistance (Table 1).

On the other hand, there are equally strong theological arguments in favor of vaccines and compliance with public health guidelines, particularly arguments which invoke "obedience to authority" and "acceptance of science." However, whereas "trust in science" by itself is a motive that can be channeled in order to break through the barrier of misinformation or the deadlock of theology vs. theology, "obedience to authority," whose ground is in Islamic political theology, has the potential to be sought as reference in order to overcome private differences of belief for the sake of public welfare and social cohesion. The following table lists each of the twenty-one reported claims alongside its cause (Da'wah Institute 2023).

One of the virtues of this study is its ability to distinguish "this-worldly" secular claims from "other-worldly" theological warrants for vaccine resistance. Looking at the breakdown between "claim" and "cause" in the table reveals, perhaps counterintuitively, just how much more influential social, cultural, "this-worldly" explanations for resisting public health efforts have been. Trust deficit in public institutions dominates the causes for vaccine resistance, and by extension, largely explains the lack of compliance with public health guidelines more broadly. Trust is implicated even in cases where the cause for vaccine resistance appears to be misinformation, such as: "COVID-19 does not exist. It is all a conspiracy theory." In some cases, there may be a legitimate difference of opinion, such as believing that the vaccine has harmful side-effects. Though this may be the view of a small minority, most subscribe to a collectivist conviction according to which the statistical advantage of adopting an approach which favors public health outweighs the risks individuals might incur. Not so believing usually indicates a trust deficit.

That there would be a lack of consensus within a society as to the degree to which public health policies proposed by the government ought to be embraced is not so strange. Elsewhere, COVID-19 has brought to the surface deep challenges for public policy where cooperation is needed on a global scale. While in the US leaders in red states are arguing for different policies that those in blue states, Sweden is offering entirely different prescriptions from its neighboring countries. All the while, scientists revise their guidelines in real time, adding to the perception that the challenges for a shared agenda are practically insurmountable.

Table 1. Reasons for vaccine resistance in Nigeria.

No.	Claim	Cause
1.	It doesn't concern me	Trust deficit
2.	Vaccine ingredients are *haram*	Trust deficit
3.	Vaccine causes COVID	Trust deficit
4.	Vaccine can lead to infertility	Trust deficit
5.	Vaccine can worsen health	Trust deficit
6.	Even medical practitioners don't take it	Trust deficit
7.	COVID affects only society's elite and wealthy	Trust deficit
8.	Vaccine is unsafe, even according to medical practitioners	Trust deficit
9.	Vaccine is nefarious means for population control	Trust deficit
10.	Vaccine is means to perform unknown tests	Trust deficit
11.	Vaccine only necessary if one has COVID	Trust deficit
12.	COVID is a conspiracy	Trust deficit
13.	Nigeria is unable to technically manage vaccines	Trust deficit
14.	Vaccine harms pregnant women and nursing mothers	Trust deficit
15.	COVID heals naturally; vaccines are unnecessary	Trust deficit
16.	Muslims do not fear death	Trust in God
17.	Vaccine can kill me	Trust deficit
18.	Allah is the only protector	Trust in God
19.	Vaccine has harmful side effects	Trust deficit
20.	Vaccine is not effective	Trust deficit
21.	Vaccine/manufacturers cannot be trusted	Trust deficit

3. Religion and Public Policy

In March 2020, a group of students from the University of Notre Dame in the American Midwest traveled to Muscat, Oman, for spring break. There, they met students who were studying at Notre Dame University, Bangladesh. The two student bodies from Notre Dame on opposite sides of the world were established by the Congregation of Holy Cross, "educators in the faith." (Congregation of Holy Cross n.d.). The cross-cultural encounter between mostly Catholics from the United States and Muslims from Bangladesh—which we playfully called "Holy Crossroads"—took place during the week that COVID-19 resulted in widespread global shutdowns.

Midweek, the American students received a message from the University administration instructing them not to return to campus after the trip. As student anxieties surged, Muscat went into near total lockdown on the morning of return: All schools were closed; daily congregational prayer in the mosques was suspended; entry of foreign nationals was banned; and Souq Muttrah, a daily thoroughfare, was shuttered. Just two months later, the University of Notre Dame, distinctive among nationally ranked research universities in the United States because of its faith-based mission, became the first institution of its kind to announce that it would reopen for in-person classes that fall. University president

Rev. John Jenkins, CSC, explained the rationale in a *New York Times* Op-Ed titled "We're Reopening Notre Dame: It's Worth the Risk" (Jenkins 2020).

Three principles guided his decision: ensuring the physical health and wellbeing of the community; educating the whole person, which requires in-person learning inside and outside the classroom; and advancing high-quality research. Would remote or in-person learning be better for flourishing within learning environments? What risks should be given the greatest consideration in a global pandemic? "No science, simply as science, can answer that question", argued Rev. Jenkins. "It is a moral question in which principles to which we are committed are in tension". The global response to the pandemic unearthed the human side of scientific problems. Why do some people believe in the efficacy of masking, and others disparage it? Why did Sweden follow a completely different public policy strategy from its European neighbors, despite following the same science? "There are", says Rev. Jenkins, "questions that a scientist, speaking strictly as a scientist, cannot answer for us". The University opened that fall with mandated masking and social distancing, and it mandated vaccines once they became available to near-total compliance.

Meanwhile, in Oman, the population by-and-large also complied with public health guidelines. Even the annual pilgrimage to Mecca, an obligation for every adult Muslim of means at least once in their lifetime, was canceled for all nonresidents (Blakemore 2020). Dissent, however, was not entirely absent, and it was even widespread in some parts of the world (Maire 2020; Piwko 2021). One case study in Bangladesh shows, unsurprisingly, that religion cut both ways, both helping and hurting to promote key public health initiatives which arose during the crisis (Roy 2022). On the one hand, extremist faith leaders used the pandemic to scapegoat others. On the other hand, many faith leaders engaged in social development projects. UNICEF estimates that "currently about 500,000 Imams and religious leaders are disseminating information about COVID-19 in Bangladesh on topics ranging from hygiene and infection prevention, social distancing, and how to benefit from the Holy Quran when in lockdown at home" (ibid, p. 3).

In both compliance and resistance, Muslim scholars have attempted to abide by the sharia, whether advancing the goals of political authorities—even if they have had to postpone or altogether miss out on the lifelong dream to attend the sacred precincts of Mecca and Medina—or thwarting them. The sharia, imperfectly translated as "Islamic law," has a moral component vis-à-vis one's obligations to God as well as a political component, which involves policymaking for the common good. Governance requires practical wisdom, the weighing of priorities, and the privileging of certain obligations over others when imperatives clash, especially in emergency circumstances. Scholars reasoning with the "objectives of Islamic law" (*maqāṣid al-sharīʿa*) offer a three-tier ranking system of priorities: necessities (*ḍarūriyyāt*), needs (*ḥājiyyāt*), and embellishments or adornments (*taḥsīniyyat*) (Abd-Allah 2007). To better understand this three-tier ranking, take the home as an example. Having some kind of home (shelter) is a necessity. Having basic amenities in the home, such as windows for natural light and fresh air and furniture for daily living, are needs. Leather couches and velvet curtains, on the other hand, are embellishments: Nice to have, but one doesn't invest in drapes if one doesn't have a home with windows, to begin with.

There are five overarching objectives of Islamic law: the preservation of life, intellect, religion, wealth, and family (sometimes referred to as lineage or dignity). Life takes precedence over everything else. Things that are otherwise forbidden become temporarily lawful in emergency circumstances in order to preserve life. A starving person, for example, is permitted to eat pork or carrion in order to survive, provided that they consume only what is minimally necessary for survival and immediately desist when lawful alternatives become once again available. Consistent with this pattern of reasoning, public policies that temporarily suspend obligatory rituals in order to preserve life—such as the congregational prayer, funeral rites, or the annual pilgrimage—are immediately comprehensible and justifiable within a sharia framework.

Muslim-majority countries classified as repressive, whether secular or religious according to Daniel Philpott's typology, can therefore expect compliance around COVID-19 policies not simply because they are authoritarian (Philpott 2019). They can also expect compliance because the decision to lockdown is religiously intelligible as a means of advancing public welfare and the objectives of Islamic law. Even dissenters, who personally may not trust scientists or the government, are obliged to comply with public health regulations as a religious obligation. That is because individual judgment does not supersede the rule of law, so long as the law is not obligating outright sin. If one considers—for whatever reason—that the vaccine is a danger to one's life and health, then one has the *moral* right to disobey political authority for the sake of preserving one's life and wellbeing, thus incurring no sin, but one will nonetheless suffer the *legal* consequences that follow in society. In cases where lockdowns harm more than they benefit, rulers and citizens may come up with different conclusions on the best course of action. The interplay between obeying authority, following science, prudence in policy and enforcement, and the right to dissent thus results in a complex faith-based posture that is both reasonable and in line with the sharia.

4. Obedience to Authority

One of the titles of an Islamic leader is *amīr al-mu'minīn*, or "commander of the faithful". The word *amīr*, "commander", is indicative of a leader's authority. "O you who believe", instructs the Quran: "Obey God and obey the Messenger and those in authority among you. And if you differ among yourselves concerning any matter, refer it to God and the Messenger" (Nasr 2015, 4:59). This verse contains layers of meaning for Muslim communal life and political thought. The sensibilities that it generates are directly relevant to understanding Islamic responses to the pandemic.

The "authority verse", as we might call it, would have been unambiguous within the lifetime of Muhammad. Since the prophet speaks in the name of God, obedience to him is obedience to God. Obedience to anyone who the prophet appoints as a leader, by implication, follows the same logic. Several questions arise on a plain sense reading of the verse in this manner for later generations: What if the leader were to issue an immoral command or order something that obviously stands against a known ruling of God and His messenger? Who are legitimate leaders after the prophet dies? Can leaders have legitimacy if they have not been directly appointed by the prophet? Can usurpers who seize political power ever be considered legitimate? These are the kinds of questions that have occupied the scholarly tradition through the ages.

Because of the eventual fragmentation of Muslims into many legal and theological sects after the passing of the prophet Muhammad, it is impossible to speak of "the" Islamic position on most issues. One can nonetheless attempt to identify general principles that most would consider representative. Among these principles is a reluctance to rebel against established rulers, even if the rulers are personally immoral, so long as they do not openly command other believers to disobey the sharia. In cases where a ruler prefers a moral opinion different from one that is held by a believer, the believer must comply in the public realm, so long as the believer does not consider the ruler's position a sin. A believer may openly disagree with the ruler but, nonetheless, be required to legally comply with rulings intended for public welfare.

After a meticulous study of the scholarly tradition on "Commanding Right, Forbidding Wrong" in Islamic thought, Michael Cook distills: "[W]ith regard to forbidding wrong in the face of the delinquency of the ruler, there is a clear mainstream position: rebuke is endorsed, but rebellion is rejected" (Cook 2001, p. 479). As *The Study Quran* summarizes:

> Some commentators cite a ḥadīth that indicates that one will be rewarded for obeying those in authority, regardless of the virtue of their character and rule ... The general statement this verse makes about obedience to authority has led some Muslims to view obedience, even to unjust rulers, as preferable to the chaos and social harm that may result from a revolt, and a well-known tradition states,

"One day of anarchy is worse than a thousand years of tyranny". (Nasr 2015, p. 219)

The right to dissent is built into the pledge of allegiance that believers offered the prophet: "We gave our pledge to the Messenger of Allah [may the peace and blessings of God be upon him], pledging to listen and obey in times of hardship and times of ease, willingly or reluctantly, and when others are shown preference over us, and that we would not dispute the order of those in charge, that we would speak the truth wherever we are, and that we would not fear the blame of anyone when acting or speaking for the sake of Allah" (Ibn Mājah n.d.a, 2866).

Islamic political thought would eventually extend legitimacy to any ruler who accepted the mandate to govern within the limits of the sharia, so long as the ruler ceded interpretive authority of the law to put the collective body of scholars. This arrangement placed ultimate authority to make the law in the hands of jurists, who remained, in principle, independent agents in civil society. It also provided a high degree of flexibility within Islamic law by enabling state appointed-judges to adjudicate legal matters while remaining mindful of local customs. One legal maxim states: "custom binds" (*al-'āda al-muḥakkamah*) (Abd-Allah 2007).

Muslims living as permanent minorities have recently begun to translate the principle of obeying authority as law-abiding citizens by developing a "jurisprudence of minorities" (Shavit 2016). The approach bears striking resemblance to the Jewish principle of *dina de-malkhuta dina*, "the halakhic rule that the law of the country is binding, and, in certain cases, is to be preferred to Jewish law" (Encyclopaedia Judaica 2008). The Shi'ah, having endured minority status through most of Islamic history, permit what is known as *taqiyyah*—typically translated as "dissimulation"—when they are in danger of persecution (Stewart 2012). *Taqiyyah*, etymologically related to the term for "protection", permits Shi'ahs to conceal their true faith identity in order to ward off unnecessary attention and possible harassment, or worse. Far from being a license to lie or deceive in order to gain an advantage—a highly negative stance, as some critics have wrongly argued—*taqiyyah* is based on two positive motivations: the protection of oneself and the preservation of public order.

Normative Islamic thinking in the jurisprudence of minorities is far from uniform. Uriya Shavit outlines two broad trends: a *salafī* approach that hems closer to the plain sense of scripture in line with the relatively conservative approach of scholars from Saudi Arabia, and a *wasaṭī* approach inflected by the more rational principles of interpretation (*uṣūl al-fiqh*) of scholars from al-Azhar. The *wasaṭīs* "broadly apply *maṣlaḥah* (safeguarding primary objectives of the sharī'a) and cross-searching within and beyond the four schools of law", justifying "radical accommodations of religious laws" in new contexts (ibid, p. 3).

In one case study on the banning of the *ḥijāb* (headscarf) in French public schools, the *wasaṭī* approach revealed the extent to which Muslim scholars are willing to compromise in order to facilitate peaceful coexistence:

> Sheikh al-Azhar Muḥammad Sayyid Ṭanṭāwī distinguished between the case of *ḥijābs* in Muslim lands and outside them. He declared that the French have the right to ban *ḥijābs* in their country and that it is permissible for Muslim women who live in France to respect such a law if compelled to do so. (ibid, p. 243)

Part of the reasoning for such accommodationist thinking, as Andrew March points out, is the acceptance of citizenship as a kind of "social contract," obligating individuals to participate in society under the implicit terms of that contract (March 2009) Hamza Yusuf, president of Zaytuna College, America's first accredited Muslim liberal arts college, exemplifies the approach of this kind of traditional Islam in the College's COVID-19 policy announced at the start of the pandemic. Yusuf's letter announcing the move to remote learning draws on the framework of the higher objectives of Islamic law and obedience to authority. "Our sacred law," writes Yusuf,

> holds preservation of life among the highest of divine objectives. During the 1918 Spanish flu epidemic, the Bay Area was spared much of the harm that afflicted other parts of the country, largely due to the precautionary measures taken. Erring on the side of caution in our current pandemic seems prudent until we better understand what we are up against. Following the advice of local authorities regarding coronavirus, we have moved all Zaytuna College classes online. (Yusuf 2020)

Among other things, such testimony underscores the degree to which public policy and religious authority are understood to be compatible. Not only is there nothing "essential" about Islam by way of authoritative resistance to the prevailing public health wisdom of the state, but ideally, as in the case Yusuf comments on, local authorities enjoy the backing of Muslim leaders.

Yusuf presents an excellent example because his letter accepts the authority of science and the mandate of local rulers, especially since both are aligned with Islam's higher objectives. In 2014, Yusuf participated in a conference on Vaccinations and Religion in Senegal (Vaccinations and Religion 2014). The chair of the scholars committee was Yusuf's Mauritanian mentor, Shaykh Abdallah Bin Bayyah, who reminded the conference attendees of "the Muslim community's leadership in disease prevention throughout history and the critical importance of being on the cutting edge of research and development moving forward".

5. Acceptance of Science

As medieval science evolved into modern science, with one manner of assessing and legitimizing knowledge eventually giving way to another, both epistemologies never stopped sharing a common foundation, namely, a commitment to a systematic inquiry into the natural world. The Quran refers to nature as an *āyah* or "sign" of God. Muslims across the board revere nature as God's creation and respect its systematic study. The aforementioned Vaccinations and Religion conference report includes the "Dakar Declaration on Vaccination", which emphatically affirms trust in science: "Vaccination remains to date the most effective method of protection against a variety of mankind's illnesses and epidemics, and safeguards the wellbeing of the body, which is God's gift to us". The source of knowledge for the efficacy of vaccines is not scripture; it is empirical evidence and experience. A well-known hadith implies that knowledge of nature and its workings are accessible independently of revelation:

> The Messenger of Allah [may the peace and blessings of God be upon him] passed by some people who were at the top of the palm trees. He said: "What are these people doing?" They said: "They are pollinating (the trees), putting the male with the female". He said: "I do not think this can help in any way". They were told about that and they stopped doing it. News of that reached the Messenger of Allah [may the peace and blessings of God be upon him] and he said: "If it will benefit them, then let them do it. It was only a passing thought. Do not blame me for a mere thought, but if I tell you anything about Allah (may He be glorified and exalted) then accept it from me, for I will never tell a lie about Allah". (Ibn Ḥanbal n.d., 1395)

According to this hadith, it is not the role of the prophet to instruct people on how things work in the natural world. Specialists—in this case, farmers who are familiar with productive patterns of pollination for favorable yields—exercise independent authority in their respective domains. Muslims are thus likely to go with the general consensus in scientific matters, despite its potential fallibility. Probabilistic reasoning is central to Islamic jurisprudence or *fiqh*, where "an agreement to disagree" based on a kind of underdetermination of evidence across different schools of thought eventually came to be the status quo (Walbridge 2011).

An alignment of natural science with political authority thus strengthens the likelihood of public policy compliance for faithful believers. However, because science is fallible, an accepted scientific theory being the best explanation of a phenomenon at any given time, believers naturally resist theories that contradict their beliefs in an attempt to hold reason and revelation together, hoping that future developments in science may confirm their faith perspectives. There are hadith about natural phenomena that the prophet did not get a chance to retract in his lifetime, such as the healing power of honey or the so-called hadith of the fly: "If a house fly falls in the drink of anyone of you, he should dip it (in the drink) and take it out, for one of its wings has a disease and the other has the cure for the disease" (Al-Bukhārī n.d.b, 3320). Fortunately, modern science mostly corroborates some therapeutic properties of honey (Mayo Clinic 2020). As for the latter, how can believers make sense of this today?

For one, such hadith have actually spawned scientific research projects spearheaded by faithful scientists (Claresta and Sari 2020). Expert exegetes, however, inevitably find ways to make sense of scripture regardless of its plain sense meaning. For example, the act of dipping the fly could be interpreted as an act of humility that, at the same time, alleviates the consumer of any doubt, thereby preventing needless waste. The disease of the first wing, then, is suspicion or pride; the cure in the second wing is reassurance or humility. The end result is pragmatic: Instead of discarding an entire vessel of food by dumping it out, one proceeds to consume it with gratitude.

On contagion, the prophet is reported to have said: "If you hear of an outbreak of plague in a land, do not enter it; but if the plague breaks out in a place while you are in it, do not leave that place" (Al-Bukhārī n.d.c, 5728). It is fortuitous that the report conforms well to the idea of isolation and quarantine. As one of many articles on the topic affirms: "As the COVID-19 outbreak continues to kill tens of thousands of people across the world, the prophet Muhammed's advice on how to respond to a pandemic offers a motivation to people to stay put in their homes and protect themselves from the deadly virus" (Sofuoglu 2020). The Dakar Declaration corroborates with another related hadith and well-known Muslim council: "Do not mix those who are sick with those who are healthy."

Consequently, while a general acceptance of the need to quarantine or isolate is undeniable, both according to science and according to a plain sense (even if somewhat selective) reading of the sources, its modes and practices can remain contested. Is it better to prioritize care for one's mother or father at the risk of one's own life? Should the psychological need for companionship—which is tangible and immediate—be prioritized over potential risk to the body by a nebulous virus? Personal convictions in such matters ultimately create space for divergence in public policy, resulting in grudging compliance or outright dissent. The fallibilism of science combined with suspicion of authority makes for a combustible mixture for public policy.

6. Right to Dissent

Alongside the tradition to "listen and obey" is a parallel tradition to dissent, rooted in countless scriptural sources and developed in robust scholarly literature (Kellison 2013). One hadith says: "The best of jihad is a just word spoken to an unjust ruler." (Ibn Mājah n.d.b, 4011). While primarily couched in terms of opposition, the right to dissent, first and foremost, promotes human responsibility. It affirms that human beings are not only capable of, but also have a duty to exercise, independent moral and prudential judgment. "Though dissent can often be understood in negative terms," writes Rosemary Kellison, "in the Islamic tradition dissent can also be construed as a positive duty." (Kellison 2013, p. 134).

"Each of you is a shepherd", instructs the prophet (Al-Sijistānī n.d., 2928). Believers have a duty to counsel others, regardless of whether they are rulers, subjects, members of a family, or fellow citizens (Al-Nawawī n.d., 7). The mandate of executive citizenship is perhaps best represented by the scriptural imperative to "command what is right and forbid what is wrong" (Cook 2001). Although this phrase appears multiple times in the Quran, the "three modes tradition", as Michael Cook calls it, is a helpful window into systematically reflecting on the implications.

> "Whoever sees a wrong (*munkar*)", says the prophet, "and is able to put it right with his hand (*an yughayyirahu bi-yadihi*), let him do so; if he can't, then with his tongue (*bi-lisānihi*); if he can't, then with [or in] his heart (*bi-qalbihi*). Which is the bare minimum of faith". (ibid, p. 33)

This hadith has been interpreted in many ways. Some scholars consider the charge to use "the hand" (a metaphor for force) reserved for the ruler alone, while the scholars are charged with use of the tongue (a metaphor for the power of the pen and the pulpit). The heart is reserved for the powerless in society, women and slaves. Others apply each of the three modes of every individual to the individual's capacity. "[T]he biographical and anecdotal record," chronicles Cook, "is full of sympathetically presented examples of pious Muslims harshly rebuking rulers, governors and their henchmen, often at great risk to themselves" (ibid, p. 476).

Believers who do not trust a government's motives are likely to follow the tradition of dissent by speaking out against lockdowns, social distancing, mask mandates, and vaccines, as the case may be. Pew research data indicates that public trust in government is at an all-time low in a place like the United States (Pew Research Center 2022). When disaggregated by race and ethnicity, the trust of the government on the part of the Black population reached an all-time low in 2019, right before the advent of the pandemic. Americans of color have good reason to suspect the government on account of its inglorious past, most notoriously on display in what was originally called the "Tuskegee Study of Untreated Syphilis in the Negro Male." (Vonderlehr et al. 1936).

One article on vaccine resistance concludes that "the epidemiological and social crises brought about by COVID-19 have magnified widely held social anxieties and trust issues that, in the unique circumstances of this global pandemic, have exacerbated skepticism toward vaccines" (Pertwee and Simas 2022). In this light, the results of the Nigeria study may in fact be an epiphenomenon of a trust deficit in government overall. Among all the nations of Africa, Nigerians trust their government the least (Bikus 2022). Likewise, Black American Muslims with historically antagonistic relations with the U.S. government strongly dissent against government issued COVID-19 guidelines. For instance, a warning against vaccines was posted by the Nation of Islam in the summer of 2020: "The Honorable Minister Louis Farrakhan warns the Black community against taking the COVID-19 Vaccine with the US Government's treacherous history of experimentation, medications and vaccines" (Nation of Islam n.d.).

Rooted in the experience of enslaved Africans seeking true emancipation, the Nation of Islam has taught that "Islam, the true religion of the black men of Asia and Africa, would liberate black people from white oppression" (Curtis 2010). It is vital to distinguish between the trust-related anti-vax positions among African-Americans and naturalistic anti-vax positions of prominent figures like the professional tennis player Novak Djokovic. While Djokovic tethers his stance to a certain view of science and nature, Farrakhan, the current leader of the Nation of Islam, bases his skepticism on the untrustworthiness of government (Pugh and Savulescu 2022). Farrakhan is by no means anti-science: "I say to those of us in America," he proclaimed, "we need to call a meeting of our skilled virologists, epidemiologists, students of biology and chemistry, and we need to look at not only what they give us. We need to give ourselves something better" (Nation of Islam n.d.). As such, although standing at the fringes of Islam, Farrakhan's position vis-à-vis COVID-19 is entirely coherent from the perspective of normative Islam.

Abdullah Ali, a faculty member at the aforementioned Zaytuna College, where Hamza Yusuf serves as president, has expressed opinions that are skeptical of mainstream government narratives. Ali runs "The Lamppost Education Initiative", an online forum that provides "a window into the rich Islamic tradition through the eyes of contemporary American Muslim scholars, intellectuals, activists, and leaders" (Lamppost Education Initiative n.d.). On 30 August 2021, the website posted a "Fatwa Against Forced Vaccinations", which is a translation of an opinion issued by scholars from Mauritania (Fatwa Against Forced Vaccinations 2021). The post is a textbook case demonstrating the balancing act between obedience to authority, trust in God, and the right to dissent. It is prefaced by the following assertion: "There is no doubt that the refusal of medical treatment, placing one's reliance upon Allah and acceptance of what He decrees, is among matters endorsed by the revealed law". Having asserted the right to refuse medical treatment, which forms the substance of the legal opinion, the post offers the following disclaimer: "The translation of this fatwa is not intended to oppose or discourage anyone from taking the COVID-19 vaccination" (ibid). While the right to dissent is upheld, whether that dissent is grounded in lack of trust in public authorities or an unflinching faith in God, there is a reluctance to endorse the non compliance of public policy.

7. Trust in God

In the early days of the pandemic, the Tablighi Jama'at ("Society for Spreading Faith") received widespread attention for flaunting government guidelines. As a group originating in India in 1926 whose purpose is the revitalization of faith through missionary activity across the Muslim world, with massive, crowded gatherings (*ijtima'*), the Tablighi Jama'at's very existence relies on human contact. Although the group eventually complied with mandates and restrictions to limit the spread of the virus—mainly to avoid mounting social stigma against the movement—one study focusing on the group's activities in Lombok, Indonesia, notes that the "leadership still teaches that COVID-19 is not a serious health risk but rather a global conspiracy created to weaken the Muslim community" (Hamdi 2022).

Given the background above, from where does the impulse to be noncompliant arise? In order to answer this question, the sources that have been cited in favor of trusting science must be historicized. Our contemporary understanding of disease is governed by an "etiological standpoint," which may be "characterized as the belief that diseases are best controlled and understood by means of causes ... that are *natural* ... *universal* ... *and necessary*" (Stearns 2011, p. 4). Causality is among the central concerns of Islamic theology, closely associated with cosmological debates on the nature of human actions, the omnipotence of God, free will, and accountability. With God being the primary cause for all things and the creator of all acts, many Muslim theologians dismissed the idea of *necessary* secondary causality in the natural world as imposing a limitation on God's omnipotence.

While debates on this topic are intricate and positions by no means uniform, they influence the thinking of groups like the Tablighi Jama'at on plagues and contagion. Such positions have resonance in classical theology, rooted in alternative scriptural sources. For example, the prophet is also reported to have said: "[There is] no contagion" (Stearns 2011, p. 15). In order to reconcile apparent contradictions between prophetic reports, worldviews come to play a major part. A contemporary worldview may privilege the achievements of modern science. But there are other possibilities.

For the deniers of contagion, the hadith counseling us neither to enter a plague-stricken area nor to flee from it is interpreted in other ways. For example, there is no point in fleeing because you can't escape God's decree. There is no point in entering, for why would you want to put your faith on trial by potentially attributing your fate to a cause other than God? Life and death are solely in the hands of God. One's lifespan has been preordained. "Truly", says the Qur'an, "the death from which you flee will surely meet you" (Nasr 2015, 62:9). Not least, why take any measures at all, for death by widespread contagion results in martyrdom, as in another hadith: "Plague is the cause of martyrdom of every Muslim (who dies because of it)" (Al-Bukhārī n.d.a, 2830).

8. Science & Society

In the second volume of his bestselling trilogy on human history, society, and future, *Homo Deus*, Yuval Noah Harari ponders what our new human agenda might be now that we have solved the pressing problems of hunger, disease, and war. The book presents broad historical trends demonstrating how today's world has, statistically speaking, less violence, less hunger, and fewer deaths from curable diseases than in the past. Whereas the plague was once considered an act of God, simply to be endured until God so decides to lift the affliction, today we consider it a technical problem. "[F]or modern people", Harari says, even "death is a technical problem that we can and should solve" (Harari 2017, p. 22).

Harari's eccentric account of possible human futures was published prior to COVID-19. "No one can guarantee that plagues won't make a comeback," he foretells, "but there are good reasons to think that in the arms race between doctors and germs, doctors run faster." (ibid, p. 12) Does this narrative still hold water as we transition back to a post-pandemic era? In a Ted Talk viewed forty-five million times, Bill Gates warned that humans were not ready to manage a global pandemic (Gates 2015). As COVID-19 was waning, he repeated: "We'll have another pandemic" (Gilchrist 2022).

There is no way to predict what will come next; historians can at best offer post hoc explanations if we survive. What is impossible to argue against is that the global response to COVID-19 should at least give us pause. Our response in many places across the globe was far from ideal, if not altogether inept everywhere. The world is not a controlled laboratory, scientific research takes time, and consensus does not come easy (Latour 1983; Schrader 2010). Even with a shared view of science, policy prescriptions vary depending on what is prioritized. Communication of evolving guidelines is often iatrogenic, creating mass confusion and facilitating the unintended spread of infection, especially when society provides market or political incentives to exploit our differences for short-term gain. Science is embedded in messy human cultures. "Man is a storytelling animal" (Gottschall 2012). Muslim responses to COVID-19 are no more and no less complicated than the responses of other communities. Seeing our differences as an illustration of our shared humanity enables us to empathize with each other, whether China or Sweden, red state or blue, secular or religious.

Sociologist of religion Robert Bellah deepened our understanding of the story-side of religion by couching religious life within the context of "big history." In his final synthetic work, *Religion in Human Evolution*, Bellah, drawing on the framework of neuro-anthropologist Merlin Donald, structures his account with the "mythic" (narrative) as the middle of three stages in the development of religion, between the "mimetic" (ritual) and "theoretic" (philosophical) (Bellah 2011). Although the cultural evolution of human beings moves from one stage to the next, "nothing is ever truly lost," informs Bellah. (ibid, p. 13). Human societies that have transitioned to the third stage of theorization are incapable of jettisoning ritual and myth, even if they pretend otherwise. We filter reality through narrative. Even scientific truth is embedded within some kind of narrative, what philosophers of science prefer to call "paradigms" (Kuhn 2012). Facts are intelligible in the backdrop of worldviews, whether these are explicitly stated or not. "Families, nations, religions (but also corporations, universities, departments of sociology)," says Bellah, "know who they are by the stories they tell" (Bellah 2011, p. 35). Change the story, change the reality.

The chaotic global response to COVID-19, on both individual and collective levels, can be understood through the "deep stories" behind these responses (Hochschild 2016). Deep stories give rise to deep complexity, what Savoj Žižek calls "heaven in disorder," by which he means "a radical and even exclusive division of the very (symbolic) universe in which we dwell" (Žižek 2021, p. 2). The disorder in heaven is, for Žižek, what explains disorder on earth: "Caught between two (or even three) sides—medical experts, business interests, and the pressures of populist COVID deniers—governments adopted a politics of compromises, proposing often inconsistent and ridiculously complex half measures" (ibid, p. 93).

Global problems need global solutions. In a free-for-all world, governing responsibly has become next to impossible. "The situation is hopeless," argues Žižek. That is why "it's time to act ruthlessly ... we need in Europe a version of something that cannot but be called 'wartime Communism.'" To those who think this is bad, Žižek warns of the alternative: "If we stick to our old way of life, we will surely end up in a new Barbarism." (ibid, pp. 93, 96) It is impossible to deny the resonance of this analysis with the famous Arab proverb: "Better sixty years of tyranny than one night of anarchy" (Feldman 2009). What is commonly presumed from this statement is Arab tolerance for tyranny, in contrast to Western love for freedom. "I think that's exactly backwards," argues Noah Feldman. "I think the point of the phrase is to tell you just how bad anarchy is" (ibid, p. 143). In other words, "obedience to authority," under the right circumstances, may be a recipe for social salvation.

9. Conclusions

A recent study conducted by the Da'wah Academy on vaccine resistance among Muslims in Nigeria reveals twenty-one distinct causes that may be aggregated into two categories: complete trust in God versus a trust deficit in government, heavily weighted toward the latter. Heeding some guidance which the survey illuminates, namely, that there is nothing essential about Islamic theology given to resisting sensible public health initiatives, this paper has offered a range of Muslim perspectives on how responses to COVID-19 might be grounded in Islamic sources: trust in science; dissent from the mainstream; absolute reliance on God; and respect for authority. In a world that requires global cooperation, how can public policy deal with such complexity? Blanket prescriptions are inadequate. Good governance requires identifying each objection by first understanding the worldview that sustains it: "evidence-based misinformation interventions" (Green et al. 2023). Evidence from Nigeria and beyond highlights the importance of religious literacy for effective interventions.

Human beings are complex creatures. The future is impossible to predict. The past has taught us enough at least to make sense of where we are, even as we struggle to contemplate where to go from here. In his final book, *Where Do We Go From Here: Chaos or Community?*, Martin Luther King, Jr. likens the human condition to that of a widely dispersed family that inherits a house in which they must learn to live together (King 2010, p. 177). With a simple stroke of the pen, King helped us understand through metaphor and story. A home is made of individuals who are not the same, but they cooperate and compromise nonetheless, for they must, after all, come to terms with the fact that they are "caught in an inescapable network of mutuality, tied in a single garment of destiny" (King 1963).

People across the globe need at least enough political overlap across their disparate worldviews to function as a family. Absolute individual freedom is a recipe for anarchy. For a world with existential crises requiring global cooperation, anarchy, in turn, is a recipe for disaster. New and more nimble political models are needed which allow societies to pivot between the poles of freedom and cooperation, between primacy of individuals and compromise for the sake of the collective, in order to respond to the challenges of particular moments. Instead of a false choice between "autocracy and democracy," the focus of the conversation should be on wellbeing. "[J]ust thinking in the old categories of democracies versus autocracies misses all the new challenges that our institutions have to face today," argues Jean-Marie Guéhenno. (Carnegie Council for Ethics in International Affairs n.d.). Islamic thought offers one framework to balance the tension by encouraging dissent while requiring obedience, so long as the trust deficit in public institutions remains below a critical threshold. Beyond that threshold, the most likely remaining choice might just be between tyranny and anarchy.

Funding: This research received no external funding.

Institutional Review Board Statement: Not applicable.

Informed Consent Statement: Not applicable.

Data Availability Statement: Not applicable.

Conflicts of Interest: The author declares no conflict of interest.

References

Abd-Allah, Umar Faruq. 2007. Living Islam with Purpose. *Nawawi Foundation*. Available online: https://www.theoasisinitiative.org/publications (accessed on 12 December 2022).

Al-Bukhārī, Muḥammad. n.d.a. *Ṣaḥīḥ al-Bukhārī*. Hadith 2830. Available online: https://sunnah.com/bukhari:2830 (accessed on 22 April 2023).

Al-Bukhārī, Muḥammad. n.d.b. *Ṣaḥīḥ al-Bukhārī*. Hadith 3320. Available online: https://sunnah.com/bukhari:3320 (accessed on 22 April 2023).

Al-Bukhārī, Muḥammad. n.d.c. *Ṣaḥīḥ al-Bukhārī*. Hadith 5728. Available online: https://sunnah.com/bukhari:5728 (accessed on 22 April 2023).

Al-Khalili, Jim. 2011. *House of Wisdom: How Arabic Science Saved Ancient Knowledge and Gave Us the Renaissance*. New York: The Penguin Press.

Al-Nawawī, Yaḥyā b. Sharaf. n.d. *Al-Arba'in al-Nawawiyyah*. Hadith 7. Available online: https://sunnah.com/nawawi40:7 (accessed on 22 April 2023).

Al-Sijistānī, Abū Dāwūd Sulaymān. n.d. *Sunan Abū Dāwūd*. Hadith 2928. Available online: https://sunnah.com/abudawud:2928 (accessed on 22 April 2023).

Al-Tabrīzī, Muḥammad b. 'Abdallah. n.d. *Mishkāt al-Maṣābīḥ*. Hadith 4538. Available online: https://sunnah.com/mishkat:4538 (accessed on 22 April 2023).

Bellah, Robert. 2011. *Religion in Human Evolution: From the Paleolithic to the Axial Age*. Cambridge: Belknap Press of Harvard University.

Bergman, Sigurd, and Martin Lindström. 2023. *Sweden's Pandemic Experiment*. New York: Routledge.

Bikus, Zach. 2022. Nigerians' Confidence in Government Falls to Lowest in Africa. June 21. Available online: https://news.gallup.com/poll/393953/nigerians-confidence-government-falls-lowest-africa.aspx (accessed on 16 April 2023).

Blakemore, Erin. 2020. Millions Barred from 2020 hajj pilgrimage to Mecca Due to Pandemic. Available online: nationalgeographic.com (accessed on 22 April 2023).

Carnegie Council for Ethics in International Affairs. n.d. Autocracy vs. Democracy. Available online: https://www.carnegiecouncil.org/explore-engage/key-terms/autocracy-vs-democracy (accessed on 16 April 2023).

Claresta, Ivena, and Dianti Desita Sari. 2020. The Right-Wing of Fly (Musca domestica) as a Neutralization of Drinks Contaminated by Microbe. *Journal of Nutritional Science and Vitaminology* 66: 283–85. [CrossRef]

Congregation of Holy Cross. n.d. About Us. Available online: https://www.holycrossusa.org/about-us/ (accessed on 10 December 2022).

Cook, Michael. 2001. *Commanding Right and Forbidding Wrong in Islamic Thought*. Cambridge: Cambridge University Press.

Curtis, Edward E., IV, ed. 2010. African American Muslims. In *Encyclopedia of Muslim American History*. New York: Facts on File, Inc., vol. 1, p. 16.

Da'wah Institute. 2023. *COVID-19 Vaccine Hesitancy: Responses to Common Doubts and Conspiracy Theories from an Islamic Perspective*. Nigeria: Islamic Education Trust, (Forthcoming).

DeWitt, Richard. 2018. *Worldviews: An Introduction to the History and Philosophy of Science*, 3rd ed. Hoboken: Wiley Blackwell.

Encyclopaedia Judaica. 2008. Dina de-Malkhuta Dina. Available online: https://www.jewishvirtuallibrary.org/dina-de-malkhuta-dina (accessed on 12 December 2022).

Fatwa Against Forced Vaccinations. 2021. August 30. Available online: https://lamppostedu.org/forced-vaccinations (accessed on 12 December 2022).

Feldman, Noah. 2009. Luncheon Speech: Better Sixty Years of Tyranny than One Night of Anarchy. *31 Loy. L.A. Int'l & Comp. L. Rev.* 31: 143–55.

Gates, Bill. 2015. The Next Outbreak? We're Not Ready. *TED*. Available online: https://www.ted.com/talks/bill_gates_the_next_outbreak_we_re_not_ready?language=dz (accessed on 16 April 2023).

Gilchrist, Karen. 2022. Bill Gates Says COVID Risks Have 'Dramatically Reduced' But Another Pandemic Is Coming. *CNBC*. February 18. Available online: https://www.cnbc.com/2022/02/18/bill-gates-covid-risks-have-reduced-but-another-pandemic-will-come.html (accessed on 16 April 2023).

Gottschall, Jonathan. 2012. *The Storytelling Amimal: How Stories Make Us Human*. New York: Mariner Books.

Green, Yasmin, Andrew Gully, Abhishek Roy, Yoel Roth, Joshua A. Tucker, and Alicia Wanless. 2023. Evidence-Based Misinformation Interventions: Challenges and Opportunities for Measurement and Collaboration. *Cargengie Endowment for International Peace*. January 9. Available online: https://carnegieendowment.org/2023/01/09/evidence-based-misinformation-interventions-challenges-and-opportunities-for-measurement-and-collaboration-pub-88661 (accessed on 29 January 2023).

Hamdi, Saipul. 2022. COVID-19, social stigma and changing religious practice in Tablighi Jamaat communities in Lombok, Indonesia. *International Journal of Disaster Risk Reduction* 15: 76. [CrossRef] [PubMed]

Harari, Yuval Noah. 2017. *Homo Deus: A Brief History of Tomorrow*. New York: HarperCollins.

Hochschild, A. R. 2016. *Strangers in Their Own Land: Anger and Mourning on the American Right*. New York: New Press.

Ibn Ḥanbal, Aḥmad. n.d. *Musnad Aḥmad*. Hadith 1395. Available online: https://sunnah.com/ahmad:1395 (accessed on 22 April 2023).

Ibn Mājah, Muḥammad b. Yazīd. n.d.a *Sunan Ibn Mājah*. Hadith 2866. Available online: https://sunnah.com/ibnmajah:2866 (accessed on 22 April 2023).

Ibn Mājah, Muḥammad b. Yazīd. n.d.b *Sunan Ibn Mājah*. Hadith 4011. Available online: https://sunnah.com/ibnmajah:4011 (accessed on 22 April 2023).

Jenkins, John. 2020. We're Re-opening Notre Dame. It's Worth the Risk. *The New York Times*. March 26. Available online: https://www.nytimes.com/2020/05/26/opinion/notre-dame-university-coronavirus.html (accessed on 12 December 2020).

JICA (Japan International Cooperation Agency). 2020. Nigeria Achieves Zero Polio Cases, Making Africa Polio-Free at Last. August 26. Available online: https://www.jica.go.jp/english/news/field/2020/20200826_02.html (accessed on 16 April 2023).

Kellison, Rosemary. 2013. Dissent, opposition, resistance. In *The Princeton Encyclopedia of Islamic Political Thought*. Edited by Gerhard Böwering. Princeton: Princeton University Press, pp. 134–35.

King, Martin Luther, Jr. 1963. *Letter from Birmingham Jail*. Available online: https://www.csuchico.edu/iege/_assets/documents/susi-letter-from-birmingham-jail.pdf (accessed on 12 December 2022).

King, Martin Luther, Jr. 2010. *Where Do We Go From Here: Chaos or Community?* Boston: Beacon.

Kuhn, Thomas S. 2012. *The Structure of Scientific Revolutions: 50th Anniversary Edition*, 4th ed. Chicago: University of Chicago Press.

Lamppost Education Initiative. n.d. About Us. Available online: https://lamppostedu.org/about (accessed on 12 December 2022).

Latour, Bruno. 1983. Give me a Laboratory and I will Raise the World. In *Science Observed: Perspectives on the Social Study of Science*. Edited by Karin Knorr-Cetina and Michael Mulkay. London and Beverly Hills: Sage, pp. 141–70.

Maire, Julien. 2020. Why Has COVID-19 Lockdown Compliance Varied between High- and Low-Income Countries? *Peterson Institute for International Economics*. August 20. Available online: https://www.piie.com/blogs/realtime-economic-issues-watch/why-has-covid-19-lockdown-compliance-varied-between-high-and (accessed on 22 April 2023).

March, Andrew F. 2009. *Islam and Liberal Citizenship: The Search for an Overlapping Consensus*. Oxford: Oxford University Press.

Mayo Clinic. 2020. Honey. November 14. Available online: https://www.mayoclinic.org/drugs-supplements-honey/art-20363819 (accessed on 12 December 2020).

Mitropoulos, Arielle. 2022. For Red and Blue America, a Glaring Divide in COVID-19 Death Rates Persists 2 Years Later. *ABC News*. March 28. Available online: https://abcnews.go.com/Health/red-blue-america-glaring-divide-COVID-19-death/story?id=83649085 (accessed on 12 December 2022).

Nasr, Seyyed Hossein, ed. 2015. *The Study Quran: A New Translation and Commentary*. New York: HarperCollins.

Nation of Islam. n.d. WARNING: Do Not Take the Experimental COVID-19 Vaccine. Available online: https://noinewyork.org/warning-do-not-take-the-experimental-covid-19-vaccine/ (accessed on 12 December 2022).

Pertwee, Ed, and Clarissa Simas. 2022. An epidemic of uncertainty: Rumors, conspiracy theories and vaccine hesitancy. *Nature Medicine* 28: 456–59. [CrossRef] [PubMed]

Pew Research Center. 2022. Public Trust in Government: 1958–2022. June 6. Available online: https://www.pewresearch.org/politics/2022/06/06/public-trust-in-government-1958-2022/ (accessed on 22 April 2023).

Philpott, Daniel. 2019. *Religious Freedom in Islam. The Fate of a Universal Human Right*. Oxford: Oxford University Press.

Piwko, Aldona Maria. 2021. Islam and the COVID-19 Pandemic: Between Religious Practice and Health Protection. *Journal of Religion and Health* 60: 3291–308. [CrossRef] [PubMed]

Pugh, Jonathan, and Julian Savulescu. 2022. The unnaturalistic fallacy: COVID-19 vaccine mandates should not discriminate against natural immunity. *Journal of Medical Ethics* 48: 371–77. [CrossRef] [PubMed]

Quraishi-Landes, Asifa. 2006. Interpreting the Qur'an and the Constitution: Similarities in the Use of Text, Tradition, and Reason in Islamic and American Jurisprudence. *Cardozo Law Review* 28: 67–121.

Roy, Sudipta. 2022. Social And Behavioral Change Communication in the Context of COVID-19: A Case Study Review From Bangladesh. *Joint Learning Initiative on Faith and Communities*. Available online: https://jliflc.com/resources/social-and-behavioral-change-communication-in-the-context-of-covid-19-a-case-study-review-from-bangladesh/ (accessed on 12 December 2022).

Schrader, Astrid. 2010. Responding to Pfiesteria piscicida (the Fish Killer): Phantomatic Ontologies, Indeterminacy, and Responsibility in Toxic Microbiology. *Social Studies of Science* 40: 275–306. [CrossRef] [PubMed]

Shavit, Uriya. 2016. *Sharīʿa and Muslim Minorities: The wasaṭī and salafī approaches to fiqh al-aqalliyyāt al-Muslima*. Oxford: Oxford University Press.

Sofuoglu, Murat. 2020. What Islam Tells us about Responding to Deadly Pandemics. *TRT World*. April 15. Available online: https://www.trtworld.com/magazine/what-islam-tells-us-about-responding-to-deadly-pandemics-35441 (accessed on 12 December 2020).

Stearns, Justin K. 2011. *Infectious Ideas: Contagion in Premodern Islamic and Christian Thought in the Western Mediterranean*. Baltimore: The Johns Hopkins University Press.

Stewart, Devin. 2012. Dissimulation. In *The Princeton Encyclopedia of Islamic Political Thought*. Edited by Gerhard Böwering. Princeton: Princeton University Press, pp. 135–37.

Taragin-Zeller, Lea, and Edward Kessler. 2021. 'It's Not Doctrine, This Is Just How It Is Happening!': Religious Creativity in the Time of COVID-19. *Religions* 12: 747. [CrossRef]

Vaccinations and Religion: Issues, Challenges, and Prospects: Conference Report. 2014. Available online: https://jliflc.com/resources/vaccinations-religion-issues-challenges-prospects-conference-report/ (accessed on 12 December 2022).

Vonderlehr, Raymond A., Taliaferro Clark, Oliver C. Wenger, and John R. Heller Jr. 1936. Untreated syphilis in the male Negro: A comparative study of treated and untreated cases. *JAMA* 107: 856–60. [CrossRef]

Walbridge, John. 2011. *God and Logic in Islam: The Caliphate of Reason*. Cambridge: Cambridge University Press.

Wilkinson, Olivia. 2020. *Secular and Religious Dynamics in Humanitarian Response*. New York: Routledge.
Yusuf, Hamza. 2020. A Message on the Current Crisis from Hamza Yusuf, President of Zaytuna College. *Zaytuna College*. March 18. Available online: https://zaytuna.edu/articles/presidentsmessage-march2020 (accessed on 12 December 2020).
Žižek, Slavoj. 2021. *Heaven in Disorder*. New York: OR Books.

religions MDPI

Article

COVID-19 and the View from Africa

Tim Davies [1,*], Kenneth Matengu [2] and Judith E. Hall [3]

1 Department of Anaesthetics, Intensive Care & Pain Medicine Cardiff University, Cardiff CF10 3AT, UK
2 Office of the Vice Chancellor, University of Namibia, Windhoek 10005, Namibia
3 Faculty of Health Sciences and Veterinary Medicine, University of Namibia, Windhoek 10005, Namibia
* Correspondence: daviest49@cardiff.ac.uk or timdavies26@hotmail.com

Abstract: In Africa, refusal of COVID-19 and other vaccines is widespread for different reasons, including disbelief in the existence of the virus itself and faith in traditional remedies. In sub-Saharan countries, refusal is often made worse by opposition to vaccines by the religious establishments. This is a pressing problem, as Africa has the highest vaccine-avoidable mortality rate for children under the age of five in the world. Dialogue between those wishing to promote vaccines and those who resist them is essential if the situation is to be improved. This article argues that Western and other aid agencies seeking to promote vaccination programs need to develop a dialogue with resisters, and in this process to embrace and commend the ancient African philosophical tradition of *Ubuntu*, incorporating it into these programs as a way to overcome such entrenched resistance. The paper concludes with concrete recommendations for how to accomplish this goal.

Keywords: COVID-19; sub-Saharan Africa; Christianity; Islam; Ubuntu; vaccination refusal; vaccine campaigns; colonialism

Citation: Davies, Tim, Kenneth Matengu, and Judith E. Hall. 2023. COVID-19 and the View from Africa. *Religions* 14: 589. https://doi.org/10.3390/rel14050589

Academic Editors: Andrew Flescher and Joel Zimbelman

Received: 17 October 2022
Revised: 21 March 2023
Accepted: 21 March 2023
Published: 29 April 2023

1. Introduction

Across the world, the COVID-19 pandemic has elicited responses from all formal religions. From the point of view of public health officials and politicians trying to mobilize an effective counter to the pandemic, these responses have at times been anomalous. Secular authorities trying to deal with the pandemic have often found religious responses to be a mixed blessing. In general, the ruling bodies of all the major religions have fallen in with the policies advocated by their own governments, only to find that, sometimes, as in Britain, India, Brazil and the United States, parishioners go their own way to defy the official and public pronouncements of their church leaders and the state. While many people have duly followed government guidelines as recommended by their religious leaders, those same people are often urged by co-religionists to ignore governmental attempts to impose upon them controlling and perceived arbitrary policies, such as the prohibition or truncating of community gatherings, restrictions on the methods of administering the sacrament, communal singing, or even total lockdowns. This tension has resulted in and contributed to inadequate or failed attempts to contain the pandemic in those regions of the world facing the most pressing public health crises. In this article, we explore the assertion that better communication–including a more diligent attempt to make global ambitions cohere with local norms–represents the most viable chance of reaching those most resistant to mitigation efforts, particularly efforts to implement successful vaccine campaigns.

There are numerous reasons why people refuse vaccines. Refusal often starts with vaccine hesitancy (VH), which has been defined as "a delay in acceptance . . . of vaccines despite availability of vaccine services", a state which has been identified by the World Health Organization (WHO) as being one of the ten top obstacles to the success of health initiatives globally (World Health Organization 2019). VH manifests itself irrespective of political boundaries, race, ethnicity and gender, social organization, and level of national development. If left unaddressed, it can progress to vaccine refusal (VR) (Mangal et al.

2014; Dubé et al. 2014; Byström et al. 2020). In the countries of the developed world, there is a long history of scandals involving drug companies. These incidents have generated significant skepticism among the citizens not only of drug companies, but also of the medical establishment engaged in clinical trials, vaccination campaigns and related activities. Government suspicion is also pervasive, and political institutions and their agents are often seen to be in collusion with the quintessentially capitalistic and Western pharmaceutical industry (Rao and Andrade 2011; Luthy et al. 2012; McIntosh et al. 2016; Jack 2008; Basham and Luik 2012; Jefferson 1998).

In the developing world there is also resistance to such medical interventions. In some settings the negative sentiments and suspicions are shared with citizens of developed nations, but often these attitudes are motivated as well by additional stimuli. These include the beliefs by many people that ancient folk remedies are superior to imported drugs; that drugs imported from the developed world are designed to harm or even kill people; that a certain amount of illness in childhood is good for strengthening the constitution (a view shared by some in the developed world); and that there are good reasons to distrust local medical facilities and personnel. Africa has among the world's highest levels of VH and VR, much of it precipitated by religious leaders who often reject the authority of Western science, medicine, and those who advocate for them. The tragedy of this attitude plays out in some grim statistics: Africa has the highest vaccine-treatable mortality rates for children under the age of 5 suffering from infectious diseases in the world, a figure that accounts for an alarming 40% of the total mortality rate for that age-group, thus making the matter one of great urgency (Bangura et al. 2020).

In this paper, we examine the reasons for the high incidence of VH and VR in the developing world with a focus on sub-Saharan Africa, consider the role that religion plays in this hesitation and refusal, and advance some concrete policy suggestions to improve the situation. We seek to demonstrate that although VR has many underlying causes, and while the conditions giving rise to a need for vaccination programs correspondingly vary greatly from one country to another, common factors can be identified in the reasons that top-down vaccination program planning does not work as effectively as strategies which go out of their way to reflexively look at the culture and context in which such strategies are meant to be implemented.

2. Vaccine Resistance in the Developed World versus Vaccine Resistance in Africa and the Legacy of Colonialism

When the first wave of COVID-19 hit Britain in early 2020, clerical responses were generally measured. The leaders of the Muslim community, the Church of England, the Hindu faith, and the Jewish diaspora all advised their adherents to follow the government's public health guidelines according to which government did not mandate the closing of places of worship, but left the decision on how to proceed to national organizations and local clergy. Government policy supported *prima facie* the practice of worshiping privately at home, reducing the risk of exposing oneself or others to infection, but allowing communities to make judgment calls about worship and attendance policy. (The Guardian 2021). By contrast, the leader of the Roman Catholic Church in Britain, Cardinal Vincent Nichols, despite broad support for mitigation efforts on the part of Roman Catholic leadership, opposed any limits on attending services. Cardinal Nichols claimed that there was no evidence that such a measure would control or restrict the spread of infection. As the progress of the pandemic advanced and vaccine development and deployment took center stage, many Catholics objected to those vaccines that may have used fetal stem cells in their development, despite a later statement from the Pope that objections on this ground were unfounded and that the Curia fully embraced vaccines (Ellis 2022).

India's government responded with alacrity to the pandemic's onslaught, progressively embracing border controls, social distancing and ultimately lockdown. The eventual vaccination rollout was severely hindered by high VR in many parts of the country, spurred mainly by beliefs in the power of local deities and the convictions that "folk remedies" were superior to vaccines. In many Hindu districts there remains a strong belief that the products of the cow (particularly its urine and feces) are sufficient, when consumed or used as an emollient, to ward off all infections (Daria and Islam 2021). In one remote area, villagers refused the vaccine because the local deity had expressed, via the mouthpiece of a "possessed" woman, disapproval of the vaccine. In another area VR was manifest in the widely held belief that anyone who worked outside in the sun was immune (Jaswal 2021). Attempts to enforce lockdown also resulted in raised communal tensions between Hindus and Muslims (Naqvi and Upmanyu 2022).

The United States provides an interesting case study in the complexities, confusion, and inconsistencies surrounding vaccine policy and ambivalence of vaccine acceptance. On the one hand, the leaders of virtually all major religions in the United States endorse COVID-19 vaccination, including Catholics, Protestants, Mormons, Buddhists, Jews, and Muslims. According to Pope Francis, receiving the vaccine was 'the moral choice because it is about your life (and) the lives of others' (Ellis op.cit.). The only American religious denominations known to officially oppose COVID-19 vaccination are the Dutch Reformed Church and Christian Scientists, whose members object on the ground that it interferes with divine providence (Wingfield 2021). In spite of a fairly unified voice and ethos in support of vaccination, the United States, for its part, has led the world in chaotic responses to the pandemic. This noted, the US federal government "offered surprisingly little effective response to the pandemic", something exacerbated by the failure of the Trump administration to take the advice of infectious disease experts. When the Biden administration came to power "infections and deaths [had heavily impacted the entire country]. A vaccination program had been started, but was poorly coordinated, resulting in far fewer vaccinations delivered ... than the initial goal" (Elflein 2022). Add to this the high resistance among evangelical republican Christians to taking any protective measures against infection, including when gathered together in congregation under anti-mask and -vaccine preachers—*'You will not wear masks in this church. I'm telling you right now, do not get vaccinated'* (Pastor 2021)—and you have one explanation for the United States having among the world's highest COVID-19 fatality numbers (Locke 2021; Mansfield 2017; Smith 2016; Hall et al. 2010).

Bolsonaro's Brazil, led by a demagogue in many ways similar to Trump in his disregard for scientific evidence, has suffered from a similar, almost mirror-like trajectory of arrogance and negation of duty in its leader, making Brazil second only to the USA in the global death-toll (the third highest is India) (Kibuuka and Gordon 2020). To be sure, certainly in the early going phases of the pandemic, and arguably still, the countries with the least excuse to shun science have had the most spurious results, and their leaders are in no position to preach. If four of the world's greatest, most economically advanced, functioning democracies have a fractured response to such a situation, how can we expect other countries to fare any better? In some ways, democracy can be its own worst enemy in the battle to gain vaccine acceptance. Religious freedom and the devolvement of power, especially in federated and parliamentary countries such as the United States, Great Britain and India, has given the proponents of VR a free hand to do their worst. Likewise, countries such as Russia, China and Japan—highly conformist societies with rigid power structures and social hierarchies—have also had to deal with a history of vaccine refusal, and they have not yet managed, for all their power, to suppress dissent (Galpin 2021; Cooper 2022; Yoda and Katsuyama 2021). It seems that VR is an ever-present factor in all types of society.

In this light, it is useful to set up a contrast between two contexts of VR, one where power and advantage counterintuitively work against nations with resources, and another where a relative absence of power and influence, perhaps less counterintuitively, provide a kind of narrative, if not justification, for refusing the vestiges of paternalism and colonialism, even those parts of colonialism which contain good. Sadly, many African countries contribute to a reality that Africa almost exclusively dominates the club of the world's least-vaccinated polities (Chakamba 2021). Two important studies, for example, show that confidence in vaccines was lowest in the world in the Democratic Republic of Congo (DRC) (Ditekemena et al. 2021; Kabamba et al. 2020). At the same time, it is somewhat specious to make direct comparisons between Africa and the developed world, as nowhere in the developed world have governments refused on principle to implement a vaccination program for COVID-19 (whether by incorporating vaccine mandates or merely by committing sufficient resources to making vaccines accessible.) By contrast, four African countries, Tanzania, Eritrea, Burundi and Madagascar, have done both of these things (though all but Eritrea had, by 9 December 2021, decided to accept COVID-19 vaccines after all) (Chakamba op.cit.).

Tanzania refused them because, in the opinion of the Tanzanian Ministry of Health, the efficacy of the vaccines on offer had not been fully verified (Makoni 2021), doubling down to assert that the developed world's drug companies would likely use Tanzanians as "guinea pigs" (Chakamba, op.cit.). Eritrea rejected vaccines on the grounds that it did not want to become a "dumping ground" for vaccines unwanted in the West (Zere 2020). Burundi claimed that its hygiene measures were sufficient to control the outbreak (Ayandele et al. 2021). Madagascar rejected vaccine programs on the grounds that vaccine efficacy had not been proven, and that the many side-effects vitiated vaccine effectiveness (Oduor 2020). Among African countries, it is routinely believed that Western, developed, "white" countries—not only the old colonial powers (Britain, France, Portugal, Belgium, Germany and Italy), but also post- or neo-colonial powers (particularly the United States)—have used Africa as a laboratory for new drugs, and Africans as guinea-pigs (Hotez 2018). For these historically relevant reasons, centered around a shared memory of colonialism, Africa was already a hotspot of resistance even before the vaccination campaigns got underway.

Whether one interprets such resistance as "ignorant", or more as an understandable reflection of being turned off by outside, top-down (even if "benevolent") paternalism, there is, either way, a problem in need of solving, but one that cannot be solved without a fresh and dialogical approach. In the same way that African-American communities were resistant to admonitions on the part of clinicians and public health officials to vaccinate when Pfizer and Moderna first announced their "miracle remedies", living in the wake of such human-subject atrocities as Tuskegee, African nations, particular those whose independence was more recent, were not so eager to take orders again from those who had betrayed them in the past. It will be helpful to separate and examine some of the components of a paternalism, perhaps well intended, which contribute to VR in the African context.

3. Factors in African Vaccine Resistance

While, as we have seen, the nature of VH and VR in Sub-Saharan Africa is fueled by a legitimate impulse to resist the continuing threat of colonialism, whether that threat is real or merely feared, this impulse is motivated by discreet and important components. First, there lingers a suspicion of all medical protocols, of which a vaccination program is one example. This is a direct consequence of activity on the part of Western, and often white, actors in the post-Colonial era whose own interests continue to govern their decision making. Second, resistance to vaccination programs derives from a suspicion which extends beyond policy making in general to medical facilities and personnel themselves, leading to a distrust of the places and people who would facilitate a vaccine program. Third, and quite understandably, access to medical care, including vaccines, is always more challenging in the developing world than elsewhere. Less exposure to something also leads to less comfort with it. Fourth, there are religious and political misgivings insiders harbor which often manifest as conspiracy theories about Western motivations for intervention. Finally, there are larger questions about worldview: in places in the world which are not so science centric, we should at least ask, is a vaccination program the best way to address a pandemic, or is something else? Because vaccines work, does this mean they ought to be the go-to weapon against the pandemic? It behooves us now to take a look at all of these factors in a little more detail.

3.1. Suspicion of Post-Imperial White Activity (Part One)

It is certainly true that while many motives for VR across Africa are based upon nothing more than unfounded suspicion, there is no shortage of documented episodes of abuse on the part of white, Western actors coming to Africa in the post-Colonial era whose interests do not align with those of African peoples. Such abuses consist both of flagrant violations of the principles of ethical research, and, more specifically, of a failure to respect the African subjects employed for research projects. Conspicuous and well publicized examples of this have occurred from the second half of the twentieth century on. In 1954, the French drug Lomidine, a treatment for sleeping sickness which had not been properly tested by either its manufacturer or the medical establishment, was responsible for the deaths of at least 32 inhabitants from the Gribi district of Cameroon (Lachenal and Tousignant 2017). Washington (2007) cites instances of recent bad, even criminal, practice on the part of white, European medical personnel in different parts of Africa. A white American doctor was convicted of murder after killing three black American patients with lethal injections of potassium, and is suspected of causing the deaths of 60 other people, many of them in Zimbabwe and Zambia during the 1980s and 1990s. In Zimbabwe, in 1995, a Scottish an anesthesiologist working in Zimbabwe was accused of five murders and convicted in the deaths of two infant patients whom he injected with lethal doses of morphine. In South Africa in 2000 a white South African doctor was fired for using excessive, lethal chemotherapy on black patients. These doctors may not have always had murder in mind when they committed their crimes, but they were white, often foreign actors wantonly, if sometimes unwittingly, sacrificing the assurance of the well-being of Africans under their care for an abstraction in the form of the "pursuit of scientific advancement".

3.2. Suspicion of Existing Medical Facilities and Personnel

In many African countries, medical facilities are skeletal, under-staffed and almost always under-resourced. Clinicians are often viewed with suspicion, figures to be avoided, sometimes treated with barely concealed hostility. In many parts of Africa, "the (local) clinic is the lowest stratum in a hierarchy of health services … " (Nxumalo et al. 2016). Compounding this impression, unfortunately, is the reality that such clinics are often the last places to receive funding, so that " … unintegrated and poorly resourced services inadvertently create barriers for poor households … " and " … impact on access and quality of care, and hence on the clients' trust that the health system will be able to assist" (ibid.).

A study in Harare found that there was a fair level of knowledge about the causative factors for cervical cancer (in large part because of effective radio broadcasting), but that only a small percentage of women would be able to utilize available services, mainly because of a lack of confidence in local services. As Lily Kumbani and colleagues note: "You walk into a rural health facility and you ask nurses about cervical cancer or cancer in general but they have no clue of what it is … " (Kumbani et al. 2013). Health workers who, through no fault of their own, are subjected to expressions of dissatisfaction from their clients are likely to become defensive or hostile, thus further worsening the cycle of inability–mistrust between caregivers and clients. The following testimony is typical of many:

> We need a team leader who will do home visits with us. The (one) that we have has never done any … We only see her at the end of the month to check on our books. We have incidents that … need her attention but she tells us that she is busy … We do not know whether we are doing things correctly because there is no one to guide us … . (ibid.)

Such complaints are both well reflected and documented in reports emerging out of Malawi, Kenya and Tanzania and South Africa, where women opt for traditional birth attendants, rather than the conventional maternal and child health services, due to concerns of competence deficiency in health staff, and to feelings of having been disrespected and undermined in health facilities. Consider the following accounts:

> "I think always of a sentence of this woman who lost her baby. She said that she lost her baby because of the midwife. The woman described the way she was treated, I was not proud of my profession . . . ."
>
> "One day, we listened on a tape to a husband's interview. I can always remember his words, 'we came with a baby alive in the womb of my wife and we left with our dead baby in a carton box.' There was a big silence in the room . . . ."
>
> "(The midwife said) yes if a person is troublesome, we beat her up. We are very annoyed with some who exaggerate and cry when giving birth." (Kumbane op.cit.: Essendi et al. 2011)

Regardless of the extent to which the clinicians and support staff charged with seeing through the successful delivery of these babies are actually at fault, there is at the very least a profound loss of trust with regard to care rendered on behalf of women's health, particularly in the area of childbirth, which is one of the most intimate areas of clinical care. Naturally, a collective memory of these experiences is likely to inform developing attitudes towards trusting externally introduced vaccination programs in these regions of Africa.

Logistical challenges and shortages of personnel do not help matters. In her article on Western and folk medicine in Kenya, Howland (2020) notes that there is one traditional healer for every 500 people in Kenya, and a single medical doctor for every 400,000. Such a troubling ratio of carers to cared-for leads to a simple truism: medicine will work best when it is administered by known and trusted practitioners. Examples abound in the literature of how important it is to trust those administering to health care needs. In Kenya, according to Howland, many do not trust doctors. The one they see in a hospital is, as likely as not, unfamiliar with the health issues of the patient's district and unlikely to form a bond of trust because that doctor is not bound, in the large urban hospitals in which they are working, to see that patient again after an initial consultation. In many settings, the doctor and patient may not even speak the same language. A local healer in the developing world, by contrast, will be known to native patients and will see them time and again, developing a bond likely to last a lifetime. (Research from the developed world has shown that communities respond in exactly the same way when there is a choice between being seen by a known and trusted practitioner or by a visiting, mobile clinic, so this appears to be a universal human dynamic (Wardle et al. 2012).) Thus, trust in a local, non-medical healer, whose traditional methods and materials may not cohere with those of the medical establishment, is more likely to be sought out by local people than any given modern medical facility.

Suspicion of visiting vaccination teams is also apparent across the developing world as well as elsewhere, and it behooves us to keep in mind that, wherever they surface, government-organized vaccination campaigns are, among other things, political projects which express state power and involve taxing, policing, and conscription, all of which arouse anxiety . . . " (Greenough 1995). In the developing world, however, the immediate spur of resistance is different. It is the question not only "What is in this vaccine?" which raises eyebrows, but also the question, "why are vaccination campaigns so well-funded and available while other health facilities, such as clinics for basic health care, are not?" (Closser 2010; Savulescu et al. 2021) The success of the Global Polio Eradication Initiative (GPEI) since 1988 is one of the great achievements of modern medicine (Gonzalez-Silva and Rabinovich 2021; Aylward and Tangermann 2011). Yet, no-one asks the local populations of developing countries what they want in terms of health care. There are arguments that coercion can and should be used to enforce the acceptance of vaccine programs (Savulescu et al., op.cit.), as well as some arguments against this idea (Pennings and Symons 2012). But there are special obstacles in rural locations in the developing world. The systematic neglect of local folk belief systems, alongside a militant local cleric telling you that vaccinations "stop you from having children", or "interfere with God's will", combine in a cocktail of ingredients for vehement vaccination refusal. Closser and colleagues report:

> in Kumbotso (in Kano state, Nigeria) and SITE Town (in Karachi, Pakistan), whose crumbling health systems' almost only functional activity was to implement polio vaccination campaigns on a near-monthly basis, refusals were common and vehement. One major contributing factor in both places is the relative *lack of availability of international aid funds for basic health services compared to disease-specific interventions* (author's italics) like polio eradication ... 'Not even a month has gone by since the last campaign, and now it has started again. Why?'. (Closser et al. op.cit.)

Clearly, there is a disconnect between foreign wisdom and local custom, manifesting as a distrust which impedes effective care at the most concrete and crucial ground level of medical intervention.

3.3. Difficulty of Access

Africa is vast, and all sub-Saharan African countries have poor road and rail infrastructure, making it difficult for people in isolated rural settlements, and in the outskirts of large informal townships, to access medical facilities. Intra-urban bus and train fares may be too expensive for the poorest people to reach central hospitals and clinics (Kumbani op.cit.). Paradoxically, improvements in major roads, such as metaling of larger trunk routes, can lead to increased isolation of the rural poor, as vehicle owners tend to keep their vehicles exclusively for the best roads, leaving far-flung rural settlements with even less transport than before (Porter 2012; Francis and Edmeston 2022). Efforts to get vaccines from medical bases in larger towns and cities out to rural towns and villages may be undone by failures in the cold-chain preservation system (Pabst and Taylor 1988). These factors and others combine to make basic access of goods and services, particularly within the area of health care, a challenge. This, in turn, feeds into a general impression that even if one is receptive to vaccination, one will have to rely on other methods for protecting oneself against the hardships of a pandemic.

3.4. Religious and Politcal Factors

"Mass vaccination campaigns (may) provoke resistance based less on secular concern than on religious belief: some will always assume that God offers better terms than the Ministry of Health, a credo that turns acquiescence in vaccination into heresy" (Greenough op.cit.). There are, as we have seen, functional reasons for the low rate of vaccination in many African countries, but the principal cognitive reason is deep suspicion of the motives of the vaccinators, a suspicion fed by religious leaders who, in the developed world, are overwhelmingly behind vaccination programs, but in sub-Saharan Africa are generally against them. The result is that most African countries have not one particular reason for VH/R, but rather harbor a combination of factors both functional and cognitive, a mix readily exploited by religious leaders who are hostile to vaccination in principle.

Nigeria, the most populous country in Africa, boycotted the polio vaccination campaign of 2003. According to Jegede (2007), Nigeria had the highest incidence of polio in the world, accounting for 45% of cases worldwide and 80% of African cases in 2003 (ibid.). Local uptake of the polio vaccine had always been poor, so Nigeria would have appeared to be a ripe candidate for the campaign. However, the leaders of the Muslim states of Northern Nigeria were convinced that the Western powers supplying the vaccines were united in a conspiracy against Islam, and had adulterated the vaccines with HIV, anti-fertility drugs and other pathogens. (A similar set of beliefs occurred in Pakistan after it became well known that the United States used the pretext of a vaccination campaign to find and kill Osama bin Laden) (Etokidem et al. 2021; Rezaei 2021). This tied in with a belief that a previous birth-control campaign was being continued covertly, using the polio vaccine as a method of delivery. Suspicion of this was not restricted to the Muslim areas. In a country with skeletal medical provision at best, the sudden appearance of an aggressive polio campaign was viewed with profound suspicion in circumstances where any measures suggestive of birth control went against dominant socio-cultural mores (Sullivan et al. 2019;

Orisaremi and Alubo 2012; Kunnuji et al. 2017; OlaOlorun et al. 2014; Oyediran 2006). It has been assumed that the cultural and religious differences between the Muslim north and Christian south account for the poor uptake of vaccine programs in Nigeria (ibid), but this is not necessarily always the case. In 2012 another anti-polio campaign was attempted. This one foundered not upon political-religious divisions, but on the ancient beliefs that either polio did not matter, or that it was sent as a scourge from God (Michael et al. 2014). In the meantime, a strain of Wild Polio Virus (WPV) spread from Nigeria to other sub-Saharan countries, including Sudan and Botswana, which previously were polio-free (Jegede 2007).

Independent laboratory tests appeared to show that tetanus vaccines sent to Kenya in 2014 by the WHO were adulterated with Human Chorionic Gonadotropin (hCG), a contraceptive agent, leading Catholic Bishops to claim that this was part of a covert campaign on the part of the WHO to reduce Kenya's population (Oller et al. 2017). Similar accusations were made against a contemporaneous anti-polio campaign (Njeru et al. 2016). As a result of this belief, albeit one not fully substantiated, vaccine refusal in Kenya rose from 6% in November 2014 to 12% in August 2015 (ibid.; Ghinai et al. 2013).

It is worth noting that Tanzania's policy of COVID-19 vaccine refusal, instituted under the previous president, John Magufuli, has been reversed since the accession in March 2021 of the current incumbent, Salia Suluhu, and that semi-autonomous Zanzibar has also now agreed to accept it (Mwai 2021). Results, though, have been patchy. Skepticism in Tanzania remains high. In September 2021, several months after Suluhu's accession to power, only an estimated 0.5% of the population of 58 million (i.e., about 300,000) had come forward for the vaccine (Makoni 2021). Much VH is due to the "traditional" resistance urged by religious leaders who deny the existence of the virus and urge trust in God to protect against infection (ibid.; Makoye 2021). Tanzania also has low compliance with HPV screening as part of the battle against cervical cancer, mainly because of a lack of confidence in provision for diagnosis and treatment (Urasa and Darj 2011). As Heyerdahl and Pugliese-Garcia note:

> Despite universal provision, evidence suggests relatively low vaccination coverage in Zambia' (Babaniyi et al. 2013; Heyerdahl et al. 2019), with the result that, despite there being provision for universal coverage of vaccinations in Zambia since the 1970s, during 2013–2014 there was only a 60% vaccination take-up rate. A systematic study showed that the principal obstacles to full vaccine coverage in Zambia were a belief in traditional remedies, general aversion to injections and distance from medical centres. (ibid.: Heyerdahl et al. 2019)

In Zimbabwe, research has shown that the rise of the Apostolic church movement has had a deleterious effect on vaccination and other modern health practices, due to the emphasis from its religious leaders on relying on Prophet-driven cures obtained via prayer, and the conviction that to seek medical help is to disrespect God and the Bible. Ha and Salama observe that "[a]postolic sect members in Zimbabwe have been associated with higher maternal mortality ... , [as] apostolicism promotes high fertility, early marriage, non-use of contraceptives and low or non-use of hospital care. It causes delays in recognizing danger signs, deciding to seek care, reaching and receiving appropriate health care" (Ha et al. 2014; Dodzo et al. 2016).

A study in South Africa unearthed similar responses to those in Zambia, Tanzania and Zimbabwe, including poor communications, parental resistance, anti-immunization policies and staffing problems, as well as the disinformation propagated by various religious factions (Machingaidze and Wiysonge 2021). DRC has one of the lowest rates of vaccine acceptance of any kind, sharing with Madagascar the world's lowest level of immunization rates for measles in 2019, partly because of the general dislocation caused by a simmering civil war, but mainly because of a distrust of medicines generally, and of vaccines in particular (Alfonso et al. 2019; Global Conflict Tracker 2021). In 2018 DRC declared its tenth outbreak of Ebola virus, but despite the virulence of this disease, and the offer of vaccinations, uptake was very low, due largely to disbelief in either the existence of the virus or of the effectiveness of the vaccine, or of both (Vinck et al. 2019).

In Benin, as Foun and Haddard note:

> Despite the efforts of health authorities, vaccination coverage of targeted child populations is still poor in many regions ... The faithful perceive vaccinating children against their parents' will to be a violation of the rights of both children and parents ... According to them, prayer is the only means of obtaining God's protection against illness ... Church members who disobey instructions and have their children vaccinated provoke their pastor's anger and discontent. One pastor, in explaining this situation, said, 'as soon as I find out this has happened, I punish these followers before the divine wrath comes down on them, because they are disobeying God'. (Fourn et al. 2009)

Resistance to all vaccines in these and other African countries has transferred to a similar disposition towards COVID-19 vaccines. In each of these examples, authority and credibility reside with local leaders. The combination of distrust of global, and often Western efforts, and the failure on the part of global leaders to convey their messages in vocabulary likely to be understood and embraced in local settings, has led to the unnecessary and devastating spread of infectious diseases across the African continent.

3.5. Suspicion of Post-Imperial White Activity (Part Two)

This brings us to the consideration of another practical and cultural factor in addressing pandemic control in the developed versus the developing world: are vaccinations in the first place the only, or even best, way to respond to the health threat posed by the pandemic? Do vaccination programs merely serve to feed the capitalist machine in developed countries by exploiting the needs of Africans? Do they, despite other benefits, perpetuate colonialism by another name? In this case, are religious leaders right to oppose vaccination? We have already seen how prominent and influential Christian and Muslim clerics in Nigeria and Kenya are militantly anti-vaccine. As Kaunda (2021) points out, "most churches in Africa today function with a neoliberal capitalist theology", which is, in fact, a kind of "Christocapitalism" because of its appropriation of church spaces in which Jesus Christ (capital good) and believers (consumers) are commodified in such a way that frames much of African Christianity as one which give rise to an alien culture of greed, individualism, and materialism. Christocapitalism, then, can be construed as a kind of "prosperity theology" through which the church's interactions with God are characterized by Christian monopolization and fundamentalist view of society that is not truly advocating for African religionists. As Kaunda observes, "some pastors deploy symbolic violence to threaten their congregants: 'if you don't give your tithes and offering, you'll be cursed. The windows of heaven will completely shut, and God will send a devourer to devour your finances, your relationships, your health and everything in your life'".

In this worldview, Christianity becomes subsumed in the wants and needs of Western capitalist paradigms, something which could explain the appeal to the large number of Africans boycotting COVID-19 vaccinations, especially in contexts where Islam is more native to populations than Christianity. In 9 out of 15 sub-Saharan countries surveyed, Muslim populations have significantly lower full immunization coverage than Christians, and Muslim women are less urbanized, poorer and less well educated than their Christian counterparts (Costa et al. 2020). Costa and colleagues note that "Greater involvement of Muslim leaders in vaccine promotion has proven to be effective in earlier studies", but this immediately begs the question of whether or not involvement of Christian leaders is less significant in breaking down VH/R than it is with Muslim leaders, and if so, why?

There are close parallels between Muslim and Christian behavior and belief when dealing with a pandemic. As Hilmy and Niam (2020) point out, in Islam there are for the most part three principles upon which Muslims base their responses to a plague: "(1) a plague is a heavenly blessing and when Muslims die due to a plague they are considered martyrs while a plague is a punishment for non-Muslims; (2) Muslims shall not enter a plague-affected land (or) leave plague infested regions; and (3) a plague cannot be contagious since all diseases come from Allah". These three principles are a result of the

Muslim response to the Tha'un 'Amwas plague of c 638-9CE in Syria, and came to be established as the normative grounds for the Muslim community in its response to a plague. Muslims in general, according to Hilmy and Niam, tend to "be more theologically fatalistic compared to their counterparts in Judaism and Christianity. While ... the Jewish and Christian population believed the theory of contagion, most Muslims did not. As a result, Muslims were not urged to flee from plague-infected lands on the grounds that it was not contagious but a heavenly blessing ... People with viewpoints that deviated from established orthodoxy were judged to be heretics".

Conversely, Christians tend to believe the opposite, namely, that one has to flee from plague-inflicted land because a plague is contagious. However, the realities of the behavior of Muslims in the real world, and the application of such beliefs to the point of *reductio ad absurdum*, show that theological discourse did not and does not prevail without dispute. Even dating back to the great Amwas plague, "Muslims fled from the scene of outbreaks quite as much as Christians, and the idea that Divine rage was behind the Wuhan outbreak is rather undone by the fact that quite as many Muslim countries have been stricken with C-19 as infidel ones (ibid.)". In fact, there is little indication that modern Muslim governments and organizations have taken any different course to dealing with the pandemic than any other types of society. If anything, arguably Christian societies, or the more militant or evangelical sections of them, have displayed greater affinity for the idea of disease being a tool in the Hand of God than any other kind.

Thus, we can see that common threads appear in all societies where vaccination is concerned. Beliefs everywhere persist, quite apart from religious factors, that vaccination is not only unnecessary, but also harmful. These common threads exist in the face of scientific proof that vaccinations work and are not harmful. The situation is made worse where religious opposition to accepting Western assistance with implementing vaccination programs is added to a pre-existing reluctance based upon mistrust of Big Pharma and the other instruments of the capitalistic medical establishment. We may conclude that vaccination programs intended to serve as go-to responses to the health threat posed by the pandemic will need to be taken up in tandem with other approaches that are not as vulnerable to being seen as part of Western exploitation of African resources or Western disregard for African mores and beliefs.

4. *Ubuntu* as a Solution for Addressing Problems of Messaging with Vaccine Hesitancy and Refusal

The threat of Christocapitalism, independent of the extent to which it is in fact pervasive in an African setting, invokes a deep historical memory, warning of religious traditions in which a Judeo-Christian character sanctions individual liberty and self-reliance over the needs of the body politic:

> The prophets were not social revolutionaries. Rather, they were religious conservatives deeply committed to the divinely established constitution of their nation, the body of laws believed by the people to have been delivered at Sinai by their God, Jahweh ... [T]hey were ordinary mortals equipped with keen social and political insight, able to discern how constitutional violations would cause social divisions, the loss of national strength, and, ultimately foreign conquest and domination ... The Book of Numbers (33:54) depicts a division of the land taking place at the time of the Israelites' entry into it from Jordan in which holdings were given to each of the twelve tribes according to their size (and then) distributed by lot to each kin group ... Once distributed, land became an unalienable sacred inheritance. (Green 2019)

Following from this Biblical foundation, in modern times, Jeffrey Stout offers the following through reference to Mill:

> ... Western liberal societies (embrace) the two key theses of John Stuart Mill's *On Liberty*: (1) our conduct can be divided into self-regarding and other-regarding acts; (2) while other-regarding actions are to be regulated by the principle of harm,

> self-regarding actions, '... *the part which merely concerns himself, his independence is, of right, absolute. Over himself, over his own body and mind, the individual is sovereign'*(author's italics). According to this way of thinking, risky behaviour in the middle of a pandemic (should be allowed) ... Mandatory face-masking is considered an aggressive and dangerous extension of automobile-seatbelt and motorcycle-helmet legislation (Nussbaum 2003). Jeffrey Stout ... describes Emersonian perfectionism as *'an ethics of virtue or self-cultivation that is always in the process of projecting a higher conception of self to be achieved and leaving one's achieved self ... behind'*. (author's italics) (Stout 2004)

Colonial powers which adhered to this "Every-Man-for-Himself-And-The-Devil-Take-The-Hindmost" approach to dealing with reform in post-colonial Africa were correspondingly not seen to take the autochthonous population's interests first. It is hard, if you are a white, European or North American, well-meaning person, not to think of a sequence of events, that goes: "Black Africa (Poor) + White European/American Powers (Rich) = Whites Go to Africa to help Poor Black Disease-Ridden Africans and Give Them What They Need". It is the baffling question of "Why-Do-They-Not-Want-What-We-Offer?" that trips up the well-meaning proselyte. But, under the self-asserting noise of benevolent white neo-colonialism, there is, and always has been, a quiet African voice repeating one simple word: "Ubuntu". *Ubuntu*, as defined by Bishop Tutu, pertains to the "the solitary human being [who] is a contradiction in terms", because that person is never one by oneself. (Tutu 2011) It is the alternative to an individualism that will not work as a successful ideological unit or norm of motivation so easily in an African setting.

We may examine vaccine hesitancy in sub-Saharan Africa in light of this understanding of Ubuntu, according to which "people depend on one another for the full realization of their humanity". As Bell and Metz clarify:

> The word ... originates in the Bantu languages and traces (back to a) precolonial life that was characterized by the following: people lived in small oral societies in which they could know everyone else in their group; shared rituals had elevated significance; livelihood revolved around the land, held in common and allocated according to need or clan membership; helping family had especial priority, but there was moral obligation to aid the community and indeed strangers ... wedding and procreating were duties; sources of wisdom, the elderly were believed to persist after death, so that continued interaction was possible; people also identified with non-human animals and the land, spiritually imbuing them. (Bell and Metz 2011)

As one widely circulated, almost Cartesian, formulation puts it: "I am because we are, and since we are, therefore I am" ... (ibid.). Vaccination programs, as introduced by Western actors, never seemed to be about a *people*, but rather about the fate of particular individuals poised to become vaccinated. Such messaging does not translate well into a metaphysical account of human existence which asserts that individual wellbeing is reciprocally tied to that of the community, making responsibility to self and others mutually and morally binding. (Nussbaum op.cit.: Ewuoso and Hall 2019). The imposition of colonialism disrupts traditional structures and belief-systems of sub-Saharan African life which trade on notions of interdependence and communal welfare.

> Ubuntu means humanness—treating other people with kindness, compassion, respect and care (and) is well captured in the Zulu adage which says *'Ubuntu ngomuntu ngabantu'*—a person is a person because of other persons. Hence, failure to act humanely towards other people is thus considered as a lack of humanness or lack of Ubuntu. (Murove and Harris 2014)

That vaccinations were presented in terms of "self-interest" rather than "communal well-being" might all by itself account for the mal-adaption of vaccination programs to sub-Saharan African environments.

Akpa-Inyang and Chima (2021), likewise, demonstrate that the Western-European concept of libertarianism, and even notions of a rights-based autonomy which emphasize individual liberties, may conflict with African cultural values and norms. "African communitarian ethics", they write, "focuses on the interests of the collective whole or community, rather than rugged individualism. Hence, collective decision-making processes take precedence over individual autonomy or consent. This apparent conflict may impact informed consent practice during biomedical research in African communities". More precisely, Ndofirepi and Shanyanana (2016) note that

> ... Values in traditional African communities have persistently been condemned for holding back modernisation ... because, in such collectivistic social arrangements, parents typically promote relatedness and interdependence in their children, stemming from a close relationship with, and strong connection to, the family. This orientation to the larger group encourages values such as respect and obedience. In contrast, parents in individualistic (e.g., Western) cultures generally encourage children to develop into independent, autonomous individuals who have less strong links to the larger groups. In such cultures, the values of personal choice, intrinsic motivation, self-esteem and self-maximisation are stressed.

How does this African body of belief translate into VH/R? Little has been researched in this area (Metz 2018), but the causative chain of beliefs leading to actions or non-actions is clear. In matters of life, the African guided by the philosophy of *Ukama*, the twin virtue of *Ubuntu*, is expected to find answers, knowledge, wisdom, reassurance and validation in the family.

Approaches by strangers promoting unheard-of nostrums for reasons unknown from an alien world are not likely to be very successful. Longstanding beliefs that Western medicines are either unnecessary or harmful, folk-memories of genocidal and racist activity (Grawe 2019), rumors of Western drug companies using Africa as a drug test-bed, or adulterating vaccines with anti-fertility drugs, in a context in which the elders of peoples adhere to the principles of *Ubuntu and Ukama*, are unlikely to promote support for initiatives such as vaccination drives. Conversely, a successful program will emphasize that local leaders prefer to keep to their own people and pay substantive tribute to ancient beliefs that historically have informed their way of life. To an extent, these native values are dismissed today by the successors of Africans' colonial oppressors.

5. Conclusions

In the ancient Polish folk tale of the Glass Mountain, a beautiful young princess is trapped by a sorcerer in a glass mountain. A young man tries to scale the mountain in order to release the princess and win her love. But the glass is slippery, and for every step up he takes, he slides back down two. So, cleverly, he turns about and climbs it backwards, gaining double elevation with each upward-downward step, until he reaches the princess and releases her (Duggan and Haase 2016).

In an article on polio campaigns in the developing world, Closser (2010) makes the important but counter-intuitive observation that vaccination campaigns were more likely to be successful if they were done less, because such campaigns were regarded as aggressive interventions by a state and funded by companies (and foreign governments) which might not have the best interests of their people at heart. They were also a reminder of how the state, and the wealthy providers of such campaigns, would rather spend money on such alien intrusions than on health centers and clinics that could address all the other issues faced every day by poor people with scarce to no access to medical assistance. As we have seen, one of the most commonly mentioned complaints about vaccination programs is "if they can be financed, why can't health centers which are designed to address basic, day to day needs also be financed"? Populations in the developing world deal with typhus, measles and polio, and no end of other infectious diseases that are not part of the medical scourges that routinely afflict the developed world. Without a fundamental reallocation of finances and resources, any future vaccination projects, however well intentioned, may be doomed to failure because they may be seen to be in bad (budgetary) faith.

In any case, no progress will be made on the matter until those most obdurate in their resistance are brought around to the view that, maybe, vaccinations are beneficial after all. Maybe the money spent on specialist vaccination programs would be better spent on building local clinics. Such a reallocation of resources could obviate the necessity for specialized "campaigns" against measles, polio, Ebola and COVID-19 because all those things—approved by elders, religious leaders and other respected members of the community, and thereby approved by the community—could be dealt with, routinely, by the local clinic and its doctors and nurses, all of whom would be known and trusted as part of the local community. This noted, some practical recommendations might be proffered for the sake of implementing better messaging:

1. Familiarity with and responsiveness to the concept of *Ubuntu* by all vaccination personnel, so that the wider mentality of sub-Saharan African populations can be understood and meaningfully engaged.
2. A willingness and ability to engage with local elders (and, on a national level, religious leaders) in order to convince them that vaccinations are beneficial.
3. Advanced warning of the arrival of visiting vaccination health-teams, incorporating a good level of accurate information for the target audience so that everyone knows what is coming and why.
4. Recruitment of local community leaders, who will be able to deliver all necessary information about the materials, methods and benefits of vaccines to everyone in the community, and in language that they can comprehend.
5. Alternative media options for those who are not literate with regard to all published written information.
6. Time carved out for people to absorb the information delivered and arrive at a decision as to whether or not the vaccine is a good thing.
7. Sustained and comprehensible education via the internet which effectively counters misinformation from the same source.
8. Transportation for people living unfeasibly large distances from health-stations, or the delivery of the service to them.

In case it might be thought that such recommendations are unachievable, Rwanda proves that they are not. In 2015, it had a 98% vaccination rate for its children (Bao et al. 2018). Rwanda is no richer than many African countries (in 2020, its GDP was 10.33 bn USD, against Malawi's 11.96 and Mozambique's 14.02) (World Bank 2020), but it shows that functioning health care systems are possible. There are several reasons for this. First, as Bao and colleagues points out, at the local level, health workers sensitize communities "on the importance of vaccinations and … health surveillance duties". Second,

> an integrated health management information system guides vaccination procurement and distribution to support vaccine delivery at the local level. Third, at the governmental level, the vaccination programme is driven by strong political will to prioritise health. Fourth implementation is sufficiently decentralized to the district and village level to tailor appropriate approaches for the local population … Finally, the Rwandan health system benefits from strong relationships with development partners and cross-over effects from global health initiatives, particularly in developing capacity for supply chain and cold chain management. The success of this approach is a result of utilizing the ancient Rwandan philosophy of Imihigo, which is very closely-related to Ubuntu in its outlook and practice. (Bao et al. op.cit.)

If Rwanda can do it, surely other African countries can follow suit.

We have seen that, in many instances, the religious establishments of any given country may be supportive of government initiatives to control the spread of diseases such as COVID-19. However, this is usually in societies where the interests of government and religious establishment cohere in their intentions towards their citizenry, and where the citizenry are generally well disposed towards both government and religious establishments. In other words, it most easily takes place in countries where there is a broad consensus (usually based upon high levels of education and embedded prosperity across the broad elements of society) between rulers and the ruled. Thus, in Britain, the Scandinavian countries and much of Europe, the role of the church echoes the aims and beliefs of the governments concerned. However, such consensus-based activity is largely passive. In such societies, religious leaders often do not so much express an opinion, much less get in the government's way. In other countries, where there is no such consensus, such as many of the countries of Africa and parts of highly federated polities such as India, and even the United States, religion can act as a negative force, disrupting efforts to control and cure diseases and ignoring or debunking scientific reason and verified fact.

In such cases, authorities intent on vaccinating the population must do one of two things to gain any measure of success. They must either suppress religious organizations and activists, or they must win them over. Given the realities of power-structures and the nature of societies in countries where religion acts as an intransigent barrier to vaccinations, suppression is neither practicable nor desirable. Highly conformist societies, with rigid power structures and social hierarchies, such as China and Japan, have also had to deal with a history of vaccine refusal, and they have not yet managed, for all their power, to suppress dissent. This leaves persuasion. The example of Rwanda shows that a properly organized, community-based structure can overcome refractory religious opposition to vaccines by incorporating them into a society where people find themselves involved in community decisions about such matters, where their voices and views are heard, and where the good sense of creating and financially supporting vaccine programs can finally be made acceptable. Until recognition is given to the observed fact that negative religious sentiments are reinforced by the perceived history of interference on the part of the developed world in the welfare of Africans, nothing is going to change.

Currently, many vaccination outreach initiatives to Africa find themselves similar to the questing lover on the Glass Mountain. Perhaps the order of things should be changed. The man in the legend reversed his approach and doubled his rate of progress. Maybe the medical establishment of the West, and the governments through which they craft their message and make their pitch in Africa, should do the same.

Author Contributions: Methodology, J.E.H.; Formal analysis, K.M.; Data curation, T.D. All authors have read and agreed to the published version of the manuscript.

Funding: This research received no external funding.

Conflicts of Interest: The authors declare no conflict of interest.

References

Akpa-Inyang, Francis, and Sylvester C. Chima. 2021. South African traditional values and beliefs regarding informed consent and limitations of the principle of respect for autonomy in African communities: A cross-cultural qualitative study. *BMC Medical Ethics* 22: 1–17. [CrossRef] [PubMed]

Alfonso, Vivian H., Anna Bratcher, Hayley Ashbaugh, Reena Doshi, Adva Gadoth, Nicole Hoff, Patrick Mukadi, Angie Ghanem, Alvan Cheng, Sue Gerber, and et al. 2019. Changes in childhood vaccination coverage over time in the Democratic Republic of The Congo. *PLoS ONE* 14: e0217426. [CrossRef]

Ayandele, Olajiunoke, Billy Agwanda, Mark O. Amankura, Gershon Dagba, and Israel N. Nyanda. 2021. Democracy and Elections amid the COVID-19 Pandemic: The Cae of Burundi. *African Security* 14: 391–409. [CrossRef]

Aylward, Bruce, and Rudolf Tangermann. 2011. The global polio eradication initiative: Lessons learned and prospects for success. *Vaccine* 29: D80–D85. [CrossRef] [PubMed]

Babaniyi, Olusegun, Seter Siziya, Victor Mukonka, Penelope Kalesha, Helen Mutambo, Belem Matapo, and Henry Musanje. 2013. Child nutrition and health campaign in 2012 in Zambia: Coverage rates for measles, oral polio vaccine, vitamin A., and de-worming. *The Open Vaccination Journal* 6: 1–8. [CrossRef]

Bangura, Joseph Benjamin, Shuiyuan Xiao, Dan Qiu, Feiyun Ouyang, and Lei Chen. 2020. Barriers to childhood immunization in sub-Saharan Africa: A systematic review. *BMC Public Health* 20: 1108. [CrossRef] [PubMed]

Bao, James, Heather McAlister, Julia Robson, Alissa Wang, Kirstyn Koswin, Felix Sayinzoga, Hassan Sibomana, Jean-Paul Uwizihiwe, Hakizimana Jean de Dieu, Jose Nyamusore, and et al. 2018. Near universal childhood vaccination rates in Rwanda: How was this achieved and can it be duplicated? *The Lancet Global Health* 6: S47. [CrossRef]

Basham, Patrick, and John C. Luik. 2012. Prescription for conflict: Why the alliance between the pharmaceutical industry and the anti-tobacco movement is not in the best interests of smokers. *Economic Affairs* 32: 41–46. [CrossRef]

Bell, Daniela A., and Thaddeus Metz. 2011. Confucianism and Ubuntu: Reflections on a Dialogue Between Chinese and African Traditions. *Journal of Chinese Philosophy* 38: 78–95. [CrossRef]

Byström, Emma, Ann Lindstrand, Jakob Bergström, Kristian Riesbeck, and Adam Roth. 2020. Confidence in the national Immunization Programme among parents in Sweden 2016—A cross-sectional survey. *Vaccine* 38: 3909–17. [CrossRef] [PubMed]

Chakamba, Rumbi. 2021. The countries that don't want the COVID-19 vaccine. *Devex*, March 10.

Closser, Svea. 2010. *Chasing Polio in Pakistan: Why the World's Largest Public Health Initiative May Fail*. Nashville: Vanderbilt University Press.

Cooper, Ryan. 2022. China's Mysterious Vaccine Failure. *The American Prospect*, April 23.

Costa, Janaína Calu, Ann M. Weber, Gary L. Darmstadt, Safa Abdalla, and Cesar G. Victora. 2020. Religious affiliation and immunization coverage in 15 countries in Sub-Saharan Africa. *Vaccine* 38: 1160–69. [CrossRef] [PubMed]

Daria, Sohel, and Md Rabiul Islam. 2021. The use of cow-dung and urine to cure COVID-19 in India: A Public health concern. *The International Journal of Health Planning and Management* 36: 1950–52. [CrossRef]

Ditekemena, John D., Dalau M. Nkamba, Armand Mutwadi, Hypolite M. Mavoko, Joseph Nelson Siewe Fodjo, Christophe Luhata, Michael Obimpeh, Stijn Van Hees, Jean B. Nachega, and Robert Colebunders. 2021. COVID-19 Vaccine Acceptance in the Democratic Republic of Congo: A Cross-Sectional Survey. *Vaccines* 9: 153. [CrossRef]

Dodzo, Kenneth Munyaradzi, Mhloyi Marvellous, Moyo Stanzia, Dodzo-Masawi Memory, and Hajo Zeeb. 2016. Praying until Death: Apostolicism, Delays and Maternal Mortality in Zimbabwe. *PLoS ONE* 11: e0160170.

Dubé, Eve, Dominique Gagnon, Emily Nickels, Stanley Jeram, and Melanie Schuster. 2014. Country-specific characteristics of a global phenomenon. *Vaccine* 32: 6649–54. [CrossRef] [PubMed]

Duggan, Anne E., and Donald Haase, eds. 2016. *Folktales and Fairy Tales: Traditions and Texts from around the World*. Westport: Greenwood Press, vol. 3, p. 935.

Elflein, John. 2022. Total number of U.S. COVID-19 cases and deaths August 26, 2022. *WebMD*, January 11.

Ellis, Ralph. 2022. Pope Says getting COVID Vaccine a Moral Obligation. *WebMD*, January 11.

Essendi, Hildah, Samuel Mills, and Jean-Christophe Fotso. 2011. Barriers to formal emergency obstetric care services' utilization. *Journal of Urban Health* 88: S356–69. [CrossRef] [PubMed]

Etokidem, Aniekan, Festus Nkpoyen, Comfort Ekanem, Enagu Mpama, and Anastasia Isika. 2021. Potential barriers to and facilitators of civil society organization engagement in increasing immunization coverage in Odukpani Local Government Area of Cross River State, Nigeria: An implementation research. *Health Research Policy and Systems* 19: 46–58. [CrossRef] [PubMed]

Ewuoso, Cornelius, and Susan Hall. 2019. Core Aspects of Ubuntu: A Systematic Review. *South African Journal of Bioethics and Law* 12: 93–103. [CrossRef]

Fourn, Léonard, Slim Haddad, Pierre Fournier, and Roméo Gansey. 2009. Determinants of parents' reticence toward vaccination in urban areas in Benin (West Africa). *BMC International Health and Human Rights* 9: S14. [CrossRef]

Francis, Kate, and Michael Edmeston. 2022. *Beyond Band-Aids: Reflections on Public and Private Health Care in South Africa*. Parktown: The Helen Suzman Foundation, pp. 41–46.

Galpin, Richard. 2021. Russia's COVID nightmare driven by vaccine rejection. *BBC News*, October 22.

Ghinai, Isaac, Chris Willott, Ibrahim Dadari, and Heidi J. Larson. 2013. Listening to the rumours: What the Northern Nigerian polio vaccine boycott can tell us ten years on. *Global Public Health* 8: 1138–50. [CrossRef]

Global Conflict Tracker. 2021. Violence in the Democratic Republic of Congo. November 19. Available online: https://www.cfr.org/global-conflict-tracker (accessed on 19 November 2021).

Gonzalez-Silva, Matiana, and N. Regina Rabinovich. 2021. Some lessons for malaria from the Global Polio Eradication Initiative. *Malaria Journal* 20: 1–13. [CrossRef] [PubMed]

Grawe, Lukas. 2019. The Prusso-German general Staff and the Herero Genocide. *Central European History* 52: 588–619. [CrossRef]

Green, Ronald M. 2019. Head, Proportional, or Progressive: An Evaluation Based on Jewish and Christian Ethics. In *Ethics and Taxation*. Edited by Robert van Brederode. Singapore: Springer, pp. 115–44.

Greenough, Paul. 1995. Intimidation, Coercion and Resistance in the final stages of the South Asian Smallpox Eradication Campaign, 1973–1975. *Social Science and Medicine* 41: 633–45. [CrossRef] [PubMed]

Ha, Wei, Peter Salama, Stanley Gwavuya, and Chifundo Kanjala. 2014. Is religion the forgotten variable in maternal and child health? Evidence from Zimbabwe. *Social Science & Medicine* 118: 80–88.

Hall, Deborah L., David C. Matz, and Wendy Wood. 2010. Why Don't We Practice What We Preach? A Meta-Analytic Review of Religious Racism. *Personality and Social Psychology Review* 14: 126–39. [CrossRef]

Heyerdahl, Leonard W., Miguel Pugliese-Garcia, Sharon Nkwemu, Taniya Tembo, Chanda Mwamba, Rachel Demolis, Roma Chilengi, Bradford D. Gessner, Elise Guillermet, and Anjali Sharma. 2019. "It depends how one understands it": A qualitative study on differential uptake of oral cholera vaccine in three compounds in Lusaka, Zambia. *BMC Infectious Diseases* 19: 421. [CrossRef]

Hilmy, Masdar, and Khoirun Niam. 2020. Winning the battle of authorities: The Muslim Disputes over the COVID-19 Pandemic Plague in Contemporary Indonesia. *Qudus International Journal of Islamic Studies (QIJIS)* 8: 293–326. [CrossRef]

Hotez, Peter J. 2018. The global fight to develop antipoverty vaccines in the anti-vaccine era. *Human Vaccines & Immunotherapeutics* 14: 2128–31.

Howland, Olivia. 2020. Fakes and Chemical: Indigenous medicine in contemporary Kenya and its implications for health equity. *International Journal for Equity in Health* 19: 199. [CrossRef]

Jack, Andrew. 2008. Drug Development: Balancing Big Pharma's Books. *British Medical Journal* 336: 418–19. [CrossRef] [PubMed]

Jaswal, Srishti. 2021. This Indian village refused COVID vaccines, fearing a god's wrath. *Al Jazeera*, June 11.

Jefferson, Tom. 1998. Vaccination and its adverse side-effects; real or perceived? *British Medical Journal* 317: 159–60. [CrossRef] [PubMed]

Jegede, Ayodele Samuel. 2007. What Led to the Nigerian Boycott of the Polio Vaccination Campaign? *PLoS Medicine* 4: e73. [CrossRef] [PubMed]

Kabamba, Nzaji Michel, Ngombe Leon Kabamba, Mwamba Guillaume Ngoie, Ndala Banza, Blood Deca, Miema Judith Mbidi, Lungoyo Christophe Luhata, and Mwimba Bertin Lora. 2020. Acceptability of Vaccination against COVID-19 among Healthcare Workers in the Democratic Republic of the Congo. *Pragmatic and Observational Research* 11: 103–9. [CrossRef] [PubMed]

Kaunda, Chammah J. 2021. The need to rethink African "Ideas of Christ" in the search for human flouring(sic) in post-COVID-19 era. *Dialog: A Journal of Theology* 60: 322–30. [CrossRef]

Kibuuka, Brian, and Lutalo Gordon. 2020. Complicity and Synergy between Bolsonaro and Brazilian Evangelicals in COVID-19 Times: Adherence to Scientific Negationism for Political-Religious Reasons. *International Journal of Latin American Religions* 4: 288–317. [CrossRef]

Kumbani, Lily, Gunnar Bjune, Ellen Chirwa, Address Malata, and Jon Øyvind Odland. 2013. Why some women fail to give birth at health facilities: A qualitative study of women's perceptions of perinatal care from rural Southern Malawi. *Reproductive Health* 10: 1–12. [CrossRef] [PubMed]

Kunnuji, Michael O. N., Rachel Sullivan Robinson, Yusra Ribhi Shawar, and Jeremy Shiffman. 2017. Variable Implementation of Sexuality Education in Three Nigerian States. *Studies in Family Planning* 48: 359–76. [CrossRef] [PubMed]

Lachenal, Guillaume, and Noémi Tousignant. 2017. *The Lomidine Files: The Untold Story of a Medical Disaster in Colonial Africa*. Baltimore: Johns Hopkins University Press.

Locke, David. 2021. Understanding consent: The importance of informed debate on COVID vaccines for children. *New Law Journal* 171: 7.

Luthy, Karlen E., Renea L. Beckstrand, Lynn C. Callister, and Spencer Cahoon. 2012. Reasons Parents Exclude Children from Receiving Immunisations. *Journal of School Nursing* 28: 153–60. [CrossRef]

Machingaidze, Shingai, and Charles S. Wiysonge. 2021. Understanding COVID-19 vaccine hesitancy. *Nature Medicine* 27: 1338–39. [CrossRef]

Makoni, Munyaradzi. 2021. Tanzania refuses COVID-19 vaccinations. *The Lancet* 397: 566. [CrossRef]

Makoye, Kizito. 2021. Tanzania struggles to dispel myths against COVID-19 vaccine. *Anadola Agency (Africa)*, August 16.

Mangal, Tara D., R. Bruce Aylward, Michael Mwanza, Alex Gasasira, Emmanuel Abanida, Muhammed A. Pate, and Nicholas C. Grassly. 2014. Key Issues in the persistence of poliomyelitis in Nigeria: A case-control study. *Lancet Global Health* 2: e90–e97. [CrossRef] [PubMed]

Mansfield, Steven. 2017. *Choosing Donald Trump: God, Anger, Hope and Why Christian Conservatives Supported Him*. Grand Rapids: Baker Publishing Group.

McIntosh, E. David G., Jan Janda, Jochen H. H. Ehrich, Massimo Pettoello-Mantovani, and Eli Somekh. 2016. Vaccine Hesitancy and Refusal. *Journal of Pediatrics* 175: 248–50. [CrossRef] [PubMed]

Metz, Thaddeus. 2018. How to deal with neglected tropical diseases in the light of an African ethic. *Developing World Bioethics* 18: 233–40. [CrossRef] [PubMed]

Michael, Charles A., Ikechukwu U. Ogbuanu, Aaron D. Storm, Chima J. Ohuabunwo, Melissa Corkum, Samra Ashenafi, Panchanan Achari, Oladayo Biya, Patrick Nguku, and Frank Mahony. 2014. An Assessment of the Reasons for Oral poliovirus Vaccine Refusals in Northern Nigeria. *The Journal of Infectious Diseases* 210: S125–30. [CrossRef] [PubMed]

Murove, Munyaradzi Felix, and Leonard Harris. 2014. Ubuntu. *Diogenes* 59: 36–47. [CrossRef]

Mwai, P. 2021. COVID in Tanzania: Vaccination campaign gets underway. *BBC Reality Check*, July 28.

Naqvi, Muneeza, and Trivedi Upmanyu. 2022. New wave of anger against Muslims threatening to hurt India's virus fight. *The Print*, February 25.

Ndofirepi, Amasa Philip, and Rachel N. Shanyanana. 2016. Rethinking *ukama* in the context of a 'Philosophy for Children' in Africa. *Research Papers in Education* 31: 428–41. [CrossRef]

Njeru, Ian, Yusuf Ajack, Charles Muitherero, Dickens Onyango, Johnny Musyoka, Iheoma Onuekusi, Jackson Kioko, Nicholas Muraguri, and Robert Davis. 2016. Did a call for boycott by the Catholic bishops affect the polio vaccination coverage in Kenya in 2015? *Pan African Medical Journal* 24: 8986. [CrossRef]

Nussbaum, Barbara. 2003. African Culture and Ubuntu: Reflections of a South African in America. *Perspectives* 17: 1–12.

Nxumalo, Nonhlana, Jane Goudge, Lucy Gilson, and John Eyles. 2016. Community health workers, recipients' experiences and constraints to care in South Africa—A pathway to trust. *Aids Care* 28: 61–71. [CrossRef]

Oduor, Michael. 2020. Madagascar takes last stand on COVID-19 vaccine, refuses immunisation. *Africa News*, November 27.
OlaOlorun, Funmilola M., Michelle J. Hindin, and Stefan Schlatt. 2014. Having a Say Matters: Influence of Decision-making Power on Contraceptive Use among Nigerian Women Aged 35–49 Years. *PLoS ONE* 9: e98702. [CrossRef] [PubMed]
Oller, John W., Christopher A. Shaw, Lucija Tomljenovic, Stephen K. Karanja, Wahome Ngare, Felicia M. Clement, and Jamie Ryan Pillette. 2017. HCG found in WHO Tetanus Vaccine in Kenya Raises Concern in the Developing World. *Open Access Library Journal* 4: 32.
Orisaremi, Titilayo Cordelia, and Ogoh Alubo. 2012. Gender and reproductive Rights of Tarok Women in Central Nigeria. *African Journal of Reproductive Health* 16: 83–96. [PubMed]
Oyediran, Kolawole Azeez. 2006. Fertility Desires of Yoruba Couples of South-Western Nigeria. *Journal of Biosocial Science* 38: 605–24. [CrossRef] [PubMed]
Pabst, Henry F., and John Taylor. 1988. Cold-Chain Breaks in Africa. *The Lancet* 331: 1466. [CrossRef]
Pastor, Greg Locke. 2021. Global Vision Bible Church, Tennessee. *NPR*, August 21.
Pennings, Susan, and Xavier Symons. 2012. Persuasion, not coercion or incentivisation, is the best means of promoting COVID-19 vaccination. *Journal of Medical Ethics* 47: 709–11. [CrossRef]
Porter, Gina. 2012. Reflections on a century of road transport development in West Africa and their (gendered) impact on the rural poor. *EchoGeo* 20: 1–17. [CrossRef]
Rao, T. S. Sathyanarayana, and Chittaranjan Andrade. 2011. The MMR vaccine and autism: Sensation, refutation, retraction and fraud. *Indian Journal of Psychiatry* 53: 95–96.
Rezaei, Nima, ed. 2021. Chapter 37. Inayat Ali; COVID-19 Amid Rumours and Conspiracy Theories: The Interplay between Local and Global Worlds. In *Coronavirus Disease—COVID 19*. Cham: Springer, pp. 673–86.
Savulescu, Julian, Alberto Giubilini, and Margie Danchin. 2021. Global Ethical Considerations Regarding Mandatory Vaccination in Children. *The Journal of Paediatrics* 231: 10–16. [CrossRef]
Smith, Tara. 2016. Religious Liberty or Religious License? Legal Schizophrenia and the Case Against Exemptions. *Journal of Law & Politics* 32: 43–93.
Stout, Jeffrey. 2004. *Democracy and Tradition*. Princeton: Princeton University Press, p. 29.
Sullivan, Kristen A., Margaret Olivia Little, Nora E. Rosenberg, Chifundo Zimba, Elana Jaffe, Sappho Gilbert, Jenell S. Coleman, Irving Hoffman, Tiwonge Mtande, Jean Anderson, and et al. 2019. Women's views about contraception requirements for biomedical research participation. *PLoS ONE* 14: e0216332. [CrossRef] [PubMed]
The Guardian. 2021. Faith Leaders in England Urge Caution Over COVID Lockdown Exemption. Available online: https://www.theguardian.com/world/2021/jan/05/faith-leaders-in-england-urge-caution-over-covid-lockdown-exemption (accessed on 31 January 2023).
Tutu, Desmond. 2011. *God Is Not a Christian and Other Provocations*. New York: HarperCollins.
Urasa, Miriam, and Elisabeth Darj. 2011. Knowledge of cervical cancer and screening practices of nurses at a regional hospital in Tanzania. *African Health Sciences* 11: 48–57.
Vinck, Patrick, Phuong N. Pham, Kennedy K. Bindu, Juliet Bedford, and Eric J. Nilles. 2019. Institutional trust and misinformation in the response to the 2018–2019 Ebola outbreak in North Kivu, DR Congo: A population-based survey. *Lancet Infectious Diseases* 19: 529–36. [CrossRef] [PubMed]
Wardle, Jon, Chi-Wai Lui, and Jon Adams. 2012. Complementary and Alternative Medicine in Rural Communities: Current Research and Future Directions. *The Journal of Rural Health* 28: 101–12. [CrossRef] [PubMed]
Washington, Harriet A. 2007. *Why Africa Fears Western Medicine*. New York: New York Times Company.
Wingfield, Mark. 2021. Looking for a religious exemption to a COVID vaccine mandate? Most denominations won't help you. *Baptist News Global*, September 16.
World Health Organization. 2019. *Ten Threats to Global Health in 2019*. Geneva: WHO.
Yoda, Takeshi, and Hironobu Katsuyama. 2021. Willingness to Receive COVID-19 Vaccine in Japan. *Vaccine* 9: 48. [CrossRef] [PubMed]
Zere, Abraham Tesfalul. 2020. Can Eritrea's government survive the coronavirus? *AL Jazeera*, May 3.

religions

MDPI

Article

Exploring the Benefits of Yoga for Mental and Physical Health during the COVID-19 Pandemic

Radhika Patel [1,*] and Daniel Veidlinger [2]

1 Program in Public Health, State University of New York, Stony Brook, NY 11794-8338, USA
2 Department of Comparative Religion and Humanities, California State University, Chico, CA 95929, USA
* Correspondence: radhika.patel@stonybrook.edu

Abstract: This article examines the efficacy of the postures, breath control techniques, and meditative states of yoga, specifically Haṭha Yoga, in promoting overall mental and physical health. It then examines whether this form of yoga could be effective in reducing morbidity or serious illness during the COVID-19 pandemic. We assess the potential efficacy of three claims made for Haṭha Yoga. They are the following: (1) breathing exercises associated with yoga may help maintain pulmonary health and protect the upper respiratory tract, the portal of entry for the SARS-CoV-2 virus infection; (2) improved immunity resulting from sustained yoga practice may help prevent COVID-19 contraction; (3) stress reduction of yoga may be effective in maintaining the mental well-being needed to combat the extra stress of living during a pandemic. Related to this claim, we examine testimony to the effect that yoga also gave people meaning and purpose in their lives during the isolating lockdown period. While exploring these beneficent advantages, we further address a serious health-related counterclaim that the community practice of yoga has the potential to create conditions that facilitate disease transmission due to heavy breathing in small, enclosed spaces. This balanced analysis introduces an interesting tension relevant to public health policy, namely that well-intended attempts to minimize indoor interaction for the sake of reducing the spread of infection may impact the effectiveness of yogic therapies and impede the freedom to practice the spiritual discipline of yoga. They may also not reduce the spread of infection enough to warrant their damaging effects on yoga practice. We suggest ways for resolving this tension and conclude with some concrete recommendations for facilitating yoga practice in future pandemics. These include (1) that public health policymakers consider programs that provide access to yoga by ensuring hospital prayer rooms appropriate in size and that, where feasible, yoga studios conduct their lessons outside in open areas; (2) that resources be devoted to providing therapeutic access to virtual yoga as a federal program, despite potential resistance to this idea of government involvement due to concerns that yoga has its origins in heterodox religious practice.

Keywords: yoga; online yoga; health benefits; COVID-19; subtle body; Hatha; Vinyasa; mental health

Citation: Patel, Radhika, and Daniel Veidlinger. 2023. Exploring the Benefits of Yoga for Mental and Physical Health during the COVID-19 Pandemic. *Religions* 14: 538. https://doi.org/10.3390/rel14040538

Academic Editors: Andrew Flescher, Joel Zimbelman and Simon Dein

Received: 1 December 2022
Revised: 31 January 2023
Accepted: 4 April 2023
Published: 17 April 2023

1. Introduction

There is power, both spiritual and therapeutic, in the incantation of *Om*. This sacred syllable that is intoned at the start and conclusion of a traditional yoga session represents an astonishing ancient Indian insight about the play between breath and mouth that creates language. *Om* encapsulates the universe, as all possible letters that can be enunciated are bookmarked by the two sounds o and m. "O" is shaped deep in the back of the throat, at the root of our language-producing anatomy when air is forced through vibrating vocal cords. "M" is produced far at the other end of the mouth, as the lips press together and utter the sound that is made by humans as they suckle on the breast of their mother. All other letters are born somewhere between the sounding points of these two utterances. As the air travels from deep in the throat through the mouth and exits the pursed lips, it journeys through the space where all other letters are produced. Every possible utterance is therefore symbolically held in this sound. In the words of the great sage Śankara, *Om* "contains within itself the entire literature" (Jha 1942, p. 10).

No civilization has put as much attention into the structure of the mouth and throat and the way that air and vibration travel through them as has ancient India. The Vedics recognized the singular importance of breath for life. Indeed, the very word for breath in Sanskrit, *prāṇa*, is the word for lifeforce or soul (Sarbacker 2021, p. 168). A deep and rich catalog of practices emerged for understanding and controlling the breath in India, making its way into techniques that are commonly used today in yoga studios around the world.

During the COVID-19 pandemic, the struggle to breathe became a widespread concern, and many people turned to yoga in order to help them cope with the perils of the disease. A consequence of the pandemic has been that people have felt reticent about seeking medical care for other ailments at healthcare facilities, fearing exposure to the virus and wishing to minimize the spread of the disease (Wadhen and Cartwright 2021, p. 331). This opened an opportunity for people to seek alternative methods of staying healthy without having to go to hospital wards which might have a high incidence of the virus and could facilitate transmission. While the subtle body outlined in many yogic texts, with its *nāḍīs* (channels) and *cakras* (energy discs), might not correspond to anatomical features that are known to the scientific community today, there is good evidence that yogic practices may nevertheless help in the fight against COVID-19, both in their effects on the physical body and on the mental health of those who have contracted it or are in danger of contracting it. Yoga's postures, breath control techniques, and meditative states have been used for millennia by millions of people around the globe to promote mental, physical, and spiritual well-being. In recent years, significant scientific research has been conducted exploring the potential benefits of these practices (Bower and Irwin 2016; Bushell et al. 2020; Cahn et al. 2017; Falkenberg et al. 2018; Groessl et al. 2015; Kuntsevich et al. 2010; Morgan et al. 2014; Pascoe et al. 2017; Shete et al. 2017).

In this paper, we assess the purported benefits of yoga for COVID-19 related prophylaxis or treatment, exploring three main areas, which we will here raise as questions: (1) is the practice of yoga effective at reducing stress and maintaining the mental well-being needed to combat the extra stress of living during a pandemic? (2) Is there any evidence that yoga boosts the practitioner's immunity, leading to reduced disease contraction? (3) Do breathing exercises associated with yoga help maintain pulmonary health and protect the upper respiratory tract, the portal of entry for the SARS-CoV-2 virus infection? In sum, we explore the claim that the overall bodily health promoted by yoga helps prevent severe illness in situations where the virus is contracted. Related to this last point, we examine the evidence for the assertion made by practitioners that yoga also gives people meaning and purpose in their lives when confronted with the challenges of an isolating lockdown. Finally, we assess these benefits in light of mitigation efforts such as social distancing, arguably disruptive to the practice of yoga, and to religious engagement generally.[1]

2. What Is Yoga?

The term "yoga" has many different meanings. Yoga comes from the Sanskrit root "yuj" meaning "to join" and therefore denotes at its core "joining" or "uniting." However, debates persist about what exactly is joined to what: is it the soul that is united with God, or consciousness united with its true identity, or something else? Over time, "yoga" has come to refer to almost *any* religious practice where an aspirant uses some method to achieve greater knowledge of the spiritual world. Historian of religion Stuart Sarbacker has recently compiled a helpful overview of the different paths that yoga has taken, etymologically and heuristically, in India and beyond over the centuries (Sarbacker 2021). In one of the usages he examines, the word yoga is translated simply as "religious practice," i.e., as a term ubiquitously referring to practices from all the Indian religions, including Hinduism, Buddhism, and Jainism. This noted, when the term yoga is used in contemporary parlance, especially in the West, it usually refers to a series of postures, breathing techniques, and modes of meditation emerging out of a system known as *Haṭha Yoga*, translated as the

"Yoga of Forceful Exertion," dating back to the twelfth century and associated with Tantric ideas of the body's relationship to the cosmos (Sarbacker 2021, p. 172).

The origins of yoga in fact go back to the earliest Indian texts, the *Vedas* (1500–500 BCE), which refer to the idea that an aspirant has the ability to tap into the generative power of the universe through self-discipline (*tapas*) and a state of celibacy (*brahmacarya*) (Sarbacker 2021, p. 56). *Tapas* is a Sanskrit word that means "heat" and is used to denote the energy generated deep within the self through the power of ascetic practices. It is conceived as a spiritual fire that can be stoked through difficult practices that deny the body of pleasure, often equated with the heat of the sacrificial fire. Sacrifice, or *yajña* in Sanskrit, is the prime mode of religious expression in the *Vedas*. All of the rituals demarcated therein ultimately drive towards sacrifice, namely the burning of an offering that is conceived variously as a gift to the gods or even as a rite whose merit impels the universe to produce good outcomes for the agent preparing the sacrifice (Jha 2018, pp. 15–18). Over time, and especially in some of the major *Upaniṣad* (500–400 BCE), which are explorations of the deeper inner-meaning of the earlier parts of the *Vedas*, the idea of reconfiguring the physical sacrifice to be a more spiritual practice emerged. This became known as the *inner sacrifice*, the sacrifice made not by taking an animal and placing it on an altar but rather by offering something of value from deep within the individual in its place (Bentor 2000). The oblation was commonly conceived as being pleasure. The aspirant offers the normal pleasures of life, such as sex, good food, grooming, and status as a sacrifice and lives thereafter as a renunciant, someone who has gone beyond the life of a householder and given up financial luxuries as well as sensual and worldly pleasure in pursuit of higher goals. This, of course, requires self-restraint, and the individual living this ascetic life is known as a *Samnyāsi*, literally "one who has given up everything" (Sarbacker 2021, p. 151).

These *Samnyāsis* took seriously the insight in many of the *Upaniṣad* that we are caught in an endless cycle of physical embodiment known as *samsāra* that is driven by ignorance of the true nature of reality (Sarbacker 2021, p. 235). We are born again and again, transmigrating from one life and one body to another, forever doomed to become sick, age, and die, only to be born again and endure the sufferings of life over and over. Yoga was developed as a salvation story to help us escape from this cycle and achieve a blissful state of disembodied union with the divine through the purification of our perception and cognition. Because ignorance of our true nature was regarded as the source of this recurrent trap, the main aim of yoga was to help us disengage from our normal cognitive state and the sense impressions fed to us by our bodily senses that fool us into believing that the world of matter is one of ultimate importance.

The ontology underlying yoga makes a distinction between two entities, not the mind and body as in Western dualistic philosophies and theologies but rather between the mind–body complex and the soul. What we normally think of as the mind is, in this case, a kind of sixth sense, related to, if more complex than, the other senses, though still part of the changing and active material of the cosmos, often known as *prakṛti*. Underlying this is the second element, the soul. Known variously as *puruṣa*, *ātman*, or *jīva*, it is unchanging, eternal, and not active in the world, forever pure and stainless and characterized by pure consciousness (Sarbacker 2021, p. 242). David White notes that "The term yoga is often used to designate the theory and practice of disengaging the higher cognitive apparatus from the thrall of matter, the body and the senses (including mind). Yoga is a regimen or discipline that trains the cognitive apparatus to perceive clearly, which leads to true cognition, which in turn leads to salvation, release from suffering existence" (White 2012, p. 7).

Yoga, then, is primarily the attempt to suppress the riot of sensory perceptions that cloud consciousness in order to let pure consciousness of the eternal soul (often equated with the Divine) shine through, just as the sun must set in order for the moon to shine through. "The self (*ātman*) is likened to a driver of a chariot made of the mind and body of the person, whose purpose is to bring restraint and control to the vehicle. Through control of the chariot of mind and body the charioteer is able to recognize the source of their manifest consciousness in the unmanifest reality of the person (*puruṣa*), the reality of brahman" (Sarbacker 2021, p. 65). Breath control, known as *prāṇāyāma,* serves as an essential practical technique for stilling the chaos of thought and turning the self's attention towards the soul. Five kinds of breath are sometimes enumerated (such as in the *Maitrī Upaniṣad* 2.6), and one can ride the breath to reach divine consciousness or *mokṣa* just as the offering of the sacrifice is sublimated by the smoke into heaven (Cowell 1935, p. 247). The *Maitrī Upaniṣad* further discusses the control of the breath by instructing the aspirant to press the *prāṇa* into the central channel (*suṣumṇā*) in order to achieve a state known as isolation (*kaivalya*) (Sarbacker 2021, p. 67; Cowell 1935, pp. 269–70). Here, isolation is understood to be a separation of the soul from its conjunction with the material world such that it will not be endlessly reborn and instead will achieve salvation.

In our normal state, the soul is radically intertwined with the material world, and our ignorance of the true nature of our spiritual and material aspects keeps these two spheres intertwined (Sarbacker 2021, p. 103). The intricate process of "teasing out" our soul from its dalliances with the material world involves a six-limbed (*ṣaḍaṅga*) or eight-limbed (*aṣṭāṅga*) system of yoga, including breath control (*prāṇāyāma*), withdrawal of the senses (*pratyāhāra*), meditation (*dhyāna*), concentration (*dhāraṇā*), inquiry (*tarka*), and contemplation (*samādhi*) as described in classical yoga texts such as Patañjali's *Yoga Sūtras* (Sarbacker 2021, p. 67). Another word often used to describe the goal of yogic practice is *amrtyu*, meaning "deathlessness." The conquest of death entails the absence of disease, and although there are differences of opinion about whether the body itself exists in a purified state in such a case, it does reflect an ancient desire to purge the body of disease and impurities. This claim about a benefit of expiation has played out in modern times as a belief that yoga can also provide medical and health benefits, releasing the body from dangerous toxins and other hazards to which it is otherwise susceptible through exposure to the outside environment.

3. Haṭha Yoga

Haṭha Yoga, the form of yoga most commonly practiced in yoga studios around the world and which has been the subject of most of the scientific studies that we will invoke below, involves a number of developments based on its conception of the body as a complicated system of pneumatic and hydraulic forces. Breath control becomes highly advanced in this form of yoga with increasingly involved practices that include precise degrees of control of the breath, sometimes leading to long periods of both extremely deep breathing and breath stoppage (White 2012, pp. 15–16). These practices are aimed at awakening and then propelling upwards the *kuṇḍalinī*, a serpentine force viewed as lying coiled, dormant at the base of the spine that represents the potential of *śakti* or energy in the body and which, when awakened, travels up through the *suṣumṇā* passage in the spine and pierces the energy *cakras* as it flies up to the top of the head, bursting into the cranium and delivering a state of ecstasy and bliss. According to Sarbacker: "This upward movement is homologized with an ascension through the cosmological process itself, from the gross elements to the subtle reality of consciousness, through the concentric circles on the vertical axis of the *suṣumṇā nāḍī*" (Sarbacker 2021, p. 163). Here, the human being is conceived of as a microcosm of the universe, with the soul equivalent to the divine power which is the ground of all being, the *nāḍīs* or channels equivalent to the great rivers that feed the world, the spine representing Mount Meru, the lofty center of the universe.

The Tantric tradition that established much of the foundation for Haṭha Yoga did not deny the body entirely but perceived it to be a vessel where the divine resides, one that could be used to experience the divine through the creation of a transubstantiated body that is the result of these practices. In contrast to earlier forms of yoga whose aim was to entirely separate the soul from the body, Haṭha Yoga accepts and uses the body in the quest for higher goals. The *Yoga-Śikā-Upaniṣad* observes that The Absolute (*Brahmatva*) has attained embodiment (*Dehatva*), even as water becomes a bubble. The phases of matter are portrayed metaphorically by water changing from a liquid form to a bubble form, which requires heat or an abundance of light (Feuerstein 2013, p. 382). The key insight of this analysis is that, here, the body is used to achieve the goals rather than being completely denied or renounced, thus producing the kind of beneficial effects outlined in some of the studies we will present below. The concept of the subtle body (*sūkṣma-śarīra*), an inner body that houses the main lifegiving functions and energies that support the gross material body, is a key player in this drama, for it is through purification and perfection of this subtle body that the beneficial effects are felt in the gross body. The "subtle body" as described as early at the 6th century BCE in the *Chāndogya Upaniṣad* (Section 8.6) includes a series of channels (*nāḍī*) that bloom out of a central channel, known as the *suṣumṇā nāḍī* (Jha 1942, pp. 441–46). The *sūkṣma-śarīra* is described as having wheels (*cakra*) or lotuses (*padma*) where the vital energy (*prāṇa*) and drops (*bīja, bindu*) of vitality move throughout the *nāḍī*. The physiology underlying Haṭha Yoga became fully developed in the medieval period and holds that the *sūkṣma-śarīra* may have knots (*granthi*) that inhibit the flow of vital energy throughout the nāḍī. To alleviate *granthi* within the *sūkṣma-śarīra, layayoga, kuṇḍalinīyoga,* and *haṭhayoga* began to be practiced in order to affect the free flow of vital force (Sarbacker 2021, p. 162).

The most popular forms of yoga practiced today are Haṭha and Vinyāsa, both of which take the traditional modalities discussed above and mix them with newer developments that were adopted from other sources, such as British calisthenics used in the Indian Army as well as the developing gymnastic and bodybuilding practices of the West (Singleton 2010). The sun salutation is an exemplification of the practice of Vinyāsa, which builds on the Haṭha Yoga practice of "victorious breath control" (*ujjāyī-prāṇāyāma*). Vinyāsa also includes other forms of breath control called the "upward flying" (*uḍḍīyāna*) abdominal and "root" (*mūla*) pelvic lock. It is also referred to as *uḍḍīyāna* "binding" (*bandha*), which means holding on to the breath after a full expiration. Vinyāsa incorporates the use of a focused gaze (*dṛṣṭi*) on a point on the body or in space while practicing the more developed form of breath control and performing certain postures (*āsana*) with movements of the body. Vinyāsa moves from one pose to the next in a fluid manner, whereas Haṭha tends to hold one in the locked poses for longer. Bikram Yoga emphasizes the ranges involved in *āsana* such as static *āsana* (seated postures) and dynamic *āsana* (standing postures) but in an extremely hot environment (Sarbacker 2021, p. 196).

The traditional views of the body explain how the thinkers who laid out the yogic system thought it worked, but their claims and insights do not necessarily correspond to modern scientific understandings of the body. While some question how verifiably measurable the benefits of the practices that are grounded in the action of yoga's postures, breathing techniques, and mental habits are, when the results of specific practices are subject to repeated testing and experimental replication, results can be affirmed as having pragmatic value even if the mechanisms of such effects are poorly understood (Van Fraassen 1980, pp. 2–5). Indeed, there is a body of clinical research supporting these observations. Yoga practices have been shown to reduce stress levels and promote a healthy lifestyle, while boosting the immune and pulmonary systems, particularly the upper respiratory tract, the portal of entry for the SARS-CoV-2 virus infection (Bushell et al. 2020, p. 547). Additionally, the health of the respiratory system is an important line of defense in preventing fatality (Beltramo et al. 2021). Finally, yoga displays few adverse side effects (Bushell et al. 2020; Agarwal and Maroko-Afek 2018; Balkrishna et al. 2021). Clinical studies have suggested that yoga has immunity-inducing, pulmonary protective, stress-reducing, well-being improving, and overall ailment-alleviating results (Naoroibam et al. 2016, p. 57). This all suggests that overall health and well-being help combat COVID-19 and are fostered by yoga. With this background about the spiritual referents and health benefits now established, we may turn our attention to the SARS-CoV-2 viral outbreak, which the World Health Organization declared to be a widespread pandemic in March 2020.

We may recall that when the WHO made this declaration, independent national governments across the globe were urged to create emergency restrictions and regulations for mitigating the alarming spread of the SARS-CoV-2 virus and its virulent impact. The biggest obstacle to this effort was the uncertainty of the mode of transmission and morbidity of COVID-19. As the pandemic progressed in 2020, differential transmission trends in various contexts became visible. Prevalence rates of transmission and the morbidity and mortality statistics varied substantially across regions, races, ages, and communities of different socioeconomic status. Social determinants of health became a focal concern as strategies in preventing transmission grew in importance. In response to this crisis and uncertainty, one form of preventive care to which many turned was yoga, specifically Haṭha or Vinyāsa Yoga, along with their associated forms of meditation. To this end, we now consider what we have long known and have recently acquired evidence for with regard to yoga's efficacy in minimizing the severity of mental health struggles, boosting immunity function, and combating pulmonary ailments of the virus responsible for COVID-19. (Tillu et al. 2020, p. 2).

4. Yoga and Mental Health

Post Traumatic Stress Disorder (PTSD) has been identified in individuals who have been affected by anxiety-producing circumstances caused by the COVID-19 pandemic. Being assaulted by an invisible enemy that could strike one or one's loved ones down at any moment is a perfect recipe for the kind of trauma that can lead to PTSD. There are many sources of trauma that operate on people infected by the disease, such as the difficulties of hospitalization, including possible intubation, stigmatization by families and friends, and the inability to be physically close to loved ones during infection. A meta-analysis of studies on the effects of COVID-19 noted that quarantine, lockdown, and the threat of severe illness and death during the pandemic have resulted in deleterious effects to the mental health of a significant number of individuals (Yunitri et al. 2022, p. 1). High levels of PTSD were noted in all sectors of society, including those infected with COVID-19, those working in hospitals, and in society at large, with the prevalence ranging around 17% across all the studies that were examined in the meta-study. Even those who did not contract the disease were shown to be at risk for PTSD due to the fear of infection and severe disruptions to social and work life effected by the pandemic. PTSD can cause serious impairment to all areas of mental function, as it impinges on the carrying out of daily routines, as well as many aspects of physical well-being (Cushing and Braun 2018, p. 21). Psychiatric consultations have soared since the pandemic began, and antidepressants have been prescribed at ever-increasing rates (Di Lorenzo et al. 2021; Rabeea et al. 2021).

In the midst of these social disruptions and traumatic assaults on mental and physical health, the practice of yoga has been shown to be effective at mitigating and even relieving many of the symptoms of PTSD. The practice is indicated in treating as well as preventing the psychiatric disorders such as anxiety, poor sleep, and depression that arise from this condition (Bushell et al. 2020, p. 5). A cross-sectional study from Brazil on the connection between yoga practice and mental well-being during the pandemic conducted in July 2021 examined the habits of practitioners of a variety of yoga modalities, such as Haṭha, Vinyāsa, Integral, Kundalini, Ashtanga, Raja, and Iyengar (Dos Santos et al. 2022, p. 127). The study surveyed 860 people and noted the length of time that a subject had been practicing yoga, the number of times per week that they had been practicing during the pandemic period, and the average length of each session. Next, the study correlated this data with assessments of mental well-being, including presentations of depression, anxiety, and stress. The results revealed a correlation between the level of yoga one had engaged in with assessed levels of depression, anxiety, and stress. The greater the level of yoga that a subject had practiced was, the lower their score related to these levels was (Kahya and Raspin 2017). Meta studies have also revealed that those who have a higher level of yogic discipline have the most improvement in mental well-being (Cushing and Braun 2018). As a result of these reported successes leading up to and now during the pandemic, more mental health care professionals and even primary caregivers are implementing yogic therapies into their existing clinical management of mental health disorders, emphasizing yoga's "relationship to distress, through mindful, non-judgmental acceptance of internal experiences through an enhanced capacity to tolerate distress and self-soothe" (Kahya and Raspin 2017, p. 116).

As a result, yoga's popularity as a psychological therapy is growing. One recent study has shown that yoga incorporating postures, breathing, and meditation administered to women suffering from treatment-resistant PTSD was able to alleviate the trauma in half of the women to levels below what would clinically be classified as PTSD, leading to a significant reduction in the severity of symptoms for those who were still clinically diagnosed (Van Der Kolk et al. 2014). This study suggests that yoga may provide a complementary approach to reducing PTSD by improving physical and emotional awareness and regulation. A second study demonstrated the efficacy of Trauma Center Trauma-Sensitive Yoga (TCTSY), which is a form of yoga that has been modified for use at trauma centers to make it accessible for people who need more gentle interventions due to trauma. In particular, TCTSY avoids requiring the instructor to physically touch and correct the student's postures and aims to give one more power over one's own body. In this study, the thirty-item Clinician Administered PTSD Scale measures dropped significantly in the trial group using yoga therapy, making them in line with the standard Cognitive Processing Therapy interventions commonly used to treat this condition. (Kelly et al. 2021, p. S-45). As the investigators report, yoga "may be an effective treatment for PTSD that yields symptom improvement more quickly, has higher retention than CPT, and has a sustained effect. TCTSY may be an effective alternative to trauma-focused therapy for women veterans with PTSD related to MST." (Kelly et al. 2021).

Telles and colleagues report that yoga was effective at improving mental health and alleviating anxiety in instances of severe trauma and loss, where symptoms of anxiety, sadness, and PTSD abated, attention span improved, and restlessness decreased among the subjects of the trials that were examined (Telles et al. 2012). Heart rates were additionally reduced when elevated, negative emotions were limited, and sleep quality was improved by sustained practice (ibid.). Physical postures were found to improve mood, and meditation was associated with increased rates of remission of depression. In the same study, yoga was also shown to help alleviate anxiety, with longer interventions lasting several months shown to be more effective than shorter interventions lasting only a few weeks. As Macy notes: "Based on the current evidence, clinicians and service providers working with individuals who are experiencing negative outcomes associated with traumatic experiences ... should consider using yoga as an intervention, but only in addition to other evidence-based and well-established treatments" (Macy et al. 2018, p. 52). (Macy et al. acknowledges that because of the holistic nature of yoga, it is difficult to isolate exactly what component of the practice is eliciting the documented efficacious outcomes and what the mechanisms for this might be. The studies were also statistically problematic by dint of their small sample sizes, poor quality baseline data, inconsistent evaluation and outcome measurements, lack of long-term follow-up to investigate the sustained effects of yoga, and poor documentation of methodological processes). Still, other significant studies are worthy of our attention. A treatment study entitled "Yoga Therapy for the Mind: Eight-Week Course" (YTFTM) addressed depression and anxiety through mindfulness-based interventions and yoga practice in female participants (Kahya and Raspin 2017, p. 123). This was followed years later by a similar study which conducted and evaluated a two-week virtual PTSD treatment of CPT for veterans with PTSD during the COVID-19 pandemic (Held et al. 2021, p. 543). Both studies uncovered multiple benefits in the target groups, including the appropriation of virtual mindfulness techniques, including trauma-sensitive yoga.

The combined take away of all of these studies suggests that those suffering from PTSD might view yoga as a long-term coping tool that could be appropriated in addition to other treatments, even if the mechanisms of yoga's functional contribution are not fully clear. It may be, as Schmalzl intimates, that breathing exercises and postures help combat PTSD by encouraging a lifestyle of self-love and self-health, a view which is reinforced by the rewiring of the subconscious away from negative coping mechanisms (Schmalzl et al. 2015, p. 235). While additional studies are needed in order to clarify these provisional explanations of yoga's efficacy, there is enough already to see the practice of yoga, though spiritual at its core, could become mainstream therapy for trauma-induced hardship as a result of COVID-19.

5. Yoga and Immunity Function

For some time there has been mounting interest in exploring the potential effects of yoga therapy on human immune systems during exposure to stress. In one prominent study assessing the association between exam-taking among students in medical school and their immune system responses, yoga was introduced as a potential mitigating factor. After screening for acute and chronic illnesses, with a sample size of 60 first-year medical students, cohorts were randomly divided equally between a control group and a test group enrolled in a yoga therapy regimen for 12 weeks during the medical examination period (Gopal et al. 2011, p. 26). The yoga curriculum was enforced for at least 35 min daily in the active study group and consisted of yogic prayer for 2 min, *sukşma vyāyama* (micro exercises) for 6 min, *sthūla vyāyama* (macro exercises) for 4 min, *āsanas* (postures) for 12 min, *prāṇāyāma* for 4 min, and *dhyāna* (meditation) for 5 min. The results of this study positively correlated yoga activity and immune health. The control group experienced a decrease in the levels of interferon gamma (a cytokine that plays an important role in immune response) as well as a significant increase in the serum cortical, heart rate, blood pressure, and respiratory rate. The experimental group did not experience a decrease in the core immunity functions and did not experience an increase in the physiological parameters that mark reduced immune response. The results of the study suggest that yoga helps resist the autonomic changes and impairment of cellular immunity seen in stressful situations (Gopal et al. 2011, p. 26).

A second, more recent study evaluated the effects of yoga on stress, sleep, diurnal cortisol, and malignant cell count on patients with metastatic breast cancer. The screening criteria ensured that the population of women selected for the study had to have at least a high school education and be diagnosed with stage IV breast cancer within 6–24 months. It consisted of a sample size of 91 women randomized into the experimental group with an integrated yoga-based stress reduction program ($n = 45$) and a control group with education and supportive therapy sessions ($n = 46$). The yoga intervention spanned a three month period that consisted of a set of *āsanas* (postures practiced with awareness), breathing exercises such as *prāṇāyāma* (voluntarily regulated nostril breathing), meditation, and yogic relaxation techniques with visuals, and the yoga intervention focused on attention diversion, awareness, and relaxation as the prominent principles to alleviate stressful experiences. The sessions included ten minutes of lectures and discussions on philosophical concepts of yoga and the importance of these in managing stressful experiences on a daily basis. The sessions were then followed by twenty minutes of warm-up by practicing easy yoga postures, breathing exercises, and yogic relaxation. The final 30 min of the sessions consisted of guided meditation based on awareness by focusing on sounds and chants from Vedic texts as well as touch and sound sensation exercises intended to produce both stimulating and calming therapeutic experiences during the sessions (Rao et al. 2017, p. 253). Participants attended the sessions of the yoga intervention at least two times per week for twelve weeks. The results showed a significant decrease in symptom distress, sleep deprivation, and waking cortisol levels. The primary stress hormone cortisol also significantly decreased compared to the control group (Rao et al. 2017, p. 253).

A third study examining some of the more stress-reducing effects of yoga therapy correlated the function of the endocrine, immune, and nervous systems to stress levels, specifically in environments where human beings experience hormone-level, cytokine-level, and neurotransmitter-level fluctuations as a result of acute stress, lowering immunity (Venkatesh et al. 2020, p. 9). The authors discovered that salivary human β-defensin 2 (HBD-2) levels increased after subjects engaged in stretching for 90 min in the context of yogic practice, a finding heralded as a breakthrough discovery because HBD-2 is an antimicrobial peptide that is expressed in epithelial cells of the oral cavity and respiratory tracts, an effect found to be decisive in lowering hormone stress levels measured in all three systems mentioned above (Venkatesh et al. 2020).

Finally, a fourth study of 19 randomized control trials consisted of a meta-analysis and systematic review (sample size of 1300). The study attempted to draw conclusions on the effectiveness of yoga therapy on people diagnosed with HIV. The study looked primarily at the serum CD4 counts, which is a test measuring the presence of white blood cells known as T-cells that are some of the main tools the body uses to fight off bacteria and viruses (Jiang et al. 2021). It found that yoga therapy was functional in significantly elevating CD4 counts (i.e., lymphocyte counts that, dependent on specific serum levels, indicative the effects of HIV have weakened) as well as in reducing stress, depression, and anxiety, while also improving the quality of life for those battling with HIV. These successful results from yoga therapy are apparent immediately post-intervention and long-term follow-up post-intervention (ibid., pp. 505–19). These same debilitating symptoms, stress, depression, and anxiety, are, as we have discussed, at issue when one is suffering from COVID-19.

6. Yoga and Pulmonary Health

Because of the long tradition in Indian yoga of deep breathing techniques, a number of recent studies have assessed the potential benefits of yoga on patients who present with chronic obstructive pulmonary disease (COPD). Patients who suffer from COPD often experience airflow blockage and breathing-related problems predominantly due to inflammation, which can be caused by numerous factors. A question of central concern with regard to yoga's focus on deep abdominal breathing has to do with the attention to the heightened awareness in every breath as potentially benefitting patient breathing and health (Dhansoia et al. 2022).

In order to assess the potential effects of yoga therapy on breathing fully, a meta-analysis was conducted in 2019 which gathered data from 11 randomized controlled trials with a total of 586 patients. The methods of the various studies analyzed yoga interventions grouped by either yoga breathing-only or by complex yoga interventions with yoga breathing added to physical postures, meditation, and/or lifestyle advice. The results of this study concluded that yoga therapy that focused on breathing exercises had beneficial effects on patients with COPD and resulted in better lung function through the measure of their forced vital capacity (FVC), forced expiratory volume (FEV), and Peak Expiratory Flow Rate (PEFR). The results of the study concluded that yoga breathing techniques can be an effective adjunct intervention for patients with COPD, as well as a beneficial preventive measure (Cramer et al. 2019, pp. 1847–62).

Acute Respiratory Distress Syndrome and Pneumonia are frequent complications of COVID-19 and surgery in elderly populations (Chiumello et al. 2022). An analysis of "upper-body yoga" in elderly patients with acute hip fracture assessed the feasibility and efficacy of yoga therapy for a population for up to four weeks post-surgery (Guo et al. 2019, pp. 1–8). The study placed forty patients in a control group that undertook abdominal breathing training, while 39 patients were placed in the yoga group and provided a regimen of yoga-related upper-body therapy. The study showed that one patient in the control group developed pneumonia post-operation whereas none of the patients in the yoga therapy group developed pneumonia post-operation (a statistically insignificant finding), and the study also found that elderly patients who participated in more than four weeks of low-intensity "upper-body yoga" training suggested higher FVC, PCF, and daily living activity than those in the control group. The findings of this study not only help show how yoga therapy can help with respiratory function but also how it protects the respiratory system from developing pneumonia. Additionally, it lays the ground for the safety and efficacy of upper-body yoga in the acute phase of hip fracture surgery and subsequent rehabilitation as a viable therapeutic intervention (ibid.).

The above studies suggest that yoga could be an effective intervention in ameliorating several key challenges that elderly patients face when infected with COVID-19. It may assist in strengthening the immune system, which can provide prophylactic protection against contracting the disease in the first place. It likely strengthens the pulmonary system, the primary system affected by COVID-19, leading to stronger, deeper breathing, which in turn has a number of ancillary benefits. Finally, yoga may lower the rate at which fragile patients contract pneumonia, reducing stress while promoting overall mental health with much lower rates of PTSD.

7. Assessment of Community Yoga

Do the benefits of yoga outweigh the perceived risks of practicing it in an indoor group setting during the pandemic? The relationship between the yoga teacher and the student, known as the *guru-śiṣya* relationship, is often cited in the ancient texts (including the *Upaniṣad*, which literally means "sitting down near" one's teacher who imparts their knowledge) as fundamental to the success of the endeavor. Some traditions developing out of the Tantric modalities that underlie Haṭha Yoga even assert that the transmission of yoga principles and practices cannot be effective without the establishment of this sacred relationship (Feuerstein 2013, pp. 11–13). The frequent claim that the teachings of yoga must be practiced and taught in person follows from these ancient teachings. The challenge in the current pandemic crisis (but in similar situations that are not difficult to imagine) is that the communal practice of yoga can create conditions that facilitate viral transmission due to heavy breathing in small, enclosed spaces. This introduces a tension in public health policy, namely that yoga may help combat symptoms of and boost immunity to COVID-19, but attempts to minimize indoor interaction during the pandemic impede the ability to practice yoga. Additionally, as a practice that has deep roots in, and is inextricably connected to, the Hindu religious tradition, restrictions on the practice of yoga might in some cases be viewed as a challenge to freedom of religion.

One study found that satisfaction amongst practitioners joining a yoga class online was lower than amongst those who attended in person in the four main outcome categories of mental health benefits, feeling physically satisfied, feeling focused, and feeling energized (Brinsley et al. 2021, Table 2). Another study suggested that there is more risk of injury to the student when practicing online because the teacher is not present to correct the postures (Sharma et al. 2022, p. 1). A further study has demonstrated that there is no respiratory inhibition when wearing a mask and performing various forms of physical exercise including yoga. Researchers found that the participants in the study had no difference in the time to exhaustion when exercising with or without a face mask (Shaw et al. 2020). Yoga practice can also accommodate an acceptable degree of social distancing, because the space needed between mats in order to provide the room for the practitioner to properly stretch and move their limbs has to be at least two arm lengths, or perhaps six feet. It may be, then, that the effects of practicing yoga in person, using masks in a well ventilated and socially distanced area, may outweigh the threat of iatrogenic disease while producing the mental and physical benefits that can keep practitioners healthier during this difficult epidemic.

There are other factors to consider as well when determining whether yoga should be practiced in person versus online during the pandemic. To fight off a pandemic, we need stronger, more resilient, and more productive communities, which can be achieved through community connectedness, which itself in turn is a byproduct of communal yoga therapy at studios, health centers/clubs, and rehabilitation centers (McGrath et al. 2017, p. 101). We have to remember that there are many situations in which the importance of being together in a physical place outweighs the risks of contagion, such as at hospitals. The health care workers have to come into contact with the patients in order to treat them, so the question then becomes whether a yoga instructor can be thought of in these terms as well. As a therapy that is recognized as having health benefits both by the National Center for Complementary and Integrative Health and the American College of Physicians (https://www.nccih.nih.gov/health/yoga-what-you-need-to-know) (accessed on 4 February 2023), it is clear that yoga instructors are important adjunct healthcare workers and should be treated as such.

Those who already live and work in congregate settings could readily find communal yoga to be a helpful tool for maintaining health. The most integral part of a resilient community during a pandemic is its healthcare workforce. Healthcare workers (HCWs) are already at a higher risk of suicide before a pandemic and at an even higher risk of suicide during a pandemic. Bismark et al. (2022) address how the pandemic magnified their pre-existing mental illness as well as issues in their personal lives such as domestic violence and financial struggles. During the pandemic, HCWs faced an increase in work obligations while facing depletion of the necessary medical resources. HCWs recommended that having a stronger sense of belonging would have been more beneficial to mitigate suicidal thoughts (Bismark et al. 2022, p. 113). Communal yoga can help provide HCWs' need for belonging and connectedness in order to quell thoughts of suicide or self-harm.

Communal yoga would not only be beneficial to HCWs but to their patients as well. In addition to maintaining HCW durability in the workplace, patients could benefit from direct access to yoga practice which has been shown to improve strength, balance, flexibility, and attention control as well as providing a greater sense of belonging, community connection, and the ability to move forward with their lives (Donnelly et al. 2020, p. 2482). Fall prevention programs that use yoga therapy have been studied for those who have Parkinson's Disease. In fact, one study, despite its small sample size, was able to find that the experimental group that received yoga therapy had a significant reduction in fall risk compared to their control group. Both groups experienced improvements in motor function, postural stability, functional gait, and freezing gait (Van Puymbroeck et al. 2018, p. 1). A study analyzing the WDEQ pregnancy-related anxiety questionnaire assessment also found yoga to be effective in reducing anxiety as a form of prenatal care (Newham et al. 2014, p. 631).

Prisons provide yet another forced congregate setting which might take advantage of in-person yoga practice. A review of the relevant literature related to yoga in prisons found that yoga helped alleviate aggression and violent behavior through its stress-reducing effects (Muirhead and Fortune 2016, p. 57). A systematic review on yoga for substance abusers found significant cessation of substance use by using yoga therapy alone or when using yoga therapy in conjunction with other pharmacological treatment modalities such as opioid substitution therapy (Walia et al. 2021, p. 964).

The above considerations lead us to surmise that for individuals who find themselves during a pandemic type situation in unavoidable congregate environments (such as various sorts of healthcare facilities, nursing facilities, and prisons), communal yoga practiced with masks and social distancing can be commended for disability rehabilitation, substance abuse rehabilitation, aggression alleviation, suicide prevention, fall prevention, prenatal care, and postnatal care and may be successful in maintaining or improving mental health and physical wellness. Public health policymakers might also consider programs that provide safe access to yoga by ensuring hospital prayer or meditation rooms appropriate in size and ventilation for yoga to be practiced with as little risk as possible.

8. Public Health Policy Implications of Yoga Practice

The evidence brought forward in this paper suggests that yoga practice can help to prevent or mitigate symptoms of COVID-19 and improve overall mental and physical health—with the caveat that additional research, maintaining rigorous experimental design standards with larger sample sizes as well as extended longitudinal and meta studies, needs to be undertaken. We have also just suggested above that in-person communal yoga practice has greater benefits and fewer adverse effects than yoga practiced alone at home, and, therefore, if people are already living in a congregate setting, then practicing communal yoga is likely to be beneficial even during a pandemic. However, if the research is more than suggestive that yoga interventions are efficacious, what public health policies might we consider appropriate to actively support therapies to enhance patient care and population well-being more broadly? Are there circumstances in which those who are not already in a congregate setting ought to practice yoga in person? How might this compare to other spiritual practices?

During the very earliest days of the COVID-19 pandemic, and frequently later during acute surges of viral transmission, many religious communities shut down their places of worship and eliminated face-to-face worship and community events. In the United States, state governments generally argued for such mandatory closures on the basis of the Supreme Court decision in Department of Human Resources Oregon vs. Alfred Smith (1989) that if a law was enacted that encroached on religious liberty but did so for the public good and did not single out any particular religion for unequal treatment, then such policies could be construed as permissible under the US Constitution (Levison and Segall 2020, p. 1). In the earliest days of the virus before vaccines and therapeutic treatments were widely available, as well as in subsequent months where large gatherings were established as transmissible events, many early cases of mass contagion were traced to religious gatherings (Linke and Jankowski 2022, p. 1641). As businesses were gradually allowed to open at reduced capacity, some states such as California still required religious institutions to remain shuttered. Legal challenges mounted and the Supreme Court ruled that the religious institutions were being treated unfairly because other buildings were allowed to reopen at limited capacity (Breslow and Totenberg 2021, p. 1). Many yoga studios closed of their own volition during the height of the pandemic and others were forced to shut down due to government regulations. Many yoga studios were forced due to economic reasons to close for good, and YogaWorks, one of the largest chains of studios, filed for Chapter 11 bankruptcy citing the effects of the pandemic (Club Industry 2020).

Curtailing the spread of COVID-19 was, and remains, a public good. However, as effective barriers to transmission have increased, as vaccination and infection have become more widespread and effective in their protection against serious reinfection, and as the benefits of prohibiting all gatherings has been offset by various costs and burdens society incurs for practicing such a restrictive policy, there have been significant shifts in public policy.

This raises the interesting ethical question of whether—with the goal of combatting COVID-19 and advancing health in more general terms—it is better to allow communal religious practices or forbid them. It is important to note in this regard that many patients have positive outlooks toward physician involvement in spiritual issues, with 77% in one study saying that physicians should consider patients' spiritual needs and 37% wanting their physicians to discuss religious beliefs with them more frequently (King and Bushwick 1994). Many religious and spiritual practices besides yoga have been shown to be linked to increased mental and physical health (Linke and Jankowski 2022, p. 1641). It has been known for some time that regular churchgoers, for example, tend to have longer life expectancy and better overall health than appropriate control groups (Mullen 1990). What might account for this? Other than reducing stress, it is likely that participation in religious services itself is not the proximate causal event that brings about the improved health noted in studies. Rather, those who attend are likely in other settings to make healthier lifestyle choices, have less substance abuse, more secure friendships and family relationships, and follow doctors' instructions more carefully. This has led some to believe that going to a place of worship such as a church or synagogue even during the pandemic (and with some of the risks that it entails) may have tangible psycho-social or health benefits.

In spite of the fact that public health analysis with respect to social distancing, viral spread, and relevant mitigation has equated studio-based yoga practice with church attendance, there may be important differences between the two that justify how we support or restrict these practices in the time of a pandemic. In the case of yoga, it is the actual practice—not just attendance—that leads to the positive health outcomes. Though studies have shown that areas with lower attendance of religious services had lower transmission (Linke and Jankowski 2022, p. 1641), there may nevertheless be some benefits to one's health from attending yoga classes, if the various benefits that we have outlined so far in this article turn out to be sufficiently effective. A central question then becomes whether the same effects can be obtained from doing yoga virtually with online instructors and whether the balance of safety with promoting health dictates that yoga should be practiced individually rather than communally in groups to avoid iatrogenic effects from yoga practice.

As the pandemic proceeded through its natural cycle over several years, many yoga practitioners continued to practice apart from their regular studio experience, setting their mats up at home and often participating in online yoga instruction. Such practice expanded significantly during the pandemic. Yoga equipment sales grew 154% during the course of the pandemic as many people sought to maintain this important part of their lives at home (Business Wire 2020, p. 1). Adriene Mishler is an example of a successful online yoga instructor. She uploaded yoga videos onto her YouTube channel Yoga with Adriene, and, within the first three months of the pandemic, video views went from 500,000 to 1.5 million views each day (Okamoto 2021, p. 1). However, as yoga instructor Amy Suplina notes, "The intimacy and reverence that occur in a studio are essential. The reason we teach yoga is that alchemy of having bodies together breathing and moving in a room, and seeing people, and connecting and sharing that experience" (Okamoto 2021, p. 1). We also noted above that the benefits of yoga when practiced at home through online instruction are not as robust as those that accrue when doing yoga in person energized (Brinsley et al. 2021, Table 2). To retain the noted benefits of group in-person practice during the pandemic, some private yoga studios held outdoor or rooftop yoga with proper social distancing in order to accommodate the needs of the community. (Similar sorts of arrangements were appropriated by various religious communities as well).

Amy Suplina's notion of the importance of practicing yoga in-person can be further evaluated in light of the fact that most people in America, regardless of the various preventive measures that were put into place, ended up contracting COVID-19 anyway. The government's strict mandated isolation requirements may not have reduced the overall number of people who contracted the disease but did become obstacles to preventive care involving religious practices such as yoga therapy. While, of course, practices such as wearing masks and keeping some distance from others are highly effective at preventing the immediate spread of COVID-19 and other similarly contagious respiratory diseases, the practical aspects of life are such that no one can be expected to actually stay away from others or wear a mask properly at all times in public. Even with all of the restrictions that have been in place, most people in America seem to have contracted the virus at some point during the pandemic. The Center for Disease Control reports that the total number of reported cases as of March 2023 was 103,672,529 (CDC Covid Data Tracker 2023). However, an earlier CDC study suggests that the majority of cases have gone unreported, finding in September 2021 that only about 1 in 4 cases since the start of the pandemic had been reported (Estimated COVID-19 Burden 2023). If these low reporting estimates are anything close to the actual reporting frequencies, this would suggest that almost everyone in America, knowingly or unknowingly, contracted COVID-19 at some point during the pandemic. The CDC also announced in April 2022 that at least 60% of the population had had COVID-19 at some point (Neel 2022), and at the time of this writing, almost a year later, the disease is still very much on the march, so the numbers must be considerably higher than that currently. Finally, we also see that there do not appear to be significant differences in the total number of cases between states with strict and lenient prevention policies. For example, California has particularly tough restrictions that include mandatory masking at healthcare facilities, homeless shelters, and jails, whereas Texas actually prohibits schools and local governments from instituting masking requirements at all (Markowitz 2023). Yet, at the time of this writing, California had a total case rate of 306,189 per million residents, whereas Texas had a total number of cases standing at 290,688 per million (United States Worldometer 2023). This suggests that while the masking and other provisions may delay the contraction of COVID-19 and flatten the curve that represents the case rate on a graph, they do not eliminate it. If masking is held to be important for attenuating the number of cases at any one time in order not to overwhelm the healthcare system, then one might also add that yoga could help in this endeavor as well. Ventilator shortages and shortages in other healthcare resources have been an ongoing problem during the pandemic, and, as such, the benefits of yoga therapy that we have laid out could help keep some people out of the hospitals, even if they did not mitigate the actual spread of the disease.

The extremely high total number of COVID-19 cases as we enter three years of pandemic thus adds yet another layer of complexity onto the question of whether yoga should be practiced in person in such a situation. If people are highly likely to eventually contract the disease no matter what they do, then are the potential benefits of practicing yoga in the traditional and most effective manner, namely in person with an experienced teacher acting as a guide, worth the risk?

If the benefits to immunity function, as well as pulmonary and mental health are indeed as robust as the studies that we have highlighted here indicate, and any given individual is likely at some point to contract the disease, then it may be that the risk of contracting the disease during any given session of communal yoga practice is outweighed by the health benefits acquired by the practice of yoga. There are a few scenarios that could play out in this situation: (a) an individual could practice yoga with a mask in a communal setting and never contract COVID-19; (b) an individual could practice yoga communally and contract COVID-19 from others at the yoga studio; (c) an individual could practice yoga communally and contract COVID-19 from other places; (d) an individual could cease practicing yoga or practice it less effectively on their own and contract COVID-19; (e) an individual could cease practicing yoga and never contract COVID-19. Out of these possibilities, only (b) involves iatrogenic disease that emerged out of the communal yoga practice itself. However, even here, if the individual did not practice yoga, based on the above mentioned case rates, it is still likely that they would have contracted the disease elsewhere eventually, but, in this case, they would not have the increased resistance that emerges from yoga practice. Moreover, the full benefits of doing communal yoga would accrue to all of the individuals in cases a, b, and c. Partial benefits might accrue in case d and none in case e (although they would not be needed).

The cost–benefit analysis of doing communal yoga is therefore extremely complex and not as straightforward as simply avoiding yoga studios. Ultimately, it may be impossible to assess the risk properly because of too many unknowable factors, but these scenarios represent an attempt to take as many factors as are now known into consideration, and it is worth noting that of the five possible scenarios, in only one case (b), does it appear that communal yoga could cause more harm than good. However, even here, there is nothing to rule out the possibility that this individual would have later found themselves contracting COVID-19 elsewhere, even if had they somehow known they would have contracted the disease at the yoga studio and ceased attending.

9. Public Health Policy Proposal

For those who are working remotely from home and are not already gathered in public places such as hospitals and prisons, the question of whether the benefits of communal yoga outweigh the dangers of being near others during a pandemic such as COVID-19 is, as shown in the previous discussion, very complicated. There are good reasons for these people to practice yoga in person because the benefits to any future contraction of the disease may outweigh the possibility that they will contract the disease at the yoga studio. However, while satisfaction with yoga was higher when practiced in person based on the study by Brinsley et al. (2021), it may be the case that to avoid iatrogenic effects, yoga practiced in isolation through video instruction can be recommended for those who are immunocompromised, elderly, or for other reasons must take the utmost caution with regard to exposure to the disease.

We would also recommend that, where feasible, yoga studios conduct their lessons outside in open areas. This is, of course, the easiest way to mitigate the spread of the disease while still experiencing the benefits of communal yoga practice with a live teacher. We also suggest resources be devoted to providing therapeutic access to virtual yoga as a federal program for those who are uncomfortable going to yoga studios in person, but we recognize that there may be some resistance to government involvement due to the concern that yoga has its origins in religious practice. However, the United States National Institute of Health (NIH) and the National Center for Complementary and Integrative Health (NCCIH 2022) have established stress-related initiatives and are considering ways in which yoga may be able to help with breathing-related diseases and future infectious threats just as the Ministry of AYUSH of the Government of India urged their people to protect their health by immune boosting techniques through yoga (Debnath and Bardhan 2020, p. 1). Despite its religious roots, yoga is nevertheless regarded as an allowable recipient of public funds and has received endorsement from the NCCIH (Black et al. 2018, p. 1).

10. Conclusions

Yoga has been practiced in different forms throughout India for millennia and is spreading globally. In both its historic and contemporary settings, it has been viewed as a path from the confines of the body to ultimate salvation. Some strands of the tradition—such as Hatha and Vinyasa Yoga—use the body itself to achieve higher states of consciousness as well as to achieve esoteric powers through the practice of various techniques of breath and body control. Clinical research has suggested that some of these techniques have health benefits with statistically significant outcomes that boost immunity and pulmonary strength as well as improve mental well-being. The practice of yoga has been recognized by the NCCIH as a legitimate form of alternative or complementary medicine. Significant research is continuing into the health benefits of yoga. As such, there are possibilities to acquire funding to provide more access and information for the practice of yoga as seen by the sponsorship for Yoga Warriors (501(c)(3)) through the 2019 Mission Act (Reddy et al. 2019, p. 1592).

In future pandemics and similar cultural challenges, we recommend that national governments sponsor yoga practices through the implementation of communication and practices similar to that advanced by India's Ministry of AYUSH during the COVID-19 pandemic (Debnath and Bardhan 2020, p. 1). The United States government should designate outdoor spaces that are amenable to social distancing and promote such areas for outdoor and appropriately distanced physical activity. The peak of the recent COVID-19 pandemic produced the promising prevalence of rooftop yoga for aspiring newcomers as well as avid practitioners. For those who are immunocompromised and are unable to risk human interaction during a pandemic, there should be government assistance for free online yoga classes through the NIH-NCCIH or appropriate websites. The NIH-NCCIH should also promote their currently free published *eBook on Yoga Health* from their website during times of severe outbreak to encourage people to practice preventative self-care. Future editions of this publication should describe how yoga can help combat any new upcoming pandemic. For those who believe yoga to be a practice grounded in faith, and not just a secular endeavor, the government should ensure prayer rooms at healthcare and community centers and have social distancing in order to allow for this practice to take place.

Author Contributions: Writing—original draft, R.P.; Writing—review & editing, D.V. All authors have read and agreed to the published version of the manuscript.

Funding: This research received no external funding.

Conflicts of Interest: The authors declare no conflict of interest.

Note

1 A word about methodology. In researching, we conducted a literature review using articles published from 2012 to 2021 utilizing the search engines PubMed and Google Scholar in order to find articles on Hatha Yoga and PTSD, Hatha Yoga and Anxiety, Hatha Yoga and Depression, Hatha Yoga and Immunity, Hatha Yoga and COPD, Hatha Yoga and Pneumonia, and Hatha Yoga and COVID-19. Articles were then filtered by sample size and clarity of methodology, with longitudinal studies and meta-analyses prioritized because of their higher level of statistical significance. If a study resulted in a finding that was not uncovered by other

researchers, then the new findings were addressed. If a given study had a distinct method for administering experimental Hatha yoga, its intercalated yoga techniques were addressed. Finally, the contribution of the longitudinal meta-analyses studies to this research was determined by the duration of their time period as well as their unique findings.

References

Agarwal, Ram P., and Adi Maroko-Afek. 2018. Yoga into cancer care: A review of the evidence-based research. *International Journal of Yoga* 11: 3. [PubMed]

Balkrishna, Acharya, Dipak Chetry, Sachin Sharma, and Shirley Telles. 2021. Benefits and adverse effects associated with yoga practice: A cross-sectional survey from India. *Complementary Therapies in Medicine* 57: 102644. [CrossRef]

Beltramo, Guillaume, Jonathan Cottenet, Anne-Sophie Mariet, Marjolaine Georges, Lionel Piroth, Pascale Tubert-Bitter, Philippe Bonniaud, and Catherine Quantin. 2021. Chronic respiratory diseases are predictors of severe outcome in COVID-19 hospitalised patients: A nationwide study. *European Respiratory Journal* 58: 2004474. [CrossRef] [PubMed]

Bentor, Yael. 2000. Interiorized Fire Rituals in India and Tibet. *Journal of the American Oriental Society* 120: 594–613. [CrossRef]

Bismark, Marie, Natasha Smallwood, Ria Jain, and Karen Willis. 2022. Thoughts of suicide or self-harm among healthcare workers during the COVID-19 pandemic: Qualitative analysis of open-ended survey responses. *BJPsych Open* 8: e113. [CrossRef]

Black, Lindsey I., Patricia M. Barnes, Tainya C. Clarke, Barbara J. Stussman, and Richard L. Nahin. 2018. *Use of Yoga, Meditation, and Chiropractors among US Children Aged 4–17 Years*; Washington, DC: US Department of Health and Human Services, Centers for Disease Control and Prevention, National Center for Health Statistics.

Bower, Julienne E., and Michael R. Irwin. 2016. Mind-body therapies and control of inflammatory biology: A descriptive review. *Brain Behavior and Immunity* 51: 1–11. [CrossRef]

Breslow, Jason, and Nina Totenberg. 2021. Supreme Court Rules against Calif. In *Doubles down on Religious Rights amid Pandemic*. Washington, DC: NPR. Available online: https://www.npr.org/2021/02/06/964822479/supreme-court-rules-against-california-ban-on-in-person-worship-amid-the-pandemi (accessed on 5 February 2023).

Brinsley, Jacinta, Matthew Smout, and Kade Davison. 2021. Satisfaction with Online Versus In-Person Yoga During COVID-19. *The Journal of Alternative and Complementary Medicine* 27: 893–6. [CrossRef]

Bushell, William, Ryan Castle, Michelle A. Williams, Kimberly C. Brouwer, Rudolph E. Tanzi, Deepak Chopra, and Paul J. Mills. 2020. Meditation and yoga practices as potential adjunctive treatment of SARS-CoV-2 infection and COVID-19: A brief overview of key subjects. *The Journal of Alternative and Complementary Medicine* 26: 547–56. [CrossRef]

Business Wire. 2020. Yoga Equipment Sees 154% Growth as Consumers Focus on Wellness at Home during COVID-19—Researchandmarkets.com. Available online: https://www.businesswire.com/news/home/20200501005330/en/Yoga-Equipment-Sees-154-Growth-as-Consumers-Focus-on-Wellness-at-Home-During- (accessed on 3 November 2022).

Cahn, B. Rael, Matthew S. Goodman, Christine T. Peterson, Raj Maturi, and Paul J. Mills. 2017. Yoga, meditation and mind-body health: Increased BDNF, cortisol awakening response, and altered inflammatory marker expression after a 3-month yoga and meditation retreat. *Frontiers in Human Neuroscience* 11: 315. [CrossRef]

CDC Covid Data Tracker. 2023. Centers for Disease Control and Prevention. Available online: https://covid.cdc.gov/covid-data-tracker/#datatracker-home (accessed on 14 March 2023).

Chiumello, Davide, Leo Modafferi, and Isabella Fratti. 2022. Risk Factors and Mortality in Elderly ARDS COVID-19 Compared to Patients without COVID-19. *Journal of Clinical Medicine* 11: 5180. [CrossRef]

Club Industry. 2020. Yoga Works Files for Chapter 11, Permanently Closes All Studios. Available online: https://www.clubindustry.com/commercial-clubs/yogaworks-files-for-chapter-11-permanently-closes-all-studios (accessed on 16 October 2020).

Cowell, E. B., trans. 1935. *The Maitrī Upaniṣad with the Commentary of Rāmatīrtha*. Calcutta: Baptist Mission Press.

Cramer, Holger, Heidemarie Haller, Petra Klose, Lesley Ward, Vincent CH Chung, and Romy Lauche. 2019. The risks and benefits of yoga for patients with chronic obstructive pulmonary disease: A systematic review and meta-analysis. *Clinical Rehabilitation* 33: 1847–62. [CrossRef] [PubMed]

Cushing, Robyn, and Kathryn Braun. 2018. Mind-Body Therapy for Military Veterans with Post Traumatic Stress Disorder: A Systematic Review. *The Journal of Alternative and Complementary Medicine* 24: 106–14. [CrossRef]

Debnath, Ramit, and Ronita Bardhan. 2020. India nudges to contain COVID-19 pandemic: A reactive public policy analysis using machine-learning based topic modelling. *PLoS ONE* 15: e0238972. [CrossRef]

Dhansoia, Vipin, Vijaya Majumdar, N. K. Manjunath, Usha Singh Gaharwar, and Deepeshwar Singh. 2022. Breathing-Focused Yoga Intervention on Respiratory Decline in Chronically Pesticide-Exposed Farmers: A Randomized Controlled Trial. *Frontiers in Medicine* 9: 453. [CrossRef] [PubMed]

Di Lorenzo, Rosaria, Gianluca Fiore, Alessandra Bruno, Margherita Pinelli, Davide Bertani, Patrizia Falcone, Donatella Marrama, Fabrizio Starace, and Paola Ferri. 2021. Urgent Psychiatric Consultations at Mental Health Center during COVID-19 Pandemic: Retrospective Observational Study. *Psychiatry Quarterly* 92: 1341–59. [CrossRef] [PubMed]

Donnelly, Kyla Z., Shari Goldberg, and Debra Fournier. 2020. A qualitative study of LoveYourBrain Yoga: A group-based yoga with psychoeducation intervention to facilitate community integration for people with traumatic brain injury and their caregivers. *Disability and Rehabilitation* 42: 2482–91. [CrossRef]

Dos Santos, Giovanna M., Rozangela Verlengia, Anna GSV Ribeiro, Cinthia A. Corrêa, Melissa Ciuldim, and Alex H. Crisp. 2022. Yoga and mental health among Brazilian practitioners during COVID-19: An internet-based cross-sectional survey. *Sports Medicine and Health Science* 4: 127–32. [CrossRef]

Estimated COVID-19 Burden. 2023. Centers for Disease Control and Prevention. Available online: https://www.cdc.gov/coronavirus/2019-ncov/cases-updates/burden.html#est-infections (accessed on 14 March 2023).

Falkenberg, R. I., C. Eising, and M. L. Peters. 2018. Yoga and immune system functioning: A systematic review of randomized controlled trials. *Journal of Behavioral Medicine* 41: 467–82. [CrossRef]

Feuerstein, Georg. 2013. *The Yoga Tradition: Its History, Literature, Philosophy, and Practice*. Prescott: Hohm Press.

Gopal, Aravind, Sunita Mondal, Asha Gandhi, Sarika Arora, and Jayashree Bhattacharjee. 2011. Effect of integrated yoga practices on immune responses in examination stress—A preliminary study. *International Journal of Yoga* 4: 26.

Groessl, E. J., D. Chopra, and P. J. Mills. 2015. An overview of yoga research for health and well-being. *Journal of Yoga and Physical Therapy* 5: 210–14. [CrossRef]

Guo, Jinli, Chaona Gao, Haifeng Xin, Jiahui Li, Bing Li, Zhuan Wei, and Yiting Yue. 2019. The application of "upper-body yoga" in elderly patients with acute hip fracture: A prospective, randomized, and single-blind study. *Journal of Orthopaedic Surgery and Research* 14: 1–8.

Held, Philip, Brian J. Klassen, Jennifer A. Coleman, Kaitlin Thompson, Thad S. Rydberg, and Rebecca Van Horn. 2021. Delivering intensive PTSD treatment virtually: The development of a 2-week intensive cognitive processing therapy–based program in response to COVID-19. *Cognitive and Behavioral Practice* 28: 543–54. [CrossRef]

Jha, Ganganatha, trans. 1942. *The Chāndogya Upaniṣad: A Treatise on the Vedanta Philosophy Translated into English with the Commentary of Śankara*. Poona: Oriental Book Agency.

Jha, Ujjwala. 2018. Mīmāṃsa Theory of Apūrva. *Journal of East-West Thought* 8: 13–18.

Jiang, Taiyi, Jianhua Hou, Runsong Sun, Lili Dai, Wen Wang, Hao Wu, Tong Zhang, and Bin Su. 2021. Immunological and psychological efficacy of meditation/yoga intervention among people living with HIV (PLWH): A systematic review and meta-analyses of 19 randomized controlled trials. *Annals of Behavioral Medicine* 55: 505–19. [CrossRef]

Kahya, Holly Hannah, and Courtney Grant Raspin. 2017. Yoga therapy for the mind eight-week course: Participants' experiences. *Explore* 13: 116–23. [CrossRef]

Kelly, Ursula, Terri Haywood, Eliza Segell, and Melinda Higgins. 2021. Trauma-sensitive yoga for post-traumatic stress disorder in women veterans who experienced military sexual trauma: Interim results from a randomized controlled trial. *The Journal of Alternative and Complementary Medicine* 27: S-45. [CrossRef] [PubMed]

King, Dana E., and Bruce Bushwick. 1994. Beliefs and attitudes of hospital inpatients about faith healing and prayer. *Journal of Family Practice* 39: 349–52.

Kuntsevich, Viktoriya, William C. Bushell, and Neil D. Theise. 2010. Mechanisms of yogic practices in health, aging, and disease. *Mt Sinai Journal of Medicine* 77: 559–69. [CrossRef]

Levison, Sanford V., and Eric J. Segall. 2020. Forced Closing of Houses of Worship During the Coronavirus: Both Legal and Right. American Constitution Society. Available online: https://www.acslaw.org/expertforum/forced-closing-of-houses-of-worship-during-the-coronavirus-both-legal-and-right/ (accessed on 7 November 2022).

Linke, Magdalena, and Konrad Jankowski. 2022. Religiosity and the Spread of COVID-19: A Multinational Comparison. *Journal of Religion and Health* 61: 1641–56. [CrossRef]

Macy, Rebecca J., Elizabeth Jones, Laurie M. Graham, and Leslie Roach. 2018. Yoga for Trauma and Related Mental Health Problems. In *Trauma, Violence & Abuse*. New York: Sage Publications, Inc., 19 vols, pp. 35–57. Available online: https://www.jstor.org/stable/10.2307/27010960 (accessed on 20 January 2023).

Markowitz, Jenny. 2023. State by State Coronavirus-Related Restrictions. AARP. Available online: https://www.aarp.org/politics-society/government-elections/info-2020/coronavirus-state-restrictions.html (accessed on 14 March 2023).

McGrath, Georgia, Laura Alfrey, and Ruth Jeanes. 2017. Community connections in health and physical education: A reflection of stakeholder experiences. *Asia-Pacific Journal of Health, Sport and Physical Education* 8: 101–14. [CrossRef]

Morgan, Nani, Michael R. Irwin, Mei Chung, and Chenchen Wang. 2014. The effects of mind-body therapies on the immune system: Meta-analysis. *PLoS ONE* 9: e100903. [CrossRef]

Muirhead, Jonathan, and Clare-Ann Fortune. 2016. Yoga in prisons: A review of the literature. *Aggression and Violent Behavior* 28: 57–63. [CrossRef]

Mullen, Kenneth. 1990. Religion and Health: A Review of the Literature. *International Journal of Sociology and Social Policy* 10: 85–96. [CrossRef]

Naoroibam, Rosy, Kashinath G. Metri, Hemant Bhargav, R. Nagaratna, and H. R. Nagendra. 2016. Effect of Integrated Yoga (IY) on psychological states and CD4 counts of HIV-1 infected patients: A randomized controlled pilot study. *International Journal of Yoga* 9: 57. [PubMed]

National Center for Complementary and Integrative Health. 2022. U.S. Department of Health and Human Services. Yoga for Health: What the Science Says. Available online: https://www.nccih.nih.gov/health/providers/digest/yoga-for-health-science (accessed on 30 November 2022).

Neel, Joe. 2022. *Most Americans Have Been Infected with the COVID-19 Virus, the CDC Reports*. Washington, DC: NPR. Available online: https://www.npr.org/2022/04/26/1094817774/covid-19-infections-us-most-americans (accessed on 26 April 2022).

Newham, James J., Anja Wittkowski, Janine Hurley, John D. Aplin, and Melissa Westwood. 2014. Effects of antenatal yoga on maternal anxiety and depression: A randomized controlled trial. *Depression and Anxiety* 31: 631–40. [CrossRef]

Okamoto, Nadya. 2021. How the Yoga Industry Has Changed with the Pandemic. ASweatLife. Available online: https://asweatlife.com/2021/06/yoga-industry-change/ (accessed on 17 June 2021).

Pascoe, Michaela C., David R. Thompson, and Chantal F. Ski. 2017. Yoga, mindfulness-based stress reduction and stress-related physiological measures: A meta-analysis. *Psychoneuroendocrinology* 86: 156–78. [CrossRef] [PubMed]

Rabeea, Shahad A., Hamid A. Merchant, Muhammad Umair Khan, Chia Siang Kow, and Syed Shahzad Hasan. 2021. Surging trends in prescriptions and costs of antidepressants in England amid COVID-19. *DARU Journal of Pharmaceutical Sciences* 29: 217–21. [CrossRef] [PubMed]

Rao, Raghavendra Mohan, H. S. Vadiraja, R. Nagaratna, K. S. Gopinath, Shekhar Patil, Ravi B. Diwakar, H. P. Shahsidhara, B. S. Ajaikumar, and H. R. Nagendra. 2017. Effect of yoga on sleep quality and neuroendocrine immune response in metastatic breast cancer patients. *Indian Journal of Palliative Care* 23: 253. [CrossRef]

Reddy, Ashok, Stephan D. Fihn, and Joshua M. Liao. 2019. The VA MISSION act-creating a center for innovation within the VA. *The New England Journal of Medicine* 380: 1592–94. [CrossRef]

Sarbacker, Stuart Ray. 2021. *Tracing the Path of Yoga: The History and Philosophy of Indian Mind-Body Discipline*. Albany: State University of New York Press.

Schmalzl, Laura, Chivon Powers, and Eva Henje Blom. 2015. Neurophysiological and neurocognitive mechanisms underlying the effects of yoga-based practices: Towards a comprehensive theoretical framework. *Frontiers in Human Neuroscience* 9: 235. [CrossRef]

Sharma, Sachin Kumar, Shirley Telles, Kumar Gandharva, and Acharya Balkrishna. 2022. Yoga instructors' reported benefits and disadvantages associated with functioning online: A convenience sampling survey. *Complementary Therapies in Clinical Practice* 46: 101509. [CrossRef]

Shaw, Keely, Scotty Butcher, Jongbum Ko, Gordon A. Zello, and Philip D. Chilibeck. 2020. Wearing of cloth or disposable surgical face masks has no effect on vigorous exercise performance in healthy individuals. *International Journal of Environmental Research and Public Health* 17: 8110. [CrossRef] [PubMed]

Shete, Sanjay Uddhav, Anita Verma, Dattatraya Devarao Kulkarni, and Ranjeet Singh Bhogal. 2017. Effect of yoga training on inflammatory cytokines and C-reactive protein in employees of small-scale industries. *Journal of Education and Health Promotion* 6: 76–82. [PubMed]

Singleton, Mark. 2010. *Yoga Body: The Origins of Modern Posture Practice*. Oxford: Oxford University Press.

Telles, Shirley, Nilkamal Singh, and Acharya Balkrishna. 2012. Managing Mental Health Disorders Resulting from Trauma through Yoga: A Review. *Depression Research and Treatment*. [CrossRef] [PubMed]

Tillu, Girish, Sarika Chaturvedi, Arvind Chopra, and Bhushan Patwardhan. 2020. Public health approach of ayurveda and yoga for COVID-19 prophylaxis. *The Journal of Alternative and Complementary Medicine* 26: 360–64. [CrossRef] [PubMed]

United States Worldometer. 2023. Available online: https://www.worldometers.info/coronavirus/country/us/ (accessed on 14 March 2023).

Van Der Kolk, Bessel A., Laura Stone, Jennifer West, Alison Rhodes, David Emerson, Michael Suvak, and Joseph Spinazzola. 2014. Yoga as an adjunctive treatment for posttraumatic stress disorder: A randomized controlled trial. *The Journal of Clinical Psychiatry* 75: 22573. [CrossRef]

Van Fraassen, Bas. 1980. *The Scientific Image*. Oxford: Clarendon Press.

Van Puymbroeck, Marieke, Alysha Walter, Brent L. Hawkins, Julia L. Sharp, Kathleen Woschkolup, Enrique Urrea-Mendoza, Fredy Revilla, Emilie V. Adams, and Arlene A. Schmid. 2018. Functional improvements in Parkinson's disease following a randomized trial of yoga. *Evidence-Based Complementary and Alternative Medicine*. [CrossRef]

Venkatesh, H. N., H. Ravish, C. R. Wilma Delphine Silvia, and H. Srinivas. 2020. Molecular signature of the immune response to yoga therapy in stress-related chronic disease conditions: An insight. *International Journal of Yoga* 13: 9.

Wadhen, Vipin, and Tina Cartwright. 2021. Feasibility and outcome of an online streamed yoga intervention on stress and wellbeing of people working from home during COVID-19. *Work* 69: 331–49. [CrossRef]

Walia, Namrata, Jennifer Matas, Acara Turner, Sandra Gonzalez, and Roger Zoorob. 2021. Yoga for substance use: A systematic review. *The Journal of the American Board of Family Medicine* 34: 964–73. [CrossRef]

White, David G. 2012. *Yoga: Brief History of an Idea*. Edited by David G. White. Princeton: Princeton University Press, pp. 1–23.

Yunitri, Ninik, Hsin Chuc, Xiao Linda Kanga, Hsiu-Ju Jena, Li-Chung Pieng, Hsiu-Ting Tsai, Abdu Rahim Kamil, and Kuei-Ru Choua. 2022. Global prevalence and associated risk factors of posttraumatic stress disorder during COVID-19 pandemic: A meta-analysis. *Journal of Nursing Studies* 126: 104136. [CrossRef] [PubMed] *religions* MDPI

Article

COVID-19, State Intervention, and Confucian Paternalism

Ellen Y. Zhang

Department of Philosophy and Religious Studies, University of Macau, E21-4101, Avenida da Universidade, Taipa, Macau, China; eyzhang@um.edu.mo

Abstract: For many in the West, paternalism manifest as state interference carries a pejorative connotation, as it is often taken to entail unjustified restrictions on autonomy and self-determination and frequently believed to precipitate bureaucracy, corruption, and inefficiency. Meanwhile, uncritical deference to policies in which individual liberties remain essentially unchecked by state oversight has faced renewed scrutiny since the outbreak of the COVID-19 pandemic, as many across the globe are now coming to believe that we must accept greater governmental intervention in our lives, particularly during times of widespread health crises. This paper explores normative considerations justifying state intervention with respect to public health policies in response to the COVID-19 pandemic through the lens of Confucian paternalism, which is distinguished from a more general concept of paternalism widely used in contemporary philosophical discourse. It argues that the "soft" paternalism apropos to Confucianism has pragmatic benefits for the development of healthcare policies due to which it is not only morally warranted but even preferable to alternatives in terms of safeguarding population health.

Keywords: paternalism; libertarianism; intervention; Confucianism; autonomy; public health; COVID-19

Citation: Zhang, Ellen Y. 2023. COVID-19, State Intervention, and Confucian Paternalism. *Religions* 14: 776. https://doi.org/10.3390/rel14060776

Academic Editors: Andrew Flescher and Joel Zimbelman

Received: 27 October 2022
Revised: 21 December 2022
Accepted: 7 June 2023
Published: 12 June 2023

1. Introduction: Libertarianism and Paternalism

Beginning in early 2020, in response to the COVID-19 pandemic, a notable wave of top-down governmentally overseen public health policies were introduced and implemented across the globe. For many in the West, especially those sympathetic to a libertarian worldview, such intervention implied an assertion of state control unduly regulating the private lives of citizens. Although this legislation was proposed on the basis of specific health and welfare calculations, it was considered to be problematic because of the degree to which new regulations were perceived to impinge on individual liberties hitherto considered sacrosanct and untouchable. Such libertarian counterarguments were based on the principle of autonomy and respect for persons, on justifications grounded in civil rights, and through well-known appeals to legislative restraint on government interference. Meanwhile, concerns about bureaucratic overreach, the corruption of political and cultural elites, and inefficiencies of state-sponsored policy initiatives lent extra support to the critical response to perceived incursions into basic freedoms.

Though written in England and more than twenty centuries removed from Confucius, John Stuart Mill's *On Liberty* reflects the sociopolitical transition from a traditional culture to modernity. Here we find the classic statement of the liberal position where "the only purpose for which power can be rightfully exercised over any member of a civilized community, against his will, is to prevent harm to others. His own good, either physical or moral, is not a sufficient warrant" (Mill 1974, p. 68). For Mill, despite the fact that governments can seek to justify their interference on an exceptional basis by asserting that they act for individual citizens' own good, paternalistic policies are problematic because they amount to an infringement of a presumptive individual liberty.

Since Mill, philosophers and political theorists in diverse cultural settings have accepted the premise that we should respect the decisions of individual agents when those decisions affect no one other than themselves. In the US, the unpopularity of paternalism is often associated with pejorative expressions such as the "nanny state." Even those who take issue with the libertarian position acknowledge the rhetorical challenge inherently posed by these utterances, which, when not heeded as the linguistic obstacles they are intended to be, can impede the realization of important public health outcomes (Carter et al. 2015, pp. 1021–29). This poses a conundrum for the one in favor of intervention during times of a public health crisis: how can we manage to overcome a libertarianism that does not prioritize the good of the population without needlessly invoking a culture war in which basic freedoms are announced to be under attack?

Complicating matters, proponents of libertarianism often announce that they are champions of "individual autonomy". The word autonomy derives from the Greek root "autos", or self, and "nomos", meaning rule or law. Those who argue against paternalism often use the concept of "autonomy" to indicate the idea of "self-governing" and "self-deciding" as the alternative to being "controlled" by external political authorities. In this respect, autonomy is construed as the power of individuals to act independently and resist coercion imposed by foreign externalities. It is a principle which leads to a normative view according to which the choices of autonomous agents should be protected from interference and intervention by institutions or government. Libertarians seek minimization of the state's encroachment on individual liberties as something to be prized for its own sake. For libertarians, freedom is an integral part of human rights. This is a view to which Robert Nozick, one of the most influential political philosophers defending a libertarian position, lent considerable heft when he likened individual freedom to what he termed "the right of self-ownership". In *Anarchy, State, and Utopia,* Nozick sees the principle of self-ownership as a first premise of a rights-based view of morality in which every person is morally entitled to full private property and expression in their own person and powers (Nozick 1974). To quote Nozick, "each person has an extensive set of moral rights ... over the use and fruits of his body and capacities" (Cohen and Graham 1990, p. 25).

Although self-ownership is identified with the right to private property (including the physical space occupied by one's body), it also indicates self-control and self-determination bereft of external coercion. Nozick's principle of self-ownership is the fundamental idea at the heart of all major versions of libertarian arguments based on freedom. It functions as a normative claim pointing to the relationship between oneself and one's action. To maximize autonomy and individual freedom, Nozick proposes the idea of a "night-watchman state" in response to the twin challenges of statism and anarchism (Nozick 1974). In this relatively minimalist conception, government should do what is necessary in order to prevent society from lapsing into a chaotic and uncivil polity. It should provide protection and security from both external and internal aggressions in order to maintain law and order and support critical public facilities, but it should not do much more.

In spite of its grounding in a durable and tested political tradition that predates even the Enlightenment, such a view has faced growing resistance since the outbreak of the pandemic, defense against which requires proactive and preventive planning. This paper explores normative consideration of the emerging case for paternalism through the lens of Confucian ethics, whose collectivist approach to crafting public policy has often been mistaken as a form of political totalitarianism in the West and elsewhere. I argue that there are dimensions in the Confucian politico-ethical position that are both unexplored and misunderstood, which, properly appreciated, can offer guidance in response to global health crises. I distinguish Confucian exemplary paternalism from the more standard concept of paternalism used in the contemporary philosophical discourse, focusing my analysis on the related concepts of character-based consequentialism, trust, and relational autonomy, suggesting, finally, that this "soft" notion of paternalism is not only morally justifiable, but also preferable for pursuing sound healthcare policies in times of exigent widespread health crises.

2. Defining Confucian Paternalism

"Paternalism" is a misused and arguably misunderstood concept. The English word "paternalism" comes from the Latin *pater*, meaning to act like a father, or to treat another person like a child. As the metaphorical language suggests, paternalism represents a parent/child relationship in which it is assumed that the child lacks the capacity to act in their best interest. The parent thus must use their presumably legitimate authority to guide the child in ways that help the child flourish. It follows that paternalistic practice involves spheres of provision and protection accompanied by restriction and control. From this much it is clear that paternalism has both general and specific meanings. At a general level, paternalism refers to government by a "benign parent" who makes decisions on behalf of those who may not be able to make good decisions for themselves (Blackburn 2008, p. 270). More specifically, paternalistic policies possess some distinct elements: (1) they involve interference in a person's opportunity or ability to choose; (2) they imply an enactment to further the person's perceived good or welfare; and (3) they are made without explicit consent of the person concerned (New 1999, p. 65).

In the modern West, especially since the Enlightenment and among secular thinkers, paternalistic political authority and governance is often rejected for a number of reasons that are not necessarily built into the strict definition of paternalism just considered, including that (1) it embraces a skeptical view of an individual's capacity to make good decisions on behalf of one's own welfare and wellbeing; (2) it is over-confident in the ability of government to make a better decision to advance that welfare and wellbeing; and (3) it holds that because of what government can do which individuals supposedly are incapable of doing, it should be given broad discretionary authority to enact policies that restrict free choice as a way to advance the welfare of the community, even when such policies run counter to the presumptive respect for autonomy and the related values of privacy and informed consent. In other words, while paternalism in all of its forms entails an authority acting on behalf of someone else, hopefully in that person's best interests, in the West and in most standard accounts the concept *also* came to imply a disparaging account of individuals, who are presumed at the outset not be able to act in their own best interests. Responding to moral arguments mustered by critics of this modified understanding, supporters of paternalistic policies affirm the legitimate authority of the state as one of the most basic and enduring types of traditional governance (Lau et al. 2019). In communitarian societies, such as those grounded in Confucian ideals and practices, "authority" is in any case not likely to be perceived as problematic because the idea of respect for authority is seldom challenged and a strong notion of individualism, as such, does not exist.

Confucius (551–479 BCE) is one of the most influential thinkers of Chinese philosophy and a representative voice of Chinese culture even up through the contemporary era. His ideas are regarded as foundational to a philosophical tradition that emphasizes respect for the elderly and the moral duties of rulers and subjects. Since the family is considered the smallest, but also the most essential, unit of state organization, and paternalistic leadership is inextricably linked to the familial model, Confucian ethics endorses a specific type of moral reasoning based on the values of familial caring and dutiful relationships. The term "paternalism," which has been increasingly used in Confucian scholarship in recent decades, makes sense when discussing classical Confucian politics and ethics given that in the Chinese tradition, government officials are literally called "parent–officials" (*fumu guan* 父母官) whose sovereignty is honored and respected. Those in positions of power have, as they do in the relationship between parents and children, the right and the obligation to act upon the best interests of those who need appropriate guidance in circumstances in which they are not otherwise capable of knowing their true interests. In Confucianism, paternalism is linked to the virtue of "filial piety" (*xiaojing* 孝敬), i.e., the attribute of respect for one's *parents*, elders, and government officials, an asset reflecting *de facto* hierarchical social relations. According to Ruiping Fan, filial respect is not simply owing to a person's maturity or rationality, but also due to one's relation to the ancestors (Fan 2010, p. 226). Thus, the interdependence between parents and children is logically and seamlessly extended to political life between rulers and their subjects.

Quite a number of scholars contend that paternalistic governance tends to limit individual autonomy. For example, during the "New Culture Movement" (*xin wenhua yun dong* 新文化運動) popular at the beginning of the last century in China, Chinese intellectuals who advocated Western-inspired notions of individualism vehemently criticized Confucian paternalism as being "oppressive" and "cruel" in the name of parental protection. By contrast, Mencius' critique of the concepts of "each for himself" held by Yang Zhu (楊朱; 440–360 BCE), and his support of the notions of being "without rulers" and "inclusive love" promoted by Mozi (墨子; 476–221 BCE), were taken to lay the grounds for a Confucian position on paternalism punctuated by the idea of "filial piety" towards one's parents and rulers. In the West, we often see a conflict between paternalism and individual autonomy. Gerald Dworkin, for example, defines paternalism as "the interference of a state or an individual with another person, against their will, ... defended or motivated by a claim that the person interfered with will be better off or protected from harm" (Dworkin 2020). By contrast, Confucian paternalism entails an implicit and more harmonious understanding of checks and balances between individual and society. In Confucianism, the "right" of individual liberty is never absolute and must be weighed against the "good" in service of which the individual interests of everyone are pursued. In other words, in the Confucian view, the right and the good cannot, and should not, so easily be distinguished. Sor-Hoon Tan notes that even if one concedes that there is a tendency toward paternalism in Confucianism, one could still maintain that paternalism could never be pushed too far on Confucian grounds because its preoccupation is with a moral transformation which could not be brought about by force alone (Tan 2010, p. 141). Tan resists identifying Confucian paternalism with authoritarian and totalitarian regimes. Joseph Chan, on the other hand, associates the foundation of Confucian political authority with the concept of perfectionism in which oversight and liberty are fused into a holistic ideal. While realizing that one of the most challenging issues that must be faced today in developing a contemporary Confucian ethical and political theory is the question of individual autonomy, Chan attempts to show that Confucian ethics entails a notion of "autonomy" baked into its foundational premises, defining autonomy as a voluntary and reflective engagement of morality (Chan 2000, p. 282).

It remains a question as to whether political perfectionism itself, in the Confucian or liberal instance, is technically paternalistic. In contrast to state neutrality, perfectionism holds that the state has a duty to take a stand on what is a worthwhile way of life in order to help people flourish. In this sense, "Confucian perfectionism," if we use this term, suggests a form of paternalism since "worthwhile conceptions of the good are what people should be guided by", and a perfectionist state is likely to provide a motivation for a wide range of paternalistic policies (Clarke 2006, pp. 111–12). John Rawls, for example, points out that perfectionism would sanction the oppressive use of state power in order to enforce a conception of the good (Rawls 1993, p. 37). If Rawls is correct in his observation, then how should Confucius' tendency to embrace some form of paternalism be assessed? To answer this question, we need to go beyond the modified definition of paternalism challenged by libertarianism and explore possible connections between state initiatives which appear as beneficial interventions and Chan's and Rawls's notion of autonomy as a voluntary and holistic morality, which assumes a positive use of state power to promote the good.

A model of Confucian paternalistic governance can be understood as a weaving together of three interrelated aspects: (1) character-based consequentialism; (2) the pivotal role of trust in explaining leadership effectiveness; and (3) relationality and reciprocity. Sarah Flavel and Brad Hall develop the term "exemplary paternalism", stating that Confucian paternalism "stresses cultivation of the people by moral exemplars to guide the people to act in ways that are in their own best interests" (Flavel and Hall 2020). They agree with Tan that Confucianism emphasizes the notion of guidance qua exemplars instead of coercion qua punishment (a method employed by the School of Legalism or *Fajia* 法家). In this respect, Confucian paternalism can be interpreted as a "soft" prod, one which simultaneously accounts for the needs of individual and society. Flavel and Hall argue that Confucian paternalism "does not advocate for a static top-down structure of governance that is incapable of reform, underscoring its non-authoritarian ideal" (Flavel and Hall 2020). This form of paternalism is "weaker" in that, to channel Dworkin, "it is legitimate to interfere with the means that agents choose to achieve their ends, if those means are likely to defeat those ends" (Dworkin 2020). Flavel's and Hall's observation is important and helps us avoid an unjustified authoritarian reading of Confucianism by raising the prior question of whether paternalism necessarily implies a coercive posture that works against the will of the person being interfered with. As the authors conclude: "To define Confucianism as authoritarian would be an unfair judgment on several counts, but especially because Confucian thinkers believe that using coercion and force of law as a primary method of control is an inferior method of overseeing and even directing the behaviors of the people" (Flavel and Hall 2020, p. 224).

We might examine some characteristics of Confucian paternalism that can be invoked to support Flavel and Hall's argument. First, exemplary paternalism denotes an idea of governance by moral exemplars which is facilitated by a merit-based political system. Authority is not given by a transcendent power, nor obtained by force, but is recognized and conferred by a person's character or virtue. In his studies of Confucian ethics, P. J. Ivanhoe coins the term "character consequentialism" (a hybrid of virtue ethics and consequentialism) to describe the virtues promoted by Confucianism that are valuable both intrinsically and instrumentally (Ivanhoe 1991, p. 55). According to Ivanhoe, a virtue-based consequentialism develops a specific sense of authority that is established on the basis of an assessment of concrete moral agents practically reasoning. In this respect, it pays attention to character development. Ivanhoe points out that such a virtue ethic might also go by "character consequentialism" insofar as it differs from a rigid utilitarianism, focusing on the long-term benefits brought to individuals and society as a whole. Writes Ivanhoe, "character consequentialism is concerned with a range of results of actions, especially the effect a given action has on the development of a person's character" (Ivanhoe 1991, p. 61). The development of moral character empowers persons in the right direction, producing "certain desirable consequences" (Ivanhoe 1991, p. 61). Confucian exemplary paternalism represents political influence based on the Confucian ideal of *ren* 仁 (humanness/benevolence), implying the existence of a benevolence which is intrinsic to legitimate authority. At the same time, this model of paternalistic meritocracy has an instrumental value that generates a mutual *xin* 信 (trust or trustworthiness) that is crucial to a functional paternalism. While *ren* points to the Confucian principle of love and respect one harbors towards others, xin helps to establish the affective and functional bond between leaders and their people.

The virtue of interpersonal trust is a second important aspect of Confucian paternalism. In Chinese, the character *xin* is a combination of the root "person" (*ren* 人) with the trait of righteous "speech" (*yan* 言), meaning a person who keeps their word. But the term in Confucianism actually indicates a moral integrity that goes beyond the specific notion of "keeping one's word," extending to a robust connotation of trust secured by psychological mechanisms underlying the relationship between paternalistic leadership and consensual performance among the people. According to Boin and colleagues, there are three factors that determine the credibility of authorities during a crisis: prior trust, the initial response, and the timing of messages (Boin et al. 2021, p. 78). Legitimate authorities should not act unilaterally, bereft of the explicit acknowledgement of those on behalf of whom they are acting. Trust requires a sensitivity both to timing and to how authoritative action is being perceived.

From a Confucian point of view, trust not only refers to the character, or *moral integrity*, of public authorities (officials and experts), but also to faith in their *professional capacities*. These concepts do not neatly fit Western distinctions between "public" and "private". For Confucians, "parent–officials" are not some arbitrary outside agents who interfere in the life of the community. Rather, they provide guidance through their exemplary actions, where "decisions are made for others (with or without their knowledge) yet perhaps with their full or implicit support" (Flavel and Hall 2020). It follows that successful Confucian paternalism seeks and affirms a political arrangement that is based on the moral trust entailed in a family model. The relationship between a government and its people is not a political contract but a moral bond. The primary purpose of Confucian paternalism is not to coerce others for their own good. Rather, it seeks a shared, reciprocal good for both parties involved.

A third aspect of Confucian paternalism follows from the previous points. Paternalistic Confucianism's commitment to relationality and reciprocity attempts to account for the rich social matrix in which individuals must inevitably exist to fulfill shared and common goals. Relationality recognizes the interconnectedness of society both at the family level and state level. Reciprocity, in turn, implies that the self and the other are deserving of equal and mutual respect. The prioritization of these attributes entails an appreciation of the collective, common good, which is emphasized over the idiosyncratic desires of individuals. Politically, Confucian leaders view themselves as integral to social relationships made up of persons who have moral duties generated through a web of connections and interdependence.

In this respect, relationality in Confucianism points to a concept of a person's self-determination that is different from that of liberal individualism in the West. The Confucian characterization might be expressed as "relational autonomy," a term that has been employed by feminist thinkers in the West to reconceptualize traditionally patriarchal notions of autonomy (Mackenzie and Stoljar 2000; Carter et al. 2015). Individual choice, while important, is always enmeshed in and responsive to the relationships in which one participates. Relationality in this context points to the idea that autonomy requires something in addition to self-sufficiency. The Chinese character *ren* 仁, a combination of the roots for "person" and "two", which denotes interpersonal relationships, emphasizes this augmentation beyond the Western notion of autonomous individualism. As Herbert Fingarette puts it: "for Confucius, unless there are at least two human beings, there are no human beings" (Fingarette 1972, p. 24). Humans are in every instance social and responsible beings. Correspondingly, the concept of self is intimately and intricately enmeshed in human relationships. A person's relational conditions are necessary for shaping who they are. Confucian paternalism focuses on the role of family as the intermediary social arrangement that connects the state and individuals.

3. Reciprocity and Relationality

More needs to be said about the complementary attributes of reciprocity and relationality in order to clarify Confucianism's resistance to dichotomizing "self" and "other", two concepts which, in contrast to Confucianism, are demarcated in both libertarianism and the version of paternalism that libertarians tend to critique. In a Confucian worldview, reciprocity's aim is not calculated self-interest, but shared aims and mutual respect. Like *ren,* reciprocity (*shu* 恕) is considered a crucial virtue that denotes two meanings: (1) mutuality and (2) interaction with sympathetic understanding. Reciprocity thus implies an "analogical extension" *(leitui* 類推), which is a movement from self to others in the sense of being empathetic towards others. It is understood as "consideration of others", "empathy", or even "altruism". In the *Analects,* when a student asks Confucius about the meaning of reciprocity, he replies: "Do not impose on others what you yourself do not want" (*Analects,* 15:24). This statement can be viewed as the converse of the principle of the golden rule often held up as the standard-bearer by scholars in the West. In the Confucian formulation, mutual interaction between self and other often focuses on not doing something. Wing-Tsit Chan and Vincent Shen also translate *shu* as "reciprocity," a direct form of perspective-taking. As Chan notes, "putting oneself in another's place is an act of compassion and moral practice of concern for the welfare of others" (Chan 1963, p. 44). Both see reciprocity as tantamount to the pursuit of the "common good" (Shen 2008, pp. 291–304). If we apply this understanding of reciprocity to Confucian paternalism, we see that the notion of coercion through threats cannot be rendered morally acceptable or even coherent.

Given the way in which reciprocity has just been spelled out, we can see that it is inherently relational, which is to say never exclusively self-regarding. If one wishes to explore what the traditional Confucian ethic of reciprocity and relationality might look like in a Western context, contemporary discussions of relational autonomy developed in modern feminist literature give us one path forward. In her book *Tough Choices: Structured Paternalism and the Landscape of Choice*, Sigal Ben-Porath offers a concretized justification for paternalism, noting that it is "an attempt to improve the well-being of others while keeping in mind their inferred needs, including the threshold conditions of civic equality and the expansion of opportunity" (Ben-Porath 2010, p. 20). For Ben-Porath, the term "inferred needs" alludes to the things that are necessary to sustain life, such as water, food, shelter, and health. The phrase "threshold conditions of civic equality" pertains to the function and availability of governmental institutions, including access to quality education, healthcare, and transparency in voting rights. This version of state paternalism reflects the classical, Western liberal aspiration of protecting the vulnerable individual who stands to be exploited, while casting communitarian ambitions as the means to this end. Thus, it attempts to balance individual liberties with the pursuit of collective goals. In making this move, the author offers a middle way between the choices of freedom-oriented anti-interventionism and equality-oriented social welfare.

Ben-Porath's modified paternalism is related to but importantly different from that of Confucius's. Confucius harbored a tendency to divide (or "sort") people into various categories in terms of different social roles, leading to an ethos of "to each according to their own needs" as opposed to the practice of loving everyone equally. In this respect Confucian paternalism is sensitive to different roles people occupy in society. Individuals situated in complex webs of familial and community relationships are understood to experience different and competing responsibilities. One might have a role simultaneously as a parent caring for one's children during a pandemic and a competing role as a governmental official tasked with the care of citizens during the same health crisis. The dilemma is how one should balance these different roles, their related responsibilities, and competing claims. How should public responsibilities be curtailed when they stand in tension with familial duties? Such adjudication is dependent on specific situations and contextual determinations, not fixed ethical rules or guidelines. Although the script determining defined roles, obligations, and norms of behavior in modern society is not as clear as it might have been in Confucius' time, the Confucian role-based ethic, if it is to be commended to modern settings, should be grounded in our empirical experience in life.

The "middle way" offered by Ben-Porath and other Confucian revisionists is worthy of serious consideration. Many today are concerned about the potential danger and overreach of a paternalistic state. Thoroughgoing, or "hard," paternalism tends to interfere pervasively in people's lives, violating the prerogative for self-regarding choice, while soft paternalism tends to interfere in specific situations when governmental prerogatives are asserted. The distinction between "hard" and "soft" can also be made in terms of the way interference is performed. Traditional Confucian ethics assumes that people live in largely role-defined relationships and in communities in which they share with everyone else common virtues and norms, language, goals, and ritual practices (*li* 禮). Indeed, the priority given in Confucianism to such ritual practices is the primary means of legitimizing power, cultivating self-virtues, and creating a communal order. As such, Confucianism speaks more of "rites" than "rights." The former gives priority to a person's duty to others (Zhang 2010, p. 260). This moral ordering is perhaps counterintuitive in a setting of contemporary urban communities in which people imagine themselves as independent entities, seeing themselves more as "moral strangers" rather than "moral friends" to others.

It should be noted that Confucius would have been sympathetic with some of the libertarian concerns about concentrated power given the Confucian critique of state coercion via legal enforcement of actions advocated by the School of Legalism, where paternalism is typically characterized by coercive power in contrast to the influence of the morally exemplary. Nevertheless, Confucius would not have absolutized individual autonomy and freedom, since solutions to many crises depend on cooperation and, by extension, some measure of subjugation of immediate individual interest. With appropriate implementation of government rules and policy, people could be better off or less harmed, but state involvement should never be considered synonymous with state coercion. Such an understanding of paternalism implies a form of epistemic privilege where it is legitimate for a morally and intellectually cultivated elite to take a leading role in engineering social policies for the human good. Thomas Metzger utilizes the term "epistemic optimism" to refer to the idea that in traditional Chinese society, people expect cultivated and professional rulers to deliberate about the most effective means for promoting social goods on behalf of those they are charged with representing (Metzger 2005, pp. 21–31). Knowledge is power, but it is also something which is earned and used for the benefit of those who are not knowledgeable.

This consideration leads to a final point about the relationship between individuals and governmental officials. "Relational autonomy" of the sort Confucius commends presumes a relationship between people and governmental officials. In this relationship, the key issue is trust, which, in the context of COVID-19, amounts to trust in authorities *qua* public health specialists and policymakers. Distrust toward authorities can be dangerous, particularly when people are limited in their access to information concerning pandemic control and limited in their disposable time to inspect such information. Frequently in life, we will have no choice, as a practical matter, but to rely on officials publicly and professionally assigned to promoting our best interests, including our health interests. This will be an easier thing to accept if there are well-established grounds for trust prior to these pivotal moments. That a population would come to rely on its designated public health officials, legitimately and over time, is a reinforcing, a buttressing, of autonomy, since such officials enable the common people to live life safely and cooperatively.

4. State Interventions during COVID-19 and the Benefits of Confucian Paternalism

The COVID-19 pandemic forced a reassessment in many places around the world of the feasibility of a rigid commitment to non-governmental interference, including revisiting policies surrounding mandatory vaccination, health passport requirements, citywide lockdowns, isolation and quarantine, and border controls. Immediately following the onset of the COVID-19 pandemic, state interventions were implemented in order to mitigate the spread of the virus and lower the death toll. These measures took the form of social distancing, mask-wearing, regional commercial and travel shutdown, sporadic isolation or quarantine, and mandatory vaccinations. In response to declared emergencies selectively incorporating these strategies, hospitals in mainland China shifted from patient-centered to population-centered healthcare provisions, predictably causing some problems for patients with chronic diseases that required medical treatment and individual oversight on a regular basis. The situation became more acute and certainly more controversial when definitions of "non-essential" and "non-urgent" service became less clearly defined to the public. This all took place amidst a debate over the feasibility of the newly adopted heavily utilitarian approach to public policies that prioritized population health needs during the pandemic over the individual "few" who stood to suffer more because of decreased targeted care and personal attention.

In spite of these tradeoffs, most Chinese citizens were nevertheless not shy to acknowledge how effective paternalism could be in response to crisis management. COVID-19 provides a distinctive and helpful test case for the line-drawing between justified and unjustified aspects of paternalism and for distinguishing among different conceptions of autonomy. Indeed, individual autonomy becomes a tricky issue when public health is suddenly placed in jeopardy. The response to government containment strategies during the initial stages of the COVID-19 pandemic was recently compared in a study of four northern European countries, Denmark, Germany, the Netherlands, and Sweden. It revealed that all four placed emphasis on expressions of governmental trust in the development of their policy responses (Perlstein and Verboord 2021, pp. 1–23). In the case of Sweden, a laissez-faire attitude once deemed acceptable by a majority was questioned as mortality rates from the pandemic began to rise. A comparable situation was seen in Hong Kong, where the idea of limited government initially had been accepted by most of Hong Kong's citizens. With the onset of the pandemic, the government of Hong Kong initiated a series of policies to control the spread of virus, such as lockdowns, restrictions on visits to hospitals and nursing homes, and the implementation of vaccination passports. Because of the vivid and painful memory of SARS in 2003, most people in Hong Kong agreed to various compromises that took the form of acquiescing to government regulations at the expense of their personal freedoms. In the summer of 2022, Hong Kong's government informed members of the public that the third stage of the Vaccine Pass was to commence on May 31. By then all members of the public aged 12 or above, except those who obtained the COVID-19 Vaccination Medical Exemption Certificate, were required to receive COVID-19 vaccination(s) to comply with government requirements.

Concurrent with these developments, the Cato Institute, a libertarian thinktank in the US, published numerous articles debating whether "state capacity" should be boosted to respond to havoc wrought by the pandemic. Thomas A. Firey wonders whether "Americans must accept much greater governmental intervention in their lives if the United States were to respond effectively to the disease," given that, practically speaking "there are no libertarians in a pandemic" (Firey 2020). While criticizing the US government's uncoordinated and incomplete efforts to control the pandemic at the federal, state and local levels, Firey contends that governments across the board could do a better job at effective intervention. Though he does not fully agree with the idea that limited government has handicapped the country's response to the crisis, he does accept the necessity of competent state intervention in the face of such a health crisis.

The debate about state intervention in the face of competing moral claims to respect autonomy highlights the appeal of the concept of the "nudge" used by Richard Thaler and Cass Sunstein in support of "libertarian paternalism." The authors develop the concept of "choice architecture," designed as a mechanism for the state to encourage modification of behavior in desired and predictable ways without overriding individual autonomy or rejecting freedom of choice. Structurally, nudge theory rules out forcing individuals to succumb to top-down regulation, as it discourages introducing economic incentives to compel governmentally mandated action. The argument rests on the belief that paternalism can encompass a certain flexibility with regard to interference. Though an oxymoron, Thaler and Sunstein deploy the phrase "libertarian paternalism" to reveal a false assumption and at least two misconceptions associated with competing notions of paternalism. The false assumption is that people usually make choices that are in their best interest, while the two misconceptions are that there are more obviously viable alternatives to paternalism and that paternalism itself always involves coercion (Thaler and Sunstein 2008). In lieu of the forced dichotomy between libertarianism and paternalism favored by some, Thaler and Sunstein hold that the libertarian paternalist approach preserves individual choice while simultaneously authorizing both private and public institutions to "steer" people by means of incentives, persuasion, education, and thought experiments intended to promote their wellbeing. "A policy counts as 'paternalistic' if it is selected with the goal of influencing the choices of affected parties in a way that will make those parties better off" (Thaler and Sunstein 2008). Other scholars similarly embrace presumptive libertarian assumptions in justifying paternalistic interventions, focusing in their approach on the failures of rational decision-making. Sarah Conly, for example, rejects the idea of autonomy as absolute or inviolable, clarifying that people are often irrational in their decision-making (Conly 2013). Because their judgments are often compromised and their choices frequently undercut the achievement of their own goals, Conly argues, we should accept some degree of governmental influence *in service* to a principle of respect for persons. In this understanding, paternalism is what establishes the ground for the enabling conditions of agency.

This view of limited, or moderate, paternalism applies similarly to the holistic Confucian conception. In Confucianism, as with the examples just considered, freedom of choice is built into the notion of moral responsibility. Chenyang Li observes that while in the West there is often a distinction posed between personal autonomy and moral action, there is an integration of these two forms of autonomy in Confucianism, with the combination including self-activation, self-cultivation, self-reflection, and self-reliance. As Li puts it, "From a Confucian perspective, personal autonomy always, more or less, carries with it a moral characteristic because of the inevitable effect our action imposes on people around us." (Li 2014, p. 906). Regarding freedom of choice, Confucius did not focus on the act of choosing per se, but the object or outcome of choice.

Li's observation reminds us of the problem we often encounter in biomedical ethics when debating the legitimacy of informed consent, according to which the attributes of voluntariness, disclosure, understanding and capacity all need to be present in order to know that consent has genuinely been offered and rendered. Among these four characteristics, voluntariness and capacity are particularly problematic, as both principles suggest the idea of an overt individual responsibility of shared decision-making, while in reality a patient often signs informed consent papers as an "act" of freedom without real understanding of what they are giving consent to. There are many reasons this might be so, including limited capacity, subject difficulty, and poor presentation. Confucian paternalism, rather than putting an unrealistic pressure on individual patients to guarantee moral compliance with their own commitments, is built on the trust of medical professionals as well as the supporting presence of family members. A patient is empowered to make a final decision with guidance from the doctor, but a prior and vetted acquiescence to medical authorities who have earned the trust of their patients also serves as a safeguard to rubberstamping which serves no one. In this respect, Confucian paternalism promotes rather than undermines autonomy.

These issues are worth exploring in the context of policies governing mandatory vaccination in countries requiring balancing public health priorities with individual liberty concerns. Even if arguments grounded in the collectivist language are eschewed, we can still defend some mandatory policies by other valid arguments in the exigent instance in which a pandemic presents a tangible risk to society. Jason Brennan contends that mandatory, government-enforced vaccination can be justified even within a libertarian political framework. He advances what he refers to as a "clean hands principle", which is a legal term that calls out the potential hypocrisy of those who uncritically call for a universally "hands-off" disposition (Brennan 2018). As Brennan notes, "hands off" is not so harmless and can lead to worsening the condition of society's most vulnerable individuals. In his prescription, those seeking equity must do equity," and "equity must come with clean hands". In other words, only a party that has done nothing wrong, including not failing to do something that might hurt another, can come to court with a lawsuit against the other person. Brennan appropriates this term to show that the potential harm to others brought by the unvaccinated violates the principle of non-aggression maintained by libertarians. After all, the core libertarian value of freedom does not just include political autonomy but also one's right to life. According even to Nozick, freedom is defined as the prevention of, and protection against, aggression by others, and protection of one's life (Nozick 1974). Based on Nozick's own assumptions, Brennan asserts: "Individuals may be forced to accept certain vaccines not because they have an enforceable duty to serve the common, and not because cost–benefit analysis recommends it, but because anti-vaxxers are wrongfully imposing undue harm upon others," thereby violating the clean hands principle (Brennan 2018, p. 37).

Apart from the "clean hands principle", Mill's "harm principle" can also be interpreted to establish that the right to free choice or self-determination is not unlimited. According to Mill, an action that results in doing harm to another is not only wrong, but also *wrong enough* that government must intervene to prevent that harm from occurring. In spite of the fact that Mill's harm principle was not designed primarily to guide the actions of individuals, its use even in the political and public health arena inevitably places restrictions on personal liberty and an individual's right to exercise free choice. This position is consistent with the Confucian view elaborated earlier that asserts that what matters is not simply the act of choice but its consequence.

This is not to say that in the Confucian account there will never be legitimate medical justifications for refusing a vaccination which we might wish to respect. As Fan notes, "Confucianism would certainly permit medical exemptions for medically difficult individuals, such as those who are immunocompromised, allergic to the components used in the vaccinations, suffering from relevant diseases, or standing other medical contraindications to vaccination" (Fan 2018, p. 27). This flexibility in vaccine restriction and response is closely associated with the Confucian idea of "appropriateness" (*yi* 義), which connotes a moral discernment that allows situational consideration. The overall point is that Confucianism allows for give and take, and for flexibility with regard to the manner in which benevolent governmental influence is imposed, even when such is deemed necessary.

5. Confucian Paternalism in the Light of the WHO's *Ethical Guidance*

The World Health Organization (WHO), in its "Guidance for Managing Ethical Issues in Infectious Disease Outbreaks," identifies the consideration of seven ethical principles for public health during epidemics: justice, benevolence, utility, respect for persons, liberty, reciprocity, and solidarity (WHO 2016). This guidance grew out of ethical concerns raised by the Ebola outbreak in West Africa in 2014–2016. These principles are perceived as cross-culturally shared despite political, religious, or cultural inflections; however, it should be noted that some derivative rules such as privacy, confidentiality, truth-telling, and informed consent provide more specific guides to action than do the more general principles identified in standard accounts of biomedical ethics (Beauchamp and Childress 2001, p. 14). This means, among other things, that despite universality, there is room for flexibility of interpretation and sensitivity to particular cultures in which universal norms are being applied.

Such an acknowledgement is one viable way of approaching the debate over the question of how specific cultures might go about integrating supposedly universalizable ethical principles. Universals exist in moral reasoning, and they can even serve as a basis for a global biomedical ethics regimen, but they must always be interpreted within specific linguistic and cultural settings. Many Chinese ethicists grapple with how best to reconcile ethical universalism with modern Chinese culture. Principles such as benevolence are relatively non-controversial, since most Confucian scholars agree that they are implied by the Confucian virtue of *ren*, i.e., doing good and not doing harm. The virtue of *ren* can be expressed both positively and negatively. The positive formulation of *ren* is "Wishing to establish one's own character, seeks also to establish others; wishing to be prominent oneself, also helps other to be prominent" (*Analects* 6:30). The negative formulation, "Not to do to others what you do not want them to do to you," denotes the notion of non-maleficence and noncoercion (*Analects* 15:23). It carries an explicit intent to prevent "moral harm" (Allinson 1985, pp. 305–15). The idea at work here is that both action and inaction have other-regarding consequences, something not adequately captured in an ethos of straightforward rule-following.

With regard to two other principles, respect for persons and justice, reconciliation with the Confucian worldview is perhaps more challenging. From a Confucian perspective, personal autonomy and freedom must be taken into consideration within a framework of the public good and prior to individualistic considerations, especially during the advent of a public health crisis. Because Confucian ethics is grounded in the notion of "relational persons," it is likely to be relatively accepting of pandemic responses that begin from the premise that human beings are social and consequently more amenable to mitigation measures which restrict personal liberty (including isolation, quarantine, travel advisories or restrictions and community-based measures to reduce contact between people, such as closing schools or prohibiting large gatherings) (WHO 2016). Because it is filial-focused rather than individualistic, Confucian ethics can accommodate paternalistic restrictions, so long as the proposed interference with individual liberty is understood as "family co-decision." For example, in the case of vaccination, parents' views on whether their children should get vaccinated or not need to be heard. No one has sole or unrestricted dominion over their choices, because those choices almost always affect more than oneself. Fan recommends that Chinese healthcare be guided by the Confucian ethical principles of *ren-yi* 仁義 (humaneness–appropriateness) and *chengxin* 誠信 (sincerity–trustworthiness), virtues that recognize interconnectedness at the outset of all moral decision-making.

In the case of disputes regarding vaccination mandates, Confucian principles may help us to reflect on the limits of over-emphasizing individual autonomy at the expense of consideration of one's moral responsibility to others. The principle of *humaneness–appropriateness* denotes the idea of "doing good", while the principle of *sincerity–trustworthiness* provides guidance for how to think about and encourage the legitimacy of political authorities, particularly given its emphasis on reducing or avoiding the mistrust that can be caused by various forms of government-backed public health measures during a health crisis. As we have seen over the past three years, a society's compliance with government restrictions, or the rejection of these interventions because of developing distrust, can make or break containment efforts. At the same time, the libertarian warning against excessive government intervention signals the risks of powerful governments asserting their control and insinuating themselves excessively into the lives of their citizens through policies such as lockdowns, mandated health passes, contact-tracing using mobile apps, and the use of related technologies, quarantines, testing, and screening.

One sense of justice emerges as another sense is contested. According to the WHO, justice, or fairness, encompasses two related concepts: substantive *equity* and *procedural justice* (WHO 2016). Equity focuses on fairness in the distribution of scarce medical resources, scarce opportunities, and undesirable burdens. Procedural justice seeks to establish a fair process for making important decisions. All social systems entail mechanisms for distributing scarce resources in health care settings by evaluating the fairness of the procedures involved. Determining who receives what, when, and how, often amounts to detailed kinds of decision-making. Should we distribute on the base of first-come-first-served, priority of one in need, a person's ability to pay, or the best overall outcome (straightforward utility)?

Confucians may have different viewpoints on what the best mechanisms are to put in place in order to guarantee just procedures for the distribution of scarce resources. For instance, should the earliest vaccines be given to the individuals who will benefit the most, or to individuals who will protect their communities the best? Instead of responding with an insensitive or imprecise notion of "equality" (e.g., give it out based on lottery or to whomever presents first at the hospital), Confucian paternalists tend to favor giving priority to seniors who are more vulnerable to the virus. At the same time, the pressure of mandatory vaccination during the second and third years of the COVID-19 epidemic was placed on the society in general but not heavily pushed on the elderly in China. As the COVID-19 pandemic unfolded, discussions took place in the professional medical, religious, and philosophical literature, not about autonomy with regard to taking the vaccine, but about access in the form of its availability, particularly in urban versus rural populations, where vaccine hesitancy varied (Wu et al. 2023, pp. 1–12). Confucians tend to agree with the WHO's position that some groups face heightened susceptibility to harm during the pandemic and thus special consideration should be given to address their needs.

The WHO's document adds three more principles which inform moral deliberations concerning crises caused by the outbreak of pandemics: utility, reciprocity, and solidarity. The principle of utility suggests that actions are right insofar as they maximize the wellbeing of individuals or communities. Efforts to maximize utility require consideration of proportionality (balancing the potential benefits of an activity against any risks of harm) and efficiency (achieving the greatest benefits at the lowest possible cost). This noted, when government officials choose to embrace the utilitarian course, according to Confucians ethics, they should have a clear understanding of what "wellbeing" actually means in the concrete, taking into account other relevant values and keeping in mind compromises that might be needed to realize these goals. Confucian ethics does not completely reject the optimality principle, but many Confucians would argue that the pursuit of short-term effectiveness should not replace the primacy of duties and virtues. Sacrificing the need of individual "few" has the potential to stand in tension with benevolence (and non-malevolence). Thus, for example, a multipronged approach is better when mandatory quarantine or citywide lockdown has to be implemented in an urgent situation, such as providing special service to the sick and the elderly instead of treating everyone "the same." At the same time, Confucians advocate the "doctrine of the mean" (*zhongyong* 中庸), maintaining that "to go beyond is as wrong as to fall short' (*guoyou bu ji* 過猶不及) [*Analects* 11:15]. The doctrine of the mean in Confucianism acknowledges how important, yet difficult, it is to take a timely action or reaction in every critical moment of decision-making. It aims at harmonizing the interest of individuals and the wellbeing of society.

The principle of reciprocity, likewise, implies that one has a moral obligation to offer a "fitting and proportional response" to the actions and contributions that another has made and from which one has benefitted. This suggests an appreciation for the role of mutual understanding in a relationship that leads to the presence of trustworthiness at both organizational and interpersonal levels. In terms of the distribution of scarce resources, reciprocity entails an obligation to ensure that healthcare workers who accept risks of exposure to infectious disease when providing care to patients have access to essential goods, such as personal protective equipment. This might mean giving priority to health care workers for scarce resources, such as intensive care beds or ventilators.

The first two principles are not in conflict within Confucian ethics, since the philosophy conceives of people fundamentally as members of social groups, including family, clan, political community, and state. With regard to the third principle, social solidarity, questions about inclusion need to be addressed. Who is the "we" a government is meant to represent, and which demographic is emphasized within this collective? Confucians emphasize the importance of helping aging generations cope with increased risk experienced during health crises. To care for the elderly is part of "filial obligation," a pivotal duty in the Confucian tradition. In Hong Kong, for example, specific regulations were established to make sure that older people had access to information, care, and medical services through familial connections and community services (Au 2022, pp. 9–25). Currently in Hong Kong, more than 90 percent of the elderly live in domestic households. (The remaining live in non-domestic households, such as residential nursing homes, hospitals, and penal institutions). Since the sense of isolation caused by social distancing measures has dramatically impacted those living alone, any support that comes from family and community (e.g., daily activities through video links and other digital means of synchronous communication) improves their welfare. Social media in Hong Kong has created a special platform where people can exchange ideas about effective ways of taking care of the elderly during the medical crisis. The principle of solidarity ensures that sub-populations within the larger population will appropriately be accounted for, just as it requires populations themselves to be regarded as their own worthwhile whole.

Paternalism in a Confucian context, then, implies moral judgment as well as detailed and nuanced estimations of what is good for the part and the whole. It will be sensitive and calibrated if, in its application, it successfully addresses the needs of the vulnerable. Only in this way can paternalism be purged of its negative connotation and build into its moral analysis the specific needs of different groups. By the same token, individualism need not be posed as the opposite of collective action. Confucianism is its own virtue ethic that has the power and flexibility to respond to the needs of human beings as they are individually revealed on a case-by-case basis by attending to collective actions that respond to health crises. Confucian paternalism can be sensitive to the needs of struggling individuals while also accommodating overarching obligations to protect the welfare and wellbeing of the larger population.

6. Conclusion

The argument of this paper has been that a soft Confucian paternalism offers an alternative way of thinking about human relationships and moral obligations during challenging times and that it serves as a way to avoid adopting policy positions that may be formulated in too individualistic a manner and with little room for the proper consideration of other dimensions of respect for persons. It eschews a position where individual autonomy is given veto power over all forms of intervention. Many national governments during the COVID-19 pandemic were called upon to introduce policies designed to contain the spread of COVID-19 which would benefit everyone in the long run. Although "relational autonomy" does not resolve every existing tension between individual freedom and public safety, solidarity and collective action proved to be relevant to the creation of sound public health policy during a time in which we confronted a transboundary crisis wrought by a virus which knows no borders.

Ideally, the aims of public health are best fulfilled when citizens voluntarily follow preventive measures without recourse to government coercion. We all wish to arrive at a point where caregivers, patients, the public, and government can arrive at a shared idea of the common good, mutually assenting to the instantiation of the good in policies which reflect compassionate care. If our moral discourse focuses on the values of trust and relationality, and we hold our leaders to aspiring to expertise and professionalism, we will move in a direction that will provide desired health outcomes. Confucian virtues, including the emphasis on family values where paternalism comes to entail individual ends, can be implemented as a needed hybrid entity effective in softening the tension between the individual and society in the management of the COVID-19 pandemic situation.

Likewise, a Confucian ethic based on familial relations and a notion of authority premised on shared decision-making can enhance a productive sense of paternalistic behaviors for all strata of society, particularly in an emergent health emergency where we hope to save as many lives as possible. Although the notions of "filial piety" and "parent–officials" in Confucian thought are sometimes perceived as authoritarian, the Confucian normative imperatives do place the needs and welfare of the people and the common good of the society at the center of deliberative policy-making. These Confucian values, translated into the ethical guidelines and practical policies of public health, encourage a degree of state intervention when high stakes decisions are involved.

Funding: This research is funded by SRG, University of Macau. Grant number: SRG2022-00043-FAH.

Data Availability Statement: Not applicable.

Conflicts of Interest: The author declares no conflict of interest.

References

Allinson, Robert E. 1985. The Confucian Golden Rule: The Negative Formation. *Journal of Chinese Philosophy* 12: 305–15. [CrossRef]

Au, Kit Sing Derrick. 2022. Ethical Issues Arising from the COVID-19 Pandemic in Hong Kong. *International Journal of Chinese and Comparative Philosophy of Medicine* 20: 9–25. [CrossRef]

Beauchamp, Thomas L., and James F. Childress. 2001. *Principles of Biomedical Ethics*, 5th ed. Oxford: Oxford University Press.

Ben-Porath, Sigal R. 2010. *Tough Choices: Structured Paternalism and the Landscape of Choice*. Princeton: Princeton University Press.

Blackburn, Simon. 2008. Paternalism. In *The Oxford Dictionary of Philosophy*. Oxford: Oxford University Press, p. 270.

Boin, Arjen, Allan McConnell, and Paul't Hart. 2021. *Governing the Pandemic: The Politics of Navigating a Mega-Crisis*. London: Palgrave Macmillan.

Brennan, Jason. 2018. A libertarian case for mandatory vaccination. *Journal of Medical Ethics* 44: 37–43. [CrossRef] [PubMed]

Carter, Stacey M., Vikki A. Entwistle, and Myles Little. 2015. Relational conceptions of paternalism: Away to rebut nanny-state accusations and evaluate public health interventions. *Public Health* 129: 1021–29. [CrossRef] [PubMed]

Chan, Joseph. 2000. Legitimacy, Unanimity and Perfectionism. *Philosophy and Public Affairs* 28: 5–42. [CrossRef]

Chan, Wing-Tsit, trans. 1963. *A Source Book in Chinese Philosophy*. Princeton: Princeton University Press.

Clarke, Simon. 2006. Debate: State Paternalism, Neutrality and Perfectionism. *The Journal of Political Philosophy* 14: 111–21. [CrossRef]

Cohen, Gerald A., and Keith Graham. 1990. Self-Ownership, Communism and Equality. *Proceedings of the Aristotelian Society, Supplementary Volumes* 64: 25–61. [CrossRef]

Conly, Sarah. 2013. *Against Autonomy: Justifying Coercive Paternalism*. Cambridge: Cambridge University Press.

Dworkin, Gerald. 2020. Paternalism. In *The Stanford Encyclopedia of Philosophy*. Edited by Edward N. Zalta. Available online: https://plato.stanford.edu/archives/sum2020/entries/paternalism/ (accessed on 6 June 2023).
Fan, Ruiping. 2010. *Reconstructionist Confucianism: Rethinking Morality after the West*. London and New York: Springer.
Fan, Ruiping. 2018. A Confucian View on Informed Consent and the Issue of Vaccination. *Studia Bioethica* 11: 23–30.
Fingarette, Herbert. 1972. *Confucius: The Secular as Sacred*. New York: Harper Torch books.
Firey, Thomas A. 2020. Government in a Pandemic. Cato Institute. (November 17). Policy Analysis No. 902. Available online: https://www.cato.org/policy-analysis/government-pandemic (accessed on 6 June 2023).
Flavel, Sarah, and Brad Hall. 2020. Exemplary Paternalism: A Consideration of Confucian Models of Moral Oversight. *Culture and Dialogue* 8: 220–50. [CrossRef]
Ivanhoe, Philip J. 1991. Character Consequentialism: An Early Confucian Contribution to Contemporary Ethical Theory. *The Journal of Religious Ethics* 9: 55–70.
Lau, Wai Kwan, Loan N. T. Pham, and Lam Dang Nguyen. 2019. Remapping the construct of paternalistic leadership. *Leadership & Organization Development Journal* 40: 764–76.
Li, Chenyang. 2014. The Confucian Conception of Freedom. *Philosophy East & West* 64: 902–19.
Mackenzie, Catriona, and Natalie Stoljar, eds. 2000. *Relational Autonomy: Feminist Perspectives on Autonomy, Agency, and the Social Self.* Oxford: Oxford University Press.
Metzger, Thomas. 2005. *Cloud across the Pacific: Essays on the Clash between Chinese and Western Political Philosophies Today*. Hong Kong: The Chinese University Press.
Mill, John. 1974. *On Liberty*. Baltimore: Penguin.
New, Bill. 1999. Paternalism and Public Policy. *Economics and Philosophy* 15: 63–83. [CrossRef]
Nozick, Robert. 1974. *Anarchy, State and Utopia*. Oxford: Blackwell.
Perlstein, Sara Grøn, and Marc Verboord. 2021. Lockdowns, lethality, and laissez-faire politics. Public discourses on political authorities in high-trust countries during the COVID-19 pandemic. *PLoS ONE* 16: 1–23. [CrossRef] [PubMed]
Rawls, John. 1993. *Political Liberalism*. New York: Columbia University Press.
Shen, Vincent. 2008. Globalization and Confucianism: The Virtue of Shu and Generosity to Many Other. In *Confucian Ethics in Retrospect and Prospect*. Edited by Vincent Shen and Kwong-Loi Shuan. Washington, DC: The Council for Research in Values and Philosophy.
Tan, Sor-Hoon. 2010. Authoritative Master Kong in an Authoritarian Age. *Dao: A Journal of Comparative Philosophy* 9: 137–49. [CrossRef]
Thaler, Richard H., and Cass R. Sunstein. 2008. *Nudge: Improving Decisions about Health, Wealth, and Happiness*. New Haven: Yale University Press.
World Health Organization. 2016. WHO Guidance For Managing Ethical Issues In Infectious Disease Outbreaks. Available online: https://pandemicethics.org/consensus-documents/who-guidance-for-managing-ethical-issues-in-infectious-disease-outbreaks/ (accessed on 6 June 2023).
Wu, Jian, Zhanlei Shen, Quanman Li, Clifford Silver Tarimo, Meiyun Wang, Jianqin Gu, Wei Wei, Xinyu Zhang, Yanli Huang, Mingze Ma, and et al. 2023. How urban versus rural residency relates to COVID-19 vaccine hesitancy: A large-scale national Chinese study. *Social Sciences & Medicine* 320: 115695. [CrossRef]
Zhang, Ellen. 2010. Community, the Common Good, and Public Healthcare—Confucianism and its Relevance to Contemporary China. *Public Health Ethics* 3: 259–66. [CrossRef]

MDPI
St. Alban-Anlage 66
4052 Basel
Switzerland
www.mdpi.com

Religions Editorial Office
E-mail: religions@mdpi.com
www.mdpi.com/journal/religions

www.ingramcontent.com/pod-product-compliance
Lightning Source LLC
Chambersburg PA
CBHW080937240926
51849CB00004BA/483
* 9 7 8 3 0 3 6 5 8 5 7 2 7 *